A History
of Religion
East and West

AN INTRODUCTION AND INTERPRETATION

Trevor Ling

PROFESSOR OF COMPARATIVE RELIGION
UNIVERSITY OF MANCHESTER

MACMILLAN

First edition 1968
Reprinted 1974, 1977, 1979, 1982, 1984, 1985

Published by
Higher and Further Education Division
MACMILLAN PUBLISHERS LTD
Houndmills, Basingstoke, Hampshire RG21 2XS
and London
Companies and representatives
throughout the world

Printed in Hong Kong

ISBN 0-333-02839-2 (hard cover)
ISBN 0-333-10172-3 (paper cover)

210842

A HISTORY OF RELIGION
EAST AND WEST

13098

By the same author

The Significance of Satan (S.P.C.K.)
Buddhism and the Mythology of Evil (ALLEN AND UNWIN)
Buddha, Marx and God (MACMILLAN)
Prophetic Religion (MACMILLAN)

Contents

CHAPTER FIVE: RELIGION AND CIVILISATION   209

ABBREVIATIONS

B.C.   Before the Christian era.
C.E.   Christian era.
E.R.E.   *Encyclopaedia of Religion and Ethics,* ed. H. G. Hastings, Edinburgh, 1905.

Acknowledgements

I would like to thank the following firms for their kindness in allowing me to use material which has already appeared in their publications:

Cambridge University Press, for material from 'Buddhist Mysticism' from *Religious Studies*, vol. i; The Society for Promoting Christian Knowledge, for material from 'The Buddhist Christian Encounter' from *Theology*, vol. lxxix, no. 554, August 1966.

Introduction: Comparative Religion Today

1

IT has been said that no man is so vain of his own religion as he who knows no other. There is another side to this: no one is more likely to be hostile to all religion than the Western sceptic who knows no other tradition than that of the West. Karl Marx's critique of religion, that it consisted of the ideological epiphenomena thrown up by the real brute facts of existence, which were economic, was based almost entirely upon his observation of the nature and workings of nineteenth-century European Protestantism. On the other hand, Max Weber, in contesting this view and offering very important modifications of it, ranged over a wide area of the world in the course of his study: ancient Judaism, China, India, the Islamic world, as well as Europe. In the present writer's view this method of Weber's is the only reputable course for any scientific study of religion to follow. What is offered here, however, does not begin to approach anything like the scale or the intensity of Weber's comparative study; it merely acknowledges that the wide area which Weber covered is the important territory, the territory that needs to be explored afresh; the student is here offered simply an introductory view of this whole area.

An extremely pious clergyman, hearing from a student that the comparative study of religion formed part of her university course, exclaimed with horror, 'My dear, I would rather you read *Lady Chatterley's Lover* than that subject!' The desperate nature of the comparison showed how strong his feelings were. He added, by way of explanation, that at least you were *aware* that the Devil was attacking you when you read D. H. Lawrence.

The same would no doubt be true of a number of other academic subjects, and perhaps he would have been equally nervous if she had been reading any of them. The comparative study of religion, however, is particularly strongly disliked by a certain type of Christian. The objection seems to be that an impartial study fails to indoctrinate the student in the way the objector wishes him to be indoctrinated. This kind of rejection by Christians of any extension of the area of study to include other traditions is very understandable in certain cases. For there are those who seem to suppose that loyalty to Christ means the blind and passionate adherence to anything which in the course of history has come to be labelled 'Christian', and unquestioning hostility towards anything which is 'non-Christian'. These attitudes themselves demand study. Such is the conceit of some Christians with whom the present writer has discussed these things that when they are confronted by evidence that Islam and Buddhism have, for example, been characterised by more tolerant attitudes and greater care for minorities under their control than has Christianity during much of its history, their reaction is to assume that this simply cannot be true.

A fair and impartial study of religious traditions means the study of their actual historical records in terms of the ideas they teach, the types of personality they have produced, and the kinds of societies found in association with them. Those who, from the standpoint of one particular religion, object to the comparative study of religion immediately raise the suspicion that they have something to hide: that their faith does not bear scrutiny alongside others, or that its historical record needs to be hushed up. If this is so, then the plight of the student who is an adherent of that faith is parlous, whatever branch of human learning he happens to be studying; the best advice to him would be not simply that he should drop the comparative study of religion but that he should withdraw from academic study altogether, give up exercising his mind and retreat into an anti-intellectual obscurantism.

The present writer's own conviction is that an appreciation of the many and varied ways men have manifested their awareness of a dimension other than the temporal and 'material' can be of the greatest value in an age which is increasingly menaced by secularism. The comparative study of religion has a more positive and constructive role than nervous piety sometimes imagines. But first it must be made clear what is being compared with what. We are not here concerned with that somewhat debased form of study in which Christianity is compared with the 'other religions', or the 'non-Christian religions'; these latter all-embracing and rather condescending terms are still in favour with some neo-orthodox theologians. In this kind of undertaking it is accepted from the start that the comparison is to be to the advantage of Christianity.

At a more respectable academic level comparative religion did mean, and to some extent still does mean, a study of the interrelationships of the major systems of religious thought and of the way in which the diffusion of religious themes and ideas has taken place. For there is a great deal of intertwining among the great religious traditions, especially of Eurasia. Judaism was affected by Zoroastrianism, and together they both contributed to Islam. Islam, expanding eastwards, hastened the demise of Buddhism from India and in turn was itself influenced by Hinduism. Christianity reaching India from Europe had its effects upon nineteenth-century Hindu and Islamic revival movements, and in Ceylon had the effect of an antibody to stimulate Buddhism to a recovery of its own intrinsic ideas. In recent decades Asian religious thought, particularly Buddhist, has had subtle effects upon Western theology. The issues are not so simple, of course, as this hasty summary of cross-currents suggests, and it is with the more complicated and delicate mechanism of the diffusion of ideas that comparative religion is partly concerned; this alone would provide it with a *raison d'être*.

The subject entails more, however, than the comparative study of religious ideas. Comparative religion has in recent years, especially in the United States, begun to mean, and needs very much more to become, the relating of the findings of two separate disciplines, the philosophy of religion and the sociology of religion, *each pursued in a world context*. These two subjects, as they are at present studied, are not always, and perhaps not often, pursued in a world context. The subject matter of courses labelled 'the philosophy of religion' frequently consists only of the philosophy of Western religion, or (even more partisan) philosophical Christian theology. The sociology of religion, moreover, much more advanced nowadays in the United States than in Europe, usually confines itself to the study of religion in contemporary American society, although there are notable exceptions, particularly in some of the studies of millenarian movements. The direction in which comparative religion has begun to develop is a corrective to this, and it is at the same time a logical advance from what was its earlier position, represented for example by the work of such scholars as E. O. James.

In this earlier period comparative religion relied to a considerable extent on the work of anthropologists; indeed it was often difficult to draw any clear line of demarcation between comparative religion and anthropology. Within the field of social science generally, sociology now tends to take over the position of importance which anthropology formally held, as more and more of the world's peoples become industrialised and urbanised, or at least, with the growth of new states, are organised in more complex societies. Certainly it is the sociologists today who are active in studying and reporting on the religious behaviour of men, on the effect which this has upon economic and social structures, and, conversely, the ways in which religious behaviour is affected by social and economic structures. However, in doing so, sociology has in recent years become increasingly empirical, to the exclusion of theory; facts are gathered from the results of field work and from sociological analysis of the data, and some kind of immediate conclusions are drawn relevant to the situation under scrutiny. There is much less concern with the construction of general theories of religion and society than there was in the days of those giants and pioneers, Max Weber and Émile Durkheim, upon whose work writers like R. H. Tawney were able to build. The recent tendency is understandable; intensive development of a subject inevitably leads to specialisation, and where circumstances virtually compel all to become specialists, who has time for constructing general theories? Even though Weber claimed not to be formulating a general theory, the fact remains that he surveyed a very much wider field than any sociologist of religion has done since – seventeenth-century Puritanism, Judaism, Hinduism, Buddhism, Islam and the religions of China all came within his purview. His American commentator and expositor, Talcott Parsons, may be a more thorough *sociological* system-builder with a lively awareness of the interaction of religion and society, but his work does not claim to have the breadth of Weber's. We may hear from Gerhard Lenski in great and very useful detail about the religious situation in the Detroit area, or from Herberg about overall American values finding expression in the three major religious communities, Protestant, Catholic, and Jewish, but in what academic discipline are these related to similar researches in neo-Shintoist Japan, or Buddhist Burma, or the Islamic society of Pakistan? More important, what other discipline exists, apart from comparative religion, which is likely not only to lead to a synoptic view of such studies, but also to bring us a little nearer to a more accurate understanding of the place of religion in the modern world?

This might be thought to be the task of what, if it existed, could be called 'the comparative sociology of religion'. But such a discipline would have certain disadvantages and limitations. For the academic sociologist works, professionally at least, within certain self-imposed limits; if he were required to investigate other aspects of religion than the sociological he might consider that he was trespassing upon the province of the philosopher of religion – or he might simply not be interested in raising these other questions. Let the philosopher, or even the theologian, raise them. But if the sociologist is not interested in at least the tentative answers or findings worked out by the philosopher, some of the potential value of the philosopher's work will be lost. And if, on the other hand, the philosophers and theologians have not really taken the pains to understand what the sociologist has been pointing out concerning the interrelation of religion and society there may remain a suspicion that their account of religious belief and religious behaviour is as unsatisfactory as that of the purely empirical sociologist.

The argument thus seems to lead to the demand for an academic discipline that might be called 'the philosophy and sociology of religion'. Some means would have to be found, however, both for ensuring, and for making clear, that the subject was to be pursued by *comparative* study, and in a *world* context. The title might therefore be 'the comparative philosophy and sociology of world religions'. If such a long-winded title were ever used it would in fact indicate what I believe are the present proper concerns of comparative religion.

To return then to the question, 'What is being compared with what?' we find that the word 'comparative' has here a double reference; it refers to the fact that the findings of sociologists need to be compared with those of philosophers of religion; and also to the fact that in each case East must be compared with West; that is, the researches of sociologists in the United States are to be set alongside those of their colleagues in, say Japan, or India; and that a similar catholicity is to be encouraged in the case of the philosophy of religion.

There is, however, yet another approach to the subject without which a good deal of the contemporary evidence might not be properly interpreted, and that is the historical. One needs to be aware of the changes which particular religious traditions and institutions have undergone, changes which are evident from *historical* comparison. One does not understand the Hindu caste system if one regards it as something which is eternally the same, having existed as it is today from time immemorial (the view which some Hindus take), and subject only to minor modifications here and there. A proper appreciation of the nature of caste in India demands an understanding of what it was (embryonically, perhaps) at the time of the Buddha, compared with what it had become some centuries later when the laws of Manu received their present codification, compared again with what it was at the beginning of the nineteenth century, and compared yet again with what it is today. Similarly one does not properly understand the religion of one's Pakistani immigrant neighbour if one attends only to the rise of Islam in seventh-century Mecca and Medina. The modern Pakistani Muslim is heir also to centuries of tradition which have moulded the Islamic tradition of the Indo-Pakistan subcontinent and have provided him with his present religious and cultural heritage. He cannot easily shake this off, nor can we properly understand his situation apart from this. One of the valuable qualities of Weber's work was his historical realism about religion; he studied religion as it actually existed – in seventeenth-century Europe, for example – and not as what its adherents claimed for it in some ideal form which they believed had existed in the past.

This, then, is the scope of comparative religion. The field begins to seem vast – perhaps too vast to be comprehended as a single area of study; too vast a subject for any one man to undertake to study or to teach. A little reflection shows, however, that the same is true of other academic subjects, including those with which this one has common frontiers, especially philosophy, sociology, history and theology. All these demand wide competence and all to some extent overlap one another; yet each has its own special contribution to make to the understanding of the world and of the human situation. So too has comparative religion; the student who works in this field will be aware of his indebtedness to researchers in many other fields; he will, moreover, be encouraged in his own special research by the conviction that this area, too, has its own particular contribution to make, in the better understanding of religion, and of what is happening today in the religious life of man.

2

Such, then, is the scope of the study to which I have endeavoured to provide an introduction in the present volume. But should an introduction be concerned also with interpretation? I can see no good reason why not. Textbooks which I have used with students in the past have been more stimulating and hence more effective when their authors have presented a subject from a particular point of view, while acknowledging that there are other points of view and indicating what these are. Quite frequently, the student who comes to a study of this sort for the first time (but concerning which he may have some general notion) is more likely to be provoked into further and more intensive study than he might otherwise have engaged in if he is confronted with what is quite clearly an interpretative presentation, which he may wish either to question or to pursue further.

In the present work the interpretative comment is mainly to be found in the summaries which follow each chapter. Within the chapters I have attempted to present the most widely-accepted findings of scholars in the various fields concerned, to indicate where fuller treatment of the subject under discussion may be found, and, where appropriate, to indicate the existence of contrasting views upon a subject.

In an introductory work of this character, a great deal of interesting detail inevitably has to go unmentioned. This is true in the treatment here of both Eastern and Western religions. Certainly, no attempt is made to present a complete account of Christian developments of the kind which is undertaken in that branch of theological study known as Church History.

Christian views of the growth of the Church, in a variety of shades of orthodoxy, are available in abundance. What is less common is a study of Christian history in the context of the history of religion, undertaken not from the point of view of Christian confessionalism, but in relation to the study of the history of other religious movements. Some Christians, as we have noted, do not regard this kind of undertaking with much favour, especially if they happen to hold the view that the Christian Church is unique and therefore not to be compared with 'other religions'. But Hindu institutions and ideas also are unique; so are Buddhist and Muslim religious practices and ideas. There is, for example, nothing quite like the Sangha, or the doctrine of anatta, outside Buddhism. Others, hostile to Christianity, view the history of the Christian Church as valuable only in confirming their own view that Christianity has been an impediment to human progress. There is, nevertheless, value in the kind of appreciative and sympathetic study of Christian religious history that a discerning and thoughtful religious man of Asia, say a Hindu or a Buddhist, might engage in; this would be the sort of study which would aim at sifting out, from among the European vanity and prejudice which have sometimes obscured it, what in Judaism and Christianity is of permanent and universal religious value. Work of this kind is beginning to be done, as the modern comparative study of religion becomes an item of university teaching and research in places as diverse as California, Jerusalem, Bengal, and Japan. What is outlined here may help to provide some indication of the kind of study which needs increasingly to be undertaken, and may, it is hoped, stimulate others to enter more thoroughly into this area of great potential importance within the general field of liberal and humane studies.

Chronological Table

B.C.

1700	Hammurabi king of Babylon
1500 (approx)	Aryan tribes invade north-west India
1230 (approx)	Exodus of Hebrew tribes from Egypt under Moses
1200–1025	Period of Hebrew settlement in Canaan and the amphictyony of Israel
1000 (approx)	Composition of later Ṛg-vedic hymns (cosmogonic)
1025	Beginning of Hebrew monarchy: Saul
1006	Beginning of reign of David.
960	Beginning of reign of Solomon
922	End of Solomon's reign: division of the Hebrew kingdom
900–700	Composition of Brāhmaṇas
750 (approx)	Beginning of prophetic activity of Amos, Hosea, and Isaiah
721	Fall of Samaria and end of northern kingdom of Israel
700–500 (approx)	Composition of earlier Upaniṣads
588	Beginning of Zarathustra's prophetic activity
587	Fall of Jerusalem and end of southern kingdom of Judah: exile of leaders to Babylon
563(?)	Birth of Buddha
551(?)	Birth of Confucius
541	Death of Zarathustra
538	Cyrus captures Babylon. Beginning of Persian period in Near East. Jews begin to return to Jerusalem
520	Darius allows more Jews to return
515	Dedication of rebuilt Temple in Jerusalem
483(?)	Death of the Buddha
479(?)	Death of Confucius
468(?)	Death of Mahāvīrā, founder of Jain movement
445	Rebuilding of the walls of Jerusalem begun
400 (approx)	Ezra active in Judah
383	Buddhist Council at Vesālī
331	Alexander conquers Palestine. Beginning of period of Greek rule
327–325	Alexander in north-west India

270 (approx)	Beginning of emperor Aśoka's reign in India
250	Buddhist Council at Patna, under Aśoka
	Hebrew Pentateuch translation into Greek begun at Alexandria
232	End of Aśoka's reign
175	Beginning of the reign of Antiochus IV (Epiphanes)
168	Antiochus IV persecutes Jews and desecrates Temple at Jerusalem
167	Revolt led by Judas Maccabeus
165	Cleansing and rededication of Temple in Jerusalem
155–130	Menander, Indo-Greek king of north-west of India (Milinda)
63	Pompey captures Jerusalem. Beginning of period of Roman rule
50 (approx)	Commencement of Roman trade with southern India
C.E.	Birth of Jesus of Nazareth
33(?)	Crucifixion of Jesus of Nazareth
	Beginning of growth of the Christian sect
65	Persecution of Christians in Rome under Nero
?	Mission of Thomas the Apostle to India
70	Fall of Jerusalem, and destruction by the Romans
115	Martyrdom in Rome of St Ignatius, bishop of Antioch
150 (approx)	Buddhist monks and missionaries enter China
180 (approx)	St Irenaeus bishop of Lyons. Anti-Gnostic writings
186 (approx)	Birth of Origen, Christian theologian and philosopher
216	Birth of Manes, inaugurator of Manichaeism
271	Death of Origen
313	Christians granted equality of rights by emperor Constantine
320	Beginning of the Gupta dynasty in India
325	Council of Nicaea, under presidency of Constantine
346	Death of Pachomius, founder of Christian monastic settlements in Egypt
354	Birth of St Augustine
387	Baptism of Augustine
395	Augustine made bishop of Hippo
410	Sack of Rome by Visigoth king Alaric
430	Invasion of North Africa by Vandals. Death of Augustine
520	Arrival in China of Bodhidharma, traditional founder of Ch'an school
550 (approx)	Buddhism introduced into Japan
570	Birth of Muhammad, the Prophet
593–621	Shotoku, Buddhist ruler of Japan
610 (approx)	Beginning of Muhammad's prophetic activity in Mecca

622	Year of Hijra (migration to Medina)
629–645	Chinese pilgrim Hsuan-tsang in India
630	Submission of Mecca to Muhammad
632	Death of Muhammad. Abu Bakr becomes successor (caliph)
634	Death of Abu Bakr; succeeded by Umar
644	Death of Umar; succeeded by Uthman
656	Death of Uthman; succeeded by Ali. Ali's claim disputed by Mu'awiya
661	Assassination of Ali. Mu'awiya proclaimed caliph
671–695	Chinese pilgrim I-Tsing in India
711	Arab Muslims under Tariq enter Spain
	Beginning of Arab conquest of Sind, north-west India
750 (approx)	Introduction of Vajrayāna Buddhism to Tibet by Padma Sambhava
788	Birth of Hindu philosopher Shankara
803	Tendai Buddhism introduced to Japan by Saicho
820	Death of Shankara
845–847	Persecution of Buddhists in China by Tang emperor
849	Founding of the Burmese kingdom of Pagan
873	Birth of Al Ashari, Muslim theologian
925	Death of Al Ashari
970	Founding by Fatimids of city of Al Qahira (Cairo)
972	Printing of the Buddhist Tripitaka in China
1000 (approx)	Beginning of Muslim Turk raids on Punjab
	Atisha's mission to Tibet
1033	Birth of St Anselm
1044	Founding of the Pagan dynasty in Burma by Anawratha
1054	Patriarch of Constantinople excommunicated by Rome. Final schism between Eastern and Western Christian Churches
1055	Baghdad taken by Seljuq Turks
1058	Birth of Al Ghazali, Muslim theologian and mystic
1093	Anselm becomes Archbishop of Canterbury
1096	First Crusade arrives in Constantinople
1109	Death of Anselm
1111	Death of Al Ghazali
1135	Birth of Maimonides
1184	Waldenses anathematised by Rome
1191	Rinzai Zen Buddhism introduced into Japan from China
1200 (approx)	Final disappearance of Buddhism from India
1204	Death of Maimonides
1206	Founding of the Sultanate of Delhi by Aibak
1222	Birth of Japanese Buddhist, Nichiren

1815	Christian missionary activity begins to be permitted in British India
1818	Birth of Karl Marx
1820	Muslim reform movement in Bengal
1827	Founding of Brāhma Samāj movement by Rām Mohan Roy
1829	Catholic Emancipation in Britain. Birth of William Booth
1833	Beginning of Oxford Movement in Church of England
1834	Birth of Rāmakrishna
1845	John Newman enters Roman Catholic Church
1854	Immaculate Conception of the Virgin Mary declared an article of faith
1859	Publication of Darwin's *Origin of Species*
1858	End of Mughal rule in India. Beginning of expansion of Christian missionary activity in Asia
1864	Syllabus of Errors published by Roman Catholic Church
1865	Founding of the Salvation Army
1868	End of Tokugawa regime: Japan opened to the West
1869–1870	Vatican Council. Birth of M. K. Gandhi
1875	Founding of the Ārya Samāj
1885	End of Burmese Buddhist kingdom of Mandalay
1886	Death of Rāmakrishna
1891	Founding of Maha Bodhi Society
1893	Parliament of Religions in Chicago
1896	Zionist Congress in Basle
	Founding of Ramakrishna Mission by Vivekananda
1906	Founding of the Muslim League in India
1910	Christian missionary conference at Edinburgh
1912	Founding of Muhammadīya movement in Indonesia
1930	Muhammad Iqbal president of Muslim League
1938	Death of Muhammad Iqbal
1941	Founding of Jama'at-i-Islami movement in Muslim India
1948	Murder of M. K. Gandhi by Hindu extremist
	World Council of Churches founded at Amsterdam
1950	World Fellowship of Buddhists founded in Ceylon
1956	'Sixth' World Buddhist Council in Rangoon

North-West India and West Pakistan

1 Nomads, Peasants and Kings

1.1 RELIGION IN THE EARLY CITY-CIVILISATIONS OF ASIA

1.10 The area of concern

'NOT in innocence, and not in Asia, was mankind born.' Such is the contention of a recent writer on the subject of man's animal origins, as he presents evidence to show that man first emerged as man somewhere in the African highlands (Ardrey, 1961; 9). Whether mankind was born in innocence, and subsequently by some kind of 'fall' became sinful, or whether man evolved from a particularly murderous species of animal and is still in the process of evolution towards some 'nobler' form of existence, is a question on which religious traditions are divided, as we shall see later in our study. It is however fairly clear that wherever *homo sapiens* may first have emerged, it is in Asia that the roots of the present great civilisations of the world are to be found. Moreover, it is in the land mass which extends from the Atlantic eastwards to the Pacific, known for convenience as Eurasia, that three-quarters of the world's present population is contained. Here the major religious and philosophical traditions of the world had their origins – Jewish, Christian, Islamic, Hindu and Buddhist – and it is these which we are concerned to trace.

Within the continental area of Eurasia certain regions are of special importance in the early development of religious traditions: these are Mesopotamia, Egypt, and the Indus valley (see Maps 1 and 3).

1.11 The making of Mesopotamia's civilisation

The primary natural importance of Mesopotamia lies in its rivers, the Euphrates and the Tigris. The wide expanse of alluvial plain has a climate which in the south is mild enough for the date palm to flourish, and in the north cold enough, with its winter frosts, for vigorous activity. The southern part of the region is the home of the most ancient civilisation known to us. The people called Sumerians were in possession of this territory from at least the middle of the third millennium B.C., that is from the earliest time at which it is possible to identify its inhabitants. Here, it is claimed, history began; that is, in the sense of the possible reconstruction of the story of human affairs on the basis of contemporary records and archaeological evidence. Here were the first schools of which we have any evidence, the first legal procedures, the first system of ethics of which we know, the first library, and even, it is claimed, the first 'war of nerves' (Kramer, 1958). Ancient Sumer appears to have consisted of a confederation of cities, all of which possessed similar patterns of culture. Each city acknowledged a god who was the 'owner' or patron of the place. From what is known of their mythology it has been suggested that the Sumerians came originally from a different kind of territory from that of lower Mesopotamia – possibly from the mountainous area of Iran, to the east. The Sumerians are usually regarded as having been more distinctively Asian than the Semitic people who began to invade the area from about 2000 B.C. The first of these were the *Accadians*, whose city, Accad, was set up in the northern part of Mesopotamia. Then came a second wave of Semitic invaders known as the *Amurru*, better known in the West by their Old Testament name of Amorites. One of the great centres which they developed was Mari, and in this Amorite state there eventually emerged the great ruler Hammurabi (eighteenth century B.C.) known to us best for the law code associated with his name. Under his rule Babylon, a village on the banks of the Euphrates, was expanded to become the capital city of the state. The new state included what had previously been Sumer and Accad, and it was in the capital that the great 'tower' of Babylon was set up (the 'House of the Foundation-Platform of Heaven and Earth'). Such towers, known as ziggurats, were a common feature of ancient Babylonia; on a high platform reached by successive tiers of masonry, a temple was placed, and in the city of Babylon this temple was dedicated to the city's patron-god, Marduk.

One of the most important waves of invasion into Mesopotamia was that of the people known as the *Hurrians* (referred to in the Old Testament as the Horites). They came from the highlands of Iran into the northern part of the region in the eighteenth and seventeenth centuries B.C. and are of special interest in that they belonged to the Aryan-speaking race, another branch of which invaded north-west India a century or two later; the Hurrian invaders of Mesopotamia worshipped gods having the same names as those worshipped by the Vedic Aryans of India, such as Mitra, Indra and Varuna (*1.33*; *1.34*).

1.12 Religious aspects of Mesopotamia's civilisation

Such waves of immigrants were successfully absorbed into the life and culture of Mesopotamia, each perhaps contributing something to the high civilisation of this land of cities, a civilisation whose fame was widespread in the ancient world. There were eventually about ten major cities, each of which was in essence a small state, each with its own god, and each subject to the central city of Babylon, as the city-gods were subject to Marduk. Marduk in time thus acquired the attributes of conqueror of the world, and the gods of other cities came to be regarded as aspects of the one supreme power. Just as each god presiding over the life of a city community was, so to speak, its unseen spirit-genius, the element of continuity from generation to generation, so Marduk, presiding over the life of the whole empire of cities, was the supernatural focus for the life of the great community, existing above the changes and chances of individual human kingship, and giving supernatural sanction to the laws by which, in the interests of justice and the welfare of the community, the human ruler, such as Hammurabi, sought to order the life of the state.

More popular forms of religion were provided by soothsayers and seers. These were men who claimed a special competence in the business of divination, warning their fellows of impending calamities and seeking ways for them out of present distresses. Here, as so often, the raw material of popular religion was the sense of the unsatisfactoriness of actual human existence and a conviction that things should be otherwise. This manifests itself also in the 'wisdom' type of literature of which there was a considerable amount in Babylonia, which attempted to deal with such problems as apparently unmerited human suffering, and the reconciling of this with the idea of divine justice and power.

There are thus found in Babylonian religion two prominent features or aspects: first, that of the high god, the supernatural ruler, the spirit of the society enduring through all human generations and providing continuity, and so nullifying the transiency of human life; and second, an attempt to answer problems arising from the actual day-to-day experience of human individuals, and to provide ways of dealing with suffering and distress.

1.13 The civilisation of Egypt

Among the reasons for the early emergence of Egyptian civilisation are, as in the case of Mesopotamia, its natural advantages of terrain and climate. The southern part of the Nile valley is a fertile alluvial strip of land set between the sides of a rift valley, which at its northern end opens out into the wide fan-shaped expanse of the delta, extending into the Mediterranean. These two territories, the 'African' Egypt of the south, and the 'Mediterranean' Egypt of the north, were made one by the necessity for centralised control of the Nile waters, and early in history the single state of Egypt came into existence. The people of Egypt similarly are made up of two main elements: African, of the Somali type found in the Sudan; and Semitic, from the Arabian peninsula. Their language also is a combination of these two elements.

Egypt thus early became one of the great 'oriental despotisms' described by Karl Wittfogel (1957), characterised by large-scale, state-controlled irrigation works and a rationalised system of agriculture made possible by the centralisation of political power in the person of the monarch. Egyptian civilisation emerged roughly contemporaneously with that of Mesopotamia, by about the beginning of the third millennium B.C., but in Egypt the institution of monarchy seems to have been more deeply rooted – possibly in African concepts of kingship (Frankfort, 1948).

1.14 The religious aspect of Egyptian civilisation

Unified political *power*: this is the important aspect of Egyptian civilisation for the purposes of our study, for it is clear that it was chiefly in terms of power that deity was thought of in Egypt. But we must now take account of the fact that Egyptian religion includes a mythology of many gods. The precise nature of ancient Egyptian religion is in fact not fully understood. Henri Frankfort has described it as a polytheism which was also a monotheism. There appear to have been two contrasting tendencies of thought: there was the particularising tendency, by which every local appearance of power was seen as a separate manifestation of the divine, a separate god; and there was the universalising tendency, by which all these were recognised as manifestations of one power. This was, however, seen in three main spheres: the power of the sun, in creation; the power residing in animal life, seen in procreation; and the power inherent in the earth, manifested in the yearly 'resurrection' of life. The one focus of these three kinds of power was the monarch himself, and in this way the Egyptian conception of deity came to be that of an absolute potentate and creator, one who had by his power produced habitable and productive territory and upon whose will the circumstances of men's daily lives depended.

Absence of clear distinction between kingship and deity: this more than any other single feature is the outstanding characteristic of Egyptian religion. Kingship and deity were so closely interconnected that each shared the nature of the other. This conception of monarchy is difficult for us to appreciate; our experience of monarchy is of an institution which survives largely as a matter of tradition and picturesque ceremony. Modern societies, it seems, can accept it or do without it. But in ancient Egypt the monarch was believed to perform a cosmic role. The life of his people and the life of nature throughout his territory was thought to be closely bound up with his life, his vigour, his virility. Chaos might ensue at his death if his natural successor were not immediately enthroned in his stead; by this was understood not only political chaos, but something more akin to cosmic chaos. The king was deity incarnate, the guarantor of life and fertility, the upholder of the whole natural order.

The correlation between monarchy and monotheism has been pointed out by a succession of anthropologists and sociologists. Whereas earlier theorists such as Max Weber were impressed by the frequency of the correlation in such societies as they had studied, recent modern studies have gone beyond these impressionistic findings, and have been based on precise factual and statistical analysis. One of the most recent of such studies is that by Guy Swanson (1960). Swanson, examining the evidence provided by fifty separate societies (Azanda, Aztec, Bemba, Carib, Cuna, ancient Egyptian, etc.), found that there was a strong correlation between societies having a clearly identifiable hierarchical structure – that is, having three or more *types* of sovereign groups ranked in hierarchical order – and monotheistic beliefs. A summary of Swanson's findings is sufficient for our purpose here. A perfect correlation, that is, one in which monotheism was always found to occur in hierarchically-structured societies, and never in simple-structured societies, would be represented by a coefficient of $+1{\cdot}0$. A result which showed the complete reverse of this, viz. that monotheism never occurs in hierarchically-structured societies, would be represented by a coefficient of $-1{\cdot}0$. A complete absence of correlation one way or the other would be represented by the coefficient 0. On the basis of the fifty societies examined, the coefficient of contingency between hierarchically-structured societies and monotheistic beliefs was found to be $+0{\cdot}81$, a result which is near enough to the absolute of positive correlation $(+1{\cdot}0)$ to be very impressive.

Moreover, among these ancient Egypt is a particularly strong case, since it satisfies other general results from Swanson's study, such as that monotheistic beliefs are most likely to occur in societies possessing normally stable sources of food, that is large-scale grain-producing agricultural societies.

Correlation must not be confused with causal connection. But in the case of Egypt the causal factors responsible for the emergence of centralised political power are overwhelmingly geographical, physical and cultural. The territory itself, as Frankfort points out, is of a kind which has much more clearly-marked natural frontiers than most, from which political power would most easily recoil to the centre. And it is clear that in Egypt it was in terms of such power that deity was thought of.

1.15 Kingship, myth and ritual in the ancient Near East

Both in Egypt and Babylon the life of the king was considered to be directly related to the life of the land, its crops, its herds and its people. Even in Babylon where the king was not regarded as himself divine, as he was in Egypt, there was a high evaluation of the person of the king as the god's representative.

In both Egypt and Babylon such ideas found expression in an annual festival. The ritual associated with the festival was intended to repel the powers hostile to life, and to safeguard and secure fertility and the continuance of life. Connected with the ritual actions was a creation myth which told of the conquest of a primeval chaos-monster and the setting up of the ordered life of nature and of the nation. At the annual festival the king personally played the chief role in the ritual which was held to be a re-enactment of the creation drama related in the myth. The common features of this festival were therefore:

1. A drama representing the death and resurrection of the deity
2. A recapitulation of the creation story
3. A ritual combat, or mimic battle, in which the god-king overthrew his enemies
4. The celebration of a sacred marriage between the deity and the land
5. A triumphal procession of the victorious god-king

This was the climax of the festival, and often took the form of the enthronement of the king. This last feature has provided the name by which scholars often refer to this ancient Near Eastern ritual, *Thronbesteigungsfest* or Enthronement-festival.

In Babylon this festival marked the beginning of a new year. The accompanying myth has become well known as the Epic of Creation: the story of Marduk, god of Babylon; of how he engaged in battle with Tiamat, the female personification of the great ocean, and her demon-host, the monsters of chaos; of how Marduk emerged triumphant, having slain Tiamat; of how he then organised the natural order of the universe. The story of the creation of man follows, which tells how man was created for the service of the god. Marduk was then confirmed in his place as 'king for ever'.

In Egypt the myth told of Osiris, the god, who was killed, and subsequently brought back to life by Isis the goddess in order that he might father Horus his successor. It has been suggested that this myth, and the accompanying ritual performance, was a dramatic representation of the annual disappearance of vegetation in Egypt, when the land was inundated by the flood-waters of the Nile, followed by the subsequent renewal of life when the waters had subsided. Thus, Osiris died and was hidden – but always with the expectation of reappearance and renewal of life. In the Egyptian form of the enthronement ritual the human king of Egypt was identified with Horus, and the previous (dead) king with Osiris. The ritual actions of the living king were deliberately made to represent those of Horus in the myth; the meaning, comments A. M. Blackman, is that 'he in whom the life of his people is centred, will ensure the fertility of his subjects, and of their fields, flocks and herds' (Hooke, 1933; 32).

1.16 Myth, ritual and magic

According to S. H. Hooke, the origin of such ritual 'lies in the attempt *to control the unpredictable element in human experience*' (present writer's italics). 'The ritual pattern represents the things which were done to and by the king in order to secure the prosperity of the community in every sense for the coming year' (Hooke, 1933; 8). In this connection it is interesting to note the distinction made by Bronislaw Malinowski between magic and religion. According to Malinowski magic is essentially practical in its scope and intention: 'It is always the affirmation of man's power to cause definite effects by a definite spell and rite' (Malinowski, 1926; 81). It is the kind of routinised activity in which men engage in face of the unpredictable, that is in situations where their empirically-based skills, such as sailing or agriculture, become insufficient, 'the domain of the unaccountable and adverse influences'. In such situations magic is resorted to, and it thus consists of 'a practical art consisting of acts which are only means to a definite end expected to follow later on'. In addition to the *acts* Malinowski points out there are also certain important *sounds*, to be chanted or recited; these constitute the spell, in which the power of the magic resides. Religious faith on the other hand is concerned not so much with producing immediate practical effects, as with establishing, fixing and enhancing 'all valuable mental attitudes, such as reverence for tradition, harmony with environment, courage and confidence in the struggle with difficulties and at the prospect of death' (Malinowski, 1926; 82).

In describing the myth-ritual state ceremonies of the ancient Near East as attempts 'to control the unpredictable element in human experience', S. H. Hooke is in effect identifying them, according to Malinowski's analysis, as magic rather than religion. It is important that in the course of a survey of religion such as we are making we should be able to distinguish the characteristically *religious* attitude from other attitudes, often closely associated and sometimes confused with it. Malinowski's distinction between *science* as an empirical body of knowledge, *magic* as a routinised method of attempting to control forces present in situations of uncertainty or unpredictability, and *religious faith* as the enhancing of certain valuable mental attitudes, although it is obviously somewhat over-simplified, nevertheless provides what is probably the clearest guide in these matters.

1.17 *Magical rituals and creation myths*

A further question which needs to be raised in connection with the myths and ritual of the ancient Near East concerns the creation myths. As S. G. F. Brandon has pointed out, so accustomed are we to the idea of the creation of the world in the Hebrew tradition of Genesis, that we have come to regard the idea as axiomatic (Brandon, 1963). We have also come to regard this idea as a necessary part of religious belief. Yet the origins of the idea in its traditional Hebrew form appear to be in the ancient myths of Egypt and Babylon, and in the realm of magic. Brandon has shown that the earliest Egyptian creation legends come from the 'first vigorous phase of its civilisation known as the Old Kingdom (2740-2270 B.C.)', when the country had first come under a centralised monarchical government. Before that time Egypt as we know it scarcely existed:

> The annual submergence of the low-lying land by the great river meant that habitation was possible only at places above the level of the inundation, while large tracts of the valley and delta must have been a permanent swamp, full of water-weed and teeming with aquatic life. Only gradually and by immense labour were these swamps drained, and irrigation works constructed to control and conserve the flood waters. Such undertakings in turn extended the area possible for settlement and so allowed the increase of a settled population, occupied in agriculture. (Brandon, 1963; 14 f.)

The connection between such an achievement and the power of the monarch who had unified the country and, in a sense, brought Egypt into existence was so strong that it is not surprising that the god-king came to be regarded as one who, by his own will and power, had created the land upon which his people lived. It is this idea of creation that forms an important element, as we have seen, in the myth and ritual pattern of Egypt, that is, in state ceremonies that are ostensibly as much magical as they are religious. This is a subject which can only be lightly touched upon here, but it is a question to be borne in mind in any historical survey of religious belief and practices: is the idea of a divine creation *ex nihilo* a necessary element in religious belief, as Westerners tend to assume? We shall see that a creation legend is not a primary feature of the formative period of Israel's characteristic religious faith (*1.20*); nor is it an element of Buddhist religious faith. On the other hand, where in Indian religion it does assume a place of prominence it is in the context of the *magical* practices of Brahmanism (*1.53*).

1.18 The Indus valley civilisation

It was not until 1920, when the excavation of two ancient and forgotten cities of the Punjab began, that any evidence of India's early history was available. Until then scholars relied on the Vedic sacred texts (*1.34*), which, so far as India is concerned, provide us with evidence only from about 1500 B.C. onwards, when the Vedic Aryan tribes entered north-west India. These facts need to be mentioned so that the student may be aware that books concerning Indian religion written before 1920 are based on the assumption that the only light that can be shed on ancient India's religious beliefs and practices is that provided in the Vedic texts. Since the early 1920s, however, it has become possible to construct a picture of conditions in north-west India before the invasion of the Indo-European or Aryan-speaking tribes. Two extensive city sites, known as Mohenjo-Daro and Harappā, have been excavated, the former on the west bank of the Indus and the latter on the south bank of the Ravi, one of the five rivers of the 'Punjab' (i.e. the 'five waters'). These excavations have revealed the existence throughout a period of at least a thousand years before the coming of the Aryans of an urban civilisation similar to those of Babylonia (*1.11*) and Egypt (*1.13*). Archaeological work has now been carried out at many other sites in the Indus valley besides Mohenjo-Daro and Harappā, and has revealed how extensive this urban civilisation was, covering as it did most of the lower Indus valley and the Punjab, that is to say an area of about a thousand miles in extent from south-west to north-east. It seems to have been roughly contemporaneous with the other two river valley civilisations, although it is possible that it emerged a little later than the other two, and may even have been due to some extent to their influence: an urban civilisation centring on a few large towns or cities was probably imposed on an earlier village economy. That is to say, a social and political pattern which was otherwise foreign to India may have been stimulated in the Indus region, in imitation of these other civilisations whose fame was widespread.

The literature describing the layout of these Indus valley cities and the kind of economy which supported them is now easily available (Piggott, 1950; Childe, 1952; H. M. Wheeler, 1959 and 1966). Briefly, what is important for our purpose is that by about the middle of the second millennium B.C. this civilisation was already a thousand years old, and in a state of decline. The type of buildings which have been unearthed, the layout of the cities, as well as the large number of small household objects such as pottery and terra-cotta and bronze figurines, and articles of a mercantile character such as seals, all indicate, says Stuart Piggott, the existence of what may be described as a largely 'middle-class' civilisation, that is one in which a comfortable standard of living was enjoyed by the maximum number; they imply 'the elaborate organisation of an urban mercantile class whose products lack not only the barbaric spontaneity of the older and more primitive cultures, but even the cheery *nouveau-riche* vulgarity of Early Dynastic Sumer . . . and display instead a dead level of bourgeois mediocrity in almost every branch of the visual arts and crafts' (Piggott, 1950; 200). There was evidently a highly organised system of central government capable of administering large-scale building and town-planning, but nothing is known for certain about the nature of this government. Some scholars have suggested that it was of a priestly-hierarchical kind, but this remains uncertain.

1.19 Religious aspects of the Indus valley civilisation

The main evidence upon which some reconstruction of religious practices may be based consists of the seals and statuettes found throughout the area. First, there are the many terra-cotta statuettes of a female figure evidently intended to suggest motherhood; so many of these have been found that they are generally regarded as evidence of the worship of a mother-goddess. In some cases vegetation is shown issuing from the womb of the figure, and this would seem to indicate the idea of a mother-earth goddess. Second, there are frequent representations on seals of a male figure seated in the characteristic posture of the Indian yogin, with crossed legs. This yogic figure is often three-faced and surrounded by various animals. There is little doubt, concludes Piggott, that this is a prototype of the (later) Hindu god Śiva, who is known as the Prince of Yogins, the Lord of Beasts, whose faces look to the four quarters of the earth (Piggott, 1950; 202). Third, there is evidence of the veneration of phallic symbols, and thus of the generative powers in the natural world; this also corresponds with what appear in later Indian practice as fertility cults. Fourth, there is evidence of the veneration of a sacred tree; this too is a feature of later Indian practice, in the worship of the pīpal, the Hindu holy tree. Fifth, there is a piece of negative evidence, in the absence of anything in the nature of a temple-building. In conjunction with the large number of mother-goddess statuettes this suggests that the religious practices of the Indus valley civilisation were largely domestic; this too corresponds with the major emphasis in later Hindu practice, even when temples do begin to play some part.

These similarities between the religious practices of the Indus valley – the mother-goddess, the yogic god, the phallic emblem, the sacred tree, the domestic emphasis – are of great interest, especially in view of the characteristic conservatism of religion in India. It may be suggested, therefore, that the Hindu cults of the post-Buddhist period do not constitute a new development, but something which in essence is to be found at least two thousand years earlier.

Little is known, or can be reconstructed, concerning the religious ideas of the Indus civilisation. One of the major obstacles here is that the script which appears on the objects discovered is unlike any other of the ancient world, and is so far undeciphered.

1.2 OUT OF MESOPOTAMIA AND OUT OF EGYPT

1.20 *The significance of Israel*

Within the whole context of ancient oriental history, Israel's place is very small; certainly it was of much less importance in the ancient world than it has come to be regarded subsequently, because of what has developed out of the religion of Israel. Even within the context of the history of the ancient Near East, the great names are Egypt, Babylon, Assyria, while Israel's role is of minor importance. Nevertheless, from the religious life of a small confederation of tribes have developed, historically, the major religions of the Western world: Judaism, Christianity, and Islam; the religious ideas of the Old Testament have, for better or worse, heavily influenced the religious thought of Europe and America. The three major systems just mentioned together constitute most of the Western stream of religious tradition, and are sometimes grouped in contrast to the other religions of the world, especially those of India, namely Hinduism, Buddhism, Jainism, and Sikhism. That there are some real differences of emphasis and outlook between these two groups or traditions cannot be denied; how these differences are to be identified or characterised, however, is not easy to decide. Some call the Western tradition prophetic, in contrast to the Eastern tradition which they describe as mystical (Zaehner, 1959). But the religion of the Buddha also has claims to the title 'prophetic' and was so regarded by the German sociologist of religion, Max Weber. Some have characterised the Western tradition as monotheistic in contrast to the Eastern tradition as pantheistic. Yet there is a strong and important element of monotheism in the religion of India, which receives classic formulation in the thought of the Hindu theologians Rāmānuja, Rāmānanda and others (*6.14–6.17*), although it did not begin with them. For these and other reasons it is difficult to find any clear differential factor between what are broadly the original religious traditions of West and East, and even these now overlap one another geographically. This overlapping came about, first, by the large-scale missionary expansion of Islam into Asia from the eighth century onwards, to be followed later by Christianity; and then in modern times by the missionary expansion of the Hindu and Buddhist systems into the Western world. It is therefore inappropriate to speak of the religious tradition of the West as monotheistic, or prophetic, and that of the East as pantheistic, or mystical, as some people especially in the West are inclined to do (and more especially if when they call something pantheistic or mystical they are thereby indicating its inferiority to what is monotheistic and prophetic). All that can strictly be said of these two broad streams of religious tradition is that one stream has its most important single source in Israel and the other in ancient India; both have received considerable accessions of thought and practice from elsewhere in the course of their progress through history.

1.21 Weber's view of the essence of Israel's religion

Another important distinction between the religious beliefs and
practices (especially the latter) of East and West was that made by Max
Weber in his studies in the sociology of religion. According to Weber
there is a fundamental contrast between oriental and occidental
religion; the former he sees as being characterised by contemplative
mysticism, and the latter by ascetic activism. He contrasts the attitude
found among Hindus with that of the Jews:

> Ritually correct conduct, i.e. conduct conforming to caste standards,
> earned for the Indian pariah castes the premium of ascent by way of
> rebirth in a caste-structured world thought to be eternal and unchange-
> able. . . . For the Jew the religious promise was the opposite. The social
> order of the world was conceived to have been turned into the opposite
> of that promised for the future, but in the future it was to be overturned
> so that Jewry could be once again dominant. The world was conceived
> as neither eternal nor unchangeable, but rather as having been created.
> Its present structures were a product of man's activities, above all those
> of the Jews, and of God's reaction to them. (Weber, 1952; 3 ff.)

Weber thus sees the cultural heritage of the religion of Israel for the
West as that of 'a highly rational religious ethic of social conduct',
which, he considers, was 'worlds apart from the paths of salvation
offered by Asiatic religions'. This alleged contrast is one of the important
issues in the modern comparative study of religion, and we shall return
to it later. Briefly, it may be observed at this point that Weber's
contrast, made in the opening pages of his *Ancient Judaism*, is far from
satisfactory as it stands for the following reason. The religion of Israel
was not a simple, uncomplicated 'rational religious ethic', as Weber
himself acknowledges. What he is here describing is the religious
attitude exemplified and commended by the ethical prophets of Israel;
over against it and in continual opposition to it was the other major
element of Israelite religion concerned with monarchy and magic.
Precisely the same dichotomy is to be observed in Indian religion,
between the ritualistic, monarchy-supporting, priestly tradition of
Brahmanism, and the rejection of this in the ethical-prophetic movements of Jainism and Buddhism. Weber's sources of information on
Indian religion were not as rich as those he was able to use for Judaism,
as we shall see; and his genius for making conceptual structures and

then applying them to actual religious systems seems to have led him astray to some extent. One further point which can be made here is that the religion of Israel bequeathed something else to Western culture besides a rational religious ethic; something equally important, far-reaching and possibly disastrous in its consequences all through Western history – the idea of the holy war. Out of the earliest most formative period of Israel's history comes the idea of a god who fights for his people against their enemies, an idea which has, in the eyes of those Jews, Christians and Muslims who have been influenced by it, provided legitimation for various courses of international, inter-cultural, and inter-religious violence, right up to the present day where its influence is still at work in such policies as those which aim at destroying communism in Asia by military might.

1.22 Sources for the study of Israel's religion

The main source for the study of the religion of ancient Israel is the Old Testament. This, however, is itself a collection of documents of various kinds whose origins range over a period of about a thousand years, so that the evidence of each part has to be used with discrimination, after its historical reliability has been evaluated. It has to be supplemented by and compared with certain other sources of historical evidence. The most important of these extra-Biblical sources are as follows.

1. *The Egyptian execration texts.* These consist of a large number of fragments of earthenware pots on which had been inscribed certain magical formulae in execration of Egypt's enemies, and which had then been smashed (to make the formulae effective). Their value as historical evidence lies in the fact that they give the names of rulers and places in the ancient Near East in the early centuries of the second millennium B.C. They have, says W. F. Albright, 'illuminated the political and demographic situation within the Egyptian empire in Asia (Palestine, Phoenicia and Southern Syria) to a previously unimagined degree.'

2. *The Mari Texts.* These relate to a period probably just after that referred to in the Execration Texts. They consist of some 20,000 tablets and fragments comprising the official records of the kings of Mari (*1.11*), at that time a powerful state; the texts provide

valuable evidence of the international Near Eastern culture of the
period (Bright, 1959; 50 f.).

3. *The El Amarna tablets.* These consist of about 400 clay tablets
dating from about the fourteenth century B.C. They began to be
discovered in 1887 in a mound, or *tell*, at El Amarna in upper
Egypt, where there was once a palace of one of the Pharaohs.
Their value lies in the fact that they consist of items of imperial
correspondence in the international script and language of the
time, namely Babylonian, and throw considerable light on the
background of Israel's early history.

4. *The Rās Shamra tablets.* These, too, belong to approximately
the fourteenth century B.C., and provide a rich source of Canaanite
religious literature in the form of epics (Rowley, 1951; 30–4).

5. Various other sources of archaeological evidence relating to the
period of Israel's origin and development, the more important of
which are: the Code of Hammurabi, the Babylonian Epics, and
certain Hittite and Assyrian tablets (Winton Thomas, 1958).

It will be seen that there is a considerable amount of independent
historical evidence outside the Hebrew documents of the Old Testament,
and it is on the basis of this kind of evidence that Old Testament
scholarship now proceeds, as well as on that of the Hebrew texts.

1.23 The earliest outline of Israel's history

When does Israel's history begin? The question is not easy to answer,
for there are a number of different possible starting points, each of
which appears in some sense to have been the real beginning. In the
Old Testament any continuous narrative of the history of a recognisable
group called Israel would appear to begin in the book of Exodus,
although this has now been prefaced by the patriarchal narratives of
Genesis, and these in turn are prefaced by stories of what purports to be
the primeval history of the world. The early chapters of Genesis are
not, however, the oldest in point of composition. For sheer contem-
poraneousness with the events described one of the best claimants is an
ancient song embedded in Judg. 5, the Song of Deborah. Another
claimant to great antiquity is the very ancient creedal confession now
found in the book of Deuteronomy (26: 5–9), the words of which are
important enough to be quoted in full here:

A wandering Aramean was my father [the speaker is any Israelite, in the period after the settlement in Canaan], and he went down into Egypt, and sojourned there, few in number; and he became there a nation, great, mighty and populous:

And the Egyptians evil entreated us, and afflicted us, and laid upon us hard bondage:

And we cried unto the LORD, the God of our fathers, and the LORD heard our voice, and saw our affliction, and our toil, and our oppression:

And the LORD brought us forth out of Egypt with a mighty hand, and with an outstretched arm, and with great terribleness, and with signs and with wonders:

And he has brought us unto this place, and he has given us this land, a land flowing with milk and honey.

Here we have words which were used as a religious confession by ancient Israel long before the Bible had come into existence, and it is important to notice, therefore, what is said and *what is not said*.

Nothing is said concerning an act of divine creation; at that time Israel's religious affirmation did not start from the doctrine of a God who had created the universe. Nothing is said concerning the patriarchs Abraham or Isaac; 'a wandering Aramean' almost certainly means Jacob (*1.24*). Nothing is said concerning the great events at Sinai, the making of the covenant between Israel and her God, and the reception of the Law. Each of these points must therefore be examined in a little more detail, together with those things which *are* affirmed in this ancient Israelite creed.

1.24 *The patriarchal background to Israel's beginnings*

For the ancient Israelite the history of the special group of tribes of which he was a member began with an eponymous ancestor, one who bore the name by which the whole group was now known, that is, Israel. 'Jacob' and 'Israel' are interchangeable, alternative names, both for the patriarch and for the group, throughout the Hebrew scriptures. Outside the Pentateuch (where one would expect to find mention of Jacob the patriarch) there are elsewhere in the Old Testament just over 130 different references to 'Jacob'; in most of these the name is used as a synonym for Israel, the nation. While 'Jacob' is thus not unusual outside the Pentateuch, the names Abraham and Isaac (surprisingly) occur only rarely. The identification of Jacob as the nation's ancestor was obviously something very characteristic of Israel's tradition. Nevertheless, even

though Israel's history proper really begins with Jacob, the figure of
Abraham also had an undeniable importance, and in course of time the
traditions about this earlier ancestor from Mesopotamia were gathered
together and given a place in the 'preface' to Israel's history which we
now call the book of Genesis. Apart from the possibility that he may
well represent a Mesopotamian ancestry for the Hebrews, Abraham has
an importance in the religious tradition quite different from that of
Jacob. He is the *ideal* Israelite whereas Jacob was so obviously the real
Israelite, scheming, shrewd, full of guile (cf. John 1: 47). To say this is
in no way to suggest that Abraham was not an historical figure: the
traditions concerning him seem to be well grounded and the incidental
details accord well with what is now known of names and customs of
Mesopotamia and Canaan at the beginning of the second millennium
B.C.; moreover the fact that Isaac appears as a link between Abraham
and Jacob (and for little other purpose, if the narrative was a pious
invention) indicates that we are dealing here with real, remembered
facts. Abraham is the *ideal* Israelite in the sense that he represents,
especially in the view of the ethical prophets, what every Israelite
should be, or should aspire to be – a man entirely obedient to God, a
man of moral uprightness and devout faith.

1.25 *The status of creation-beliefs among the Hebrews*

Another ancient creedal confession, similar to that which is now
embedded in the narrative of Deut. 26, is to be found in Josh. 24: 2–13.
This is similar, but slightly longer. Already the process of elaboration
can be seen at work; the process of filling out the original basic creed
had begun, which was eventually to result in the present Pentateuch.
The narrative in Josh. 24 consists of words attributed to Joshua on the
solemn occasion of the covenant with various other tribes who had not
been present at the original covenant occasion at Sinai (*1.28*); Joshua is
reminding the whole community of Israel, the original members and
the newcomers, of the essentials of their faith. The narrative statement
begins: 'Your fathers dwelt of old time beyond the River [that is, the
river Euphrates; thus, in Mesopotamia], even Terah, the father of
Abraham, and the father of Nahor: and they served other gods. And I
took your father Abraham from beyond the River, and led him
throughout all the land of Canaan. . . .'

It will be noticed that in neither of these two very ancient formulae setting out the essentials of the faith of Israel is there any introductory statement concerning God as creator of the universe. For Israel, their history began with Jacob, or possibly with Abraham. And this is how the book of Genesis very naturally and easily divides: the historical material begins in chapter 12, with Abraham's sense of a divine call to him to leave Mesopotamia and journey into some new territory; before that now stand the eleven chapters which consist largely of ancient Near Eastern mythology, modified and adapted by later Hebrew thought. The fact that later on in Israel's history it was felt to be necessary to preface the 'salvation-history' which began at Abraham with a cosmological introduction reveals the extent to which the Hebrews were influenced by the culture of the rest of the ancient Near East, particularly of Mesopotamia and Egypt. For it was in these countries most notably (and, indeed, with their hydraulic-agrarian despotisms, understandably), that creation ideas had developed. Especially in Egypt it was the god-king who was regarded as having, by his will and activity, created the land upon which his people lived; here the centre of political power *had* indeed been the creative factor in producing land for cultivation by flood control and co-ordinated planning. In Mesopotamia the central power had achieved this through an overall scheme of irrigation works. We have seen, too, that creation stories in these lands were integrally related to a national ritual-magic in which the king as the embodiment of the nation's life procured through the process of the ritual the continuance of the life of this created world each new year.

The religion of Israel did not spring primarily from such roots. Its major impetus was not a desire for the safeguarding and continuance of the life of the land, the crops, and the herds. The doctrine of divine production of the land was therefore of less primary importance, as were also the rituals by which the life of the land was yearly maintained, although both these elements did later come to be features of the complex which is known as Hebrew religion.

1.26 The distinctive character of Yahwism

Essentially the religion of Israel differed from that of other nations of the ancient Near East in that it was at its most characteristic not a royal ritual-magic, nor a popular system of divination and wisdom for enabling men to pick a trouble-free way through the changes and chances of mortal life (*1.12*), but had the character which Talcott Parsons, in translating the works of Weber into English, calls '*prophetic breakthrough*' (Weber, 1963; xxix).

It is because Weber's '*primary* interest is in religion as a source of the dynamics of social change, not religion as a reinforcement of the stability of societies' (Weber, 1963; xxx), as it was in Egypt and Babylonia, that he regards the prophetic religion of Israel as a crucial factor in the development of Western society. We have, therefore, to examine the circumstances in which this prophetic breakthrough occurred.

Out of Egypt came Israel. A group of tribes, by tradition herdsmen rather than cultivators, whose ancestors had perhaps taken refuge in this land where food supply was more secure because of skilful centralised administration, had by that same administration been forced to toil as slaves, contributing to some of the vast state enterprises of the Egyptian monarch. But at last there emerged among them a man of great charisma under whose leadership they escaped from this oppressive rule, from this land of highly organised agriculture, with its great urban centres and massive temples which a potentate had built and where power was worshipped. Out of Egypt came Israel, at first glad to shake Egypt's dust from their feet, reviling everything Egyptian, and most of all perhaps, monarchical rule, against which, it must not be forgotten, the Exodus was a revolt. To Israel escaping there came the awareness of spiritual reality of another kind, formulated in other terms. It came to them through their own prophet-leader; the awareness first experienced by him of personal encounter with a spiritual being whose nature was supremely that of *compassion*, one who had heard the cry of the afflicted Hebrews and knew their sorrows (Exod. 3: 7), and whose only name was *I am what I am*, or *I will be what I will be*, that is, one whose nature was disclosed in the course of ongoing relationship. Between this holy one and themselves the Hebrews believed there now existed a firm and unbreakable relationship, a covenant, not initiated by them but to which they, out of gratitude, must be faithful. This became the cohesive factor for a confederation of Hebrew tribes, including not only those who had come out of Egypt but others who appear to have been already settled in central Canaan, and to whom the covenant relationship was now extended upon the acceptance by them of its implications – loyalty to and worship of the holy one of Israel (see Josh. 24: 14–15).

In the early creedal confession (*1.23*) deliverance from Egypt is the central affirmation; around this other statements are grouped by way of introduction and consequence. From the fact of what the Hebrews held to have been a divine act of deliverance the subsequent statements in the confession take their significance. Three aspects of this deliverance which forms the basis of Israel's faith demand our attention: the event itself; the man who is notably associated with the event, i.e. Moses; and the interpretation and subsequent understanding of the event.

1.27 *The event of the Exodus*

It is clear that later piety has been at work on the tradition concerning the Exodus, as often elsewhere, embroidering and magnifying the marvellous nature of the event. When the early creed found in Deut. 26 (*1.23*) is compared with the somewhat later and already amplified form found in Josh. 24, it will be seen that certain features in the older statement have been considerably expanded, in the direction of thaumaturgy, or heightening the element of the marvellous. Deut. 26 speaks simply of 'signs and wonders'; whereas in Josh. 24 these are spelt out in detail, in connection with the Egyptian army's miraculous destruction in the waters of the Red Sea after the Hebrews' equally miraculous safe crossing. When the book of Exodus (a still later stage in the development of the tradition) is consulted we find a further magnification of marvels. In the earlier version, 'a strong east wind' opened a way through a lagoon (Exod. 14: 21), whereas in what is generally regarded on linguistic grounds as being a later version, the waters are said to stand up like walls on either side of the Israelites (Exod. 14: 22). In what is a later tradition still, Ps. 114: 3, the trend continues, for we are told that 'the sea fled'. Perhaps the ultimate is reached in the treatment given to the incident by modern Hollywood film-makers.

But whatever 'really happened' it is obvious that it made a deep impression on those who experienced it, and the interpretation of its significance by Moses became the central religious tradition of Israel. The tradition that the Hebrew people had been serfs in Egypt is very strong, and it accords with what is known of Egyptian history. There is on the other hand the equally strong and well-attested tradition among the Hebrews that when they entered Canaanite territory it was as conquerors – disciplined and well organised, and thus able to overcome the resistance of the inhabitants of the land in their strongholds. Some historical experience of outstanding quality has to be postulated to explain the transformation which a comparison of these two traditions implies, from serfs to disciplined conquerors of superior forces. We have to consider how much of this was due to Moses, and what was his most characteristic role.

1.28 *The prophetic role of Moses*

Walter Eichrodt says of Moses that he does not easily fit into any one category as leader of the Hebrew tribes, but combines several functions: tribal chieftain, leader of an army, priest, inspired seer, legislator. Eichrodt considers that in the tradition of Israel it is only later that Moses comes to be regarded as a prophet, 'when there had been time to reflect on the analogy between Moses and prophetism' (Eichrodt, 1961; 290). But this is simply to say that *the word* 'prophet' was applied to Moses only later on, when it had come into general use and when there were a number of exemplars in what are called the classical prophets, that is, from Amos onwards (*2.13*). To deny Moses the *nature* or *religious function* of prophet is a purely arbitrary decision based on the assumption that Hebrew prophecy occurred only from the eighth century B.C. onwards. In fact, he has a number of the characteristic marks of the classical prophet.

1. There is first of all the strong tradition of a profound personal experience of an inaugural kind – inaugural, that is, to his activity as a charismatic leader – the tradition which is contained in the narrative of Exod. 3. The vision of the bush which glowed as with fire and yet was not consumed; the overwhelming consciousness of a divine presence; the awareness that he was being personally addressed by this divine reality whose name (that is, whose *nature*) he did not as yet know; the enigmatic name which was conveyed to him in this experience – YHWH, meaning possibly 'I will be what I will be' or 'I am what I am' or even simply 'He who is' (the name which in the English

translation of the Old Testament is indicated by the word 'LORD' in upper-case letters): all these are characteristic features of the initial vision and 'call' of a prophet in Hebrew tradition. In this kind of experience the constant elements are the sense of being confronted by transcendent reality as never before, and the sense that this reality is of a personal kind, making unavoidable demands and promising the individual who is thus confronted a special endowment of the qualities necessary for the fulfilment of the task which is now laid upon him.

2. Besides the knowledge of the name (nature) of the divine being which comes to Moses in this experience there is also the disclosure concerning something that is about to happen, something which Yahweh (this is the accepted modern vocalisation of YHWH) is going to bring to pass. This, too, is characteristic of the Hebrew prophets; their role was to make known something which Yahweh was about to do.

3. Moses is represented as being himself the human agent of this happening – the deliverance of the Hebrews from their Egyptian serfdom. This involvement in the action is also characteristic of the classical Hebrew prophets: Elijah, Elisha, Isaiah, Jeremiah; these were certainly men of action as well as of words.

4. Above all, Moses is the human agent through whom the events are interpreted to the people as the activity of God; it is he who invests them with meaning for Israel, meaning which it is given to the prophet to perceive.

There is, however, another aspect of the activity of Moses according to Hebrew tradition, namely that of lawgiver. The fact that the large complex of events which later tradition places at Sinai (the communication of the divine law and the making of a sacred covenant between Yahweh and the Hebrew tribes) is not mentioned at all in the early summaries of Israel's history, in Deut. 26 (*1.23*) and Josh. 24 (*1.25*), is certainly on the face of it a very curious fact. This has led some modern German scholars (Noth, 1960; Von Rad, 1962) to suggest that the association of Moses with the law-giving at Sinai is a later embellishment; that originally there were two separate groups of tribes, one of which experienced the deliverance from Egypt and whose tradition is represented in the early creedal summaries; while the other group experienced a theophany at a sacred mountain somewhere outside

Canaan, an experience later formulated in terms of a covenant-making and law-giving. These two groups, it is suggested, later joined forces on Canaanite soil, and their originally separate traditions of deliverance from Egypt and covenant at Sinai became fused into one tradition which was from then on common to both. According to this theory Moses was the leader of the group which came out of Egypt and originally had no connection with the reception of the sacred law. There is, however, an alternative explanation for the absence of any mention of Sinai from the earliest creedal confessions, namely, that the sheer bulk of the Sinai tradition, and its special nature, meant that it was transmitted independently, in a separate parallel form from the summaries of the 'salvation history'. Moreover, it is the event of the deliverance from Egypt which provides the basis for the covenant between Yahweh and the Hebrew tribes; if this was not the basis for the very powerful covenant idea, then some other event very like it would have to be discovered in order to account for what is a most strongly attested and persistent and peculiar idea among the ancient Hebrews – that the divine being, Yahweh, had in some way given outstanding proof of the relation which was to be regarded as existing between him and the Hebrews.

On the whole, therefore, the connection of Moses with the communication to the tribes of the sacred law which was henceforth to govern their common life may be regarded as genuine and trustworthy tradition. The prophet who made known to the Hebrew tribes what had been revealed to him concerning the nature and purposes of the divine being, also made known to them in precise detail the pattern of life which this entailed for them, as the beneficiaries of Yahweh's saving action. Here, in fact, we see another characteristic mark of Hebrew prophecy throughout its history, namely the insistence that to be the recipients of divine revelation means also for the Hebrews that their common life is to exhibit a certain pattern of ethical conduct.

1.29 *Prophetic interpretation of historical events*

The role of Moses in relation to the Exodus of the Hebrew tribes from Egypt is, then, essentially that of prophet, as this is understood in subsequent Hebrew tradition. He who interprets certain significant events of human history and points out to men the revelation of

Yahweh's nature which these events constitute is, in the tradition of Israel, a prophet. Whether or not it is proper to speak of Moses as the *founder* of Israel's religion is debatable. But certainly it is with Moses that we can first clearly recognise the emergence of a religious tradition which is markedly different from other major religious traditions of the ancient Near East. It is a tradition whose most characteristic bearers are such men as Moses, who appear from time to time as inspired leaders and interpreters of the great events of human history; who appeal to their fellows to see in the course of events what they have seen, the manifestation of the purposes of a personal, transcendent, holy being, who can only be known as 'He who is', but with whom, the prophets declare, it is possible for men to enter into a relation of personal communion as they observe and fulfil the demands which he makes upon them; in Hebrew prophetic religion such relationship is itself the *summum bonum*, a self-authenticating experience which in prophetic terms is 'to know the LORD' (Jer. 31: 34). The effects of the kind of innovation which Yahwism represented, even although the prophet doctrine was never fully comprehended or adhered to by all of Israel, were sufficiently radical in the situation of the time to justify the modern description of it as a 'prophetic breakthrough'. Nothing corresponding to this is found in contemporary Babylonian or Egyptian culture; nor in Persia until the sixth century B.C. when something like it appears in the prophetic activity of Zarathustra (*2.2*); nor in India either until (also in the sixth century) there appear the Mahāvīra and the Buddha. At this point, however, we have still to trace certain developments which took place in India in the second half of the second millennium B.C., that is, the period immediately before and after the events which have just been related were taking place in Egypt and Canaan.

1.3 RELIGION IN INDIA DURING THE EARLY VEDIC PERIOD (*1500–1000* B.C. approx.)

1.30 Pre-Aryan India

One of the earliest chapters of Indian history of which we have any record at all, that of the Indus valley civilisation (*1.18*), came to an end as other subsequent chapters of Indian history have done, partly because

of internal decay, partly because of invasion from without. In this case it was the Aryans who were the invaders. More precisely, it was a wave of Nordic peoples speaking an Aryan language; and this Aryan language and culture, from the middle of the second millennium B.C., was gradually to impose itself on the earlier, Dravidian culture, and extend further and further into India from the river plains of the Punjab; this is a process which has continued for centuries and is still going on today. Because the chief feature of the process is the acceptance of the Aryan language, Sanskrit, or at least of names and terms derived from Sanskrit, it is sometimes called 'Sanskritisation'. Another principal feature of the process has been the recognition of the special status of the Aryan priestly class, or brāhmans; hence it is sometimes also called 'brahmanisation'. What we need to enquire at this point is: What kind of culture, and what kind of people were (and still are) being subjected to this process?

Before the coming of the Nordics there had already been considerable intermixture of the ethnic types in the Indian subcontinent: Negrito is perhaps the earliest known, followed by Australoid, Mediterranean and Mongolian races. The Australoid peoples are represented by small pockets of Munda-speaking tribes. The Mediterranean element is broadly represented by the Dravidian language-groups of South India. Mongolian stock is found largely in the north along the Himālayan foothills, but has spread into other areas as well.

1.31 Religious features of pre-Aryan India

What we know of the religious practices of the Indus valley civilisation provides a rough, rather indistinct picture from which we may possibly infer a little about the religion of the other parts of pre-Aryan India. The Indus valley civilisation was essentially urban; its one or two large cities determined the pattern of its life. But as we have seen this pattern had probably been imposed on an earlier one in which the village was the characteristic unit of society. Outside the Indus valley, throughout the rest of India, this village economy was probably the general pattern at the coming of the Aryans. The village-pattern is still most characteristic of India, and is even now only gradually giving place to larger, overall regional and national patterns. A further point which we have to note is that over most of India from at least the time of the Indus valley civilisation until now agriculture has provided the characteristic basis of Indian life. With this village society based on an agricultural economy goes yet one more characteristic feature – the cult of the village goddess. In nomadic, pastoral, herd-keeping societies the male principle predominates; among agricultural peoples, aware of the fertile earth which brings forth from itself and nourishes its progeny upon its broad bosom, it is the mother-principle which seems important, unless, as in Egypt, some other factor intervenes. Among Semitic peoples therefore, whose traditions are those of herdsmen, the sacred is thought of in male terms: God the father. Among Indian peoples whose tradition has been for many centuries, and even millennia, agricultural, it is in female terms that the sacred is understood: God the mother. Throughout the more Dravidian area of South India the grāmadevata, the village goddess, still constitutes the most characteristic cult-object. Eliade notes such names for these village deities as Ellamma, Mari-yamma, Ambika, formed from a Dravidian root 'amma', meaning 'mother' (Eliade, 1958; 349). D. D. Kosambi also draws attention to the 'strong, highly localised cult' of goddesses bearing names with the termination 'ai', meaning mother: Mengai, Mandhrai, Songjai, Udalai, and so on (Kosambi, 1965; 48).

Here then is one of the dominant features which we shall notice again and again in the history of Indian religion, a persistent tendency to think of the sacred in terms of motherhood. It is a characteristic which seems to belong to the soul of India itself – or India *herself*, we should say, since the country is commonly referred to by her children as Mother-India. It is *not* a characteristic of the religious ideas of the invading Aryans, whose gods, as we shall see, were almost exclusively male.

1.32 The Dravidians and the notion of karma

Another thoroughly characteristic feature of Indian religious belief is that of karma. By this is meant a law of moral cause and effect which operates automatically and externally throughout the whole universe. It is in its relation to human beings, however, that the significance of this notion comes out most clearly, and provides one of the major factors in the development of Indian religious ideas. At the human level karma means that what a man is in this present life has been determined by his conduct in previous lives. Similarly, his conduct in this life will determine the kind of life he will lead in his next existence. This is sometimes known as the theory of transmigration, or metempsychosis. While it is not unknown elsewhere it is specially strong and persistent in India. Like the tendency to conceive of deity as feminine, this does not appear to have been characteristic of the Aryan invaders of India, but to have been learnt by them from the peoples whose land they invaded.

In his book, *The Dravidian Element in Indian Culture*, Gilbert Slater suggested that the roots of this idea are possibly to be found in the period when there was as yet no understanding of the facts of human reproduction; in particular, when the connection between intercourse and conception had not been perceived. Such was the case, Slater said, even in modern times among certain Australian aboriginal tribes. Among primitive tribes at this stage of development it was thought that conception was due to the entry of a spirit into the body of a young woman. Spirits commonly lurked in lonely and secluded places, it was held, and young women who resorted to such places were liable to become pregnant. The next stage in the development of the notion was to ask where the spirit came from which thus entered the woman's body and produced the embryo. The answer that would have been given was that the spirit came from some person who had recently died. In this way the idea arose of spirits passing through a series of human bodies, through one life after another. The important development which took place in India, however, was the linking of this attempt at biological explanation with moral ideas, that is, the introducing of the notion that the spirit in the course of its transmigration from one body to another carried with it its moral guilt or its merit, and that this explained the bad or good fortune which appeared, otherwise in-explicably, to mark the life of the new human being. Thus was evolved a satisfying solution to the problem of why men appeared to suffer misfortune undeservedly or, equally undeservedly perhaps, to enjoy good fortune and immunity from harm. If a man suffered misfortune without apparent cause, it was because of evil which he had done in a previous existence. If he committed countless wrongs and yet went unscathed this immunity was only for a while; in a future existence his moral guilt would bring its entail of suffering. So satisfying an explanation was this theory of karma, once developed, that even when the process of reproduction and the role of the father were better understood, the idea of a transmigrating spirit which was the bearer of a man's *moral* constitution persisted. This idea still does persist in India and South-East Asia, and one of the strongest reasons in its favour, so those who hold the theory maintain, is that no other explanation can account, as this does, for the apparent inequalities of human fortunes on the one hand, and the demand for justice in human affairs on the other. To abandon this idea, it is said, would be to attribute meaninglessness and injustice to the structure of human existence.

1.33 The coming of the Aryans

The Nordic, Aryan-speaking tribes who invaded the Indus valley and the Punjab in the middle of the second millennium B.C. came probably from the area of central Asia which lies to the south of Russia. They may have migrated from even further north. They called themselves Aryans, a name that in another form appears in 'Iran'. What is known of them is largely contained in the very ancient collection of chants or hymns to the gods known as the Rg-veda, the language of which is an earlier form of Sanskrit usually referred to as Vedic. In these hymns is found a different conception of man's destiny after death from that of karma and rebirth, one which has closer affinities with the ideas of northern Europe. (It is even possible that the name Arya is connected also with the name 'Eire', and that another branch of this same linguistic group may have found its way to Ireland.) There was among the Aryans when they first began to move into north-west India no belief that man's destiny consisted in an eternal round of transmigration; rather, those who had sinned were banished by the high god Varuna to the 'House of Clay', a gloomy place beneath the earth, rather like the Hebrew Sheol, while those who had lived worthily and earned Varuna's approval passed into the 'World of the Fathers', a celestial realm where they lived a life of bliss.

Here we have one of a number of indications that the religious ideas of the Aryans when they entered India differed considerably from those of the Dravidians already settled there. Another of these is the nature of the Aryan gods.

1.34 The gods of the Ṛg-veda

The prefix 'ṛg' means that which is concerned with *praise*, that is, the
praise of the Aryan gods. The Rg-veda collection of hymns, 1,017 in
number (or 1,028 by another reckoning), is arranged in ten maṇḍalas,
or cycles. The grouping of the hymns in maṇḍalas ii–viii is according
to their reputed authorship, all the hymns ascribed to one author being
placed together. Maṇḍala ix is in praise of the sacred soma plant which
is regarded virtually as a deity (see below). The first and tenth maṇḍalas
contain hymns composed by a variety of authors, and incorporate
compositions which are undoubtedly later in date than the bulk of the
hymns; something more will be said subsequently about the more
important of these later hymns (*1.52*), but first we must consider the
nature of the Aryan gods as this appears in the majority of the hymns,
which belong to the earlier period.

Whereas the worship of the mother-goddess is so prominent a
feature of Dravidian culture, the gods worshipped by the Aryans were
predominantly male. Their names show that they belong to a common
stock of Aryan, non-Indian religious ideas. (The generic name for these
beings, devas, is cognate with Latin deus, god.) Varuna, whom we have
just mentioned, is in his concern with moral rectitude not unlike
Yahweh of the Hebrews (*1.26*). The hymns in the Ṛg-veda which are
addressed to Varuna are characterised by a spirit of penitence on the
part of the worshipper which, it has been said, is very reminiscent of the
Hebrew penitential psalms (Basham, 1954; 237). Varuna is, literally,
the 'heavenly' deity, and his name is cognate with that of a similar deity
in ancient Greece, Ouranos, the god of the heavens. Other of the Vedic
deities' names also reveal linguistic connections with Greece, Rome and
Iran. Dyaus, for example, is the sky-god who is also the father (pitar) of
the gods. In Greek mythology this is Zeus, and in Roman Ju-piter.
Mitra the sun-god is also associated with Varuna in Vedic religion; by
his Greek and Iranian name of Mithras he was worshipped in the Middle
East and the Mediterranean region. Another of the powers of nature to
which deity was attributed by the Aryans was soma, the king of plants,
the source of a very potent drug which was ritually prepared from the
plant and drunk by the worshipper, upon whom it seems to have had,
to say the least, a most invigorating effect. In its Iranian form soma was
known as haoma, and in Iran too was used in a similar way. Another
Vedic deity whose name is Aryan in form is Agni, that is, fire as a

sacred power (cognate with the Latin word for fire, ignis). Agni was the bearer of the sacrifice between men and the gods – fire was the 'power' which consumed the oblation and carried it upwards to the heavens. An interesting problem in connection with Agni is at what point he came to be regarded as the power who also conveyed mortal man to the heavens after death; this is connected with another question, namely at what point did the Indo-Aryans abandon the practice of burying their dead in favour of cremation? Two passages in the Rg-veda provide evidence that burial had formerly been the Aryan practice (namely, maṇḍala x, hymn 15, verse 14; and x, 18, 10); whereas by the time the Rg-vedic collection of hymns was assembled cremation seems to have become the custom (Brandon, 1963; 310). The transition from one custom to the other may have been an aspect of the general Dravidianisation of Aryan culture which occurred in the later Vedic period, about which more will be said later (*1.50*). But the fact that the sacred power of fire has an Aryan name suggests that the deifying of fire belongs to the pre-Indian history of Vedic religion. Agni is also *par excellence* the priestly deity; with him especially the Vedic priest co-operated in the performance of the sacrificial ritual.

1.35 Vedic sacrifice

The sacrificial ritual provides the *raison d'être* of the Rg-vedic hymns. The recent tendency among Sanskrit scholars is to emphasise that it is a liturgical purpose which has shaped many of these hymns, certainly in the form in which they have survived, and that even those which were not in the first place composed with such a purpose in view have been pressed into the service of the cultic ritual and given a liturgical form (Renou, 1953; 11). Like a great deal of Sanskritic religious literature they are often highly allusive (and many of the allusions are now lost upon modern ears, Indian or other); sometimes they are undoubtedly esoteric. This may be due partly to their poetic character, in that they embody certain inspired correspondences between the sacred and the secular which the Vedic poet (the vipra, or, literally, the 'quivering one') had seized upon and expressed. It may also be due partly to the liturgical context in which they were to be used, which alone would supply the sense which otherwise remains hidden.

It is impossible, says Renou, to reconstruct this early cult. It is, however, possible to assert that it 'was in the charge of a priestly *élite* who served a military aristocracy' (Renou, 1953; 6). It was essentially a *ceremonial* rather than a private or *domestic* cult, although it was not a public cult in the sense of being congregational. Its purpose seems to have been to gratify the heavenly power or powers being invoked, and to whom the sacrifice was offered. On the principle of a supposed reciprocity between gods and men, the worshipper, through the priests, offered oblations on an open-air altar specially set up in an area carefully marked out for the purpose, and the gods in return bestowed upon the worshipper such boons as he was seeking – victory in battle, offspring, increase of herds, or other largely mundane benefits. But as Basham points out, of guilt-offerings and thank-offerings, such as the Hebrews offered, practically nothing is heard in the Ṛg-veda (Basham, 1954; 239). Priestly roles in the performance of the cultus were clearly differentiated; while one was concerned with the manual tasks of the sacrifice another would be responsible for the chanting of the sacred hymns, invoking the god and imploring the desired blessing, while yet another would supervise the whole procedure. In the later Vedic period it was the chanting of the hymns which became supremely important, and the utterance itself (brahman) came to be invested with a magical power, as we shall see later (*1.54*).

The differentiation of priestly roles is reflected to some extent in two other forms of Vedic literature: the *Sāma-veda*, or 'song' veda, a collection of Ṛg-vedic hymns rearranged for a priest to sing; and the *Yajur-veda*, or 'sacrificial' veda, a collection of supplementary sacrificial formulae to be used by the priest who is responsible for the manual action. A fourth collection of a somewhat different kind was the *Atharva-veda*, which will be discussed later (*1.59*). At this point it may be mentioned that the word 'veda' implies something akin to 'revelation'; the word means literally 'that which been (supernaturally) perceived'; perceived, that is, by the ṛṣi or seer of old. These seers are legendary and largely unknown figures, but this in no way detracts from the revelational status which the Vedic hymns and chants are given throughout subsequent Indian history.

1.36 Career patterns of the Vedic gods

The deities worshipped by the Vedic Aryans have been likened to planets in the sky: some are low on the horizon and about to disappear from view; others are at their zenith; others again have only recently appeared over the horizon, or are in the ascendant. In the first category, among deities already old in Vedic times and soon to be lost to view, was Dyaus, a deity who belongs to a pre-Indian stage of development, the great 'sky-father' of the Indo-Europeans. Another whose prestige was waning was Varuna, who is known as an asura (lord), a word which links Varuna with Iran, for the Iranian form ahura was the Zoroastrian designation of the great 'Lord of light', Ahura Mazdā. We have already noted that the name Varuna has a linguistic connection with the Greek sky-god, Ouranos. In Vedic India Varuna continued to be of importance for some time, but already he had yielded pride of place to Indra, who is undoubtedly the greatest god of the Vedic pantheon, a war-god and of great importance to the Aryan warrior. Varuna on the other hand is the most 'ethical' of the Vedic gods; the ideas of moral rectitude and moral retribution which were associated with him never again attached themselves to any Indian deity in quite the same unambiguous way – possibly because other conceptions of retribution (karma) took their place as Aryans became slowly Dravidianised (*1.50*). Another deity who is beginning to make an appearance in the Vedic period, but is not yet very prominent, is Viṣṇu (anglicised, Vishnu), who seems to have some of the characteristics of a solar deity. In later Hinduism Vishnu becomes one of the two or three most important names for the supreme god.

1.37 *The importance of Indra*

It has been suggested that the Vedic god Indra may possibly be a deified hero, and that there had been a human warrior-leader of the Aryan invaders of this name. Certainly he is a war-god, and Vedic hymns ascribe to Indra the credit for the successful conquest by the Aryans of their enemies; it was he who enabled them to overcome the city-dwelling, dark-skinned aboriginals, whom they called the Dāsas. He was, however, associated also with the storm; his characteristic weapon was the vajra, or thunderbolt. Even in this stern role he is still beneficent, for it is he who looses the pent-up rain in the thundercloud and brings refreshment to the parched earth, and thus sustenance to its human inhabitants. The worship of a deity of this name is not confined to the Indian Aryans, moreover; he was known as a god among the Kassites who conquered Babylon. He is mentioned in the Boghazkoi list of gods worshipped by the Mittani (1400 B.C.?); together with Varuna and Mitra, Indra is mentioned as one of the gods of the 'Hurrians' (Aryans) who entered Mesopotamia possibly from Iran. While it is unlikely therefore that the name originally belonged to a human leader of the Indo-Aryans, it is easy to see that a warrior-god would be likely to be held in high honour by a largely warrior community, engaged in the early Vedic period in the invasion, conquest and colonisation of the river plains of the Punjab.

1.38 *Indo-Aryan social structure*

Rudimentary division into social classes was already a feature of the Aryan tribes before they entered north-west India; this is the view of a number of modern orientalists. Dumézil has argued that a threefold social structure is reflected in Aryan mythology: the concerns of the three classes were respectively religious and juridical, military and temporal, and economic. Émile Benveniste (1938) also found evidence of a three-class social system in the Vedic literature. Basham points out that in the earliest Vedic hymns there appears to be a simple twofold division into nobility (*kṣatra*) and ordinary tribesmen (*viś*) (Basham, 1954; 34 f.). During the period we are at present concerned with the priests (*brāhmans*) were developing a special social role for themselves, and something of a tripartite division of Aryan society can be said to have existed almost from the time of the Aryans' entry into India. Here, then, is to be found *one* of the contributory factors which led, in a later period, to the gradual emergence of the caste system of Hindu India.

The basic social unit was the family, and in Vedic society the family was patrilinear, and a patriarchal system of authority was recognised. Unlike the people of the Indus valley whose civilisation they overthrew, the Aryans were not dwellers in towns; rather, kinship-groups of families, each of which was called a grāma, formed the usual pattern of social organisation; as the Aryans settled down these kinship-groups became village communities and this remained the characteristic form of their civilisation during the early Vedic period. Families and village kinship-groups existed within the larger context of the tribe. The tribal ruler was the rāja (cognate with Latin rex, king) who was not, however, an absolute monarch, but shared the governing of the tribe with a tribal council or assembly (sabhā). The rāja was primarily a leader, especially in war and in the defence of the tribe. Even although there is little foundation for the idea that the Vedic god Indra was a deified hero-warrior, it is nevertheless not without significance that in this period of conquest and consolidation of new territory the sacred was conceived of in terms of Indra, the warrior; a deity belonging to the pre-Indian period of Aryan tradition, he was by nature specially suited for elevation into a primary position in the Vedic pantheon during this period.

1.39 Aryan expansion eastwards

During the earlier Vedic period the Aryan tribes had consolidated their position in the north-west river plains, the area today known as the Punjab, and had probably not penetrated further eastwards than the Jumna river (on which modern Delhi stands). During the later period, however, the tribes moved eastwards into the Ganges valley, and continued their advance as far as the area now known as Bihar, and the western borders of Bengal. They do not seem to have penetrated the area to the south of the Ganges, and it has been suggested that as the Ganges plain was at this time a jungle-covered swamp, the Aryan advance may have been confined to the Himālayan foothills along the northern side of the Ganges, where the going was less arduous and the territory slightly easier to bring under cultivation. For by this time the Aryans had certainly become as much an agricultural as a pastoral, herd-keeping people. Agriculture only with difficulty established itself among them as a respectable occupation, however, and seems to have been looked upon as a rather demeaning activity, at least by those whose interests are reflected in the hymns – the aristocracy of horse-riding warriors and hereditary priests. A certain amount of intermarriage was now taking place between some of the Aryan tribesmen and the dark-skinned Dravidian women, and in this way a lower class of Aryan society, less hostile to agricultural pursuits, was gradually developing. A further factor which has to be mentioned is that in moving south-eastwards down the Ganges valley the Aryans were leaving behind the somewhat cooler climate of the Punjab for the hot, humid and more enervating atmosphere of the Indian midland plain. This does not mean

L.H.R.

that they soon settled down into less vigorous ways and into the contemplative habits of a hot climate: the energetic way of life which modern Americans and Europeans continue to carry on in such tropical regions is an indication of how attitudes to work and vigorous activity persist even when conditions are against them. But in the course of time climate may be regarded as having had its effect on the Aryans, as we shall see.

1.4 YAHWEH AND THE HEBREW MONARCHY, TO 926 B.C.

1.40 The Settlement, and the emerging tension in Yahwistic religion

The important formative period in the history of Israel's religion is that of the early centuries of the settlement in Canaan. The wording of the basic summaries of Israel's faith which have been referred to (*1.23, 1.25*) postulates a Canaanite situation ('And he has brought us unto this place, and has given us this land . . .'). The very fact of settlement in a certain territory which the Hebrew tribes now regarded as their own introduced a tension into Israelite religion. How this tension arose may be briefly outlined as follows. The basis of the unity of the tribal confederation was the prophetic-interpretative activity of Moses. It is important to notice that it was this, rather than the actual remembered experience of deliverance from Egypt. Not all those who took part in the settlement on Canaanite soil had been present at the Exodus; some had not been born, other tribal groups had attached themselves to the main body somewhere along the line between Egypt and Canaan. The principle of cohesion among them was acceptance of what had been proclaimed by Moses the prophet: namely, that there existed a divine being whose nature was compassion, who was also the director of human history (even although his purposes might be inscrutable), and who had pledged himself to this group of tribes to whom his nature had thus been revealed, and had led the nucleus of the group out of Egypt; and that they were therefore pledged to serve him and order their common life according to his will, together with such others as might join with them in the acceptance of this faith. There seems to have been a considerable accession in Canaan to the original Exodus group of tribes, mainly from other Hebrew tribes already settled in the land. The incorporation of these others is probably the main reason for what seems to have been a repetition at Shechem, under Joshua's leadership, of the original covenant-making occasion at Sinai. This is related in Josh. 24, and it was in that context at Shechem that the essentials of Israel's faith were rehearsed by the whole company of tribes, original and newly acceded, and were accepted by them all. The principle of unity was thus acceptance of the Mosaic interpretation of history, and common allegiance to, and worship of, the divine being to whom this interpretation testified. The principle of unity, that is to say, was primarily religious. This unity had also a very loose political expression from the time of the Shechem covenant-making onwards, for the tribes who thus acknowledged a common allegiance to Yahweh formed a religious confederation or league. This confederation is sometimes described as an amphictyony, because its unity consisted in a common cultus, or worship. The fact that the tribes of this religious league also possessed a certain territorial or geographical unity is, from the religious point of view, of secondary importance. However, it was the defence and preservation of the territorial area which before long became a major consideration, and the cause of the tension which now entered Yahwistic religion.

1.41 Yahwism, and Israel's territorial integrity

It in no way detracts from the status of Moses as a prophet that not all the tribesmen of Israel comprehended the nature of the divine being as Moses had done; indeed this is part of the common experience of prophets, that their message is often only half-comprehended. The fact that this happened in early Israel, and that Moses is by tradition represented as being aware of how far the average Israelite fell short of the prophetic experience ('Would God that all the LORD's people were prophets, that the LORD would put his spirit upon them!'), at least enables us to understand the limitations of Yahwistic religion in ancient Israel. To the extent to which the Hebrew tribesmen had responded to the prophetic message they had acquired a new solidarity, and it was as a result of this that they were transformed from fugitive serfs to disciplined conquerors (*1.27*). Religious cohesion had as its consequence military success, as centuries later it had also in the case of Islam (*5.15, 5.16*).

We find therefore that the conception of Yahweh which emerged during the early settlement period was that of a war-god, one who fights on behalf of his people against their territorial rivals. In the Song of Deborah, possibly almost contemporary with the events it records, Yahweh is described as a god of thunder, rain and earthquake (Judg. 5: 4). One is here strongly reminded of the thunder- and war-god Indra of the Aryans. In this way the security of Yahwistic religion came to be identified with the security of Israelite territory, an identification which was to have far-reaching consequences, down to modern times.

1.42 *The theocratic character of the Israelite league*

During the period following the settlement in Canaan and the setting-up of the tribal league or confederation of Israel, the affairs of the tribes were largely in the hands of inspired leaders and men of wisdom, known to English readers by the misleading name of 'judges'; more precisely, they were 'deliverers'; an even more accurate term would be the modern 'charismatic leaders'. The book of Judges presents a round number of twelve of such 'deliverers': six 'minor' and six 'major'. At first sight the minor ones do not seem to have been markedly charismatic or to have provided much leadership; they appear more as local worthies, persons of substance, pillars of society, men who administered the laws, perhaps rather like justices of the peace in English society. But their function was not quite so localised as this; they probably constituted something more like a higher court of appeal, or were men who could be entrusted with the making of decisions which affected the tribal confederation as a whole, men who knew the law of Yahweh and could apply it to a new situation. It begins thus to look as though they would have needed to be men possessed of special gifts, and the tradition linking them all, minor and major, in one category is not lightly to be set aside. Of the same kind, although not included as one of the twelve, was Deborah; it is noteworthy that she is described as a 'prophetess'. That is to say she was an 'inspired person', a person of special charisma.

What is indisputable is the importance which the tradition accords to these leaders, men 'raised up' by Yahweh from time to time, men upon whom the spirit of Yahweh came. The fact that those who interpreted and administered the divine law were the most important figures in the community is an indication that the tribal league was virtually a theocracy. A common cultus was the practical unifying force, and associated with this cultus was the sacred law, and behind both of these lay the covenant between the tribes and Yahweh. Cultus, law and charisma; all three at this period seem to have been closely integrated and interrelated.

1.43 Early demands for a monarchy

One of the most outstanding of these charismatic leaders was the major 'judge', Gideon. In the stories of Gideon's successful defence of Israel's territory against neighbouring tribes we have a number of clues concerning popular religious attitudes in Israel as they existed at that time. Before the settlement in Canaan under Joshua's leadership the Hebrew tribes who were the bearers of Yahwistic religion were nomadic in character, wanderers without special attachment or claim to any particular territory. But after the setting-up of the confederation the bearers of Yahwistic religion become also the claimants to and inhabitants of a certain territory into which they had intruded and where they had established themselves at the expense of the former inhabitants ('the Amorites, in whose land you dwell . . .', Judg. 6: 10). Their success in this enterprise they regarded as a consequence of their adherence to the worship of Yahweh, so that Yahweh was regarded as having 'given' them the land (Judg. 6: 9). Its sacred places were now taken over for the purpose of the Yahweh cultus and made into Yahwistic sacred places. The Hebrews took to agriculture and fruit growing, and becoming thus dependent on the land adopted the seasonal festivals that were associated with agriculture: the spring festival of unleavened bread at the beginning of the barley harvest (upon which the nomadic 'passover' spring-festival was also imposed); the midsummer festival of Weeks, at the wheat harvest (made the occasion also for celebrating the giving of the Law at Sinai); and at the autumn (i.e. New Year) vine harvest, the feast of Booths (perhaps originally the bridal bowers of the sacred marriage between the Canaanite god and the land), which was also made the occasion for remembering the time when Israel dwelt in tents in the wilderness. Yahwistic religion, in its original Mosaic, prophetic character as the worship of one who was the lord of history, was thus both territorialised (i.e. it became associated with particular localities), and modified in the direction of Canaanite agricultural religion. A prophetic religious movement had acquired economic interests; although it was not inevitable that Yahwism should have been brought into partnership with these economic interests, this in fact is what happened.

A further development was a need for a political system better fitted for the defence of these economic interests than was the loose structure of the Yahwistic cult-league. In other words, there arose the demand for a king such as other nations had. The associations of Egypt had not been entirely thrown off. Just as in the migratory period, in times of hardship, there had been those who looked back longingly to the fleshpots of Egypt, so there were those who in times of trouble tended to see as the only solution to the problem of threats to their security, the idea of monarchy. The knowledge of this was not only kept alive in the folk-memory of tribes who had once lived under a monarchy, but was also directly available to them in Canaan, since it was a pattern widespread throughout the ancient Near East. So when one of the tribal confederation's prophet-deliverers was acclaimed for his success in unifying and inspiring the Hebrew tribes, there arose a demand that he should be set up as monarch and inaugurate a kingly dynasty. Gideon's answer to this demand is one which expresses the prophetic attitude throughout this period: 'I will not rule over you, nor shall my son rule over you' (the rejection of the idea of an hereditary kingship) – 'Yahweh shall rule over you' (Judg. 8: 23). Here we see, in this rejection of the demand for a kingly dynasty, a representative of Yahwism, a charismatic person, one upon whom 'the spirit of Yahweh' had come, reaffirming the earlier Yahwistic principle of theocracy.

1.44 Samuel, and the twilight of Yahwistic theocracy

The sanctuary of Shiloh is given considerable prominence in connection with Samuel. It was there, before his birth, that he was dedicated to the service of Yahweh by Hannah his mother. It was to the sanctuary at Shiloh that as a young child he was brought and presented; and it was there that he ministered, assisting Eli the priest in the sacrificial cultus. It was in the sanctuary precincts of Shiloh that there occurred his inaugural experience as a seer, that is, one to whom were disclosed the immediate purposes of Yahweh. One could hardly ask for more evidence that Samuel was regarded in ancient Hebrew tradition as a cultic figure. But he was also a seer (rōeh) which, we are told, (1 Sam. 9: 10–16) was the name by which at an earlier period prophets were known. In Samuel we have a powerful reminder of something which has been emphasised by modern scholarship, that in ancient Israel prophets were closely connected with the cultus; that is to say, there was not a rigid dichotomy of priest and prophet, such as a superficial reading of some passages from the canonical prophets might suggest. Samuel had another role also, that of judge; we are told that he went on annual circuit as a judge, a decider of difficult issues. He went from Ramah to Bethel, from Bethel to Gilgal, from Gilgal to Mizpeh, and from Mizpeh back to Ramah, where his home was and where he served as priest (1 Sam. 7: 15). He is represented as a man of considerable authority, authority exercised by virtue of his charisma and his cultic office. So venerable a figure had he become that during the last years of his life the question arose of who could possibly succeed him. It became clear that his sons were not worthy successors, and this seems to have provided the opportunity for those hankering after the establishment of a monarchy to raise their demands once again, as in the time of Gideon (*1 43*). This demand for a king is represented as having initially met the same response from Samuel as from Gideon.

However, circumstances combined to make this rejection by the Yahwistic priest-prophet of the idea of a monarch in Israel more difficult to sustain. The demand was sharpened now by the pressure of events; in particular by the hostile presence of the Philistines on the western borders of Israel's territory. These were peoples from the islands of the Greek archipelago, Crete, Cyprus and possibly Asia Minor, who in the latter part of the second millennium B.C. had been forced to migrate by the advance of the Aryan-speaking peoples from the north (*1.33*). (The Aryan language in India developed into Sanskrit; among the invaders who displaced the Philistines it took the form we know as Greek.) One of the ways in which the Philistines were distinguished from the Semitic and Egyptian peoples as being of an alien culture was that they were 'uncircumcised'. They settled at first in the coastal plain of Palestine, and then began to advance into the hill territory of the interior. The Hebrew tribes tried to resist this advance but were defeated in the violent encounters they had with the Philistines. The occupation by the Philistines of the central area, until then held by the tribes of Ephraim and Benjamin, seemed to threaten the whole confederation, and it is probably this which explains the serious step which was taken, of carrying the sacred ark out from Shiloh, with the idea of ensuring the presence of Yahweh among the defenders of what had now come to be regarded as his territory. The defeat of the Hebrew forces, the capture of the ark, and the destruction by the Philistines of the sanctuary at Shiloh, presented itself as a situation of the most alarming seriousness and horror.

In these circumstances the demand for a king made itself felt with much greater urgency, and it was within this general situation that the decision was taken to set up Saul as king. But it was not a decision that was easily reached, and there remained within Israel a strong current of opposition to the institution of monarchy, which in later periods became much more vocal than it could be at that time. Something of the memory of the controversy remains in the narrative found in the first book of Samuel.

1.45 The controversy over kingship

It has been suggested that in the narrative contained in chapters 9–11 of the first book of Samuel two originally separate traditions have been combined: one pro-royalist and the other anti-royalist. This is perhaps to draw the distinction too sharply; it would be better to speak of two slightly different emphases in the points of view. One represents an uncompromisingly Yahwistic, theocratic point of view: theocracy is the proper form of common life for the worshippers of Yahweh, and should not be abandoned. The other is the compromise view, which recognised the difficulties of Israel's political situation and saw a need for some modification of the old theocracy in the direction of monarchy. This view was based on the assumptions that Israel was Yahweh's people, and that her territory was Yahweh's land, and that the preservation of the one was bound up with the preservation of the other. What was required, in this view, was a *theocratic king*, one who would rule in the name of Yahweh, and lead Israel against her enemies in the power of Yahweh. Such a king, it was hoped, Saul would prove to be. His charismatic qualities were emphasised by the upholders of this point of view – for example, in the incident described in 1 Sam. 10: 9–13. The situation demanded the handing over of centralised control to a charismatic military leader, a servant of Yahweh. The upholders of the other point of view questioned whether it was right to introduce the alien religious institution of kingship – associated with the religious-state systems of Egypt and Babylon – into the life of the people of Yahweh. Perhaps both these different emphases, found side by side within the present form of the narrative, represent the interpretations of two differing schools of thought in later times, both looking at the event with historical hindsight.

1.46 The reign of Saul

What in fact we see in the ongoing course of Saul's reign is how Saul the ecstatic, the man subject to the impulse of the spirit of Yahweh, becomes Saul the arrogant official and would-be autocrat. There appears to have been a change in Saul's character, perhaps as a result of his assuming power. But there seems also to have been a certain ambiguity in the situation: Samuel remained very much a central and powerful figure even after Saul's consecration as king. Saul is not allowed to unite sacred and secular affairs; he is the military leader, but Samuel remains supreme in the administration of the sacred (1 Sam. 13). Again, in sparing the life of Agag the king of the Amalekites (1 Sam. 15: 9) Saul found himself in conflict with the theocratic commands of Samuel the representative of Yahweh. The estrangement between the two men seems to have gradually deepened, and it may well have coincided with an estrangement between the holders of the two points of view within Israel. What this phase of Israel's history seems to show is the extreme difficulty of combining in a single control the ultimate interests which are at stake in the religious life with the immediate and pressing concerns which are involved in the government and defence of a particular state or territory. It is a difficulty which we shall encounter again in the later history of Islam. Certainly the attempt to solve it which the Saul–Samuel partnership represented was a failure. Yet, granted the assumption that was being made concerning the need to preserve 'Yahweh's' territory, some solution had to be found. It might be thought that the kingship of David provided the answer, since in David we see Israel's ideal of a king who preserves both religion and land. We need to be clear, however, about how David achieved this, and what happened to the prophetic Yahwistic religion in the process.

1.47 The reign of David

The naïve, superficial and sentimental view of David is that he was a harp-playing shepherd boy who made good; an upright man who because of his skill and virtue was chosen to be king, and who also, incidentally, wrote many of the psalms. This idealised picture does not quite square with what Hebrew tradition tells us about this particular monarch. His reign falls into roughly two periods: first, seven years during which he reigned from Hebron, first as king of Judah only and then of both Judah and Israel; second, thirty-three years as king of Judah and Israel in Jerusalem.

At the death of Saul, Abner, who had been his officer-in-chief, took it into his hands to make Saul's son Eshbaal (also, in later tradition called Ishbosheth) king of Israel. The men of Judah had proclaimed their warrior-leader David king of Judah. King Eshbaal then fell out with Abner the general over the matter of a concubine, and Abner decided to throw in Israel's lot with that of Judah, and support David. David strengthened his position by taking Saul's daughter Michal as his wife. David's earlier marriage to her had been annulled by Saul, and she was now in fact the wife of another man. Abner arranged the remarriage as one of the conditions for a united kingdom, and Michal took her place alongside the two other wives David already had – the wealthy widow Abigail, and Ahinoam. Shortly after, Abner was murdered by Joab, one of David's officers, in revenge for his own brother's death. On hearing the news of Abner's murder David uttered an impressive curse on his murderer's descendants: 'May there never be lacking one of them who is ill, or a leper, or slain by the sword or hungry.' Before his own death David charged Solomon his son that he should not allow Joab's 'gray head to go down to Sheol [the place of the dead] in peace'. Eshbaal, now unsupported in his capital at Mahanaim, was also murdered, during his midday siesta by two brigands who bore a grudge against his father. This left David without a serious rival to the leadership of the tribes of Israel and Judah. These, then, were the circumstances in which the Hebrews acquired their greatest king.

The immediate result was that the Philistines, now confronted with a united Israel, had to contend with a stiffer opposition; the rest of the period of David's rule from Hebron was taken up with removing the

Philistine threat to Israel's territorial security. Having strengthened his position thus, the king went on to strengthen it further by acquiring a new capital, namely Jerusalem, a city which until then had no Hebrew associations at all, but which he now annexed from the Jebusites. It had the double advantage of being a natural stronghold and also an ancient Canaanite cultic centre, the place where the deity El-Elyon was worshipped. This Canaanite god was known also by the names Sedek and Shalem; the latter appears in the name of David's son, Solomon, as well as in the name of the city. Since it was a place that had no previous connection with either the northern or southern Hebrew tribes it was a particularly appropriate symbol of the king's personal prowess and military achievement. Whether or not its cultic importance was an additional advantage from the king's point of view, the fact is that it now became the new centre for the Yahweh cult, which was possibly superimposed on the El-Elyon cult. According to the tradition David's intention was to set up there a temple; this in fact was not done until the time of his son and successor Solomon, but it is evident what the trend had already become. Yahwistic religion, first of all identified with a certain territory, and a tribal confederation, was now further assimilated to the pattern of the state religions of the Near East by its association with monarchical government. The logical end of this process was the establishment of an urban temple cult like those of Babylon and Egypt. As a first step, the Ark, the ancient symbol of Yahwism, was solemnly brought from Kiriath-Jearim in a festal procession led by the king, performing a ritual dance. It was the king as priest (after the Near Eastern pattern) who then offered sacrifice and gave the people his blessing, presumably at the Canaanite city-shrine where the Ark was now installed, and where it was now to be served by priests who were royal officials (Noth, 1960; 191).

1.48 The reign of Solomon

All the main ingredients of the reign of Solomon as a minor oriental potentate had thus been provided by his warrior father David: an expanded territory gained by military aggression; an hereditary monarchy; a royal city-capital; a temple cult with its official priesthood. All this Solomon consolidated into a centralised system of autocratic power after the Egyptian model.

A superficial view of the reign of Solomon is that it was for Israel a time of unparalleled peace, prosperity and security. 1 Kgs. 4: 20 presents an idyllic picture of all Judah and Israel eating, drinking and enjoying general happiness. This is difficult to reconcile with the repercussions which followed Solomon's death, in the revolt of Jeroboam. Then, we are told, the whole assembly of Israel were smarting under the repressive measures which Solomon had carried out. They expressed their resentment to Rehoboam thus: 'Your father made our yoke grievous.' Of the wealth and prosperity of the court there can be no doubt. We are told that the Queen of Sheba was breathless with admiration at all she saw of Solomon's court, his organisation, his beautiful wives and his magnificent staff. Allowance has to be made for the fact that she was a neighbouring chieftain who had come probably with some commercial purpose in view, and that this may account for such oriental hyperbole as she uttered, but even so there can be little doubt that Solomon's court and city were characterised by a good deal of vain ostentation and display and that this was a far remove from the life of the peasants and artificers upon whom the economic burden of all this ultimately rested. The timber for the new city temple in Jerusalem, for example, was obtained from King Hiram of Tyre at the cost of an annual export of wheat of 220,000 bushels of wheat and a considerable quantity of oil. Again, Solomon's civil servants alone consumed nearly 400,000 bushels of grain yearly, and it has been estimated that in a country of the size and productivity of Israel at that time, this, together with the wheat export to Tyre, would alone have constituted a heavy burden on the peasant population. The forced labour of Canaanites whom Solomon was holding in captivity as state slaves would have gone part of the way to meet the labour problem which Solomon's many ambitious state building plans entailed, but not all his needs could have been met thus.

The Temple became both the political and religious centre of the state, with Solomon exercising a royal priestly function. The close association of the Temple cult with the royal court and its luxurious life enables us to understand how the Jewish priesthood of Jerusalem came to be characterised by aristocratic and courtly attitudes, both at this period and in the post-Exilic period (just as the high-priestly vestments were an adaptation of the royal vesture). The capital was also the place where Canaanite and foreign deities were worshipped, as a concession to Solomon's many foreign wives and paramours.

1.49 Yahwistic religion during the early monarchy

In the shrines of the tribal confederation outside Jerusalem the local priests continued the worship of Yahweh in accordance with the earlier tradition. If the extent to which they fell under the influence of Canaanite nature-religion increased during the early monarchy, it has to be admitted that they had every encouragement from Solomon's introduction into Jerusalem of the cults of Egyptian, Moabite, Ammonite, Phoenician and Hittite gods.

Religious opposition to the monarchy among those who remained faithful to the prophetic Yahwism of the earlier period would by no means have diminished during this formative period of the Jerusalem dynasty. The building of the Temple was itself a great innovation in Hebrew religion, and was inspired by religious ideas alien to Yahwism – those of the Egyptian and Babylonian systems centring around the god-kings. The fact of the Temple's existence later came to be accepted and reconciled with Yahwistic ideas: the present narrative concerning its building is coloured by such an attitude of accommodation. But at the time there was a genuine protest against it – represented no doubt in the words of reproach of Nathan the prophet addressed to King David: 'Thus saith Yahweh, Shalt thou build me an house for me to dwell in? For I have not dwelt in an house since the day that I brought up the children of Israel out of Egypt, even to this day, but have walked in a tent and in a tabernacle.' Von Rad has suggested that 'in speaking as he did, Nathan was acting as a spokesman of the old tradition of the "tent of meeting", with its completely different ideas of the presence of Yahweh', that is, a tradition in which Yahweh was thought of as moving about among the Hebrew tribes, rather than solidly established in one special place (Von Rad, 1962; 61). But the Yahwistic protest represented by Nathan came to nothing; the Temple was built, after the Near Eastern style, the worship of God became linked with a political capital, and the seeds were sown of the Jewish religious attitude which in the modern world we know as Zionism.

1.5 RELIGION IN INDIA DURING THE LATER VEDIC PERIOD (*1000–500* B.C. approx.)

1.50 *The Dravidianisation of Aryan culture*

Undoubtedly the Aryans were being affected by their migration farther into the heart of India. Probably the intermarriage with Dravidians which has already been mentioned was one of the chief factors. One of the most important ways in which this is indicated is to be found in some innovations in Aryan language which occurred during this period. Alone among the Indo-European or Aryan group of languages, Sanskrit has a number of consonants which are peculiarly Indian. These are the 'cerebral' or 'retroflex' consonants, usually transliterated with a subscript dot to indicate the retroflex form: thus, ṭ, ḍ, ṇ, ṛ, ḷ, ṣ. They represent consonants which do not come naturally to a European, and are made by attempting to speak the consonant indicated while keeping the tip of the tongue turned inwards against the back of the palate. These are sounds which are Dravidian in origin, and we have here one indication, from the realm of language, of the process of Dravidianisation which the Aryans now began to undergo.

In the same way that they absorbed this non-Aryan and characteristically Dravidian consonant-sound, it is safe to assume they would be absorbing other elements of Dravidian culture, and to a consideration of some of the more important of these we now turn.

1.51 *Religious speculation in the later Vedic age*

Among the hymns in the tenth maṇḍala of the Ṛg-veda, that is, those which belong to a later period than the bulk of the hymns (*1.34*), are three which may be selected for special attention. These are: x.90, 'The Sacrifice of Primal Man'; x.121, 'Prajāpati', i.e. 'The Lord of Creation'; and x.129, 'In the Beginning' (Zaehner, 1966; 8–12). They reveal a mood of cosmic speculation, of enquiry into the nature of the universe, and even of scepticism concerning any possible answer, which is not found in the earlier hymns. Hymn 90, 'The Sacrifice of Primal Man', will be examined later in connection with the emergence of classes in Vedic society (*1.55*). It is the other two which indicate most clearly the trend of thought among the Aryans during this later period; at least, among the brāhman or priestly class. Hymn 121, 'The Lord of Creation" asks the question: 'What god shall we revere with the oblation? . . . Who by his might has ever been the One King of all that breathes?' This question is repeated in various forms all through the hymn. By whom are heaven and earth held in place? By whom does the sun shed its light? Who generated heaven, and gave birth to the water? In the tenth and last verse of the hymn the answer is given – Prajāpati! ('Lord of Creation'). As R. C. Zaehner comments (1966; vi), the polytheism of the Indo-Europeans has here taken a different turning and developed into something very characteristically Indian. No single one of the many gods has achieved real supremacy in the way that happened elsewhere; rather, the gods have coalesced, losing their separate identities and even their relevance. By what name the Supreme is known makes no difference: 'What is but One the wise call by manifold names' (*Ṛg-veda* i. 164, 46). Even Prajāpati, here worshipped as the Lord of Creation, has other names: Viśvakarman, the Maker of All; or Brihaspati, the Lord of brahman, the sacred power of the chant. In these ideas found in the last book of the Ṛg-veda, Aryan thought is already moving towards the pantheistic monism which is characteristic of India, and which appears plainly in the later form of Vedic literature known as the Upaniṣads (*1.57*).

In the hymn entitled 'In the Beginning' the mood of religious speculation becomes virtual scepticism about the relevance of the old gods. This hymn asks the question: 'How did everything really come into being? What existed before Being and Not-Being, before there was death or immortality, night or day, darkness or light? Who knows truly? Who can here declare it?' So the questioning goes on, until in the last verse speculation goes so far as to say, 'Only he who is its overseer in highest heaven knows', and then withdraws in the last line into an ultimate, knowledge-shattering scepticism: '. . . *or perhaps he does not know!*'

How far this is a natural development of principles inherent in the Aryan polytheism of the earlier period it is difficult to say; one can only point to the fact that it does not seem to have happened in any of the other areas into which Aryan polytheism moved. One is entitled to suspect that it is a peculiarly Indian development. It might possibly be explained as the effect of the north Indian environment: geographical – with its vast, flat, and apparently unending plains, conditioning thought in the direction of undifferentiated unity; or climatic – the merciless heat which is a disincentive to vigorous pursuits, and an encouragement to more contemplative habits. On the other hand we have to remember that subsequent immigrants into India have more successfully resisted any such effect of the Indian environment upon their religious ideas – Muslims, Parsees, Jews and Christians, *especially* (as in the case of Parsees and Jews) where there was a minimum of intermarriage with the already settled Indian inhabitants, but less so (as the case of Muslims) where there was such intermarriage. This point will need to be raised again in connection with Indian Islam in the Mughal period (*6.56*). So far as the Aryans are concerned intermarriage with Dravidians certainly does seem to have occurred and may be one of the more important factors in the development of hitherto new trends in Aryan religious attitudes.

1.52 The brāhmans and the cosmic order

In the remaining one of these later hymns of the Ṛg-veda which have been mentioned (*1.51*), namely 'The Sacrifice of Primal Man' (*Ṛg-veda* x.90), the origination of the universe is represented as having been a process of sacrifice. What can be detected here is the elevating of the very act of sacrifice to a place of supreme importance in the religious scheme, so that it became more important even than the gods themselves, to whom the sacrifice was ostensibly offered. The notion which we see emerging here is one in which sacrifice, the very process by which the universe came into existence, is regarded as the really effective factor. Seen from another perspective this is the enhancement by the brāhmans, the priests, of that activity of which they alone in Vedic society were the practitioners and controllers; with this point we shall be concerned again (*1.53*). This emphasis on the importance of the sacrificial activity had the effect not only of relegating the gods to a subordinate position in the religious scheme of things, but also of investing sacrifice with something of the character of magic. It became the vital element in the cosmic machinery; the maintenance of the cosmic order was now seen as being dependent on the due and proper performance of the sacrificial ritual. This conception of the sacrifice, and the effects which in due course it was believed to produce, as it were automatically, is one which, says Dasgupta, is 'like the fulfilment of a natural law in the physical world'.

1.53 The concept of ṛta, or cosmic law

Also to be found in the Ṛg-veda is the conception of a cosmic law by which all things are maintained in existence and in accordance with which certain results must always duly, automatically, and inevitably, follow from any given action. This cosmic law is known as ṛta in the Vedic hymns; Basham sees it as 'perhaps the highest flight of Ṛg-vedic thought'; it may represent a development from the belief in the magical and automatic operation of sacrificial ritual, or it may be a conception which the Aryans learnt from the earlier inhabitants of the land. Dasgupta takes the view that in the sacrificial magic and in this concept of cosmic law, ṛta, are to be found the origins of the law of karma, that is, of action as causal, inevitably entailing effects that can never be averted or postponed once their due season of fruition has been reached – a conception which, especially in its moral form, dominates the mind of India right up to modern times (Dasgupta, 1922; 22).

The immediate result of this development was the enormously enhanced prestige of the brāhman priest who alone had the professional knowledge necessary for the scrupulously correct performance of the sacrificial ritual (for if either the least syllable in the chanting or the slightest action were incorrect, chaos might ensue, it was held). D. D. Kosambi sees another reason for the increasing importance of sacrifice in the later Vedic period: 'society had begun to exhaust its means of subsistence' (Kosambi, 1965; 87). Since prosperity and good fortune were believed to be dependent on the sacrifice, a threatened scarcity of cattle or food would lead to an increase in the number of sacrifices offered and in aggressive activity on the part of the warriors; success in this latter enterprise also required sacrificial offerings beforehand, so there would be a further reason for increasing the frequency of sacrifice. The brāhman priests would thus grow in wealth and prestige. This had two immediate results, one literary, the other social: the composition of the treatises called the Brāhmaṇas, and the sharpening of class distinctions in the rudimentary caste-system.

1.54 The Brāhmaṇas

The Brāhmaṇas are treatises which embody the notion of the magical efficacy of sacrifice that has just been described. They take the form of commentary or exposition of the text of the Vedic hymns. In this respect they are the forerunners of a long tradition of Indian religious literature in which new developments of thought are presented as expositions of some earlier text, even though in fact the new literature may embody ideas which differ very greatly from those found in the older text. In the case of the Brāhmaṇas we find all kinds of fanciful speculations concerning the nature of the sacrificial ritual, its symbolism, its cosmic significance, and so on. Entirely speculative though this thinking might be, its authors did not attempt to set it out as such, but sought to legitimate it by presenting it as exposition of the hymns used in the course of the ritual. It is not so much that the ideas expressed in the Vedic hymns are regarded as important and therefore expounded; it is rather that the very sound of the syllables themselves has become invested with a sacred quality, a magical power. This it is which constitutes brahman, a supernatural force similar to that which in primitive religion is called *mana*. The possessor or controller of this sacred power of brahman residing in the sound of the chant is the brāhman (often transliterated in English as 'brahmin') or priest. The Brāhmaṇas, then, are the 'priestly' writings which set forth and elaborate the many aspects of this sacred (or, more correctly, magical) power.

1.55 The emergent caste system

The growing importance of the brāhman, and his special status as the controller of the magic of the chant, are already to be seen in one of the hymns of the tenth maṇḍala of the Ṛg-veda which we have already noticed, namely number 90, 'The Sacrifice of Primal Man'. The singer asks, 'When they divided primal man, with how many parts did they divide him?' The answer is then given: 'The brāhman was his mouth, the arms were made the prince (kṣatriya), his thighs the common people (vaiśya), and from his feet the serf (sudra) was born' (Zaehner, 1966; 9 f.). It is appropriate that the brāhman should be represented by the mouth, that is the *sound-uttering* part of the primal man, for this at once connects the brāhman with the most potent of the faculties of man in this way of thinking. Moreover, in this hymn of the later Vedic period we see how the earlier twofold differentiation of the *élite* (*kṣatriya*) and the ordinary tribesmen (*viś*) has now developed into a fourfold division of society, with the brāhman as the first in rank-order, having a status higher even than that of the warrior, or kṣatriya. At the same time some of the ordinary tribesmen have sunk to a lower place, that of *sudras*, or serfs. It is usually held that these consisted of those of the indigenous peoples who had been forced to labour for the conquering and territory-occupying Aryans, and possibly also the offspring of the mixed marriages between these natives and their Aryan conquerors. The fact that the four classes of society are described in this way in a Vedic hymn indicates that by the later Vedic period this division of society was already regarded as having religious legitimation – that is, it was represented as part of the ordained structure of the universe proceeding from a primeval sacrifice. Since speculative religious thought seems to have been the prerogative of the brāhmans at this period we may safely infer that this particular rank-order (first brāhmans, then kṣatriyas, then vaiśyas and last of all sudras) reflects the brāhman point of view; hence it was this order which was credited with religious sanction. From this brāhman-inspired hymn we are simply left to guess whether the kṣatriya class would have concurred in the order of the classes. The fact that the sudras are the lowest class, and that this class was drawn largely from autochthonous groups does not mean, however, that the *class* structure was based on *racial* discrimination. For there is evidence that the brāhman priesthood of the later Vedic period was drawn from both Aryan and non-Aryan sources. Some of the major brāhman clan groups are curiously described as having been 'born of a jar'. This probably means that they were sons of a human representative of a mother-goddess; the 'jar', according to Kosambi, represents the womb of the mother-goddess. The adoption of such non-Aryan sages into the Aryan priesthood was, he says, an innovation, but it had the great value of assimilating 'otherwise hostile groups, along with their many new cults, into one society worshipping common gods' (Kosambi, 1965; 83); in this way a new, highly-specialised priesthood developed.

1.56 The forest-dwellers

Were there some among the Vedic Aryans who did not fully concur with the priests' high estimation of their own activities and place in society? It is sometimes suggested that evidence of this may perhaps be found in the type of treatise which follows the priestly Brāhmaṇas, namely the Forest-Writings, or Āraṇyakas. These writings represent a turning away from ritual towards a more mystical and ascetic type of religious life. The name Āraṇyaka certainly implies a connection of some kind with the forest (araṇya). Dasgupta suggests that these treatises originated as compositions intended for old men who were no longer capable of performing the sacrificial ritual and had instead retired to the forest to meditate; the symbolism of the sacrificial ritual provided the subject matter for their meditation (Dasgupta, 1922; 14). The Āraṇyakas may be said to represent a transitional stage between the earlier situation, in which the actual performance of the sacrifice was all-important, and the later situation represented by the Upaniṣads (*1.57*) where thought-activity, in the form of meditation on the mystical correspondences and symbolism of the ritual, takes the place of cultic activity. While this trend may have originated among the old men of the priestly class, it seems to have been taken up by others, among whom the Āraṇyaka type of treatise develops into the Upaniṣad. 'Sacrifice in itself was losing value in the eyes of these men and diverse mystical significances and imports were beginning to be considered as their real truth' (Dasgupta, 1922; 35). But whether or not the Āraṇyakas represent a reaction of the kṣatriya class against the prestige claimed by the priests for the sacrificial ritual is a question on which scholarship is divided. Such a reaction did arise later, in the form of the Jain and Buddhist movements. The Āraṇyaka treatises may perhaps be said to represent an intermediate position between the all-importance of the cultic ritual and the rejection of it by these later heterodox movements.

1.57 The emergence of the Upaniṣads

The Upaniṣadic literature, into which the Āraṇyaka treatises developed, is regarded by some scholars as being broadly orthodox so far as the sacrificial cult is concerned; that is to say, in the Upaniṣads cultic activity is not opposed or repudiated. Rather, it is seen as having even greater importance as a basis or starting point for metaphysical speculation, and it is this speculation which is pursued with such thoroughness in the Upaniṣads. Basham maintains that these represent the position of the *orthodox* mystics; they 'in no way oppose the sacrificial cult but maintain its qualified validity' (Basham, 1954; 246). Similarly Dasgupta holds 'there seems to be no definite evidence for thinking that the Upaniṣad philosophy originated among the Kṣatriyas' (Dasgupta, 1922; 35). But other scholars, in Europe and India, have taken a different view: for instance, Garbe, and Winternitz, whose arguments are examined by Dasgupta. More recently D. D. Kosambi has suggested that the Upaniṣads represent an entirely different development from that found in the Brāhmaṇas. He inclines to the view that while the Upaniṣads are brāhman books they embody ideas which brāhmans were learning from kṣatriyas; this, in fact, is what is actually suggested in the text of some of the Upaniṣads, where brāhmans are found receiving instruction concerning the mystical significance of the sacrifice and the nature of the universal Self; such a case is that of the five brāhmans who approach the kṣatriya ruler Aśvapati Paikeya, who had a reputation as a teacher of such matters (*Chāndogya Upaniṣad*, v, xi–xviii). As Dasgupta points out, in other cases it was the brāhmans themselves who were discussing such matters and instructing others concerning them. This, however, does not rule out the possibility that the initiative in setting forth such new theories may have come in the first place from non-brāhmans, and Dasgupta himself acknowledges that among the kṣatriyas in general 'there existed earnest philosophic enquiries which must be regarded as having exerted an important influence in the formation of the Upaniṣadic doctrines' (Dasgupta, 1922; 31).

The effect of the emerging ideas concerning the universal Self would certainly seem to be to direct attention away from the sacrifice to other means of gaining religious ends. This was partly because the ends themselves were changing. The sacrifice was intended to secure prosperity, success, and earthly good fortune. But other goals were now being sought. The reasons for this are various and complicated, but the most important feature in the situation seems to be that the Aryan attitude to life had changed; life had come to be accepted as basically miserable, so that men longed to escape into some kind of dreamless sleep. With this went a new emphasis on asceticism, developed by the forest-dwellers and communicated by them even to brāhmans; this consisted of a rejection of the transitory, so-called pleasures of the senses in order to acquire and accumulate tapas, or spiritual 'heat'. Finally, the old Vedic ideas concerning man's destiny after death had now given place to the theory of an endless succession of lives, that is, the theory of transmigration.

1.58 The religious ideas of the Upaniṣads

In the collection of disputations and discourses that go to make up the Upaniṣads there is no systematic arrangement or single doctrinal position. Certain general assumptions, however, seem to be present in all the Upaniṣads, the most important and fundamental of which is, in Dasgupta's words, 'that underlying the exterior world of change there is an unchangeable reality which is identical with that which underlies the essence in man' (Dasgupta, 1922; 42). The goal towards which the Upaniṣads point men is the realisation by the human individual of this identity between his own spirit or self (ātman) and the world-spirit or Self (*brahman*). Not all men would be capable of realising this identity, it was recognised, but only those who had been initiated and prepared by a spiritual master or guru. The word Upaniṣad signifies teaching that is esoteric. This idea of 'secret instruction' is confirmed by many passages in the Upaniṣads themselves (Dasgupta, 1922; 38). It is therefore hardly surprising that when the Western reader learns that the one underlying doctrine is the equation of ātman with brahman, this may not mean very much to him; he does not immediately appreciate the spiritual release which this was held to entail among those who received and *practised* the Upaniṣadic religious doctrine. It certainly was understood by them as release, however, for this is what men had begun to seek; release, that is, from the prison-house of karma and transmigration. It was the spread and the acceptance of this notion, in place of the older Vedic idea that man's destiny after death was either heaven (the Abode of the Fathers) or hell (the House of Clay), which paved the way for various doctrines of release or mokṣa, of which the Upaniṣadic way of release through esoteric knowledge of the identity of ātman and brahman was one. It is in the Upaniṣads that the first real evidence of belief in karma and transmigration is found in Aryan literature. The fact that this now became orthodox doctrine among the brāhmans, and that asceticism and meditational practices were accepted by them as being among the principal methods for attaining such release, indicates the extent of the change in religious attitudes among brāhmans even within the later Vedic period.

1.59 The Atharva-veda

For many people, however, such doctrines would have been beyond comprehension; for them, religious goals were more immediate and more restricted. This was probably true of the majority of the population, the lower classes of society, both Aryan and non-Aryan, who were principally engaged in agriculture. Among them, religion appears to have been virtually identical with magic. The evidence for this is found in the collection of texts known as the Atharva-veda. As the fourth collection of Vedic hymns and chants this was added later than the Ṛg-veda, the Yajur-veda, and the Sāma-veda, but it incorporates material which is probably just as ancient as the hymns of the other collections. Some of this material may have originated among the lower class of the Aryan tribesmen; much of it is probably derived from aboriginal sources, and consists of magical spells and incantations, expiatory charms, exorcisms and so on. The Vedic gods of the Aryans have little place here, if any; there is some cosmology, but it has more affinities with that of the Upaniṣads than with early hymns of the Ṛg-veda. Such, for instance, is the hymn to the Goddess Earth, a composition which is one of the most characteristic and most attractive of the Atharvan hymns, 'rising at times to poetic conceptions of no mean merit', as Bloomfield comments. But by and large the concerns of the Atharva-veda are domestic, and if they extend beyond that, they still remain within the realm of social relationships and functions. The subjects dealt with are: charms to cure diseases and to promote health and immunity from disease; imprecations against demons and sorcerers; charms for the benefit of women – for the obtaining of a husband, or a son; charms for the benefit of men – to secure a woman's love, to cause the return of a truant wife; charms relating to kings, their consecration, and success in their enterprises; charms relating to personal relationships in general – the securing of harmony, the allaying of discord, the appeasement of anger and so on. Many of the hymns are of such a kind that we can understand, as Bloomfield says, that 'they cannot have been otherwise than highly esteemed', so obviously auspicious are the intentions and aims. Perhaps it is significant that a class of person mentioned frequently in the Atharva-veda is the vrātya. They were apparently priests of non-Aryan indigenous fertility cults; Basham comments that 'great efforts were made to convert them to the

Aryan faith, and to find room for them in the orthodox cult' (Basham, 1954; 244). On the other hand the word 'vrātya' comes in later times to mean one who did not honour the Vedas, that is, one who adheres to non-Vedic ideas and practices. The prominence of the vrātya in the Atharva-veda would therefore seem to suggest that in this Atharvan material we come nearer than in any other surviving *literary* source to the religious ideas and attitudes of pre-Aryan and early non-Aryan India.

SUMMARY AND COMMENT ON CHAPTER ONE

In this chapter we have looked at some of the principal features of religion in eastern and western Asia from the beginning of its *known* history. It must be emphasised that we have not been concerned here to investigate the historical origins of religion, for these lie far back in the period of mankind's early history, where evidence is scanty and more ambiguous and speculative theories flourish. What we have examined are the historical roots of some of the more important religious beliefs and practices of the traditions of Europe and Asia.

In the period with which we have been dealing human belief in a supernatural power or powers, or a human sense of that which was sacred, was already old. One of the earliest forms which such belief took was that of the earth as mother, or mother-goddess, a form of belief which has persisted in India more strongly than in the Near East (although it has never completely died out, even there). It is not difficult to understand why, if men were to regard anything at all as uniquely venerable, or sacred, it should be either the earth which bore them and supported them, or else the sun, which was evidently the prime source of physical life and light and the other dominant phenomenon of man's existence. In some societies it was one, in some it was the other which was venerated; primitive Japanese religion, which is an example of the latter kind, will be dealt with in the next chapter (*2.48*). It should be remembered that we are concerned here mainly to describe, in the sense that we simply note that men have from earliest times apparently felt constrained to express a sense either of dependence, a need to affirm what it was which for them was of the utmost value, or even what was for them sacred; but in noting this we still have not explained why it should be so. We may note also that there existed in these ancient civilisations a need for some view of life's changes and chances, in the light of which men might hope to take appropriate action to secure their welfare and avoid the experiences of suffering and the sense of injustice. This demand men sought to satisfy in ancient Mesopotamia, for example, by resort to the soothsayer and seer and the explanations offered in the traditional wisdom; and in ancient India by the theory of karma and rebirth, and by conduct appropriate to a good rebirth: this demand for meaning is one of the major constituent features of other religious systems, as we shall see.

More immediately germane to our study is the coincidence of two facts concerning these ancient societies and their religious beliefs. First, in the Near East the third millennium B.C. was the period of the emergence of autocratic empire-states in Egypt and in Babylon, a feature of which was the worship of territorial deities, and a state-priesthood, or city-priesthood, responsible for the cults of these deities. Second, alongside this fact we have to note that, as S. G. F. Brandon has written, while 'the fundamental concepts of cosmogonic speculation were laid far back in the preliterary period', it appears that 'true cosmogonic speculation concerning the origin of the world or the universe was probably little developed before the third millennium B.C., when the earliest known cosmogonic texts were composed.' Doctrines of creation by an omnipotent being thus have their rise within recorded history, and are seen to have been associated with certain kinds of political structures, of which the Egyptian and Babylonian states are outstanding examples.

In the case of the Indus valley civilisation knowledge of such beliefs is hindered by the present indecipherability of the script. In any case, it is not certain that the political structure there was of exactly the same kind as in Egypt and Babylon; in general the Indus valley civilisation appears to have been an assimilation to the Near Eastern river valley civilisations, but not by any means an exact reproduction. It has also to be remembered that the earlier village cultures of north-west India upon which this pattern was imposed would have made their own contribution to the special nature of the Indus valley civilisation. What may be called the 'theology' of the mother-goddess appears to have persisted more strongly in the case of the Indian civilisation than it did in the Near East, although it persisted there also. In India the first evidence we have of cosmogonic speculation is that provided by the

Aryan culture at a time when the brāhman priests were as a class beginning to establish their position of superiority in Aryan society. The creation legend here was thus not one of divine fiat, the word of an omnipotent ruler; it was a doctrine of creation by primeval sacrifice, that is to say, by a priestly type of activity. This association of cosmogonic ideas with brāhman priesthood had the important consequence later that the challenging of brāhman priestly claims (by the Buddhists, most notably) entailed also the challenging of this creation-theory which was associated with the brāhmans.

In the ancient Near East religious ideas and practices were clearly bound up with the idea of a definite territory. The assertion of territorial rights, one of the most basic features of animal and human life, here received what may be described as sacralisation. In both Egypt and Babylon it was the territory that was the primary element, together with the king who was its human protector and maintainer. The relationship between the king and his territory (including the inhabitants) was given a ritual expression, and this constituted the dominant feature of the religion in these two areas. The other subsidiary but important feature, as we have seen, consisted of the whole range of practices by which men sought to obtain, in ways other than purely logical, comfort in this life and possibly assurance of some ultimately happy destiny hereafter.

In contrast to this whole pattern of religious belief and practice was the life of ancient Israel. Founded upon an act of revolt against the territorial royal theocracy of Egypt, the metaphysical context in which this group of tribes was led by the prophet-leader Moses to see their common life was that of a *people*, rather than the inhabitants of a certain territory, a people, moreover, whose welfare depended upon a particularly vivid relationship with a deity who could be known only as 'He who is', or 'I will be that I will be'. But this situation of the early days of Israel's history gave way to another in which the people and their deity became territorialised. Yahwism became the religion of a territory, interpreted as the 'promised land', and before long assimilated to the territorial-religious systems of the Near East. The idea emerged of Yahweh as the territorial ruler or king, and also of Yahweh as the omnipotent creator by his royal-divine fiat. However, in early Israelite religion the conception of Yahweh as deliverer from Egypt, protector of his people, the One who stood in special relation to them, remained primary; the conception of Yahweh as creator-king was still only secondary to this. The assimilation of Yahwism to other Near Eastern systems was carried further by the establishment of a monarchy; nevertheless there remained some adherents to the older tradition of Israel's life who, by their charismatic authority, were able to challenge the more blatant of the developments towards the Near Eastern pattern of a royal deity and a king-god and the autochthonous and magical practices which were associated with such a culture. For the prophetic tradition within Israel Yahweh remained pre-eminently the lord of history rather than the lord of a territory, and the supreme purpose of man's life was 'to know Yahweh', that is, to realise the special relationship which was capable of existing between men and Yahweh, which was life's proper fulfilment. Nevertheless, the conjunction between Yahweh and Near Eastern kingship *had* been made, and was increasingly accepted within Israel, a conjunction which was to have important consequences in the subsequent history of Western religion.

2 Prophets and Philosophers

2.1 THE PROPHETIC TRADITION OF ISRAEL (926–520 B.C.)

2.10 The parting of the ways within Hebrew religion

ONE of the main effects of the Jerusalem monarchy was, as a modern Jewish writer has said (Epstein, 1959), the disruption of the religious unity of the old tribal confederation. That unity had been broken after the death of Saul, but was restored temporarily by the military prowess of King David; at the death of Solomon it was broken again, finally. The most important single reason for this, apart from the oppressive rule of Solomon (1.48) which was the immediate cause, was the imposition upon the earlier form of Yahwism, as it existed to the time of Samuel, of what was ultimately alien to it – the institution of monarchy. The characteristically Yahwistic figure, the great prophet, the man who by virtue of religious charisma combined the roles of seer, priest and judge, and was accepted as leader of the cultic confederation, had now been displaced by that characteristically Near Eastern figure, the king, who from now on very often owed his position to hereditary succession. It is true that the Davidic dynasty was an attempt to modify oriental monarchy and make it a Yahwistic institution, but the attempt did not meet with great success; its chief permanent result was that it eventually gave rise to the notion of an ideal monarch who would succeed in leading Israel in accordance with the religious spirit of Yahwism, where actual monarchs so far had failed. Those who tried to be both faithful Yahweh-worshippers and faithful royalists held on to the conviction that such a combination was not impossible. When the monarchy finally came to an end (and in all it lasted only just over four centuries) this notion of the ideal monarch, the Anointed One, or Messiah, who was to appear in the future and set up an enduring and righteous kingdom, became the focus of Jewish religious aspiration.

2.11 Prophetic opposition to the monarchy

There were, however, those worshippers of Yahweh who did not so easily succumb to the idea, who continued to reject the notion of monarchy and to resist the policies of actual monarchs, who more often than not seemed to the faithful to be acting in opposition to the will of Yahweh. A dichotomy had developed within Hebrew religion, a dichotomy which is not always recognised by readers of the Bible (Ringgren, 1966; 220). It would perhaps be carrying historical analysis too far to say that there were now *two religions*: one faithful to the principle that the worship of Yahweh and acknowledgement of his law was the only real basis for Hebrew unity; the other committed to loyalty not only to Yahweh but also to the king as his representative. There was, however, some approximation to this in the difference which undoubtedly existed between the religion of the royal court, and that of the areas outside Jerusalem, where the earlier Yahwistic traditions remained stronger and the cultic prophets at the local sanctuaries preserved the ethos of Yahwism.

Certainly there was a tension, and it manifested itself from time to time in conflict between Yahwistic prophets and the royal house. An outstanding example is the encounter of Elijah with King Ahab, and more especially with his queen. Early in the ninth century B.C. an army officer named Omri seized the throne of the now separate northern kingdom. His reign lasted for twelve years and was notable for the building of a new, well-placed and well-fortified capital, Samaria. (Excavations on the site of Samaria in the 1930s indicated that there had been an elaborate palace and strong fortifications belonging to the time of Omri.) Omri's son Ahab strengthened the economic and political position of the northern kingdom by a diplomatic marriage with a Phoenician princess, Jezebel, daughter of the king of Tyre. The narrative in I Kings presents us with a picture of a weak king and a forceful, determined queen, intent on imposing upon Israel both the Baal-worship of Tyre and the thoroughly autocratic Phoenician style of government. This resulted in the spirited challenge to such trends presented by Elijah, as the loyal representative of Yahweh and the traditional faith of Israel.

Just as Solomon had built shrines for the gods of his foreign wives, so now Ahab consented to the building in Samaria of a temple for

Jezebel's god, Melkart, the Baal of Tyre. Ahab could have considered he had a good precedent in the action of Solomon. The prophetic attitude to Ahab and Jezebel and their religious policy is depicted very clearly in the collection of Elijah-stories found in chapters 17–19 of the first book of Kings. A feature of these stories is the frequent occurrence of miracles; for instance, the prophet is hungry; he is miraculously fed by ravens. It is only straining the evidence of the text to say that 'ravens' is a misreading for 'merchants' or 'Arabs', just as it is misinterpreting the plain intention of the narrative to say that perhaps the child of the woman of Zarephath did not really die but only swooned; or that the meaning of the miraculous supply of meal and oil is simply an eking out of a small, continuing supply. The narrator clearly intends to present us with miracles – this is one of the places in the Hebrew scriptures where they cluster together – and in doing so he is seeking to enhance the prestige of Elijah as a man of God, a servant of Yahweh. He is indicating where the true Yahwist's interest and sympathy should lie, in disputes between syncretising kings such as Solomon and Ahab, and all loyal upholders of the traditional faith of Israel.

Having thus been introduced to us, Elijah's role in the religious drama is then indicated. We are told, in two asides, of the activities of Jezebel: she persecuted the *prophets* of Yahweh (I Kgs 18: 4), and she had the *altars* of Yahweh overthrown (I Kgs 18: 30). The fact that her action was directed against these places and these people – altars and prophets – suggests that there was an important connection between them at the time, and is generally taken to mean that there had been some kind of popular demonstration at these altars, led by the prophets of Yahweh, against the royal institution of the cult of Melkart. In the dramatic confrontation on Mount Carmel between Elijah and the prophets of Baal it is, again, the prophets who are the cultic functionaries. The offering of sacrifice on the respective altars of Baal and Yahweh was performed by the prophets of Baal (without success) and by the one prophet of Yahweh (with resounding success). In order to do this Elijah had to rebuild the Yahweh-altar which had been thrown down on Jezebel's orders. In all this, it is to be noted, Elijah is acting in a priestly role. He was also acting, as the prophet-priest of Yahweh, in direct defiance of the religious policy of the royal house. The fire from the sky, followed by a torrential downpour of rain, was regarded as a confirmation of the faithfulness and integrity of Elijah in acting thus. This vindication of Elijah in the eyes of the people only served to infuriate Jezebel, however, and Elijah found it necessary to withdraw in order to preserve his life. It is clear that in travelling to the far south of Palestine, to the mountain of Horeb, Elijah was not simply putting the greatest possible distance between himself and Jezebel. Horeb has another, and in this context most important, significance. In the earlier tradition of Israel it was the place of Yahweh's abode, and with it was associated the original revelation of Yahweh as the lord of history which had been delivered to Israel in the wilderness period. In withdrawing to Horeb, Elijah was symbolically returning to the sources of Israel's faith.

2.12 The significance of Elijah

In assessing the significance of Elijah, Fleming James pointed out that in him 'the religion of Moses lived again'. Certainly in Hebrew prophetic tradition the two figures are closely associated. Elijah was pre-eminently one who was faithful to the religious ideas and traditions associated with the great name of Moses. He has also been hailed as a true forerunner of the Hebrew prophets of the eighth and seventh centuries B.C. The fact that he adhered so firmly to the cultic worship of Yahweh and that he regarded the pure Yahwistic cultus as of such importance accords well with the concerns of the eighth-century B.C. prophets. It is significant that it was the figure of Elijah which suggested itself to the prophet of an even later age, whom we know as Malachi, as the one who would prepare Israel for the coming great day of the divine consummation: 'Behold I will send you Elijah the prophet before the great and terrible day of Yahweh comes' (Mal. 4:5). To this day at their celebration of the Passover the Jews set aside 'a cup of wine for Elijah' in case he should come.

2.13 Hebrew prophets of the eighth century B.C.

We have now to consider how to regard the remarkable growth of prophetic activity in the eighth century B.C., of which the great names are Amos, Micah, Hosea and Isaiah. Why did this happen? And why when it did? Was it because, as G. F. Moore suggested, 'it was not until the eighth century B.C. that the men came who thought through what the moral idea of God involves, and had the courage to proclaim its consequences'? (Moore, 1948; 128). Was it a newly emergent individualism which produced these great religious geniuses? Such an explanation postulates a new kind of development in what had until this time been guilds or companies of prophets, when, as T. H. Robinson suggested, 'one of the individuals in the band separated himself and delivered a message out of harmony with the rest' (Robinson; 1923). Yet another distinction that is sometimes claimed for the eighth-century B.C. prophets is that in their desire to communicate their message by every means possible certain inspired men adopted the novel procedure of writing down what they had proclaimed, thus giving a more permanent character to their prophetic outpourings. It is possible that there is a certain amount of truth in each of these three ideas. In the first place there certainly would have been some kind of reflective thought in the life of a prophet of Yahweh. But the important question is why such reflective activity was so strongly marked a feature of eighth-century B.C. Israel and Judah. It cannot have been that the capacity for religious and moral thought had only just developed; the reason more probably lies in the fact that the monarchical systems of the two kingdoms were by this time producing a religious and social situation such as would make any faithful Yahwist think pretty hard. Again, it is no doubt true that the results of religious reflection might most effectively be expressed in the form of an individual utterance. The faithful worshipper of Yahweh might well feel himself under a strong compulsion to declare to his contemporaries what the spirit of Yahweh forced him to say, and in thus speaking out he might appear in the role of an isolated preacher. But this does not mean that he was not in fact one of a guild or company of men, all of whom were in some way associated with him in his declaration: it simply means that the strong individual voice was more natural and more urgent than a joint statement would have been. The historical picture of Hebrew prophecy which has been built up in recent years has as one of its striking features, as Eissfeldt has written, 'the close linking up of the prophets (like Amos, Hosea, Isaiah and Jeremiah), with the cultus, and their membership in organised cultic associations . . .' (Rowley, 1951; 117). So far as the third suggestion is concerned, that the prophets set out to write, as conscious apologists of the Yahwistic faith, so that writing can be said to have been their deliberate and avowed purpose – this has now been seen as very improbable. The literary form of the collections that bear their names suggests that their words in each case, 'were treasured in the memories of the disciples; i.e., the members of the associations of cultic prophets to which the Master had belonged, and were transmitted to later times within the cult-prophetic association by word of mouth alone' (Rowley, 1951; 117).

To return to the original question, why was Hebrew prophetic activity of this kind so prominent a feature of the eighth century B.C.? It will be seen that we have still to seek a satisfactory answer to the questions, Why? and Why at that time? The answer suggested here is that as in so many other similar situations in religious history there was at that time a special combination of, on the one hand, socio-political unease, and on the other, men conscious of a divine message to their distressed contemporary world. In this case, the social and psychological malaise was seen by the prophets to be closely connected with the institution of monarchy. In the preceding century it had been royal policies which had frequently stimulated prophetic protests; examples of this are Nathan (2 Sam. 12), Micaiah ben Imlah (1 Kgs 22) and Elijah, already mentioned (*2.12*). In each case the prophet is chiefly remembered for his opposition, in the name of Yahweh, to the policy or the conduct of the monarch concerned.

2.14 The prophets and the corruption of worship

In the case of the eighth-century B.C. prophets, however, there is something more. Not only is there criticism of, or opposition to, royal policies or attitudes, or conduct, but also to those of the people, especially the chief citizens and courtiers, that is, those whose moral and religious attitudes were derived from those of the court. If the words of these eighth-century B.C. prophets which have come down to us sometimes give the impression that the entire nation was being rebuked, it is important to remember that the matters for which the nation was being criticised were more often than not closely connected with, or the direct result of, the monarchical system which had been imposed on Yahwistic religion. The chief of these, in the prophetic view, was the debased and degenerate state of the worship of Yahweh, and this was the result very largely of syncretism; we have already noted the large share which certain kings, such as Solomon and Ahab, had had in the process of incorporating into the cultus at Jerusalem and Samaria elements of foreign nature-religion and magic. It was this debasement

D

and distortion of the worship of Yahweh which, in the prophetic view, lay at the root of a good deal of Israel's malaise.

2.15 The prophets and social corruption

There had been a distortion also in the structure of Israelite society: the townsman had prospered at the expense of the peasant. The peasant, burdened with the economic impositions made necessary by the various state schemes of the monarchy, had become more and more impoverished. The evils of usury, to which the peasant became a victim, led to the situation where, being unable to pay, he had to forfeit his land and possibly even become a slave. Land passed increasingly into the hands of a minority group of urban rich men, with all the evil social consequences that were denounced by prophets such as Amos and Isaiah. The rich, moreover, found ways and means of influencing legal decisions in their favour should the poor man make any attempt to resort to law for the redress of his grievances. Thus Israel ceased to be a society of equals before Yahweh and become instead a nation of extremes: of wealth and poverty, luxury and misery, urban ostentation and rural depression. The rich, while outwardly conforming to the ritual of the royal temple cult, could say inwardly, 'There is no God'; no God, that is, to take any account of injustice and exploitation. The extremist reaction to all this on the part of certain minority groups such as the Rechabites was to renounce altogether a settled form of civilisation. The classical Hebrew prophets, however, proclaimed that Israel must return to a just order of society, in accordance with the religious ideals and principles of earlier Yahwism.

2.16 The prophets and political opportunism

A third aspect of Israel's falling away from the earlier faith, according to the prophets of Yahweh, was her involvement in Near Eastern international politics. The transformation of Israel from a cultic confederation to a monarchy had facilitated the provision of armaments and alliances as a defence of her life – with correspondingly less apparent need for reliance on the guidance and protection of Yahweh. With the idleness and ostentation of the ruling class went, apparently, a spirit of jingoism and national pride – ridiculous, as it turned out, but none the less real. As T. H. Robinson pointed out, there was a striking comparison between the spirit of the ruling classes in Israel in the eighth and seventh centuries B.C. and that of the French aristocracy before the Revolution.

A further factor in the development of the prophetic interpretation of contemporary affairs was the rise of Assyria to a position of dominance in Western Asia. The Assyrian empire had been extended to include much of the ancient Near East and Middle East. Confronted by the existence of this new international giant Israel began to be aware of world history in a new way. The god of Israel might, it seemed, have to give way to the mighty gods of Assyria; for it was in the name of these gods, the Assyrian generals solemnly declared in the inscriptions, that Assyria waged her campaigns. This constituted a crisis of belief in the reality and power of Yahweh. The prophets interpreted the international events of their day as the work of Yahweh, whose sphere of activity they now saw as enormously extended beyond what had been envisaged earlier. They were convinced that the divine being whom they worshipped was the lord of history – even though he might not intervene to save faithless Israel, and even though Israel might have to suffer in the events that now loomed on the international horizon, in which or beyond which the prophets saw 'the day of Yahweh' – the day of retribution and disaster. But for the faithful and the righteous it might even, according to some of the prophets such as Jeremiah, be a day to be hoped for and welcomed. The monarchy might be overthrown, the Temple whose precincts the men of Judah thought to be inviolable might be destroyed, the nation might suffer defeat and even enslavement – and yet, claimed the prophets, in all this the name of Yahweh as lord of history would only be magnified and the true worshippers would be vindicated. Jerusalem would be destroyed, Micah proclaimed, but Yahweh was concerned more with the righteousness of his people than with the Temple and its cultus. 'What does Yahweh require of you, but to do justice, and to love kindness, and to walk humbly with your God?' It is this expectation of ill fortune by means of which religious apostasy was to be condemned that marks off the prophets of Yahweh from the royal prophets, and indeed from all the soothsayers and the givers of oracles in the ancient world. When the event foretold by the prophets happened, the national disaster in which first the northern tribes were defeated and their

capital Samaria captured, in 721, and then the southern kingdom
overthrown and the city of Jerusalem abandoned and many of the
leaders of the nation carried off into exile in Babylon, in 587, the prophetic message was powerfully vindicated. The result was a measure of
recovery of the authentic religious faith of Israel. As Max Weber
wrote: 'It is a stupendous paradox, that a god does not only fail to
protect his chosen people against its enemies but allows them to fall, or
pushes them himself, into ignominy and enslavement, yet is worshipped
only the more ardently. This is unexampled in history and is only to be
explained by the powerful prestige of the prophetic message' (Weber,
1952; 364).

2.17 The traditionalist character of eighth-century prophecy

It is thus possible to see that it is the religious tradition manifested in the
prophets that is both the original and the enduring central element in
Hebrew religion. In the eighth-century situation it might well have
seemed that such men as Amos were marginal to the main streams of
Hebrew life and thought – as indeed at the time they probably were.
But one has to distinguish between the short-term and the long-term
effects and consequences of the prophetic witness. Indeed, it is in the
perspective of subsequent religious history that the effect upon Israel of
the prophetic message is fully appreciated; for this reason they are
sometimes regarded as innovators, men who laid the foundations of
a new religious attitude. But Amos, for example, speaks of himself as the
upholder of an *ancient* faith, faith in Yahweh as the God who is active in
the affairs of history. 'Thus says Yahweh, I brought you up out of the
land of Egypt, and led you forty years in the wilderness. . . . Is it not so
indeed, O people of Israel?' (Amos 2: 10; 3: 1). The indictment which
Amos brings is that in the past Israel has attempted to silence the
prophets (Amos 2: 12). Obviously, then, the prophetic tradition in
which Amos was conscious of standing was not something new.
According to Amos the essential element in Yahwistic religion is the
existence of the prophet as the declarer and interpreter of the divine
purposes: 'Surely the Lord God does nothing without revealing his
secret to his servants the prophets' (Amos 3: 7). One of the principal
roles of the prophet, illustrated in the message of Amos and of Hosea,
for example, is the call to men to turn back from secular ways of

thought and conduct, to seek to know the will of God: 'Seek Yahweh, and you shall live.' 'Seek good and not evil, that you may live.' 'Come, let us return to Yahweh. . . .' What is clear is that such men were not consciously setting forth, in the eighth century B.C., a new form of religion; they believed they were calling men to return to religious attitudes, a religious way of life, and a religious structure of society, which had been the original basis and *raison d'être* of the community of Israel but which had been corrupted and distorted in more recent times by the introduction of an alien element, the oriental pattern of despotic monarchy.

2.18 The growth of the idea of God as potentate

Once introduced into the life of Israel, however, the institution of monarchy left its permanent imprint on Israel's religion. This is to be seen not so much in the dominant place held by the royal temple-cultus from the time of Solomon onwards – fraught with serious and enduring consequences though this was – but in the influence which the institution of monarchy had upon the Hebrew conception of God. By the sixth century B.C. even the prophetic conception of Yahweh's nature had been affected; the utterances of Jeremiah, for example, reveal the extent to which ideas associated with monarchical government had entered into the mainstream of Hebrew thought. One of the significant changes in the Hebrew conception of God is from the earlier idea of Yahweh as dwelling in the holy mountain of the wilderness where the Hebrews first became his covenant people – an idea which survives in Ps. 68 and Hab. 3, where Yahweh is described as coming from Sinai – to the later idea in which he is regarded as having his dwelling in Zion, the capital city of King David, whence he 'shines forth' against his enemies (Ps. 50: 2–4; 48: 2–7). He is, in this later stratum of pre-Exilic thought, regarded as dwelling in Canaan only, the ruler of the land; beyond this territory other gods hold sway. The situation is one in which 'the worship of other gods by foreign nations is accepted as an empirical fact, while Yahweh alone is of significance for the Israelites' (Ringgren, 1966; 99). During the pre-Exilic period he is described also as 'Yahweh Sabaoth'. The word 'Sabaoth' is of uncertain meaning in this connection, but underlying the various possible interpretations is the idea of heavenly hosts or armies, or possibly a heavenly court. In this, too, we see how the divine being is thought of in terms of a mighty king.

Important though this conception of God as a powerful national monarch became, however, other aspects of his nature were also emphasised alongside this. Outstanding was the apprehension of Yahweh's holiness. The roots of this sense of the holiness of God lie far back in the early history of the Hebrews, and, in particular, in the experience of certain outstanding figures such as Moses and Samuel. An element in the sense of the holy is, as Otto has demonstrated in his famous book *The Idea of the Holy*, a feeling of awe and dread, as well as of fascination, in the presence of the *mysterium tremendum*. Yet it is easy to see how even this conception provided the basis for a transition into the idea of Yahweh as a majestic potentate. For the holiness of God 'signifies the unapproachability, the awesomeness, even the dangerousness of the God who is wholly other' (Ringgren, 1966; 74). This has obvious affinities with the unapproachability by ordinary men of the great and powerful monarch. Belief in the divine holiness could thus, in the context of monarchical government, very easily lead by yet another path to the idea of God as a king. Significantly it is Isaiah of Jerusalem who makes the transition. 'Holy, holy, holy, is Yahweh Sabaoth . . . I am a man of unclean lips, and . . . my eyes have seen the King, Yahweh Sabaoth!' (Isa. 6: 3,5). The relationship of the humble subject and the mighty king is thus transposed into religious thought; the concept of Yahweh's holiness imperceptibly becomes the concept of Yahweh's kingship.

Nevertheless, there was something more that was denoted by the word 'holy', and this remained, unassimilated to the symbolism of kingship. Hosea represents Yahweh as saying 'I am the Holy One in your midst', that is the one who is kindly and compassionate, who has mercy, and is present among his people. Something of this sense of a shared nature, between God and men, is found in the so-called Holiness Code: 'You shall be holy, for I Yahweh your God am holy' (Lev. 19: 2), where the injunction very clearly has a moral and ethical connotation.

2.19 The divine monarch, and the Hebrew idea of sin

Something of this same duality has affected the Hebrew notion of sin, which received its formative development during the pre-Exilic period.

It is not always realised that the idea of sin is by no means universal among mankind; for instance it is not a prominent or even important feature of ancient Chinese and Japanese religion (*2.45; 2.48*). So far as the Western world in general is concerned, the popular understanding of the idea of sin is in the form in which it has been bequeathed to the West by Hebrew religion. And in so far as the original Hebrew idea is twofold, the consequences of the acceptance of this twofold idea may be seen to have been, to say the least, ambiguous.

One main root, perhaps the major one, is almost certainly man's sense of moral inadequacy. This seems to have depended in turn on the emergence of an awareness of good and evil; of good and evil, that is to say, of an external and objective character, other than what is immediately the 'good' for the individual or group concerned. We shall see that such an awareness emerged also in Iranian religion (*2.23*), just as it had to some extent in the Ṛg-vedic hymns addressed to Varuna (*1.34*). Obviously in such situations there is some criterion by which men decide what kind of conduct and attitudes are good, and what are evil. In the broadest general terms it can be said that in the history of religion the criterion is related to the ultimate religious goal, whatever that may be. The religious goal may be peace, or inward harmony, or union with God, or eternal life; then that is 'good' which most surely leads to the desired end. In Hebrew religion, in the pre-Exilic period, the religious goal at the highest level was 'to know God'. A secondary but perhaps more common goal, regarded as the supreme blessing bestowed on men by God, was long life on earth, while sudden and premature death was regarded as a divine punishment upon the wicked and godless (Prov. 10: 21; 11: 9; Ps. 73: 18f.; Job 20: 6ff.). The dead were thought to have some kind of continued existence in the subterranean region or Sheol, but in pre-Exilic Hebrew thought this was the bourn from which no traveller returned; in Sheol a man was soon forgotten by the living and cut off from the presence of God. Yet there was also a conviction that the Holy One was stronger than death and Sheol, and it was for this reason that the pre-Exilic worshipper of Yahweh believed that God could 'deliver' him from the threat of death: 'Thou dost not give me up to Sheol, or let thy godly one see the Pit' (Ps. 16: 10). This conviction that the power of God was greater than the power of death which threatened to claim a man provided the basis, in post-Exilic times, for the development of the idea of resurrection (*3.17*). But that development waited upon the influence of another

religious tradition, that of Persia, which we shall shortly be considering
(2.20).

Meanwhile, the ideas of good and evil associated with the belief that
to know God and to enjoy life on earth in his presence for as long as
possible was the ultimate goal of man's existence, would be of the kind
which placed a high value on conduct and attitudes which contributed
to physical and mental health and to harmony in human relationships.
This was the good; this was what Yahweh desired from his people. Evil
was seen to lie in conduct and attitudes which were destructive of the
good, and to act in such ways and to adopt such attitudes was to have
chosen wrongly, and had as its consequence a sense of failure to live as
Yahweh required and in a way that would mean forfeiting his blessing.
Here then is one of the basic roots of the idea of sin in pre-Exilic Israel:
the sense of *failure*, of having fallen short of what might have been.
The commonest word for 'sin' in the Old Testament (*ḥēṭ*) is connected
with a root that means 'to miss', in the sense of failure (Ringgren, 1966;
138).

There is, however, another very common Hebrew word for undesirable moral conduct and attitudes (pesa), and this is connected with
the idea of *rebellion*. Here the basic meaning is that of having flouted the
commands of a monarch, or of having the desire to throw off his rule.
There is, of course, an underlying affinity of meaning between these
two words of sin. But in the second there lies the germ of the idea that
a man who is conscious of moral failure may not rest there but must
also regard himself as a rebel, or as one who had displeased a powerful
monarch. Now it is one of the truisms of the philosophy of religion that
men have scarcely ever escaped from thinking of the divine, the holy,
the eternal, in some kind of human terms. But while anthropo-
morphism may be inevitable there is a variety of possible kinds, and
upon the *kind* that gains acceptance depends what kind of religious life
and community will develop. What we have to record here is that in
pre-Exilic Israel the institution of monarchy of the ancient oriental kind
seems to have had an important influence on the shaping of Hebrew
religious ideas; among these was the conception that developed during
this period of God as an arbitrary oriental monarch, and of the sinner
as a rebel against the dictates of autocratic power. This is certainly
something which is characteristic of the Western tradition of religion;
it is much less characteristic of the religious thought of India, where the
idea of moral evil remains more closely related in a causal fashion to the

perceived religious goal: a certain kind of conduct will lead to this religious goal. In the Western tradition the idea of moral evil as rebellion against autocratic power exists alongside other ways of regarding the matter which are more akin to the Indian, and to earlier Hebrew conception: it is the idea of God as an absolute monarch which had led to some of the difficulties which attend Western theology at the present time.

2.2 ZARATHUSTRA, THE PROPHET OF IRAN (618–541 B.C. approx.)

2.20 The historical importance of Zarathustra

In the year 586 B.C., when many of the leading families of the kingdom of Judah were deported into Babylonia and the Jerusalem monarchy came to an end, in Persia a young man of about thirty had just begun to be active as a prophet (Zaehner, 1959; 209). This was Zarathustra, to give him the Iranian form of his name, although he is better known as Zoroaster, which is the Greek form. Tradition records that the Prophet of Iran commenced his prophetic work '258 years before Alexander', that is, in 588 B.C. Zarathustra belongs in the category of prophet, in that he appears to have undergone religious experiences which led him to proclaim certain truths which had been disclosed to him about the nature of the spiritual world. The period of his prophetic ministry covers roughly the period of fifty years the Jews were in exile in Babylonia, for his death occurred about 541 B.C., just three years before the Persian King Cyrus captured Babylon, incorporating it into the Persian empire and making it possible for the Jewish exiles in Babylonia to think of returning to Jerusalem. By this time Zarathustra's religious teaching had exerted a wide enough influence in Persia for the Jewish exiles to have become 'thoroughly impregnated with Zoroastrian ideas' (Zaehner, 1959; 209). The difference which these ideas made to Jewish religious thinking will be evident when post-Exilic Judaism (3.1) is compared with the religion of the pre-Exilic period. Through Judaism many of these ideas passed into Christianity in its early formative period. While Zoroastrianism now exists only as the religion of a small minority in Persia and in western India (the Parsees) the Prophet of Iran has exercised a much wider influence than this would suggest, and it is important to trace the emergence in ancient Persia of some of the ideas which have subsequently held so central a place in Western religious thought.

2.21 Light from the East?

Persia, as R. C. Zaehner points out (1955; 3), is the true Middle East; it is the meeting ground of East and West, the bridge between the culture of the Mediterranean world and that of India, the link between two widely differing civilisations. Zarathustra appears to have been indebted to a tradition of thought which is characteristic of India and China, but which his own prophetic genius transformed, thus making possible its easier transmission westwards. For a long time Western scholars, particularly Christian, were reluctant to admit that the Prophet of Iran had bequeathed anything in the way of religious ideas to Judaism. That he did so is more readily conceded now, but there is still considerable difference of opinion about Zarathustra's own beliefs, compared with those of later Zoroastrianism. An excellent and comprehensive account of the oscillation of scholarly views on this subject will be found in J. Duchesne-Guillemin's work, *The Western Response to Zoroaster* (1958), in the last sentence of which we are cautioned that 'the West has not said its last word on Zoroaster'. We must therefore leave speculation on one side and confine ourselves to what is known of the prophet's teaching, what elements of this undeniably found their way into Judaism, and how, if at all, these can be said to constitute a positive and helpful contribution from the East to the problems of religious thought encountered by the West.

2.22 Zarathustra as prophet-reformer

The source of our knowledge of Zarathustra's religious teaching are the 'Gāthās', or songs which are now found within the *Yasna*, the great liturgical text of Zoroastrianism, one of the three main parts of the Zoroastrian scriptures. (The other two parts are the *Yasts*, sacrificial hymns addressed to specific spirits; and the Vidēvdāt, the laws of ritual purification.) The Gāthās are composed in the first person, and are generally regarded as utterances of Zarathustra himself. In these the prophet speaks as one who is conscious both of having been chosen by God to communicate the Truth to men, and who having himself contemplated God's holiness freely chooses to be 'the friend of Truth' and to follow the way of holiness. His mission is to call his contemporaries from their worship of many deities, a worship which often involved bloody sacrifices, to the worship of the one 'Wise Lord' – Ahura Mazdā. The background to his prophetic message is the Indo-Iranian religion, another form of which we have already noted in the early Vedic period in India (*1.33–1.35*). We saw in that connection that the Aryans conceived of two classes of supernatural beings, *asuras* (in Iran, ahuras) and *devas* (in Iran, daēvas). Whereas in India the word 'asura' gradually came to be used for a demonic being, and 'deva' for a divine being, in Iran it was the other way round: the daēvas, probably under the influence of Zarathustra, come to be regarded as demonic, while from the ahura class one great Ahura (Lord) emerges as the Lord of Light or Wise Lord, Ahura Mazdā.

2.23 Zarathustra's cosmic dualism

Nevertheless it is not as a proclaimer of monotheistic ideas that Zarathustra is chiefly to be remembered. Rather it is for the dualism that is characteristic of his system. This, as R. C. Zaehner describes it, 'was a dualism of spirit, postulating two principles at the origin of the Universe – the Spirit of Good or Ohrmazd, and the Spirit of Evil or Ahriman. This extremely original idea', comments Zaehner, 'dates back to Zoroaster himself, and it is his basic contribution to the philosophy of religion' (Zaehner, 1955; 4). Zarathustra represented these two opposed spirits as twins, one of whom chose good, while the other chose evil. He seems to have regarded the twin cosmic principles as having had their origin in the one supreme Wise Lord, Ahura Mazdā. They are designated in the Zoroastrian scriptures by the names *Spenta Mainyu* (Holy Spirit) and *Angra Mainyu* (Evil Spirit). The relationship of the former to Ahura Mazdā was obviously closer than was that of the latter. It is for this reason that in later tradition the Holy Spirit comes to be identified with Ahura Mazdā (or in the alternative form Ohrmazd). While logic demands that Ahura Mazdā must be regarded as father of the Evil Spirit also (if the spirits were twins), Zoroastrian thought does not require Ahura Mazdā to be responsible in any way for the principle of evil. What is emphasised in Zarathustra's teaching is the complete freedom of choice exercised by the spirits, and the consequent responsibility that rested entirely upon the choice. The same emphasis is laid in Zoroastrian thought on human freedom of choice. Man is not God's servant or his slave, as in Semitic religion, and especially in Islam, but a being who has complete freedom of moral choice.

2.24 The special nature of Zoroastrian dualism

It is important to distinguish between two usages of the word 'dualism' in connection with religious idea. There is the dualism which has for its best-known example the system of thought called Manichaeism (*4.18*), in which the material, physical world is regarded as wholly evil and all goodness is confined to what is spiritual. But in Zoroastrian thought it is within the spiritual world that the ultimate dualism of good and evil has its origin. The spiritual is not wholly good; it can also be evil. On the other hand the material realm is not dismissed as the arena of evil; instead it is regarded as basically good. This is because it is thought of as the work of Ahura Mazdā himself. The physical world being thus regarded as inherently good by Zoroastrians, it is by them reverenced and respected; the material things of the earth are to be used and enjoyed by man in wise ways, that is in ways that will contribute to the holy life. Asceticism, in the sense of the rejection of certain physical aspects of life as opposed to the pursuit of holiness, has thus no place in Zoroastrianism.

The other feature of Zarathustra's teaching which qualifies it to be regarded as unique is the fact that it envisages not a single ultimate principle in the Universe, but two. It is, as Zaehner says, 'a dualism of two rival spiritual and moral forces – good and evil, light and darkness, order and disorder' (1955; 4). And behind these opposed forces lies an original, primeval *choice*. If there is in any sense an ultimate principle in Zoroastrianism it would appear to be the ultimacy of moral choice – for truth, light and order, or for untruth, darkness and chaos: this is a choice of free agents, whether spirits or men.

2.25 The question of the originality of Zarathustra's dualism

It has been suggested that the religious ideas of Zarathustra, and in particular his unique moral dualism, owe their origin to antecedent ideas, from which they represent a logical development. In the first place there is the contention of W. B. Henning that Zoroastrian ideas depend on an earlier monotheism. 'As are most dualistic movements, it is perhaps best understood as a protest against monotheism.' As a fuller exposition of this point of view Duchesne-Guillemin quotes the words of Fr. Spiegal:

> It is only when one has come to admit one omnipotent, omniscient creator, who created the world with all there is in it, that the question arises why everything in the world does not go according to the will of the creator and ruler, why not only praiseworthy undertakings of the creatures go wrong but also things happen of which he cannot possibly approve. In one word: the question arises as to how evil came into the world. An attempt to answer this question: such is dualism in its different forms. (Duchesne-Guillemin, 1958; 1)

This line of thought can be pursued in two different directions: one conclusion would be that since moral dualism of the Zoroastrian kind may well be a protest against monotheism, this relegates such dualism to a secondary, dependent or inferior position; the other conclusion would be that since the idea of moral dualism is necessary in order to attempt to explain what monotheism fails to explain, this constitutes a damaging criticism of monotheism, and indicates its inherent weakness. It is therefore at least an open question whether or not, because Zoroastrian dualism may postulate an earlier monotheism, it is therefore philosophically or religiously inferior to monotheism. But it is in fact entirely uncertain whether any form of monotheistic thought already existed in Iran; it is very unlikely that Zarathustra would have come into contact with Jewish monotheism, although not impossible. His prophetic activities were located in the north-eastern area of Persia, bordering on what is now Afghanistan and the Turkmen region of the U.S.S.R.; whereas contact with the Jewish exiles would have required him to be in Babylonia, to the south-west of Persia. The possibility remains, however, that Zarathustra himself developed a monotheistic form of belief – that of the Ahura Mazdā, which he subsequently modified into the dualism which is the special characteristic of his teaching.

This brings us to the other sense in which Zoroastrian thought may owe something to earlier ideas, a point which has already been touched on in passing (2.22). An understanding of the world in terms of an absolute, moral dualism is not entirely peculiar to Zoroastrianism. It was, by Zarathustra's time, already present in Indo-Iranian religion, with its fundamental dichotomy of asuras and devas. This seems to have been so deep-rooted a conception of Indian thought, for example, that it endured even within the Buddhist tradition; it was so popular a way of understanding the nature of the world that frequent references occur in the discourses of the Buddha (in the Pali canon) to these asura-hosts and deva-hosts, who wage constant war with one another (Ling, 1962; 21–6). Even so, there is no clear *moral* distinction between their natures; the asura-deva mythology represents an earlier stage of development, before one group had been identified as good and the other as evil. In Iranian religion it seems to have been in the teaching of Zarathustra that these opposing forces were raised to a cosmic moral dualism. Thus Zarathustra owes something to these earlier ideas, but his teaching represents also a new interpretation, the introduction of a new dimension.

2.26 The social factor in Zarathustra's dualism

An interesting and important feature of the Prophet's utterances contained in the Gāthās is the conflict to which he refers between settled herdsmen and predatory warriors. The settled community of herdsmen are identified as followers of the Truth, while the raiders are followers of the Lie, and engage in sanguinary sacrifices in honour of the daēvas (devas). It is possible that these latter were in fact the warrior-class in Iranian society, corresponding to the kṣatriya class in ancient India; they were upholders of the traditional, pagan religion of the Indo-Iranians, worshippers of the daēvas. The settled herdsmen, whose labour was devoted to the pastoral care of the herds, were the class in Iranian society who were the real producers of wealth, and would thus correspond to the vaiśya class among the Indian Aryans. These, rather than the warrior class, responding to the teaching of the prophet would have formed the basis of the new Zoroastrian community, and since their oppressors and enemies were traditionally devoted to the daēvas, it would follow that the ahuras would necessarily become the spirit-forces to be venerated by those who accepted the new prophetic religion. The fact that the hostile warrior class were by tradition worshipp ers of the many daēvas might have provided a stimulus to any incipient tendency in Zarathustra's religious thought towards belief in the One rather than the many; that is, the One Ahura, rather than the many ahuras. Certainly the opposition of warrior classes towards ethical prophetic religion is a common feature of the history of religions, and would provide a further reason in favour of the suggested analysis of the situation in social terms.

2.27 The ethical element in the religion of Zarathustra

An important feature of the religious ideas proclaimed by the Prophet of Iran is that which we have just referred to, namely their strongly ethical character. Nietzsche recognised this, in commenting on the public's enormous misapprehension of the irony contained in his *Thus Spake Zarathustra* (*Also sprach Zarathustra*, 1885–7): 'I should have been asked what the name Zarathustra means in my mouth, the mouth of the first Immoralist: for what makes up the enormous uniqueness of that Persian in history is exactly the opposite of it' (Duchesne-Guillemin, 1958; 21 f.). Nietzsche's 'immoralism' was the exact opposite of Zarathustra's teaching; the Prophet of Iran's achievement was to provide a sound and logical metaphysical basis for morality. The elaboration of the Zoroastrian system of ethics belongs to a later period of history, the Sassanian era (from A.D. 236), but the foundations were laid in the teaching of the Prophet. The presupposition of the Zoroastrian ethic is that man is free to choose his course of action, and that the wise will choose that which is consonant with truth, light, and order, that which will identify him with the forces of good, and assist their triumph over the forces of evil. Man's part in the cosmic struggle, therefore, is to think good thoughts, speak good words, and perform good actions. In practice this manifested itself in a way of life that is best summed up as urbane and moderate.

2.28 Zoroastrian eschatology

Initially the Prophet's hope seems to have been for the victory of the forces of good and the establishment of a realm of righteousness on earth. Later, however, another perspective emerges: 'Powerful in immortality shall be the soul of the follower of Truth, but lasting

torment shall there be for the man who cleaves to the Lie.' Both
Zarathustra and his followers looked forward to a life beyond death,
and since life was essentially life in the body, this hope demanded a
doctrine of resurrection of the body. Thus in later Zoroastrianism the
idea of a restored physical world appears, a world 'most excellent,
unageing, undecaying, neither passing away nor falling into corruption. . . .' Associated with this was the doctrine of the coming of
the Saoshyant, or Saviour, who was to appear at the end of time, when
all the forces of evil in the universe would be finally overcome and
rendered eternally powerless. These ideas received their full formulation
among the Prophet's followers after his death, but they had already
been adumbrated in the Prophet's teaching, or were implications of
principles which the Prophet himself had taught. They were sufficiently
well formulated during the period when Jews were in close contact with
Persia for them to pass into the religious life of Judaism.

2.29 The Zoroastrian sacrament

One point remains to be dealt with, and that is the curious history of
the central rite in Zoroastrian religion, the drinking of the haoma
juice. We have already noted (*1.34*) that the Indian branch of the Indo-
Iranian peoples deified the juice of the soma (Iranian, haoma) plant, the
drinking of which constituted an important Vedic ritual, and produced
in the worshipper a state of great exaltation. The same practice seems
to have been a feature of the religion of the Iranian branch of the
Aryans, among whom also the haoma juice was regarded as a god,
able to bestow immortality on those who partook of this rite. One of
the unsolved problems of the study of Zoroastrianism is whether this
practice was tolerated by the Prophet, or whether, after being pro-
scribed by the Prophet (who we know was opposed to the practice in
its earlier context in the bull-sacrifice) it was later reintroduced by his
followers. Certainly in later Zoroastrianism it held a central place; the
haoma was regarded as the 'son' of Ahura Mazdā, and in a ritual which,
as Zaehner comments, is curiously like the Catholic Mass, it was
ceremonially offered up to the heavenly Father, after which priest and
people partook of the drink, an act which was regarded as a proleptic
form of participation in life eternal.

2.3 GAUTAMA THE BUDDHA, THE PROPHET OF INDIA (*563–483* B.C.)

2.30 *The social situation in India in the sixth century* B.C.

We return now to the India of the sixth century B.C. Some of the features of that situation have already been sketched in (*1.57, 1.58, 1.59*). Recent historical studies, such as those of D. D. Kosambi, have given us a clearer picture of the social and political conditions in northern India in the sixth century B.C., and have enabled us to understand why answers were being sought to the problems which then exercised men's minds. The older form of society, that of the tribe or group of tribes ruled over by an assembly of elders, was everywhere in north India breaking down before the advance of a few great, new monarchies, especially those of Kashi, Kosala and Magadha (Map 2). The older tribal republics were being conquered and brought into the territory and under the dominion of these new autocratic monarchies (*2.38*). The old, familiar structure of society was, for many men at that time, being replaced by a more impersonal machinery of government; the individual frequently felt himself adrift, socially and morally, and unable to find in the new autocratic society the meaningful structure he had known formerly. The problems which were, as Kosambi has said, 'in the air' in sixth-century B.C. north India were: What is the soul? What is man's destiny after death? Why do men suffer, apparently undeservedly? How is suffering to be escaped? What is the supreme good, and how is it attained?

2.31 *The Buddha, his life and ministry*

Into this situation in about the year 563 B.C., when Zarathustra was still active in Persia, was born Gautama, later to be known by the religious title of *the Buddha* (the Enlightened, or Awakened, One). He was a member of the Sakya clan, whose territory lay along what is now the border between Nepal and India. His father was a kṣatriya chieftain; later piety has magnified his position to that of a great king. In these mountainous areas to the north of the Ganges plain the old tribal confederations survived most strongly, although they too were

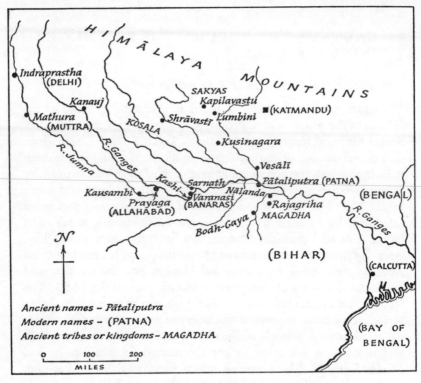

North India in early Buddhist times

threatened by the continually expanding monarchies of the Ganges plain, especially by Magadha, whose kings, Bimbisara and his son Ajatasattu, are frequently mentioned in the Buddhist canonical writings. Gautama thus grew up in an environment which to some extent protected him from the psychological malaise of the monarchical societies, but he became acutely aware of it before long. In Buddhist legend it is said that in the course of a single day he encountered an old man in the last stages of senility, then a person wasted with a foul disease, and then a dead man being carried to the burning ghat, followed by sorrowing friends. These sights made him think deeply about the nature of human existence, its meaning and its purpose. Finally, on the same day, he saw an ascetic man walking calmly and confidently along the road, and this convinced him of the supreme value of the holy life. He set out, leaving his home, to find a teacher and guide who would be able to point him to the Truth and instruct him in spiritual disciplines. After a long period of such searching, during which he practised severe asceticism and became extremely thin and weak, he finally attained supreme enlightenment while he was engaged in deep and strenuous meditation on the nature of the self and the causes of man's decay and death. In his meditation he experienced a strong spiritual opposition, which in Buddhist terminology has come to be known as Māra, the Evil One (literally 'the killer'). The Buddha's conquest of Māra has in later Buddhist tradition been embellished with much spectacular and mythological detail, especially in the Mahāyāna school (4.32). The tradition that the great enlightenment occurred near Gaya (in modern Bihar) on the bank of the river Neranjara, a tributary of the Ganges, is strong and ancient, and can probably be accepted as historically authentic. For the Buddha all the evil passions that are at the root of men's suffering had been overcome, and all doubts and fears concerning his future destiny were at rest. According to the tradition, he spent a further four weeks there in meditation beneath the sacred pīpal tree, henceforth known as the bodhi (enlightenment), or simply bo, tree. Then he sat out to make known to others the way to the enlightenment which he had gained. Traditionally, the first preaching of these truths, now known as the Buddha's *Dhamma* (Sanskrit, Dharma) or doctrine, took place at Sarnath, near Banaras. Like many other religious teachers in contemporary India he gathered a group of disciples and converts, the nucleus of the Buddhist order of monks or *Sangha*. For about forty years he and his disciples travelled about north-east India until finally at Kusinagara at about the age of eighty the Buddha's life-span came to an end and, in Buddhist terminology, the entry into complete nibbāna occurred (2.36).

The traditional dating of the Buddha's life in the countries of South-East Asia gives 623 B.C. as the year of his birth and 543 as the year of his entry into complete nibbāna (parinibbāna). On this reckoning the year 1957 C.E. was the completion of 2,500 years of Buddhist history and as such it was celebrated in the various Buddhist countries of South Asia. Modern scholars, however, are inclined to date the Buddha's life slightly later, with his birth in 563 B.C. and his decease in 483 B.C. This agrees, says Kosambi, with a record taken in Canton in a known Chinese year; the record, on a palm-leaf manuscript, gives one dot per year from the Buddha's decease to the date of writing, that is, the known year (Kosambi, 1965; 109).

2.32 The essentials of early Buddhist doctrine

The Buddha's doctrine (Dhamma) began from an analysis of the conditions of human existence. There are three major characteristics of all existence: first, *dukkha*, a word which is variously translated as 'evil' or 'ill' or 'suffering', and means any or all of these as they are expressions of the general unsatisfactoriness of ordinary empirical existence, the sense that things are not as they should be; second, *anicca* or impermanence, that is, the transient quality of all earthly experiences, especially the so-called 'pleasures' of life, and the un-relenting law of change and decay observable in all things; third, *anatta*, or the absence of a permanent enduring private 'self' (atta) within the human individual. This last is the doctrine which most clearly distinguished the teaching of the Buddha from other contemporary schools of thought, and especially from Upaniṣadic thought, in which the affirmation of the soul or self (Sanskrit, *ātman*; Pali, *atta*) within the human individual and its identification with the world-soul, or brahman, was the central doctrine (1.58). It was an error, according to the Buddha, to find the basis of that which was eternal within the human individual. The Buddha did not deny that there was something which is eternal; only it was not to be found in the temporary agglo-meration of factors, physical and psychical, which produce the appear-ance of an 'individual'. The so-called individual, he taught, is in fact a flux of material and mental events. Analysis of individual 'selfhood' can be made at various levels of complexity: the most simple analysis is into five Khandhas, or groups (literally 'heaps'). These are, outward form (the physical body), sensation, perception, volition, and consciousness, that is, consciousness especially of the preceding four. The physical body is most obviously impermanent, for it is continually changing throughout its life-span; but no less impermanent are the other factors. Together they produce the temporary illusion of an enduring reality, but it is an illusion. What is permanent and enduring must be sought elsewhere.

What then was the enduring reality to which the Buddha pointed men, and which he bade them seek? In one sense it was the Dhamma. This is a word virtually incapable of being translated into English. Conze, in his *Buddhist Thought in India*, distinguishes seven main senses of the word. The fundamental meaning of dhamma is that which is self-subsistent, that which alone exists in its own right and without dependence on any prior reality. In this sense it is strongly akin to the Greek notion of the Logos, that which upholds all things. The Pali word dhamma has passed into the vocabulary of South-East Asian languages, such as Burmese, where it is used by Christians to render into Burmese the word 'Logos' in the opening sentences of St John's Gospel: 'In the beginning was the *Dhamma*. . . .'

Ultimate, full and real knowledge of the Dhamma is the goal to which the Buddha advised men to direct all their efforts. The immediate way of encountering the Dhamma is in that form of it which is the Buddha's doctrine. Another way of describing the *ultimate* reality, however, is nibbāna (Sanskrit, nirvāna). What was meant by this term will be discussed a little later (*2.35*; *2.37*). Meanwhile it has to be noted that the basic teaching of the Buddha was expressed in another form, that of the Four Holy Truths. These were, first, that all life is dukkha (see above); second, that the cause of dukkha is desire (tanhā); third, that the bringing to an end of desire means the bringing to an end of dukkha; and fourth, that there is a way of doing so, namely, the Buddhist way, outlined in the teaching of the Buddha, that is the Dhamma. The Four Holy Truths are expressed in terms of what was probably a contemporary medical procedure, from prognosis and diagnosis, through to the therapeutic measures necessary for a cure, which is announced as possible.

2.33 The Buddhist way

Various terms are used to describe these 'therapeutic' measures which
man needs to follow. Since it is a method that avoids the extremes
(practised in the Buddha's day) of sensuous pleasure and austere
asceticism, it was called 'the Middle Way'. It was also known as the
Buddha-dhamma (the Buddha-doctrine) or the Buddha-sasana (the
Buddha-discipline). The last of these is most commonly used in Asia
to refer to what in the West is called 'Buddhist religion' or simply
'Buddhism'.

The Buddhist way has three principal features: morality, meditation
and wisdom. Morality is the indispensable basis of the system. The
essence of Buddhist morality is contained in the five precepts (pañca-
śīlā): to abstain from taking life, from falsehood, from taking what is
not given (i.e. theft), from sexual misconduct, and from using in-
toxicants and drugs, which tend to cloud the mind. Upon the foundation of a serious resolve to keep these precepts can then be built the
practice of meditation, or concentration (samādhi). This is the central
and most characteristic feature of the Buddhist way, and the most that
can be offered in a general study of this kind is a brief reference to its
methods and purpose. (For a fuller description the student should
consult E. Conze's *Buddhist Meditation*.) The ultimate purpose is to
enable the Buddhist to perceive directly and immediately the reality of
which the Buddha spoke, and which is hidden from men who are
immersed in ordinary existence; in these circumstances perception of
reality is distorted by avijja (Sanskrit, avidya), that is, ignorance, or
failure to perceive aright. A man has first of all therefore to accept in
faith the fact there is a direct perception, or knowledge, vijja (Sanskrit,
vidya) to which the Buddha himself attained, and to which others may
attain who are prepared to follow his counsel. Such knowledge is
obscured in the ordinary 'worldling' (putthu-janu, the Buddhist term
for those who have not yet began to seek enlightenment) by the
perpetual agitation that takes place on the surface of the mind, an
agitation due to constant distraction of every kind by the senses and the
uncontrolled impulses of the mind. The first step in meditation, therefore, in order to direct consciousness away from this surface agitation
to calmer depths below, is to cut off discursive thinking and the
pursuit of this or that thought at random, which can lead nowhere,

certainly not, says the Buddhist, to a cure of the human condition. The initial practice of meditation then, is the cutting off of discursive thought, by 'concentration', that is by narrowing the field of attention. Another major concern of Buddhist meditation is to damp down, as it were, and extinguish the fires or evil forces of lobha, dosa and moha, or greed, hatred and illusion, which are regarded as endemic in the human situation. There must also be a fostering of their opposites, generosity, love and insight. What mental object is to occupy the attention of the meditator is the next important question, and the answer to this will vary with different types of person. For some, one object of meditation will be specially suitable for his condition or constitution, for another it will be something different. Guidance in the procedures of meditation and in the selection of the right focus for meditation is the indispensable function of the meditation master. This is why Buddhist meditation cannot be undertaken in isolation, and is one of the main reasons why Buddhism cannot be a 'private' religion. More than this it is not possible to say here concerning Buddhist meditation; in any case this, like the central practice in all religion, can never properly be understood from outside. Suffice it that the aim of the practice is the gaining of the third stage of the Buddhist way, transcendental wisdom, or paññā (Sanskrit, prajñā). At this stage, what was formerly accepted in faith and on trust is now perceived and apprehended directly and immediately, and the result, it is claimed, will be the emergence of the truly enlightened man.

2.34 Buddhist monks and laymen

As we have already noted, one of the earliest results of the Buddha's preaching was the formation of the Sangha, the group of men who devoted themselves full-time to the practice of meditation and the pursuit of transcendental wisdom under the guidance of the Buddha as their master. Like other holy men in the India of their day they were content to live on whatever in the way of food they might be offered by sympathetic householders. There were many such wandering ascetics, philosophers, and holy men in sixth-century B.C. India; only in the case of the Buddhists, however, did a permanent, settled, institutional life develop. It probably had its origin in the practice of these wandering seekers after salvation of gathering together in a common place of shelter during the monsoon period, when heavy and often continuous rain, day after day, made travelling impossible. After the rains such assemblies of ascetics would normally disperse and go their several ways again, but in the case of the Buddhists these rainy-season retreats developed into permanent settlements (āvasas). Each such local settlement would welcome Buddhist monks from elsewhere, but each had its own 'parish' that is, the area from which it could expect alms, in the form of daily contributions of food from the local householders. The members of the Sangha came to be known as bhikkhus (Sanskrit, bhikshus), that is 'sharesmen' or 'almsmen', those who were given a 'share' of food by the local people. These latter did so out of admiration for the holiness of life and seriousness of purpose of the members of the Sangha, and were themselves often drawn towards the teachings and practices of the monks. Those who acknowledged the Buddha and wished to prepare themselves, as laymen, for eventual admission into the Order, were known as adherents, or upāsakas. The Buddha himself is represented as having offered them his teaching and guidance, and as having laid down proper duties for the householder who was a upāsaka. The class system which was emerging within Indian society (*1.55*) was totally disregarded by the Buddha, whose followers and adherents were drawn from various social classes, but notably from the vaiśya or trading class. The form of teaching given by the Buddha, as it is contained in the canonical Pali texts, reflects a popular orientation: it is not for a few initiates within an esoteric group, as the Upaniṣadic teaching was originally; the Buddha's teaching was addressed to all and sundry, in the form of parables, stories, proverbs and illustrations that all could understand. As Kosambi points out, 'this was the most social of religions'; its doctrine continued to spread 'because it was eminently fitted to the needs of a rapidly evolving society' (Kosambi, 1965; 106, 114). This view of early Buddhism conflicts with earlier judgments made by Westerners, largely on the basis of inadequate knowledge: judgments such as that of Max Weber, that Buddhism was essentially mystical and a-social. The question of the nature of Buddhist mysticism and its social implications must therefore be investigated in some detail.

2.35 Nibbāna, the Buddhist summum bonum

It is sometimes said that Buddhism is a religion without a God. This is
not strictly true. Early Buddhist texts contain numerous references to
the gods, and these are not only the Vedic gods (some mention of
whom would be understandable in the ancient Indian situation), but
also gods of a peculiarly Buddhist character, such as Sakka, who is a
milder, more humane Buddhist version of the Vedic Indra. Buddhism
has its own mythology of gods, but they are really to be regarded as
picturesque items of the celestial scenery rather than beings of any very
great or ultimate importance. Certainly Buddhist thought is not
committed to, or in any way dependent on, the idea of a divine being
who as Creator is to be held responsible for all that exists, good and
evil, as we have seen was the case with the ancient Near Eastern
religions. In Buddhist thought the universe itself is the given fact; no
explanation for its existence is offered or sought; any attempt to
provide one, said the Buddha, could only be idle speculation. Buddhism
is more accurately described, therefore, as a system of thought which,
so far as the notion of a Creator is concerned, is agnostic; it is uncommitted one way or the other.

Nevertheless, Buddhism has a *summum bonum*, that which, while it
transcends the normal limits of human experience, is yet held to be the
goal of the Buddhist way, namely nibbāna; to use Tillich's description,
this is the Buddhist's 'ultimate concern'. This has led some observers to
describe Buddhism as a form of mysticism; but it is a term which needs
to be used with care.

It is characteristic of Western investigations in this connection to
begin by asking 'What is nibbāna?' with the further question in view:
'Can it be related to Christian concepts such as God or heaven?'
Edward Conze has very rightly warned Western readers against 'the
custom of trying to ascertain the meaning of Nibbāna by collecting
and examining many disconnected quotations' (Conze, 1962; 77). A
more reliable approach to an understanding of the concept nibbāna is
to examine all that is said about it in one text; one in particular which
suggests itself as suitable for this purpose is the Sutta Nipāta, since it is
generally agreed to contain some of the most ancient material in the
Pali canon.

This has recently been subjected to very careful and close textual examination by Professor Jayawickrama of the University of Ceylon, and one of his general conclusions is to confirm that in the Sutta Nipāta we get as near as possible perhaps to some of the earliest forms of Buddhist teaching.

There are some eighteen references to nibbāna in the Sutta Nipāta. E. M. Hare, in his English translation first published in 1945, renders the word nibbāna as 'the cool'. One can think of objections to this rendering, but it does have the advantage of representing the fact that the Pali word nibbāna, like the English word 'cool', can be used both as a noun and as an adjective.

In the case of nibbāna it is the noun sense which is primary, and so one can say that basically nibbāna is 'the coolness'. But this in itself is obviously not a sufficient explanation. We need to pursue the matter further.

2.36 The Buddhist ideal: the man who is nibbuta

Even more frequent than references to nibbāna in this early Buddhist text are references which use another form of the word – nibbuta – to describe the ideal man. This word is sometimes applied to the Buddha himself, sometimes to the man whom the Buddha describes as the ideal type of humanity, the muni or sage. Such a man is nibbuta, i.e., one who has 'become cool'. He it is, the muni, says the Buddha addressing the brāhman Bharadvaja, who is worthy of oblation. Upon hearing this Bharadvaja proceeds to offer to the Buddha the brāhmanic oblation of the sacred cake. This the Buddha declines to accept, replying that it is not for a Buddha to enjoy fare won in this way, as brāhmans do from chanting hymns. 'To whom then shall the oblation be offered?' asks the perplexed Bharadvaja. The Buddha then describes once again the worthy recipient of oblation, the ideal man, 'the unprovokable, him of unclouded mind, freed from all lustfulness, void of all indolence, guide to those of passionate nature, master of life and death', and so on. He it is who should be venerated and worshipped, and in making such oblation the offerer himself will find blessing. 'But,' cries Bharadvaja, 'who else is this but thou, O Buddha, most meet recipient of all the world as an offering!' The Sutta thus ends and the inference seems clear: the Buddha is the type of the ideal man, the muni, the nibbuta-man. Not as an individual, however, is he to be venerated, but simply as the ideal man, the type.

This brings us to a point which needs to be strongly emphasised, namely that the large number of references in this early text to the man who is nibbuta suggests that this was the practical focus of early Buddhism. The abstract idea of nibbāna appears to be secondary to the notion of the ideal man, the nibbuta-man. This suggests that it is when the term 'nibbāna' becomes separated from the conception of the ideal man, the nibbuta, that we are likely to run into difficulties in understanding the meaning of 'nibbāna'. As we shall see shortly, 'nibbāna' has a transcendental meaning, but it is misleading to concentrate too much attention on this, or at least, to make this our starting point in seeking to understand the term.

When the final state of holiness has been achieved, when all the fires of greed, hate, and illusion have been extinguished (*2.33*), then one is nibbuta. But this plainly does not mean the extinction of life or annihilation. The nibbuta-man continues to live, to move about in the world, to proclaim the truth, as, for example, the Buddha did from his enlightenment until the age of eighty. The distinction between entering into the state of coolness in this life and the final state which follows at the dissolution of the body is one which is given formal expression in the distinction made in the Abhidhamma literature between *kilesa nibbāna*, the dying away of the moral defilements, and *khanda nibbāna*, the dying away of the constituents of empirical existence.

2.37 Nibbāna as transcendent

We come now to the important point that nibbāna is sometimes referred to in the Sutta Nipāta in terms that make it quite clear that it is regarded as a transcendental state. It is sometimes referred to simply as 'the beyond' (paramam). It is also said that those who know that nibbāna is a transcendent state (the 'the island of *ne plus ultra*') are by this knowledge 'exceedingly cooled' (abhinibbuta). 'Where no thing is, where no grasping is, that is the isle of no-beyond, nibbāna, where decay and death are no more; this I declare to you.' Elsewhere in the Sutta Nipāta we find nibbāna described as *amatam*, that is, characterised by the absence of death, *santim*, tranquil or peaceful, and *accutam*, permanent – that is, characterised by no passing from one existence to another.

All this and more concerning nibbāna is to be found in other Buddhist works, from the five Nikayas to such later compendia as the Visuddhimagga (*4.39*) and the Abhidhammattha-Sangaha (*6.43*). What is significant about these Sutta Nipāta references is, on the one hand, the extent of the references to nibbāna in this life as the present, realis-able goal of Buddhist living (and with this the references to the con-dition of being nibbuta), compared with, on the other hand, the relatively small number of references to nibbāna as a transcendent state. This may provide us with a clue to where attention was focused in early Buddhism, namely, on the condition of being nibbuta, ideal man, perfected man; and then, secondarily, on the transcendental nature of the condition into which man thus enters. The order reflects the practical concern that characterises so much of the Buddha's teaching. The transcendent nature of nibbāna is not being relegated to a position of unimportance because it is less often spoken of; it is simply that the cooling of the fires of greed, hatred and delusion is a more important task for the generality of men. It is more important for most men to know how to become nibbuta than to be able to expatiate on the nature of nibbāna.

To return now to the subject of mysticism, it will be seen more readily that there are difficulties in the way of any attempt to categorise Buddhist religion in terms of mysticism or non-mysticism. Certainly in the early Buddhist thought represented in the Sutta Nipāta one does not begin by postulating a transcendent Absolute, with which the individual is to seek communion or identity. One begins with the empirical condition of man. Yet one cannot say that the transcendent has no place in Buddhist religious life and thought. More of a positive nature is said concerning nibbāna than is sometimes recognised by Western writers. Long lists of epithets of nibbāna occur in the canonical writings. In particular, nibbāna is often said to be *suññatā, apranihita,* and *animita*; those terms especially suggest that the Buddhist way has affinities with other forms of mysticism. The Buddhist goal, nibbāna, is suññatā, or 'void'. This is a way of referring to the fact that the path to nibbāna involves affirming the non-existence of the empirical self, nibbāna is 'void' of all notions of the ego. Nibbāna is also apranihita, that is, it is without longing or hankering, it is characterised by contentment. Again, it is animita, that is to say, without an image, non-conceptual. It is not a 'concept' that can be recognised; one cannot say, 'Ah! there is a nibbāna'. This must be so necessarily, since nibbāna is the goal of the Buddhist life, and cannot be known until it is reached.

That this is the goal is the clear evidence of the Pali canon and its commentaries. Buddhaghosa (*4.29*) makes it explicit in the opening sentences of his great work, the Visuddhimagga: 'The goal is purification, and by purification is meant nibbāna.' What is clear throughout the whole of Buddhaghosa's summary and interpretation of Buddhist teaching is that the purification to which he refers, and which is the Buddhist goal, could also be described as a deep and radical moral change. Above all, it must be noted that in Buddhist tradition this remains a very high ideal; nibbuta-man is not commonly found; such men are rare, and highly to be esteemed.

2.38 The social dimension of Buddhist doctrine

We are now in a position to consider the second main point to be made concerning Buddhist mysticism, namely, the question of whether the Buddhist way is to be characterised as one of world-renunciation, for in the view of some this would be a characteristic of any true mysticism. Max Weber, for example, in the course of his sociological analysis of Indian religion categorised Buddhism as mystical and a-social. Salvation in Buddhism, says Weber, is 'an absolutely personal performance of the self-reliant individual' (Weber, 1958; 213). This statement indicates Weber's failure to take proper account of the anatta doctrine and properly to understand the nature of the Buddhist way. However, from this he goes on to comment on Buddhism that 'the specific a-social character of all genuine mysticism is here carried to its maximum.' It is not surprising that he finds the creation of the Buddhist Order of monks a 'contradiction' of this principle, a contradiction which has somehow to be explained; perhaps, he says, it is the work of later Buddhists.

The significance of the Buddhist Sangha (*2.31*), the Order (or literally 'assembly') of monks, has attracted some attention in recent historical and sociological studies of the early Buddhist movement. It is true that there is something of a contradiction in the fact that a Sangha should have emerged in sixth-century B.C. India, but the contradiction is with the orthodox Indian religions of salvation, not with Buddhist doctrine or principles. The ancient Indian tradition was certainly one of solitude for mystics and ascetics; it was so strong a tradition that traces of it are to be found in early Buddhist practice. But in spite of this, the positively and characteristically Buddhist development so far as the social dimension is concerned, was the Sangha. Its development is all the more notable because it runs counter to the rest of ancient Indian religious tradition.

In the Mahā Parinibbāna Sutta, which deals with the last days of the Buddha's life, a direct connection is established between the old republican assemblies (*1.38, 2.30*) and the Buddhist Sangha. On the eve of his attack on the Vajjian republic King Ajatasattu asks the Buddha to make some pronouncement concerning the future of the Vajji. The Buddha is represented as making the strange reply that if the Vajji continued to meet regularly in their tribal assemblies, if their assemblies began and ended in a spirit of unanimity, if they observed the ancient traditions, and honoured the elders among them, then they might expect to prosper. The Buddha then goes on to apply this prophecy to the Buddhist Sangha also. If the monks continue to meet regularly in their assembly, if they begin and end their assemblies in a spirit of unanimity, if they observe the traditions and honour their elders, their assembly (sangha) may expect to prosper.

In fact, the Vajji were defeated by Ajatasattu; by the time these words of the Buddha were being transmitted in the oral tradition the fate of the tribes was known: the Vajjian republic had been destroyed. It may seem curious that the Buddha should have pronounced in favour of the losing side, and even more curious that his words foretelling their prosperity should go on being repeated. Some have therefore seen in these words of approval from the Buddha of a republican-assembly form of rule a *post-eventu* way of affirming that the Buddhist Sangha was the successor or substitute for the old tribal structure of society that was, in sixth-century B.C. India, being destroyed and re-placed by autocratic monarchies. In the social distress and insecurity which this engendered the Buddhist Sangha, it is said, was the ark of salvation for the individual adrift from his old social moorings, and that is why so many individuals found refuge within it. This, for example, is the view of Debiprasad Chattopadhyaya, an Indian Marxist, in his book *Lokayata: A Study in Ancient Indian Materialism* (1959). He maintains that in this situation of social malaise, in a society experiencing a bitter struggle for power and an increasing class-stratification, the Buddhist Sangha provided men with the only experience they could have of true collective living; based on an illusion (i.e. religion), it was nevertheless, according to Chattopadhyaya, the best remedy available until Marxism appeared.

Another student of ancient India, Charles Drekmeier, in his book *Kingship and Community in Early India*, has examined the situation from a similar point of view, but has come up with a Freudian explanation of the Buddhist movement. In the disturbed and perplexing conditions of the time, he says, the Buddha's teaching regarding nibbāna, and the life of the Buddhist Sangha, can together be seen as the expression of a desire to withdraw from the difficult situation in an increasingly individualistic society and to seek refuge in a primeval state of undifferentiated being, a desire akin to that of the individual who in any age cannot adjust to the condition of being a separate individual, and unconsciously longs to return to the womb, to the condition preceding the state of individuation.

Neither of these views is to be dismissed lightly, and they may point towards an explanation of which they are both to some extent travesties – travesties, because (in the Freudian case particularly) the mistake is made of saying that because A is like B, than A is in fact B; that is, they confuse resemblance with identity. But the resemblance is important, and what these explanations may point to is another, slightly different explanation, which may be outlined as follows.

2.39 The significance of the Buddhist Sangha

From the earliest days of the Buddhist movement, as we have seen, the ideal has been the nibbuta-man, the muni, he who is 'cooled' of all egoistic desires and illusions, one in whom anatta is a manifest reality. Towards this ideal Buddhist teaching and practice directs and leads men. From the start one of the most important ways of achieving this was membership of the Buddhist Sangha. For life in the Sangha would indeed be a school of anatta, a continuous exercise in ridding oneself of the illusion of the empirical self and its importance; life in the Sangha is a mode of existence in which one has no private or personal possessions except the bare minimum of necessities allowed by the rule of the Sangha, and in which one is continually subject to the common mind and judgment of the Sangha. The Sangha thus provides the optimum conditions for the realising of anatta; it makes available a new and different kind of social existence not possible in mundane society, least of all in the society that was already becoming increasingly common in sixth-century B.C. northern India (2.30). Moreover, this new kind of social structure went beyond the collective life that men had known in the tribal system, for the Sangha was in principle of universal dimensions. To put this another way, the Buddhist Sangha differed from the old tribal sanghas in that it was non-territorial, or rather was supra-territorial. The member of this Sangha had entered into a different, a transcendent kind of kinship. This is referred to in the term that occurs in the later Nikayas and in subsequent Buddhist literature, the term 'gotrabhu', that is, 'to have become one of the clan' (and by this is understood, the clan of the Buddha). He who enters the Sangha enters a new gotra or clan-structure. Buddhaghosa (4.29) comments that this term 'gotrabhu' indicates a 'change-of-lineage'; he says it is the transcending of the (old), what he calls 'sense-sphere' lineage, which brings one into the (new) 'fine-sphere' lineage – or as we might render it approximately, into a new, spiritual lineage, or perhaps better, a transcendental lineage.

This indicates a high view of the nature of the Sangha; it is no mere accidental historical feature of the Buddhist movement as it chanced to develop: the Sangha is integral to the pursuit of the Buddhist ideal, and this explains why the Sangha is linked with the Buddha and the Dhamma in the triple-gem formula; this is why a man goes 'for refuge to the Buddha, the Dhamma and the Sangha'.

2.4 THE SOPHISTICATION OF PRIMITIVE RELIGION

2.40 The emergence of Jainism

Somewhat similar to the religious movement inaugurated by the Buddha was that which has come to be known as Jainism. In the disturbed situation of north India of the sixth century B.C. (2.30) a number of religious teachers arose, each claiming to present a more satisfactory version of the truth concerning the human situation, and a more effective way of release from human troubles than was to be found in the contemporary ritualistic Brahmanism. Some of the teachings of these sects are known to us from references in the Buddhist

Suttas. Most of them have vanished, but Jainism has survived. A much greater antiquity is claimed for this system by its followers than the sixth and fifth centuries B.C. when Vardhamāna Mahāvīra (d.? 468 B.C.) taught its doctrines, and modern scholars are inclined to accept the possibility of an earlier teacher, Pārśva, whose doctrines were developed by Mahāvīra. Like the many other heterodox (that is, non-brāhman) systems of the time, this was basically a system of psychic discipline supported by its own metaphysical doctrine. Its fundamental viewpoint is that the whole universe is animated by countless individual souls; not only human beings but all living things are believed to be inhabited by souls. This applies to animals, insects and even plants. Each of these souls may be said to inhabit a material body, but more precisely this is an imprisonment from which the soul seeks to escape. It was in this view of existence and in the method of escape taught by the Mahāvīra that his doctrine differed from both Brahmanism and Buddhism.

2.41 Distinction of Jainism from Brahmanism

On the one hand Jainism was sharply distinguished from Brahmanism, and on the other from Buddhism. It was distinguished from the former by its doctrine of ahimsa or non-violence. Since every living thing is inhabited by a soul, it is important to avoid doing violence to, and above all killing, any living being. In practical terms this meant a rejection of the brāhmanical system of animal sacrifice. The reason for such non-violence towards animal life was metaphysical rather than sentimental. The escape of the soul from the body to the realm where the soul would dwell eternally in bliss was the goal of the Jain system. This was to be achieved, it was held, by the avoidance of karma. In the Jain view, karma was a substance which adhered to the soul as a result of activity of any kind, but more especially activity of a cruel or violent kind; it was the adherence of karma which clouded over the soul and gave it a solid material body, a kind of encrustation. This could be gradually broken down and dissolved by ascetic discipline and meditation, and the avoidance of harmful activity. For this reason Jains were, and have always continued to be, the very strictest of vegetarians; eating plants rather than animals is held to reduce the degree of harmful activity one engages in. For this reason also Jains have been unable to follow agricultural occupations, for fear of doing

E   L.H.R.

violence to the small creatures of the earth with the plough. (This occupation being barred to them they have become traders, and in modern times merchants and industrialists.) While thus rejecting Brahmanism, the Jains did, however, accept the notion of gods, as beings of a more exalted kind who could bestow temporal blessings. This would seem to be a compromise with popular Indian religion rather than as something inherent in the Jain view of things. It should be noted, however, that the Jains remained fundamentally atheistic in their doctrine, in the sense that there was no place or no need for the conception of an omnipotent divine creator. In their compromise with Hinduism, moreover, there was nothing in their history comparable to the compromise which occurred in Buddhism, known as the Mahāyāna (*4.31–4.35*), especially in its Tantric form (*5.26*).

2.42 Distinction of Jainism from Buddhism

The method of ascetic discipline was much more austere among the Jains than among the Buddhists. It consisted not only of fasting but also of self-mortification, including nudity, and deliberate castigation of the body by long exposure to sun or cold. Early in their history, during the third century B.C., a schism developed between those ascetics who insisted on the old practice of nudity and some others who took to wearing a simple white garment. The former more conservative group came to be known as the *Digambaras*, or 'space-clad' (i.e. clothed with air only), while the latter were known as *Śvetāmbaras*, or 'white-clad'. Not only their greater austerity distinguished the Jains from the Buddhists, but also and possibly more significantly eventually, their doctrine of a universe made up of an infinity of separate individual souls, each requiring to gain individual salvation. The Buddhist view, as we have seen (*2.32*), consisted in the rejection of the idea of a permanent individual entity known as a soul. Moreover, the Jain view of karma was of a materialistic kind: karma was a film or cloud deposited on the soul which became the soul's corporeal prison. (Jains would have agreed in calling it 'this too too solid flesh'.) To the Buddhist, however, karma is the system of moral causal relationships by which, so to speak, the actions of one life go on echoing down the years, through countless other lives (whether lives of the same 'individual' or not being in the original Buddhist view a question that has no meaning), until the echo dies away or is silenced by contrary karma.

2.43 Confucius

Contemporary with the Buddha and Mahāvīra in India was Confucius in China. The only justification for including his name in a history of religion is that Westerners have mistakenly supposed that there was an affinity between other prophetic religious figures of the sixth century B.C. in Israel, Persia and India, such as we have already considered, and this important figure in the cultural history of China. It has even been supposed that there was a form of Chinese religion which could be termed 'Confucianism', which included a cult of Confucius-worship. K'ung Fu-tzu, (to give the Chinese form of his name, of which 'Confucius' is a Latinisation made by Jesuits in China) was an aristocrat, a teacher, and for part of his life a public administrator, whose doctrines were primarily political and social, and religious only in so far as they dealt with ethical matters. The reverence afforded Confucius was not so much a religious cult as a special example of the reverence which Chinese people have generally afforded their ancestors in proper acknowledgment of their indebtedness to them. The proper context for a consideration of the life and teaching of Confucius would therefore be a history of political and philosophical thought; it does not properly fall within the scope of a history of religion, nor can Confucius justifiably be included among those figures of the sixth century B.C. who may be described as 'prophets' because they claimed to be transmitting to their fellow men doctrines which were in some sense or another revealed. Some kind of prophetic role has, however, sometimes been claimed for Confucius (Rowley, 1956), but even apart from the fact that it is difficult to imagine Confucius behaving like some of the Hebrew prophets, it is doubtful whether this can be upheld.

2.44 Confucius and the popular religion of ancient China

Confucius was a member of the upper class of Chinese society. His teaching was characterised by the distinction between two classes of men, the 'superior man' and the 'lesser man'. Originally a social-class distinction, this was given by Confucius a certain ethical content also. The pursuit of Confucian policies and doctrines has been the concern primarily of the upper class of Chinese society. The lower classes, however, while they have been influenced indirectly by the Confucian ethic, have more immediately had recourse to practices of a popular character to which the name religion may be applied, linked as they are with certain beliefs about the nature of the universe in general and of the spirit-world in particular. If Confucius from time to time made references to the gods, or to Heaven as a quasi-deity, this was because it was natural for a man of China of that period to do so in certain contexts. The people of China, like those of many other regions, practised an ancient form of worship of the powers of nature, and concerning this Confucius appears to have been non-committal. It was accepted by him as part of the inherited order of things, and because it had the aura of antiquity. But it should not be confused with the practice of the Chinese in venerating their ancestors, which is essentially an aspect of the great emphasis in Chinese life on the *family*, whether the family of the present or past. The 'way of the sages' or the 'way of the ancients' is similarly venerated, and of these Confucius is held to have been one of the most outstanding (Shryock, 1932).

2.45 Popular religion in ancient China: ancestors and nature-spirits

The religion of ancient China has frequently been described as a combination of the worship of deified powers of nature with worship of the spirits of departed ancestors. Whether the cult of the ancestors was a religious phenomenon has, however, been questioned by some modern writers (Shryock, 1932). To some extent this tendency to separate the veneration of ancestors from the nature-cults may be seen as part of general trend among Western Sinologues to play down the importance of religion in Chinese society and to assert that the Chinese are by nature non-religious (Yang, 1961; 4–6), so that wherever a secular interpretation of Chinese customs can be offered, as in this case, the opportunity is seized to add one more item of evidence concerning Chinese non-religiousness. It may be also that earlier scholars were predisposed to see ancestor-veneration as one of the roots of Chinese religion because they were influenced by the then popular theory of euhemerism (from the name of the Latin writer Euhemerus, who held that the gods were but dead heroes elevated to the status of supernatural beings). At a period when many scholars were confident that the origins of religion were to be found by historical research this was an attractive theory by which to explain the origin of religious beliefs. It may be also that modern Sinologues, in denying the religious nature of the ancestor cult, are partly right; certainly there is less disposition nowadays to find examples everywhere to prove Euhemerus's theory. But the answer to the question whether or not ancestor veneration in China is to be thought of as a religious phenomenon will depend ultimately on one's understanding of what religion is; this will determine what is to be included as religious and what is to be excluded as non-religious.

Leaving the cult of the ancestors on one side for the present, it is clear that from earliest times the Chinese people engaged in the worship of numerous spirits of various kinds, of the earth and of the air, and that sacrifices to these spirits were of the greatest importance; this certainly cannot be said to have been marginal to ancient Chinese culture. So far as the destiny of man was concerned, the earliest traceable Chinese belief appears to be that man must ultimately return to the darkness from which he came. This was described as the 'gate of the dark female', that is, the orifice of some vast ancient earth-goddess, a dark cosmic womb from which all things came and which would receive all things again at the last. Within the bounds of this encompassing darkness man's life was lived, and it is in this context that such popular religious practices as were characteristic of ancient China have to be seen, practices which were aimed at alleviating suffering and enhancing man's temporal welfare during the span of his mortal existence.

In these practices, the offering of sacrifices to gods and spirits of earth and air, the people of ancient China were at one with many other primitive peoples in every part of the world. What is significant in the case of China is the direction in which such primitive practices developed.

2.46 The Chinese state cult

By what appears to have been a gradual process, the system of sacrifice in which the people of China engaged, as they made offerings to the local spirit-powers on whom they believed their welfare depended, was assimilated to the hierarchical system of early Chinese feudalism. This may be regarded as having developed by the beginning of the period of the Chou dynasty, about 1150 B.C. Sacrifice was gradually taken up into the processes by means of which it was considered that the life of man was to be preserved. The great sacrifice for the nation was offered to Heaven by the king; sacrifices for subordinate territories were offered by officials of subordinate grades, down to the sacrifices offered by the villager to the local deity or spirit. The sacrificial system became so moulded that it was above all else a reflection in the realm of religion of the hierarchical organisation of the state. Confucius later commented on this system to the effect that whoever understood the meaning of the Great Sacrifice possessed the key to understanding the whole cosmic system (Wilhelm, 1929; 108). Primitive Chinese religion was thus forced into two separate channels: into a sophisticated cult of the state on the one hand, and a multitude of cults of local village godlings to whom appeal was made for immediate temporal benefits on the other. This had the consequence that in the first case religious belief and practice eventually disappeared in a secularised state theory and ethic; in the second case religious beliefs and practices were effectively isolated from any wider concerns, were kept local, and inhibited from being brought into relationship with any universalist religious idea; the only acknowledged universal in this system was the idea of Heaven, the approach to which remained the prerogative of the king aided by the state ministers. In remaining at the primitive level of local cults the popular religion thus had nothing by which in later periods it could command the respect of more thoughtful minds, and hence has tended to come into disrepute. There was, however, one notable exception to this, namely, the religious system known as Taoism, to which we now turn.

2.47 Taoist development of primitive Chinese religion

The nearest Chinese approach to a religious concept of a universalist character was that of the *Tao*. The system of belief known as Taoism emerged gradually, although it had certain well known exponents, notably Lao-tzu (Laocius), an older contemporary of Confucius. Taoism coexisted uneasily with the state cult, the latter being undergirded by the Confucian system of ethics. The concept of Tao was in essence a natural development of the older idea of the primeval darkness from which all living things had emerged (2.45). In the classic book of the Tao, the *Tao-te-ching*, it is said: 'There was a living thing, a mixture of all potentialities but perfect in itself, before the skies and the earth were formed. It was tranquil and empty ... and may be regarded as the mother of the universe. I do not know its proper name, but choosing a written character for it, I take the character *Tao*, the Way.' Tao was thought of as undifferentiated being, and, because undifferentiated, eternally at rest. Since the people of ancient China had no doctrine of a life following the death of the body, the only kind of immortality that could possibly be sought was the indefinite physical prolongation of life. The position was not unlike that which was found in Hebrew religion during the pre-Exilic period when the boon sought was 'length of days'. In the case of China the quest for physical immortality became one of the major concerns or even obsessions of Taoist religion. Since Tao was the origin of all being, it was itself the essence of life; it was life *par excellence*; it was not subject to corruption, since it had no growth or decay but was eternally the same. For a human being to become immortal, to prolong his existence indefinitely, it was necessary, so it was believed, for him to become physically transformed into a fine, non-corruptible body not subject to the incidence of disease or decay. In order to develop such a body one had to become as much like Tao as possible, or even become united with Tao. This demanded withdrawal from all normal activity. One had to remain quiet, and empty oneself of all desires. These were the characteristically Taoist ideas developed by the teachers Lao-tzu, Lieh-tzu, and Chuang-tzu. It is clear that such doctrines, unlike the ethical political doctrines of Confucius, reached down to the lower classes of Chinese society, as well as having an attraction for more advanced and educated minds. The doctrines of Taoism became, in fact, the basis of a widespread popular religious movement.

It is important to notice two aspects of Taoism which were the potential causes of its subsequent degradation and the reason for the hostility it encountered. Its overriding concern with the problem how to gain physical immortality led to a preoccupation with alchemy, in the search for the elixir of life, and to various kinds of crude rituals and practices of a quasi-magical kind. The other aspect of Tao which led to its decline was its quietism, the other essential requirement for the achievement of immortality. Such quietism encouraged a wholly negative attitude towards the affairs of the state (even in the case of some emperors who became Taoists) and indeed towards all temporal affairs; in other words, social inaction and lethargy were necessary virtues. It is because of what Taoism became, for such reasons as these, that Liang Ch'i-ch'ao, a modern Chinese writer, observed that 'Taoism is the only religion indigenous to China . . . but to include it in a Chinese history of religion is indeed a great humiliation. [The Taoists'] activities have not benefited the nation at all. Moreover, down through the centuries, they have repeatedly misled the people by their pagan magic and disturbed the peace' (Yang, 1961; 5).

2.48 The religion of ancient Japan

The religion of Japan prior to the coming of Buddhism shows some of the same features as that of ancient China, but with some important differences also. The people of Japan at the beginning of the country's known history consisted of an ethnic mixture of three main groups: the indigenous Ainu and two waves of immigrants – one from the west, men of more advanced type than the Ainu, taller in build and sharper features; and the other from the south, possibly from Malaya, flat-faced and vigorous. Aboriginals and immigrants appear to have been integrated without much difficulty, and a national community developed in which there was little sense of racial antagonism, but with a wide variety of folk practices and beliefs from various sources. The common characteristic of these appears to have been a keen awareness of and sympathy with the natural environment. It is said that the Japanese are most at ease when they are close to natural things; certainly it is sensitiveness to and love of nature which is more characteristic of Shinto, as the indigenous religion is called, rather than artificiality or abstract speculation. This naturalness expressed itself in terms of belief in powers of nature whom the Japanese called *Kami*, a word of disputed etymology, but which is generally held to refer to some kind of 'superior beings' or superior powers. In general the kami were regarded by the Japanese people as beneficent; there is very little *fear* of supernatural powers in the national religion. Among the more prominent of the kami was the sun goddess, Amaterasu; the sun as the stimulant of life and growth was thought of as beneficent. The feature which is most characteristic of Shinto is the dualism between what belongs to life and health, cleanness and fertility, and what contrasts with these, namely death, disease, pollution and barrenness. The realm of the sun and light is contrasted with the realm of darkness which is the place of decay and of the dead. It was this keenly felt contrast which gave rise to the major concerns of ancient Japanese religion: promotion of fertility and cleansing from pollution. Creation was thought of as the result of sexual union of two partners, themselves spontaneously generated: Izanagi, the male, and Izanami, the female. The notion that the world itself was the product of their fertility, and regarded as basically good, is in accord with the general tenor of Shinto ideas. Similar ideas were reflected in the mythology. One of the ancient myths tells how the sun-goddess Amaterasu (daughter of Izanagi and Izanami) was offended by the unruly and violent behaviour of her brother Susanoo (the rough wind of late summer) and in order to avoid him withdrew into a cave, thus depriving the world of light. After some time a vast crowd of the kami gathered outside the cave in order to entice her out again. One of them, a goddess, then began to dance outside the cave, and in the ecstasy of the dance threw off all her clothes. The roar of laughter and the cheers which greeted this caused Amaterasu to peep out to see what was happening, whereupon two of the kami stretched a rope behind her to prevent her from retiring again into the cave. It has been suggested that this myth is an expression of ideas associated with a fertility cult, and was perhaps recited in connection with such a ritual. The withdrawal of the sun in autumn following the fierce wind of late summer leads to winter; the restoration of light and warmth in the springtime was associated with ritual dances of a kind which might now be regarded as obscene, but characterised also by cheerfulness and rejoicing at the return of spring, as the sun-goddess appears once again from hiding.

The major rites of Shinto were certainly those of cleansing from pollution, in whatever form this had been encountered; typically polluting were contact with the dead, or with excrement, disease, menstruation, and so on. The pollution envisaged was, however, always of an external and 'biological' kind; it was seldom, if ever, of an internal or moral kind. This can be seen very clearly in the fact that in the case of the wounding of a person pollution was thought to occur simply because of the spilling of blood; the guilt or otherwise of the one who may have caused the wound was of no account; the pollution consisted entirely in the fact that blood had flowed. However and for

whatever reason the flowing of blood occurred it would be polluting.
Moral rights and wrongs had no bearing on the matter.

2.49 The development of state Shinto

Whether this system of primitive fertility rites and taboos would ever
have developed beyond this stage apart from the influence first of
Confucianism (from about 400 c.e.) and then of Buddhism (from about
550 c.e.) must remain entirely a matter of speculation, but from the
nature of Shinto and the conservatism it has shown up to the present
time the possibility that any radically new developments would have
occurred from within the system seems very unlikely. One direction in
which Shinto may however be said to have moved is towards the
veneration of the emperor of Japan, and of past emperors, as kami.
This is a tendency which is closely akin to the worship of the state,
especially as the emperors who are singled out for special veneration are
those under whom the national life was most greatly enhanced (Holtom,
1938; 175). The national cult aspect of Shinto was already to be seen in
the Ceremony of the Great Purification, a ritual in which the whole
nation was required to take part twice a year for plenary cleansing of
the national life and territory from all corruption. This had developed
at least by the eighth century c.e. and the observance may go back
earlier than that. In considering this development we have been forced
to jump ahead of our period by thirteen centuries; the fact that
remarkably little development had taken place in the general nature of
Shinto in the ancient period is itself significant: no prophetic movement,
no philosophical or theological development of thought comparable
even with the rise of the Tao school in China or the emergence of Jain
ideas in India are to be found. The theory and the practice remain
basically the same over a very long period, and even after fourteen
centuries of the presence of Buddhism in Japan, the methods used in
the Great Purification ritual are today virtually what they were before
the advent of Buddhism (Holtom, 1938; 30).

SUMMARY AND COMMENT ON CHAPTER TWO

It is often observed that the period from the eighth to the sixth
centuries B.C. was particularly rich in charismatic religious personalities.

In Israel during this period there were the prophets Amos, Hosea, Micah, Isaiah and Jeremiah, to name the more outstanding; in Persia there was Zarathustra, and in India the Buddha and Mahāvīra. We noted reasons for deciding that Confucius is probably not to be included in this company, but on the other hand it could possibly be argued that the early Taoist thinkers and teachers, Lao-tzu, Lieh-tzu and Chuang-tzu, should be. These last named, however, together with Mahāvīra the Jain teacher, were responsible not so much for the promulgation of radically new and challenging doctrines as for the developing of elements of thought already present in more primitive forms. In the case of the Hebrew prophets one of their most radical and challenging ideas was that of the universalism of Yahweh, that he was not a territorial god, and that he was not bound to preserve inviolate the territory of Israel, the royal city of Jerusalem or even its Temple. In this they were in a sense cutting through the accretions which, under the influence of monarchical institutions, had gathered round the earlier Yahwism of the Exodus period. In the case of Zarathustra, the new doctrine for which he seems to have been responsible was that of the two single spiritual principles of good and evil which underlay the universe and the human situation – rather than an inchoate mass of spirits of indeterminate and unreliable character as in the earlier daēva–ahura mythology. In the case of the Buddha the outstandingly novel doctrine which he announced was one which challenged the whole essentially self-contained individualism of the karma and rebirth theory; his doctrine of anatta, that the self-contained individual does not constitute the ultimately real, the eternal, but that this is to be found in the state into which the perfected man enters, the state of being which by the Buddhist is called nibbāna.

All of these are characterised as *prophets* by the fact that they spoke to their contemporaries as they did, proclaiming these radically new ideas out of a sense of constraint. In each case there was the conception of a power or a being greater than themselves, the nature of which compelled them to share with other men their new vision even though it would have been safer or easier or more logical to keep quiet. This is a point which is sometimes missed in the case of the Buddha. There is no logical reason why the enlightened, or 'awakened' man should want to awaken others; he might assume that they would awaken themselves in due time. But there is a strong tradition, represented in various forms, that the Buddha was under a constraint to proclaim the Dhamma, a constraint which in the last analysis was due to the nature of the Dhamma, of which he was the historical representative or voice.

The other important point to be noted in connection with this period is that such prophetic breakthrough did not inevitably occur in every society. In some traditions, as in the Jain and the Taoist, there was what may be better described as a gradual sophistication of certain features of more primitive religion; in others, as in Shinto, there appears to have been a total lack not only of anything like a prophetic breakthrough but even of anything that really approaches a sophistication of the primitive religious ideas and practices. Again, why there should be this disparity, why prophetic breakthrough occurs in one place and not in another, it is not our concern to attempt to explain. We note that it is so, but in a later chapter we shall see how the prophetic breakthrough of one area does not remain confined to that area, but is conveyed to other areas besides – an important fact to be reckoned with in any consideration of the historical development of religion.

3 Scribes, Monks and Priests

3.1 JUDAISM FROM THE EXILE TO THE FALL OF JERUSALEM (587 B.C.–70 C.E.)

3.10 Historical perspective

JUST as the early, uniquely Yahwistic cultic confederation of Israel (1.40) had been superseded by the monarchical religion which had its centres in the royal temples of Jerusalem and Samaria, and which shared many features with the religion of neighbouring oriental monarchies, so in turn this was superseded, so far as Judah, the southern kingdom, was concerned, by the emerging form of religion which has since become known as Judaism. In 587 B.C. the kingdom of Judah came to an end, the capital city Jerusalem was largely destroyed and the region became a Babylonian province. For just over 400 years Jerusalem had been ruled by the Davidic dynasty; in 587 B.C. this chapter ended, and Judah was successively under the rule of Babylonians, Persians, Greeks, Romans, Arabs, and Turks, and finally in the First World War, almost exactly 2,500 years later, became a British mandated territory. The period with which we are now concerned is that covered by the six and a half centuries of Babylonian (586–539), Persian (539–333), Greek (333–63), and Roman rule (63 B.C.–C.E. 70), for during this period the foundations of the religion known as Judaism were laid. The new developments which occurred during that period may be summarised as scripture, Sabbath and synagogue, together also with certain developments in the realm of theology, notably the growth of dualism, belief in angels, the doctrine of resurrection, and ideas of an apocalyptic kind concerning the future.

It is important to remember that by the middle of the sixth century B.C. the people of Judah, the Jews, had already begun to spread and settle outside the confines of their original territory: there were sizeable settlements in Egypt; there were the leading Jews and their families who had been deported to Babylonia and were by then settled there and living in not too great discomfort; there were some, largely peasants, who remained in Judah itself. In the development of Judaism the Babylonian and Egyptian communities played the major part.

3.11 Religious developments during the Exile

An important factor in the situation of the Jews who were deported to Babylonia was that they were able to take with them their sacred writings. The extent of these in the early sixth century B.C. is not known with certainty. In order to understand something of the probable nature of the collection of scripture as it existed at that time it is necessary to go back to the earlier period, before the Exile.

The formation of the Hebrew religious historical narratives had been going on throughout the pre-Exilic period. At first it would have been in oral form that the traditions concerning Israel were put together; later these would have begun to be put into writing. The underlying motive for the assembling of these traditions can be seen from what is perhaps the earliest form of the Hebrew historical narrative, namely, the creedal confession of Deut. 26: 5-9 (*1.23*). This was a solemn recapitulation of the great facts which constituted the religious faith of this group of tribes known as Israel. Historical narrative was not indulged in simply for the sake of historiography, that is, in order that posterity in general might have a record of certain events; rather it was because there was an immediate religious or theological purpose, namely the kindling of faith, and the strengthening of loyalty to Yahweh. The story which was unfolded in the Old Testament narrative was one which, in a sense, was *numinous* in quality: the kind which produces, and is intended to produce, an awesome shudder, a thrill of horror, or of pride, or of humble gratitude. It has often been pointed out that the narratives of the Bible are not of the same order as the so-called factual reporting found in daily newspapers, yet many modern readers of these narratives still regard them as though they were. The difference between mere chronicle and theologically-coloured history is implicitly recognised in the formula which occurs from time to time in the theological history found in the book of Kings: 'Now the rest of the acts of [for example] Jehoash . . . are they not written in the book of the chronicles of the Kings of Israel?' 'Now the rest of the acts of [for example] Amaziah, are they not written in the book of the chronicles of the

Kings of Judah?' In other words, if the reader wants historical information, the standard chronicles will provide that; here he is reading a
theological interpretation, a treatment of the history from a certain
point of view, and with a certain purpose.

By the time of the Exile the theological narratives which make up a
substantial amount of the Old Testament from the book of Genesis to
the books of the Kings had already begun to take shape, and to be put
into written form. Precisely what stage in the literary formation of the
Old Testament had been reached by the time of the Exile is not clear;
the older strata which scholars have identified within these writings
would almost certainly by this time have existed in written form; the
strata which are identified as later literary products might then have
existed only in oral tradition. What is fairly certain is that those deported
Jews from the kingdom of Judah who went into exile in Babylonia
were able to take with them certain sacred writings, and that during the
time they were in exile certain of the oral traditions were committed to
writing and added to the existing literature as the concept of 'scripture'
became more and more important.

The reason for this was that the downgrading of the local Yahwistic
sanctuaries at the expense of the central, royal sanctuary of Jerusalem
had concentrated the cultic life of the pre-Exilic Hebrews in one place.
When that one place was destroyed, in 586 B.C., and the Jews were
removed from proximity to it, the only central rallying point that was
left to them were the sacred writings. Special occasions for the reading
of these sacred writings were developed, the most important being the
seventh day of the week (sabbath), originally a *tabu* day rather than a
special day of devotional practice. In Babylonia, however, it became
much more the latter type of day. On this day assemblies were held
where the scriptures were read and expounded, prayers were offered,
and possibly some existing psalms were sung. In the course of time the
circumstances of the Jewish exiles allowed them to erect special
buildings for such devotional occasions; the name for these was 'the
house of assembly' (beth ha-keneseth); they later came to be known by
the Greek form of the name, synagogue. A similar institution developed
also among the Jews in Egypt; synagogues are mentioned there in the
third century B.C.

3.12 *The revival of the priestly tradition*

In 538 B.C. the Babylonian empire was overthrown by Cyrus, the Persian. This event had effects of several kinds upon Jewish religion. In the first place the lenient policy of the Persian ruler made possible the despatch of an expedition to Jerusalem in order to set about the rebuilding of what had been destroyed in 586. An altar was set up on the Temple site and the sacrificial cultus was restored. Although there was an abortive attempt to rebuild the Temple, conditions in the ruined city made the work difficult, and it was not until about 520, under the influence of Haggai and Zechariah, that the work was begun which resulted in the dedication of the rebuilt Temple in 515. But interest in the priestly tradition had been reviving for some years before this, possibly even in the period immediately before Cyrus's victory, when it was foreseen as an imminent possibility. That stratum of the Old Testament scriptures which is generally characterised as predominantly 'priestly' in its outlook and emphasis was therefore probably passing into written form during this period, and to some extent also through the ensuing years. It is to this stratum, for example, that the first chapter of Genesis belongs, with its account of the creation of the universe, an account which incorporates details which are Mesopotamian rather than Palestinian in character, and which leads up to the sanctifying of the sabbath day as the day of rest (Gen. 2: 2–3). For a discussion of the difference between this 'priestly' account of creation and the older, more characteristically Canaanite account found in Gen. 2: 4ff., the reader must be referred to the specialist literature. A particularly useful and careful study has been made by S. G. F. Brandon (1963). On the wider subject of the identification of the various strata within the Old Testament narratives a valuable summary of recent scholarship has been made available by C. R. North (1951).

3.13 *The growing importance of the Torah and the scribes*

Alongside the revived priestly emphasis which accompanied the rebuilding of the Jerusalem Temple there was also from now on a very strong emphasis on the body of the Jewish scriptures as normative for Jewish life and religion, and in particular on the body of law, or Torah, which the scriptures contained. Here we see emerging another of the great characteristic features of Judaism. Associated with this trend was Nehemiah, who arrived in Jerusalem from Babylonia (about 445 B.C.) with permission and resources from the Persian ruler Artaxerxes (probably Artaxerxes I), to rebuild the city walls of Jerusalem and organise the life of the Jewish community now resettling there. Another leader followed from Babylon, namely Ezra, a scribe who continued the organising work of Nehemiah and in particular set up the Torah as the standard by which the life of the Jewish community was to be governed. From now on the *scribe*, as the one who was learned in the law and able to expound and interpret it, became an increasingly important religious functionary in Judaism. In Jerusalem the restored cultus and its subsequent aggrandisement resulted in the growth in prestige of the Jerusalem priesthood; alongside this, both in Jerusalem and in the surrounding territory of Judah it was the Law and its expounders which provided the other major feature of post-Exilic Judaism.

3.14 The emergence of dualistic ideas

It is easy to understand that during this period, in view of the recent course of events, the Jews would have been generally well disposed towards Persia, and things Persian. This was the second main effect of the Persian overthrow of the Babylonian empire. Proud though the Jews were of their own tradition, they nevertheless accepted, whether consciously or not, a good deal that they had acquired, and still were acquiring, from Persian religion. This becomes apparent in the Jewish literature of the post-Exilic period. Most of these ideas, such as those of the millennium, the resurrection of the body, the last judgment and the final transformation of the earth, awaited a slightly later age and other, more bitter experiences before they finally came into their own among the Jews (3.17). But already in the Persian period of Jewish history a tendency began to show itself towards a modification of Hebrew monotheism in terms of Persian dualism. The process of development of thought which can be observed in this case lends weight to the view that dualism, of the Persian kind, is likely to emerge from an antecedent, more rigidly monotheistic form of belief (2.25). It is possible to conceive that the universe is the work of a supreme potentate who brought it

into existence and who continually directs the course of its affairs. If,
however, into such a conception there is introduced the idea of moral
goodness a tension arises: how can the apparent injustices of life, the
undeserved suffering which man experiences, be explained if the ruler
of all things, who can do whatever he pleases, is to be thought of as
morally good? It is this problem which underlies the book of Job.
While this book is usually considered to be a product of the post-Exilic
period, there is no compelling reason for regarding it as such; the
problem which the book poses was one for which all the ingredients
were present in the pre-Exilic period, when the two forms of belief,
first that Yahweh is morally good, the compassionate one who cares for
his people Israel, and second that he is a king or potentate, had already
been brought into juxtaposition in the course of the development of
Hebrew thought under the monarchy (2.18). The problem to which
these two conceptions give rise is difficult of solution; some might say,
impossible. Certainly the book of Job does not appear to provide any
logical way out of the impasse, but rather gives a hint that the solution
lies outside logic, in the existential experience of the Holy such as came
to Job (Job 38–41, and especially 42: 1–6).

Another way of living with this problem is that which is provided by
dualism of the Persian kind. The greater the emphasis upon the goodness
and compassion of God, such for example as is found in the great
prophet of the Exilic period who is usually known as Deutero-Isaiah
(Isa. 40–54), the greater becomes the problem of accounting for men's
actual experience of evil and suffering, and the greater the tendency to
find the origin of evil elsewhere than in the direct will of God. At this
point the conception of a hostile spirit-power can provide a useful way
out of theological difficulties, and it was this which Persian thought
provided. Not until the period of Greek rule, however, did these ideas
develop *fully* into the dualism of spirit-hosts, good and evil; at least, it
was not until late in the Greek period that they found expression in
literary form (3.19).

3.15 Greek rule and Jewish resistance

In the latter half of the fourth century B.C. the Macedonian forces of
Alexander the Great replaced Persian rule throughout most of the Near
East, Persia, and even as far east as the Indus valley and the Punjab in

India. It has been said of Alexander that 'he lifted the civilised world out of one groove and put it in another; he started a new epoch; nothing could again be as it had been' (*Cambridge Ancient History*, vol. vi, p. 436). Certainly this was so for the Jews, who were now exposed to Greek culture and civilisation in a way that seemed to many of them to threaten the very existence of Judaism as a way of life and belief. It was not, however, until the time of the Seleucids, one of the three Hellenistic dynasties which succeeded to the empire of Alexander, that the full force of Hellenisation was felt, and especially during the reign of Antiochus IV, known also by the title 'Epiphanes', the 'manifestation' (that is, of God).

The structure of the Jewish community during the period of Greek rule has been characterised by Edwyn Bevan as one which was dominated by an aristocracy; this was an hereditary aristocracy, and it was an aristocracy of priestly families; the high-priest was the chief Jewish official (Bevan, 1904; 6). Even within the context of the Jewish community, however, and apart from Greek political dominance, there was another power in Judaism, superior even to that of the priests, and that was the Law. Nevertheless, under the Law the priesthood held a highly privileged position, and enjoyed a great source of material wealth from the offerings which the people were obliged by the Law to pay them. 'Fear the Lord and glorify the priest'; thus we read in one of the Jewish writings of this period, the book of Ecclesiasticus.

3.16 Jewish piety of the old school: Ben Sira

Besides the priest, however, there was another type of Jew influential and characteristic of this period, the sage, the kind of man whose attitude to life is contained in the Jewish 'Wisdom' literature (of which the book of Proverbs is an early example). Such a man was Ben Sira, the author of Ecclesiasticus, a wise man, or scribe, rich in the traditional piety of the grey-beards of Jerusalem. For him right conduct, according to the Law of God, carried its own reward in this life; indeed, there was no other. Concerning the dead he says, 'Turn not thy heart after him, let him go his way and remember the last end. Forget not that he hath no more expectation. ... Consider his lot that it is thy lot also, his yesterday and thine today. When the dead resteth, let thy thoughts of him also rest, and be comforted in the going away of his soul.' Such was the counsel of the wise man, who held that man has to make the best of this present life, the only life he has, by securing the approval of God. The good man is always rewarded by God in this life; the wicked is always punished in this life; any other view is based on deceptive appearances, asserts Ben Sira. The great advantage which the good man has when he dies at last is the good name which he leaves behind: 'Take thought for the name, for that it is that remaineth to thee, longer than thousands of goodly treasures. The good things of life are only for a tale of days; but the good of the name is for days untold.' It was this view of life which was soon to be shattered by the unprecedented persecutions which the Jews were to suffer under Antiochus Epiphanes.

3.17 The desecration of the Temple and the Maccabean revolt

By the year 175 B.C. when Antiochus IV Epiphanes became ruler of the Seleucid portion of the Hellenistic empire, the aristocratic families of Jerusalem had already begun to suffer division on account of Hellenistic culture. There was a strong Hellenising party who sought to bring Jewish life into line with Hellenistic culture and to make Jerusalem a new Antioch. It is important to notice that the Hellenism with which the Jews came into contact at this time was not the classical Hellenism of Alexandria, the Hellenism of Greece, and of Plato, but the debased, more voluptuous and sensuous Hellenism of Antioch, the capital of the Syrian, Seleucid empire. Some of the Jewish aristocrats of Jerusalem were prepared to come to terms with the new culture, but they were opposed in this by other members of the priestly class, as well as by the sect or party known as the Hasidim, the 'godly' or 'pious' ones. These, remaining faithful to the Law of Yahweh and the religious traditions of Judaism, regarded the Hellenising activities of some of the aristocrats with grief and abhorrence. Among the priestly families the situation became one of intrigue and jockeying for power, and in 169 B.C., when Antiochus Epiphanes was campaigning in Egypt, one of these factions saw the opportunity to rebel and attempt to seize political power in Jerusalem. Antiochus returned and dealt savagely with those in Jerusalem who had been responsible for the rebellion. He went further, and raided the sanctuary of the Temple, appropriating its wealth of gold vessels. But even this was not enough; he decided to stamp out this troublesome and bizarre Jewish religion altogether. He built a fortress on the hill opposite the Temple (the Akra), and stationed a garrison there to keep control of the area. The Temple he dedicated in 167 B.C. to the service of Zeus, an image of whom was set up in the sanctuary, and on the Temple altar swine and other animals unclean according to Jewish law were sacrificed to Zeus. Circumcision and other Jewish practices were forbidden; the observance of the Jewish Sabbath became punishable with death. A gymnasium was set up in Jerusalem, where, in accordance with Greek custom, exercises were performed in the nude; this too gave great offence to the Jews. The resistance of the Jewish people to these things was at first passive, then fiercely and zealously active.

Any success which the attempt to impose Antiochene Hellenism upon the Jews may have had was confined to Jerusalem, and to those of the upper classes to whom it was an advantage to preserve the peace. In the Judean countryside this Hellenisation was more difficult to carry out, and among the Jews who lived outside the city it was resisted. Their resistance took the form of staunch loyalty to the Torah, even to the point of refusing to defend themselves on the Sabbath day, and thus suffering death for their obedience.

All this presented a serious challenge to the old type of piety represented by Ben Sira. Jews were now suffering for their loyalty to Yahweh, and in many cases their loyalty led only to sudden and violent death at the hands of their Hellenic persecutors. Edwyn Bevan describes their bitter perplexity:

> Death, remember, had not been to their thinking the gate into life, but a darkness which God, in the case of His faithful servants, held back till they had enjoyed their full measure of days. And now – ? How did the old easy comfortable doctrine of the happy end of the righteous sound to those carried to the tormentors? . . . To the faithful it must have seemed that the ground was gone from under their feet and that before their eyes was only a void of darkness. (Bevan, 1904; 84)

It is of this situation, it is now generally agreed, that the book of Daniel spoke. Through the name of a great hero of old who had resisted every attempt of Gentile rulers to make him abandon his faith in Yahweh came this contemporary message to Jews to follow the example of Daniel now. Moreover, a large part of the book's message was concerned with the inevitable God-ordained destiny in the affairs of men that would at last, through all the suffering of the present, lead to the coming of the kingdom of the saints, when through a representative figure described as a *Son of Man* the saints would rule for ever. Stand fast then; be faithful, even to death – this was the message of Daniel to the Jews of the second century B.C. But more than this: here for the first time in Jewish literature is found the doctrine of the resurrection of the faithful to eternal life: 'And many of them that sleep in the dust of the earth shall awake, some to everlasting life, and some to shame and everlasting contempt. And they that be wise shall shine as the brightness of the firmament; and they that turn many to righteousness as the stars for ever and ever' (Dan. 12: 2–3). Ideas which had perhaps first come to the Jews from Persia, from the religious teaching of the Prophet of Iran (*2.28*) were now in a time of persecution and distress accepted as a true insight into human destiny, an authentic revelation.

A more active spirit of resistance began to show itself, however, under the influence of the Hashmon family, one of those families of the priestly class which had not succumbed to the Hellenising trend. Of the five brothers of this family the most outstanding was Judas, who was given the additional name Maccabeus, meaning 'hammer'. These brothers became the leaders of a revolt which took the form of guerrilla warfare throughout the countryside; an initial success led to increasing numbers of the Jews of the countryside rallying to their support. Another possible factor in the strength of Jewish resistance outside the capital may by this time have been the local centres of religious zeal which the synagogues provided. Support for the Maccabees was thus probably of two kinds: from those Jews whose concern was for religious liberty, the element in Judaism represented by the Hasidim, 'the pious ones'; and from those whose concern was primarily for political independence. In the course of the struggle the Maccabees were helped by external events: the Greek commander had to withdraw to Antioch, and this made possible the return of the Temple to Jewish hands. In December 165 B.C. it was restored to its proper use at a ceremony of cleansing and rededication (Hanukkah) celebrated still by Jews every December, as a festival of lights.

Thus we see that the attempt to Hellenise Judah by force resulted in a violent reaction on the part of the majority of the Jews against what was to them a vile form of heathenism. It was elsewhere, notably in Egypt, that Hellenism had a more positive influence on Judaism.

Judas Maccabeus died in the spring of 160 B.C. His brothers Jonathan and Simon played the leading role thereafter. As E. Bevan pointed out, it is difficult to know how to assess the achievement of Judas. His brothers who succeeded him certainly pursued a thoroughly worldly policy. Perhaps Judas has suffered by the reflection upon him of their shortcomings, but it may also be significant that Judaism did not include the book of Maccabees in its sacred canon.

3.18 Pharisees and Sadducees

The ideas which were expressed in the book of Daniel (*3.17*) were henceforth accepted by some as an essential feature of the Jew's faith in God; by others, more conservative, they were rejected. Among those who accepted them were, most notably, the sect which is first mentioned during the time of Simon Maccabeus's son and successor John Hyrcanus, namely the Pharisees. They appear in conflict with this high-priest and civil ruler of Jerusalem (134–104 B.C.) as the upholders of an unwritten law, men who accepted 'the tradition of the fathers'. Among those who rejected the newer ideas were, most notably, the party of traditionalist, high-priestly aristocrats, the Sadducees.

The Pharisees were in general in the tradition of the Hasidim, 'the pious' (*3.17*). Their name indicates that they 'separated' themselves, though from what is not clear; possibly from the priesthood, or from impurity, or from all contemporary secularising or Hellenistic trends. They, like the Hasidim, sought to live scrupulously in accordance with the Law, but in their case with the additional guidance of an accumulated body of oral tradition. They formed only a minority of the Jewish people as a whole, but appear to have been regarded by the people with great reverence on account of their piety. Cronbach (1963) points out that the Pharisees have had a bad press among Christians. To some extent this may be because certain of the authors of the New Testament writings were Pharisees who had broken with the movement, and hence regarded it with a violently critical dislike, just as today the ex-communist, the ex-Catholic, the ex-Jew is the most violent critic of the system he has just renounced. The ideals and the practice of the Pharisees were by no means always what the New Testament represents them to have been: patience and sincerity, puritan and ascetic personal living, concern for the life of the common people, these were the characteristics of the Pharisees in the earlier period, and in these matters they provided a striking contrast with the Sadducees. Their openness to progressive ideas and their readiness to allow an ongoing, developing tradition of religious thought resulted, as we have already noted, in their acceptance of the originally Persian doctrine of resurrection and final judgment. They were also upholders of the belief in angels which was characteristic of later Judaism, a belief which can be seen to be related to the increasing tendency to think of God as majestic, remote and utterly exalted, who must therefore employ intermediaries in order to communicate with men.

The Sadducees, shunning what was to them such religious extremism and enthusiasm (as socially superior classes frequently do) continued to take their stand on the old, conventional morality of Ben Sira, a morality very congenial to men to whom life was now once again fairly generous. When the Greek persecution had passed away the priestly families regained their old positions of prestige and influence, and became for a while the virtual rulers of Jerusalem. It was during the reign of one of them, bearing the Greek name of Alexander, that the Pharisees had become so powerful a force among the people that at his death Alexander advised his queen and successor Salome to admit them to a major share of influence in the affairs of Judea. This she did, so that the Pharisees now became a party enjoying political power, and once having entered upon it they were reluctant to give it up. It is this situation, in which the Pharisees and the Sadducees are not only opposing religious factions, but also rival political parties, that forms the background to the rise of Christianity.

3.19 Roman rule and Jewish apocalyptic ideas

In the early years of the first century B.C. a new European power had appeared on the Jewish horizon, namely Rome. The rivalries and intrigues which characterised the rule of the priestly, Sadducean families eventually led to their appealing to Rome for help. In 63 B.C. Pompey occupied Jerusalem, and from then Judea was a province of the Roman empire, at first ruled by local kings set up by Rome, of whom Herod the Great was the most outstanding, and then by procurators appointed from Rome, until the Jewish revolt in the year 66 of the Christian era, followed by the destruction of Jerusalem four years later. Like their European predecessors the Greeks, the Romans were inclined to despise the Jews for their religious bigotry and curious customs; the Jews replied with varying degrees of dislike and scorn for their Gentile overlords. It was a situation which led to the emergence of a number of extremist Jewish factions, in addition to the already existing three main divisions who are mentioned by the Jewish historian Josephus; the Pharisees, the Sadducees, and the Essenes. The last-named group appear to have been religious pietists of a nonconformist kind, possibly of the same type, if not identical with, the Qumran sect, about whom a good deal has been learnt from the discovery of the Dead Sea Scrolls in 1947 (Burrows, 1956). The extremist factions, however, such as the Zealots, the Galileans and others, were political activists who, in the tradition of the Maccabeans, sought opportunities of throwing off foreign rule.

It is during this period, the first century B.C., that the type of Jewish religious literature known as 'apocalyptic' comes into prominence. By this time the Jews regarded the sacred writings as consisting of the *Torah*, (the Law, or first five books, attributed to Moses) and the *Prophets*. The latter included as 'former prophets' those books which have since come to be regarded as the 'historical' narratives. In addition to these there existed 'the Writings', consisting of collections of psalms, proverbs, didactic books such as Job and other examples of 'wisdom' literature. The prophetic literature was regarded as complete and closed with Malachi. Hence the kind of 'revelational' writing (for that is what is meant by the Greek word 'apocalypsis') that was now being produced by seers, visionaries and similar men who believed they were writing under inspiration found acceptance in so far as the authors of these writings believed they were functioning as the mouthpieces of great heroes of old, to whom their works were therefore attributed. The first example of this kind is to be found in the book of Daniel, which in its present form dates from the middle of the second century B.C.; here we see the beginning of that type of literature characterised by prophetic visions of 'the future' ascribed to some great figure in Israel's past, such as Daniel, or Ezra, or Enoch; but which in fact may have consisted of a description of what, in the second or first century B.C., was actually recent history, with a narrative continued into the immediate future in order to show how in the final consummation the forces of evil will be overthrown and the forces of good will prevail. Dualism of the Persian kind is a very marked characteristic of this literature, and so also is an emphasis upon the idea of some extra-mundane or supernatural event which will usher in salvation for the faithful, and the consummation of human history. In connection with these eschatological ideas there developed, in the apocalyptic literature, the doctrines of warring hosts of good and evil spirits, under the command of spirit-princes. These princes of evil were known by various names – Azazel, Mastema, Beliar, and others. In earlier Hebrew thought there had existed, outside the doctrine of Yahweh as supreme ruler, a body of popular belief in various, random evil spirits. The demonology of the apocalyptic literature is distinguished from this by its development towards a unitary concept of evil: a development which reached its climax in the Satan of the New Testament. The demonology of this period has another importance also: it provides a way of explaining the nature of evil within human life which does not require that this be attributed to God, and yet does not on the other hand need to explain any ill that the individual may suffer as due to his own previous sinful action. The view found in the apocalyptic literature allows for the fact that evil may befall a man for which he is not personally responsible; it also points to the fact that such experiences may be due to an exterior collective force of evil (the demonic hosts), which is yet itself a consequence of sinful human existence, for the Jewish apocalyptic view of the origin of the demonic hosts is that their 'fall' was subsequent to the appearance of human life in the Universe (Ling, 1961; 10 f.).

While the basic features of this moral dualism were derived from Zoroastrian religion, it is significant that it is not until the second and first centuries B.C. that it really began to develop vigorously within Jewish thought. The clash of warring forces – Greek, Jewish, Roman – in the earthly, political sphere suggested to the religious mind a conflict of a more fundamental kind, between those who were described in the Dead Sea Scrolls as the Children of Light and the Children of Darkness, between the spirit of truth and the spirit of error. Contemporary political realities thus brought the Iranian doctrines to life in a very vivid and impressive way, and thus it was that the Iranian dualism came into its own with all the force of an idea when its time has come.

Partly from the Iranian conception of the eschatological saviour, and partly from the Jewish hope of the ideal Davidic king (2.10) there developed also in this period the concept of the Messiah, a prominent feature of the apocalyptic literature. Sometimes he is referred to as a coming great and wonderful king; sometimes as Lord Messiah, or by such titles as 'the Chosen One', 'the Son of David' and so on (Ringgren,

1966; 337). Elsewhere a universal saviour, the 'son of Man' (Aramaic, bar enasa, literally, a member of the human race), is spoken of. He is, however, of more than human nature, pre-existent before creation and transcending human existence. Mowinckel has suggested that this is a conception which was derived from the Iranian notion of the Primordial Man (Mowinckel, 1956; 427 f.).

The various elements of thought found in the apocalyptic literature had gained fairly widespread popular currency among the Jews by the end of the first century B.C. The overall pattern is summarised by A. D. Nock as follows:

> The approaching end of the present world order, in which the heathen triumphed and the chosen people were afflicted, would be heralded by certain signs. On the one hand, God would send certain forerunners – a returning Moses and Elijah. On the other, the forces of evil would, as it were, be intensified and would push their ascendancy to the length of a second profanation of the Holy Place at Jerusalem, comparable with that for which Antiochus Epiphanes had been responsible. Then, at what seemed the darkest hour, God's Anointed would appear to captain God's people, and to lead them in that desperate struggle which must end in victory. (Nock, 1946; 36 f.)

Such was the background of Jewish thought at the beginning of the Christian era; it will be recognised by the reader of the New Testament as the background of those writings also. It is from this context of Roman rule and Jewish apocalyptic literature that we shall later consider the rise of the Christian movement.

3.2 EARLY BUDDHISM (*500* B.C.–*70* C.E.)

3.20 *The Buddhist Sangha after the Buddha's decease*

During five centuries which followed the Buddha's decease Buddhism developed most of the characteristic features by which it is now known. These centuries were also the period during which Judaism was developing its normative features, as we have just observed (*3.1*), and the two systems were thus roughly contemporaneous in their development. India, like Palestine, had an encounter with the Greek civilisation of Alexander the Great, but in India the encounter was slight and scarcely noticeable compared with the effects which Hellenism produced in Palestine.

The first five centuries of Buddhist history from the decease of the Buddha are conveniently divided by the reign of the Indian emperor Aśoka, and the Buddhist council held at Pātaliputra (Patna) during his reign, in the year approximately 250 B.C. Aśoka's reign is also in certain respects, as we shall see (*3.26*), an important period of transition in Buddhist history.

The situation in north India immediately after 483 B.C. was one in which three major factors can be discerned, so far as the history of Indian religion is concerned. The first is the growing strength and size of the kingdom of Magadha, which by the time king Ajatasattu (*2.31*) died, in 461 B.C., had become the largest and most powerful of the newly emerged kingdoms of the Ganges plain. Iron was easily obtainable from the ore found in the vicinity of Rajgir; control of the eastern end of the Ganges valley made possible the development of sea trade with areas to the east; the forests of the Ganges plain were being steadily pushed back to provide more land for agriculture; and added to this, and perhaps because of it, Magadhan military power increased throughout this period, so that after Alexander the Great's brief raid on the Punjab (for that is all it was) the Magadhan king, Chandragupta (321–297 B.C.), founder of the Maurya dynasty, was able to move into the north-west after the retreating Greek forces and take advantage of the situation to bring yet further large territories under Magadhan control. By the time Chandragupta's grandson Aśoka succeeded to the position of ruler of this Magadhan empire in 272 B.C., it formed the largest single political unit India had known, and covered the whole area of the subcontinent southwards from the Khyber pass, with the exception of the extreme tip of the peninsula south of the river Krishna, and of the area in the north-east now known as Assam.

The second major factor was the gradual spread of the Buddhist community (i.e. the Sangha) throughout the ever-expanding territory of this Magadhan empire. Just as the political unit had grown outwards from a relatively small territory in the eastern part of the Ganges valley, expanding westward and southward, so also did the religious community of the Buddha. The same social condition which underlay the initial success of the Buddha's religion, namely the transition from tribal society to monarchy (*2.30*), continued to operate in favour of

Buddhism wherever the Magadhan state extended to engulf former tribal territories.

The third major factor during this period was the response of the brāhmans to the situation just described, throughout north India. With the details of this response we shall be concerned in the next section (*3.3*); at this point we may note that while Buddhism was in the ascendant and had the initiative, up to the time of Aśoka, the brāhmans also quickly learnt to adapt themselves to the new circumstances and were throughout this period finding new ways of validating and maintaining their position of privilege. Broadly speaking the heartland of Brāhmanism was in the western, upper reaches of the Ganges valley; the heartland of Buddhism was in the eastern, lower half. The west remained the stronghold of brāhman learning and especially of the priestly Sanskrit language, the east was the centre of the non-brāhman philosophies and of the vernacular or dialect forms of Sanskrit. The centuries we are at present considering were a period in which these two cultures were gradually interpenetrating each other; the result in the case of Brahmanism was the taking over of ideas and practices that were in origin Buddhist, and in the case of Buddhism the development of the later, Sanskritic, semi-Brahmanised form of Buddhism which came to be known as the Mahāyāna (*3.28*).

3.21 The routinisation of Buddhist religion

Buddhism, during the early centuries, was essentially the community of monks, the Sangha. No successor to the Buddha was appointed, or looked for, or indeed needed, although there were greatly-respected elders, such as Sariputta and Moggallana. The Buddha had been the exemplar and teacher of the Dhamma; it was the Dhamma that was eternal, and it was to this that the community of monks owed their allegiance. The Buddha himself is represented as having charged the monks, shortly before his death, to make the Dhamma their guide when he had gone. In addition to the Dhamma, contained in the discourses of the Buddha which were carefully preserved in oral tradition by the monks, there was also the body of regulations governing the life of the Sangha, rulings which had accumulated during the Buddha's lifetime, and which now came to be known as the Vinaya, or Discipline. In early Buddhism, then, it was the *Dhamma-Vinaya*, the

Doctrine and the Discipline, which provided the basis for the community's religious life – together, of course, with the all-important practice of meditation.

It is probably impossible now to discover exactly what was the form of the Buddha's teaching and of the monastic discipline as it existed at the time of the Buddha's decease; the tradition would undoubtedly have suffered a certain amount of accretion and modification in the course of transmission. But one need not be too sceptical. The oldest form of the tradition is that of the Pali canon – the sacred scriptures of Theravāda Buddhism. In general the Theravādins and the Sthaviras, the school from which the Theravādins developed, were noted for their strict adherence to the letter of the tradition, which they guarded with the utmost devotion. Moreover, Buddhism does not rest exclusively and entirely upon the historical veracity of *all* the stories about the Buddha, (any more than the Christian religion rests upon the veracity of *all* the stories about Jesus); the essentials are (1) the general themes are repeated so often and in so many ways in the Pali canon that there can be no doubt about them; and (2) the fact that a man existed who exemplified this teaching, and who, because of what he was, persuaded others to make the Buddhist experiment for themselves. Of these things there need be no doubt.

As for the Vinaya, this seems very early to have reached a stage when it was impious to question or challenge its details and when it was venerated as a quasi-sacred tradition. During the Buddha's lifetime the rules for the life of the community seem to have been adjusted from time to time as need arose, with considerable flexibility; to some extent this kind of flexibility may have continued for a while after his decease, but it was not long before the codification of the rules was complete, and any departure from them was regarded as a serious breach of Buddhist morality. Within this final codification, which constitutes the Vinaya proper, there is embedded, it is generally agreed, a very old set of monastic rules known as the Pattimokkha (Sanskrit, Pratimoksa). These are about 250 in number (the exact number varying with different recensions), and from the earliest days seem to have been recited at the meeting of monks held every new moon and full moon. The rules are arranged in order of gravity: the first group deal with offences punishable by permanent expulsion from the Sangha; the next group with offences meriting only temporary expulsion, and so on, down to minor matters of etiquette.

The first major example known to us of a serious breach of the Vinaya rules is dated about one hundred years after the Buddha's parinibbāna, and was the occasion of the calling together of what is commonly known as the second Buddhist Council, the Council of Vesāli. (The First Council had been held immediately after the parinibbāna of the Buddha, at Rajgir, to give definitive form to the Doctrine and the Discipline; this was attended by five hundred monks, and was presided over by Mahākassapa.) According to the account of the Second Council given in the Cullavagga (a narrative section of the Vinaya added later) it was attended by seven hundred monks, gathered to consider ten points on which the monks of the Vajji territory were said to be contravening the rules of the Vinaya. An elder monk named Yasa had called the council, inviting monks from the 'Western Country', the 'Southern Country' and the 'Eastern Country'. Vesāli, where the Council was held, was on Vajjian territory. After a great deal of fruitless discussion about these ten points of infringement, the matter was referred to a committee of four monks from the Eastern Country and four from the Western. The committee reported that the conduct of the Vajjian monks was unlawful on all ten points, and the full assembly of the Council endorsed their view. The defeated party did not accept the decision, and is said to have held another council of their own. Whether the story of this other Vajjian council is authentic or not, it seems clear that from about this time there was in some places a trend towards a relaxation of the monastic rules, in favour of a more 'lay' type of Buddhist life. Those who followed this trend called themselves the 'Great Sangha party' (Mahā-sanghika). The orthodox were thenceforth known, in distinction from this new party, as 'the Elders' (Sthaviras). In the threefold scheme of Buddhist life, morality, meditation and wisdom, the more conservative Sthaviras were concerned to place great emphasis on morality as a prerequisite of monastic life, and by this they meant the morality laid down in the Vinaya rules. The Great Sangha party, drawing their support much more from lay Buddhists, were disposed to pass lightly over the requirements for monastic morality, and place more emphasis on meditation. In this attitude of the Great Sangha party lay the seeds of two subsequent developments in Mahāyāna Buddhism: first, the great importance given to philosophical speculation, as a result of their heavy emphasis on the priority of meditation; and second, the introduction of indigenous cults, such as the worship of mother-goddesses, through the popularising tendency of the Great Sangha, with its much greater concessions to the religious needs of the lay follower.

3.22 The development of Abhidhamma

It is necessary at this point to embark upon an aspect of Buddhist thought which may to the Western reader seem excessively tedious, and possibly rather remote from what are generally understood to be the concerns of religion. The subject belongs as much to philosophy as religion, as those terms are commonly used in the West; in India, however, there has always been a much less clearly marked distinction between them. What has always to be remembered, moreover, in connection with Indian philosophical ideas is that they almost all have what in the West would be called a religious or spiritual end in view, namely the overcoming of the present ills of empirical existence, and entry into the *summum bonum*, however that may be conceived. All this is certainly true of the systematic analysis of existence which in Buddhism is known as Abhidhamma, and has remained for over two thousand years the basis of monastic Buddhism, first in India, and then in Ceylon and South-East Asia.

At the time of the Buddha's decease, the characteristic form in which Buddhist doctrine was contained was that of the *Sutta*; that is to say, a dialogue or discourse, usually between the Buddha and an enquirer, or disciple, or representative of some rival school of thought. Through each discourse there usually ran a 'thread' or main topic and it is from this that the sutta is so named (Sanskrit, sutra; Pali, sutta; c.f. English, suture). The dialogue form was one which would have had a popular appeal, and so it is possible to say that in the Suttas we have Buddhist thought wrapped up in a form useful for apologetic and explanatory purposes; we hear how the Buddha, on a certain occasion and in a certain place became involved in conversation with such-and-such a person, and what they said, usually in relation to some particular topic or idea. The title of the Sutta indicates the subject of the conversation (as for example, the Sammana-phala Sutta, which is about 'the fruits of the life of an ascetic' (Sammana-phala)); or it indicates the name of the Buddha's questioner (as in the Kutadanta Sutta, a conversation with a brāhman named Kutadanta).

Stripped of this local, topical and personal detail, however, the

Suttas taken together embody a scheme of analytical thought which is capable of being set out in a more severe schematic form. The essential point on which the Buddha's teaching differs from that of other schools of Indian thought is his denial of 'a permanent unchanging individual "self"' (ātman). This was analysed into its five component factors, or khandhas, namely, outward form, feelings, perceptions, impulses and consciousness. The last of these is the most important, and is itself capable of analysis into its various constituent 'factors'. Such factors may be listed in groups according to their nature, whether wholesome, unwholesome or neutral. In each of these groups there may be many 'states' of consciousness, and it is these that are regarded in early Buddhist thought as the 'ultimates' of this kind of analysis; they are known as dhammas, the ultimately real factors of existence. The listing of all these factors of every kind, for catechetical and instructional purposes, is a feature which emerged fairly early in the course of Buddhist history, and such catechetical lists, summaries of the ultimately real factors, are already to be seen in some of the Sutta literature, as for example, the Sangīti Sutta, found in the collection of Long Discourses (the Dīgha Nikaya). The name 'Sangīti' indicates that it is for 'chanting together', that is, by a group of monks or disciples engaged in learning the Buddhist way. Another name for such catechetical summaries is mātikā, a Pali word which is cognate with 'matrix', and indicates that this is the 'mould' in which Buddhist thought and teaching is cast.

In the collecting of such matrix-material, and its further classification and schematisation, the Abhidhamma literature was formed. This was a process which seems to have been going on throughout the first two or three centuries of Buddhist history. Although the sacred literature of the Buddhists is now generally recognised as threefold in its arrangement, namely, the Vinaya-pitaka, the Sutta-pitaka, and the Abhidhamma-pitaka, this was not its earliest form. The Vinaya is the corpus of rules governing the life of the monks in the Sangha. The Sutta collection is, as we have seen, the corpus of the Buddha's doctrine. In the early period Buddhism was comprised in these two alone, the Vinaya and the Suttas (or Dhamma, i.e. the doctrine). Thus it was that the term Dhamma-Vinaya, referring to these two main aspects of the Buddhist way, was used from early times; it occurs in the Suttas themselves. The addition of the third pitaka or collection of literature, the Abhidhamma, probably did not occur at least until after the split around 300 B.C. between the Analysers (*Vibhajya-vādins*) and the Pan-realists (*Sarvāsti-vādins*), about which more later (*3.24*). This is suggested by the fact that each of these two schools has its own Abhidhamma-pitaka, and that each differs slightly from the other in the books included, whereas their Vinaya-pitakas and Sutta-pitakas are the same.

But although the actual formation of a third collection of Buddhist texts, the Abhidhamma books, did not take place until about the third century B.C., the production of this *kind* of material, in the form of analytical schemes, was certainly going on well before that time, and probably soon after the decease of the Buddha. And behind the production of the mātikā (or lists) themselves there was, of course, the development of this analytical way of thinking which the Buddha had initiated, and which the monks were refining and sophisticating to an extreme degree. Abhidhamma may be taken to mean the 'ultimate-Dhamma or doctrine', that is, the essence of the Buddha's teaching, abstracted from the more popular form in which it is found in the Suttas. Or it may be taken to mean the study of ultimate reality as consisting in the dhammas or psychic factors into which, we have seen, Buddhist thought analysed all existence. In either case, this is what is found in the Abhidhamma, and it was this relentless breaking down of 'commonsense' conceptions which was engaging the critical faculties of Buddhist monks throughout the fifth and fourth centuries B.C.

Besides this analytical method there is, however, a second aspect to the Abhidhamma, and that is the rearrangement of the dhammas (into which existence has been analysed) into new patterns. These new patterns are, in a sense, improvements on the old; they are more wholesome; more likely to lead towards the ultimate goal of nibbāna. But first of all it is necessary to investigate the correlational system to which any single *dhamma*, (moment of consciousness, or mental event), belongs. As Nyanaponika puts it, 'thorough analysis implies an acknowledgment of relationship' (1949; 4). No mental event arises singly, but within a network of factors both 'internal' to it and also 'external'; that is, factors of which its internal structure is made up, some stronger, some weaker; and factors which act upon consciousness from outside. It is not to be expected that the reader who is being introduced to Buddhist Abhidhamma will master its principles im-mediately; the important thing is to recognise that the Abhidhamma method does not stop when it has broken human existence down into a number of separate mental and physical 'atoms'; it involves also the viewing of those atoms in relationship to each other – both their actual present relationship and their potential, improved, and more wholesome relationships. For the goal of the Buddhist method is not a bleak, ultimate 'atomism', but a wider, deeper, perfect consciousness beyond the constraints and corruption of ordinary individual existence (see also *4.29*).

3.23 The Personalists (Pudgala-vādins)

The Abhidhamma (*3.22*) was a reflective, analytical and relational approach to human psychology of a kind which the Buddha had taught his disciples to use. The aim of this method was ultimate enlightenment and nibbāna; the immediate effect of it among those who used it was to undermine the commonsense notion of an individual *self* that transmigrated from one existence, through rebirth to another, and another, and so on. But this was a notion which was very deeply rooted indeed (and still is) in Indian thought, and there were some, even among Buddhists, to whom the denial of the reality of *any* kind of real entity that passes from one existence to another was too hard to accept. Hence, as the Abhidhamma analysis was pursued more and more rigorously it produced a reaction, somewhere towards the end of the fourth century B.C., that is, about two hundred years after the Buddha's parinibbāna, in the form of a school of thought which came to be known as Pudgala-vādin, that is, those who assert (vādin) the existence of a *person* (pudgala) as a real entity. Ancient India believed that justice in human affairs was possible only if there was a permanent unchanging ātman that transmigrated and received reward or punishment in each succeeding existence. If, however, doubt was thrown upon this notion of an unchanging, permanent ātman, then what happened to the notion of justice? Obviously there was none. Such a conclusion was unacceptable, for what motive would then remain for acting rightly? Moral chaos would ensue, it was feared. Hence there emerged the attempt among Buddhists, under the very strong pressure of the idea of rebirth and karma, to assert the existence of *something* that persisted, even if it was not the ātman. It was, they maintained, the 'person' or pudgala that was the enduring entity, and they claimed in support of their contention the use by the Buddha himself of this word pudgala in a positive sense.

The emergence of this point of view, even among early Buddhists, is of interest because it indicates how strong was the popular belief in rebirth and karma, especially in the more Dravidian region of Bihar and West Bengal where early Buddhism flourished. By the majority of Buddhist monks, however, the view was rejected as contrary to the Buddha-Dhamma. It was admitted that there were instances of the use of the term pudgala by the Buddha, but he was on these occasions only making concessions to the 'common-sense' point of view of those who had not perceived the truth of the anatta doctrine. The Personalists had simply brought in at the back door the very notion (of ātman) which had been driven out at the front. Their view never prevailed completely among the Buddhists of India. Nevertheless, some nine hundred years or so later, when Hsuan-tsang (5.20), the Chinese pilgrim, visited India in the seventh century C.E. he reckoned that there were about a quarter of a million Buddhist monks in India, and that a quarter of these belonged to the Personalist school of thought.

3.24 The Pan-realists (Sarvāstivādins)

About a century and a half after the emergence of the Personalist view, the second major difference of opinion occurred among the Sthaviras, that is, about three hundred and forty years after the decease of the Buddha. This concerned the 'reality' or otherwise of past events. The development of the Abhidhamma type of analysis (3.22) was still being rigorously pursued by the Sthavira monks. Dukkha (ill) anatta and anicca are the three 'marks' of existence, according to Buddhist thought. All is momentariness, impermanence, anicca. The present, once it is past, has no reality, but perishes entirely. Nothing is necessary to bring this about; it is in the nature of reality to be thus instantaneous, non-durable. But each moment arises out of the preceding; hence there is moral continuity since each is determined by its antecedent. This was how the notion of anicca was expounded by that wing of the monks who rejected the Abhidhamma; they took their stand on the Suttas (Sanskrit, Sūtras) and the doctrine of the Buddha expounded there without the aid of the Abhidhamma analysis, and so were known as the Sautrantikas (those for whom the Sutras are the anta or end, or final word). Those on the other hand who adhered to the Abhidhamma analytical method were inclined to a different view, especially those who affirmed the reality of all three kinds of dhammas – past, present, and future. Once a dhamma had occurred it did not pass into unreality, they declared, but continued to have a real existence and to produce real effects. Similarly the dhammic events which were still future were none the less real. Hence this school of thought was known as the Pan-realist.

3.25 Monks, laymen and devotional practices

The Western reader may find it difficult to understand how abstractions of the kind which have just been outlined could possibly continue to command the loyalty of Buddhist monks for century after century and in increasing numbers. The answer lies in the fact that such abstract concerns were not the whole of the Buddhist life, even for the monk. There were also those aspects which made it a *religious* faith, namely, its devotional places and practices. The characteristic religious *practice* for Buddhist monks is meditation, but in addition to this there are certain devotional exercises, usually in honour of the Buddha and the Dhamma, which go back to a very early period in Buddhist history. The characteristic religious *place* for all Buddhists is the pagoda, or shrine, which has developed from what in ancient India was known as a stupa. This was originally a burial mound, but in early Buddhist times it had become conventionalised into a large semi-spherical solid mound of stone or brick, within which was contained a sacred relic of some kind. This sacred mound or stupa, because of the relic which it enshrined, was regarded as a focus for devotional activity. The building of such shrines was not the concern of Buddhist monks, but of the laymen who had the necessary resources. It was regarded as a work of great merit, and is so still in the Buddhist countries of South-East Asia. In general the principle which has been observed throughout Buddhist history is that the monks provide the necessary sacred relics, the laymen provide the pagoda; but all alike, monks and laymen, will use a pagoda as a convenient focus for devotional exercises and possibly meditation. Certainly the pagoda is the earlier and more characteristic object of devotion than the Buddha-rupa, or stylised representation of the Buddha in stone or metal (sometimes loosely called in the West 'a Buddha-image'). In the early centuries there was no plastic or pictorial representation of the Buddha; the practice of making such Buddha-rupas began in north-west India (Gandhāra) and reflects Greek influence (that is, in the period after Alexander's visit of 327–325 B.C.). Before that the Buddha had been represented in iconography by a bo-tree, with an unoccupied space beneath it. But at the pagoda from an early date flowers, lights, and incense were offered in honour of the Buddha and his teaching, and it was such devotional practices as these which were certainly spreading during the period we are now considering, between the decease of the Buddha and the reign of the emperor Aśoka.

3.26 Buddhism and the emperor Aśoka

The Buddhist repudiation of the principle of selfish individuality resulted in the emergence of the Sangha, the new community where men could realise the doctrine of anatta (*2.39*). In a more widely diffused form, moreover, Buddhism gradually penetrated the fabric of Magadhan society as a social philosophy. For the discourses of the Buddha contained in the Buddhist Suttas were, as Kosambi has pointed out, 'addressed to the whole of contemporary society, not reserved for a few learned initiates and adepts' (1965; 113). The social policies that were set forth in the Suttas were of a kind which envisaged a wise use of the resources of the state for the benefit of all its citizens. As an Indian historian has recently put it, Buddhism in the early centuries in India was 'a social and intellectual movement at many levels, influencing many aspects of society. Obviously any statesman worth the name would have had to come to terms with it' (Thapar, 1966; 85).

The emperor Aśoka showed himself to be such a statesman. His rule of the Magadhan empire, from about 270 to 232 B.C., was outstanding for its attempt to put into practice the social principles of Buddhism. He himself became a Buddhist about eight years after his accession, and undertook to fulfil the duties of a pious layman, such as the building of stupas (*3.25*) which he did at a number of important sacred places. But while he himself was a Buddhist, he did not use his authority to persecute or even ban other religious sects; he made substantial donations for the support of brāhman and other religious groups and their institutions. His policies and achievements have become known to modern historians from the inscriptions which have been discovered in many parts of India, and it is generally acknowledged that his achievements for the welfare of his subjects were considerable. A minority of the edicts were addressed to the members of the Buddhist Sangha, but the majority were to all his subjects. In one of these he says: 'Whatever exertion I make, I strive only to discharge the debt that I owe to all living creatures.' 'This was a startlingly new and inspiring ideal of kingship, completely strange to earlier Magadhan statecraft, where the king symbolised the state's absolute power', comments Kosambi. 'With Aśoka the social philosophy expressed in the sixth century Magadhan religions (Buddhism and Jainism) had at last penetrated the state mechanism' (1965; 159).

From the edicts addressed to the Sangha it appears that some of its members were beginning to be in need of advice on the manner of life and behaviour proper to Buddhist monks. This was to some extent no doubt due to the rapid expansion of the Sangha and the favoured position which it held in Magadhan society, which in turn would have resulted in its attracting into its membership men whose motives for entry were not always of the highest – a trend which the less strict attitudes of the Great Sangha party (*3.21*) would have done nothing to offset.

It was during Aśoka's reign that the Third Buddhist Council was held, at the imperial capital, Pātaliputra (Patna). The leading figure among the Sthaviras at this time was a senior monk by the name of Moggaliputta Tissa, for whom Aśoka evidently had a deep respect; he it was who under Aśoka's patronage was concerned at the Council to refute the doctrines of the Sarvāstivādins, or Pan-realists (*3.24*). Aśoka's concern for the strict observance of the Vinaya, a concern which may be inferred from his edict to monks on the matter of their life and conduct, is possibly another aspect of his general support for the Sthaviras, whom he now supported against the Sarvāstivādins. The latter, sensing that they were not in an altogether favourable situation in the Pātaliputra area, removed westwards, settling first at Mathurā, on the upper Jumna river, and eventually making Kashmir and Gandhāra their strongholds.

Another result of the Third Council was the official agreement by the assembled monks on the contents of the Pali canon of scripture, or Ti-pitaka as it was now called. 'Ti-pitaka' means 'three-baskets' (or three-collections), that is the Vinaya-pitaka, the Sutta-pitaka, and the Abhidhamma-pitaka (*3.22*).

3.27 Buddhist missionary activity in Aśoka's reign

Yet another result of the Council at Pātaliputra was the decision to send Buddhist monks as missionaries to various neighbouring territories of the Magadhan empire. Of the various destinations mentioned in the Pali chronicles, the best attested is that of Lanka, or Ceylon. Aśoka's son Mahinda was the leader of the mission, and he and his fellow Buddhists appear to have met with remarkable success. The king of Ceylon, Devānampiya Tissa (Tissa Beloved-of-the-Gods), is represented as having been immediately and strongly attracted to Buddhism; many of his subjects followed him, and before long the Sangha had been established on the island of Lanka, its members consisting now not only of missionary monks from the Magadhan kingdom but men of the island also. From that time Buddhism has had a continuous history in Ceylon, the longest continuous history now of any Buddhist country. The Buddhist chronicles record that similar missions were despatched to Kashmir and Gandhāra and the Himālayan regions, to western India, to southern India, and to a land described as Suvanna-bhūmi, 'the Land of Gold'; this is sometimes thought to be Burma, but more probably the name refers to Malaya and Sumatra. Aśoka's own rock edicts also mention the efforts made to spread the Dhamma in neighbouring territories, especially in the Greek-ruled areas to the north-west of Aśoka's frontier. Even although there is little remaining of Buddhism in these one-time Greek dominions, it is by no means impossible that Buddhist influences did make their way towards the Mediterranean world, and may have been a factor in the development of monastic settlements such as those of the Therapeutæ in Egypt – the land in which Christian monasticism had its origin (4.19).

The prestige which Buddhism had acquired in the Indo-Greek kingdom of north-west India is well attested by the interest in Buddhist ideas shown by a Greek from Alexandria who was ruler of the Indo-Greek area in the early second century B.C., namely Menander. The Indian form of his name is Milinda, and the Theravādin Pali work entitled 'The Questions of Milinda' (Milinda-panha) indicates the keen interest in Buddhist doctrine which this king displayed. The book takes the form of a discussion between a learned monk, Nāgasena, and the king on the kind of questions that would have arisen in the mind of a sympathetic and intelligent non-Buddhist who had made an initial acquaintance with the Buddha's doctrine and the life of the Sangha.

3.28 The Brāhmanisation of the Buddhist Sangha

Another major consequence of the benign atmosphere which the Buddhist Sangha enjoyed in the Mauryan empire has already been referred to in passing; namely, that the Sangha became materially prosperous, both from Aśoka's benefactions and from those of other wealthy citizens who followed his example; this in turn meant that life in the Sangha was comfortable and easy and increasingly attracted recruits for the wrong reasons. Another result of the increasing respectability of the Buddhist Order was that more entrants to its ranks now came from the upper classes of society than formerly. More precisely, it attracted more men of brāhman family and upbringing. These new entrants brought with them much of their traditional brāhman learning and ways of thought, and it is this which partly explains some of the philosophical developments within Buddhism during the century or so immediately before Christ, developments which go to make up a good deal of the Mahāyāna system. Moreover, in spreading into southern India, Buddhism was entering one of the strongest areas for the cult of female deities, or mother-goddesses. This too was not without very important consequences for the future development of the Buddhist religion in India.

3.29 The early phases of the Mahāyāna

We have seen that one of the major differences between the Sthaviras and the Mahāsanghikās (3.21) was that the former held to a more strictly literal interpretation of the Vinaya rules, and placed a greater importance on the necessity of monastic life for the achievement of the Buddhist goal. By the Mahāsanghikās this was held to be of relatively less importance; for them the Sangha was the great community, or 'assembly' of monks *and* laymen; hence their name, Great Sangha party. In the course of time they developed a strongly critical attitude towards the conservative and orthodox Sthaviras on the grounds of the Sthaviras' general literalism and dogmatism, apart from their attitude to the Vinaya rules. They were charged with being too dogmatic on the subject of the Buddhist ideal. The Sthaviras held that the only type of Buddhist perfection was that of the arhat, by which they meant the Buddhist monk who had reached sainthood by the strictest adherence to the letter of the law. We have seen that in the early period the nibbuta-man, the nibbāna-minded man, was the ideal type of humanity, both for monks and for the wider society and culture in which the Sangha was established (*2.36*). The use of the term 'arhat' (literally 'worthy') in early Buddhism is evidence of this fact; used in the earlier texts in a fairly general sense, it meant that the nibbuta-man was a 'worthy', a man worthy of respect, and as we have noted (*2.36*) even of oblation. In its later more formal or technical sense it has a meaning something like the English 'your worship' or 'his worship'. With the conventionalising of the term there had undoubtedly gone also a conventionalising of the ideal itself, and some of those who claimed to be arhats were probably not deserving of such a title. Such debasement of religious meaning is not infrequently the result of rigid literalism in the interpretation of sacred scriptures, once a religious tradition's essential principles have been embodied in scriptural form. Certainly this seems to have been the case with Buddhism at the point in its history we are considering.

The Mahāsanghikās therefore sought to revive the original ideal of the nibbuta-man by coming forward with a new term to replace the devalued arhat conception. More precisely they gave a new use to a term which had already been used to describe the stage which immediately precedes that of Buddhahood, namely, the term 'bodhisattva', or 'one who is possessed of bodhi' (enlightenment), one who is about to enter into the final human existence in which he will be a Buddha. This notion implies the possibility, not always fully understood by non-Buddhists, that there have been, and will be, many Buddhas; each one has appeared or will appear at an appropriate period of the world's history, a period of great need for the re-proclaiming of the eternal Dhamma. This view of things opens up the possibility that even now there are in existence bodhisattvas each of whom will, at some future period, appear as the Buddha for that era.

It was this term, and this notion, which the Mahāsanghikās took up and developed: in their view the goal of Buddhist living was the emergence of the bodhisattva, the one who in all respects possessed the qualities of the nibbuta-man (*2.36*). An important new idea, however, had also been introduced, namely that he can for the benefit of his fellow-men, indefinitely prolong his existence as bodhisattva. The development of the bodhisattva ideal in the centuries just before the Christian era emphasises not only the relative spiritual bankruptcy which had afflicted the Sthaviras by this time, but also that there was a realisation by ordinary people of the value to common humanity of the ideal man, the actual historical nibbuta; he so benefits mankind that the conviction is reached by the generality of men that such a being *must* remain in this realm, among men, in order that he may continue to bestow upon them spiritual benefits. In other words, the development of the bodhisattva conception reveals a desire among men for the indefinite prolongation of the presence of the saintly man. It was this ideal, therefore, which now began to replace the debased coinage called arhatship. An important new trend in this kind of thought, as it developed in those areas of India which had more recently become Buddhist, was the implication that the bodhisattva's spiritual attainments were of such a quality that his delayed entry into nibbāna for the sake of his fellow-men took the form of a supernatural kind of existence in which he was something more than a mortal man. The bodhisattva conception certainly had its roots in early Buddhism, in the notion of the ideal man, the saint, the nibbuta; but it also developed a wholly new and hitherto unknown dimension which it owed more to non-Buddhist influences in India, the dimension of the supernatural, quasi-divine.

The other major point on which the Sthaviras were criticised for their literalism was on the analysis of human existence into its constituent dhammas (3.22). The Sthaviras appear to have believed in the real objective existence of these dhammas, as constituting as it were the ultimate ontological 'atoms' of existence. The Mahāsanghikā schools held that analysis into dhammas was primarily the demonstration of a *method*; to stop at dhammas was to stop short at a purely arbitrary point in the analysis, and for no good reason. The analytical process must be continued indefinitely: even dhammas could not provide an ultimate resting place; analysis thus relentlessly pursued must lead to a view of all substantial entities as being *śūnya*, that is, void. It was this trend of thought which eventually became the basis of the *Śūnyatā* doctrine in the Mahāyāna form of Buddhism (4.33). But before the history of Buddhism is pursued any farther we must first consider the nature of the developments that were taking place within Brahmanism.

3.3 THE REORIENTATION OF BRAHMANISM
(*500* B.C.–*70* C.E.)

3.30 *Non-Buddhist India, from the rise of the Magadhan empire*

In this section we shall be concerned with the non-Buddhist aspects of the religious situation in India during the five centuries before the rise of Christianity. If this seems a rather negative way of describing our subject, it is because there is no other really satisfactory way of referring to the complex of factors to be dealt with. 'The non-Buddhist religious situation' might be taken to mean, broadly, Hinduism. But the latter is a term which cannot properly be applied to Indian religion during this period; first, because 'Hindu' was the term used by the Muslim Arabs of the eighth century to describe those who lived beyond the Sind or Indus valley and is therefore an anachronistic term from that point of view; and secondly, because what is later identified as Hinduism had as yet not come into existence, but was in the process of developing. Nor would it be appropriate to call the non-Buddhist religion of India in these centuries simply 'Brahmanism', since we shall be concerned not only with the religious ideas and institutions over which the brāhmans exercised control, but also with the vast range of aboriginal cults which were at this time being brought into varying degrees of relationship with Brahmanism.

3.31 *'Great' and 'Little' Traditions in India*

The situation during these centuries is a very good example of what Robert Redfield the anthropologist has described as the interaction of 'Great' and 'Little' Traditions (1956). By a 'great' tradition is meant a culture (often closely associated with a religion) which is spread over a wide area, usually embodied in some literary form, and whose typical representatives or carriers form a learned special class recognisable throughout the area, such as priests or monks. The 'little' tradition is of local origin and localised, limited extent; it is less usually a literate tradition, and if it has any special representative this will be a man whose authority or status is recognised in his own village or locality only. Between these two, the great and the little traditions, there is likely to be some kind of interaction. This may take the form of the *universalisation* of elements from many little traditions, until these come to constitute a new element of great tradition; or it may be of the reverse kind, when it is known as *parochialisation*, that is, when elements of the great tradition are accepted within a little tradition, but are broken down, modified and adapted to suit local needs and beliefs.

In non-Buddhist Indian religion during the period of the Magadhan empire and the following centuries the Great Tradition was represented by the brāhmans, their Vedic lore, and their prestige language, Sanskrit. The Little Tradition was represented by the various local, village cults varying from region to region, even from village to village, each with its local priests, usually non-brāhmans.

3.32 The brāhmans at a disadvantage

The brāhman priests were, during the early period of the Buddhist ascendancy, having to find new ways of maintaining their position and asserting their importance and indispensability. Formerly their clients had been principally from the kṣatriya class, for whom they had performed the Vedic sacrifices and rituals. Now, in addition to the kṣatriya class, a new and increasingly important section of Magadhan society was the mercantile class. The extent of the Magadhan empire, covering most of the subcontinent, meant greatly increased possibilities of trade. Even after the Mauryan dynasty came to an end in 185 B.C. and the empire was broken up, the trading went on. In the north-west, the Indo-Greek area of Gandhāra was a gateway to Western Asia and the Mediterranean world. The Mediterranean world was eager to receive the spices of South-East Asia and the silks of China, and Indian merchants became the great middlemen of Asia. The evidence of inscriptions and of contemporary literature indicates the prosperity of the merchant community everywhere in India at this time (Thapar, 1966; 109).

The ascendancy of Buddhism and Jainism had had the effect of further undermining the importance of the Vedic sacrificial system, a process which, as we have seen, had already begun by about the sixth century B.C. (*1.56*). The Buddha is represented in the Suttas as having directly criticised the sacrificial system, on the grounds that it involved the unnecessary slaughter of animals, and entailed undue hardship for the labourers who were forced (often on penalty of flogging) to prepare the very elaborate sacrificial enclosures, and represented a lavish and pointless waste of resources. Much better, says the Buddha in reply to the brāhman Kūtadanta, is the sacrifice of almsgiving to holy men, or even regular almsgiving to all; better still to follow the Buddhist way, practise the five moral precepts, deny self and gain enlightenment. The spread of Buddhism would thus inevitably have meant the further decline of Vedic sacrifices. Aśoka proclaimed throughout his realm the futility of animal sacrifice and the respect due to animal life. From this time onward the prohibition of meat eating which began in Buddhism gradually began to spread and eventually became a prominent feature of the Vaishnavite and Shaivite sects of Hinduism.

The prestige of the brāhman priest was thus being assailed on two fronts: (1) a new mercantile class was arising which had not the same traditional religious relationship with the brāhmans as had the kṣatriyas, and either continued in the practice of the local cults (which were the more normal religious milieu for the lower classes of society), or else gave their support to the Buddhist and Jain communities; (2) Vedic sacrifice was certainly not likely to be a service which this new class would require the brāhmans to minister to them, at a time when it was everywhere in decline.

3.33 New roles for the brāhman

Nevertheless, the brāhmans retained their position of prestige. That they were able to do so was due in no small measure to their own adaptability and determination. If their role as administrants of the sacrificial ritual had been downgraded, their role as public educators and the preservers of culture and learning was at this period being upgraded, and they took full advantage of the fact. The brāhman technique of memorising the sacred books had become a mental achievement of a high order, and the basis of all learning. Moreover, Sanskrit was now established as the prestige language of India; brāhmans, such as Pānini (first half of the second century B.C.) were the great grammarians, and the teaching of Sanskrit was a closely guarded privilege of the brāhman. Here then was the brāhman's continuing claim to importance so far as the educated upper classes were concerned.

So far as the ordinary householders of an agrarian and mercantile society were concerned, the brāhman learnt new ways of establishing his own social utility. The new tribes and social groups that were being brought within the scope of the Magadhan empire had their own local cults and rites; these, the little traditions, the brāhmans soon learnt to penetrate, and thus to take them over for the Great Tradition of Brahmanism, providing them with new rituals which they would represent as being superior to the old rituals, giving Sanskritic names to the village gods, thus increasing their dignity and status; with the increase of dignity of their gods, the village householders would feel, went an increase in their own status. In return the villagers would offer due respect to brāhman institutions and nominal deference to the Vedic sacred writings.

In this way the brāhmans became the integrative element in Indian society. While preserving local tribal customs and mythology in their role as the new priests, they also transmitted to the local tribe the overall values of Brahmanism, sometimes providing suitable brāhman myths to make old tribal gods assimilable. It was this process which 'enabled Indian society to be formed out of many diverse and even discordant elements, with the minimum use of violence' (Kosambi, 1965: 172); it was this process which more than any other single factor produced the caste system as it has emerged in historical times.

3.34 Bhakti: or Hindu popular devotion

The kind of popular religious devotion whose emergence can be recognised in India during the centuries immediately before the Christian era, and which was given validation by the brāhmans, is commonly known as bhakti. This is one of a group of words connected with the Sanskrit root bhaj, meaning adoration or devotion. *Bhakti* can mean adorable, or the practice of devotion. A *bhakta* is a devotee. The *Bhāgavat* is the one to whom devotion is given, and is sometimes translated 'Lord' or 'blessed one'. *Bhāgavata* is that which appertains to the 'blessed one', and is used as a general name for the system of bhakti, and was the name of a sect at this period, who may thus be called 'the Devotionalists'. The name Bhāgavat is frequently used in the Pali canonical scriptures of Buddhism as a synonym for the Buddha, and it is possible that the word was borrowed from Buddhist usage.

When this cult of worshipful devotion to a god (rather than the relationship of sacrificial ritual) began it is difficult to ascertain. An early example is provided by the cult of the god Vasudeva, which is attested in a statement made by the Seleucid Greek ambassador Megasthenes, who lived at the Indian capital, Pātaliputra, in the time of the first Maurya emperor Chandragupta (*3.20*). The Mauryan dynasty was succeeded by that of the Sungas (183 B.C. to approximately 71 B.C.); a Greek ambassador to one of the Sunga kings seems to have accommodated himself to Indian religion to the extent of declaring himself a devotee of Vasudeva. In honour of this god he erected a column at Besnagar, near Bhilsa in central India, which is still to be seen; in the inscription on the column Heliodorus describes himself as a Bhāgavata.

3.35 The cult of Vishnu

In the period we are considering there was evidently a tendency for the gods who were worshipped in different regions under different names, such as Vasudeva (just mentioned), Hari, Narayana, and others, all to be renamed and known henceforth by the name Viṣṇu (anglicised, Vishnu). This was an aspect of the process of universalisation (*3.31*) of which the brāhmans were the agents (*3.33*). Viṣṇu as we noted earlier (*1.36*) was the name of a minor god of the Ṛg-Veda, who had the characteristics of a solar deity. Now, centuries later, in the period immediately before the Christian era, his prestige had grown considerably and by means of brāhman influence he was absorbing other, non-Aryan, regional deities. His cult was destined to go on increasing in importance. Towards the end of the pre-Christian era a trinity of brāhman deities had emerged: Brahmā, who created the world; Viṣṇu who preserves and protects the world; and Śiva, who destroys. This trinitarian doctrine was unstable and short-lived, however; Brahmā's importance waned, and either Viṣṇu or Śiva became the all-important god, according to the inclination of the worshipper.

3.36 The cult of Krishna

An important development in connection with Viṣṇu which took place during the period we are considering was the incorporation into the

Viṣṇu cult of the figure of Kṛṣṇa (anglicised, Krishna). The Greeks who invaded northern India in the fourth century B.C. found that a demi-god was worshipped there whom they equated with their Herakles; this clearly was Krishna, whose cult had by then become widespread in the Punjab (Kosambi, 1965; 117). Krishna was closely connected with herdsmen and was the protector of cattle. It is possible that the origin of the Krishna cult lay in the veneration of an historical figure who had become a legendary hero; certainly by this time a copious Krishna mythology was developing. In this mythology the hero is, comments Kosambi:

> all things to all men and everything to most women: divine and lovable infant, mischievous shepherd boy; lover of all the milkmaids in the herders' camp, husband of innumerable goddesses, most promiscuously virile of bed-mates; yet devoted to [his wife] Radha alone in mystic union, and an exponent of ascetic renunciation withal. ... The whole Krishna saga is a magnificent example of what a true believer can manage to swallow, a perfect setting of opportunism for the specious arguments of the Gītā. (Kosambi, 1965; 114 f.)

3.37 The doctrine of avataras

Krishna eventually came to be regarded as a manifestation of the supreme god Vishnu. In this case however, it was not by the process of renaming the local god by henceforth calling him Vishnu (as in the case of Narayana, Vasudeva and other regional gods) but by regarding Krishna as a human manifestation, or avatara (literally 'descent') of the supreme god Vishnu. This is possibly because the tradition of the human origins of the hero Krishna still constituted a sufficiently strong element of the legends to make it necessary for him to be regarded as a god in *human* form. The doctrine of avataras is one which made its appearance in Vaishnavism during this period; it is set forth in the Bhagavad-Gītā (4.22) as consisting of a periodical reappearance of the great god Vishnu (i e. the Bhāgavat, or Lord) in an earthly body or appearance whenever evil and injustice prevails in the affairs of men, in order to set things right again. Beliefs about these various appearances of Vishnu were eventually systematised: it was held that there had so far been nine such avataras. The first three had been manifestations of the god Vishnu in the form of animal beings who had, in various ways, saved the world from disaster; it is possible that historically the origin of these avataras is to be found in cults of sacred animals. The fourth avatara was half-lion, half-man; the fifth was a dwarf, and the sixth was a brāhman, Paraśu-Rāma, who according to the legend destroyed the kṣatriya-class when the world was in danger of being dominated by them. The seventh and eighth avataras are the most important in point of popularity, that is, the extent of devotion which they receive from Vaishnavites: these are Rāma, or Rāma-candra, and Krishna. Rāma is the hero of the great epic, the Rāmāyana (4.24). It is interesting to notice that there are two more avataras, beyond Krishna. The ninth avatara is the Buddha, who seems to have been incorporated into the Vaishnavite scheme as a result of the tolerance which undoubtedly existed between the adherents of the two traditions (and in the later period the dividing line was not always very clear) and possibly in acknowledgement, conscious or unconscious, of what the Vishnu cult had taken over from Buddhism. The tenth avatara is the Kalkin – who is yet to come, at the close of the present dark age, to destroy evil and bring back goodness.

3.38 Factors in the emergence of bhakti mythology

The notion of a periodical reappearance of one who embodies the truth was very probably derived from the Buddhist doctrine of the regular appearance, in every era, of a Buddha (3.29). The character which each of these avataras possesses, namely that of a divine saviour, may possibly owe something to the Zoroastrian doctrine of the Saoshyant (2.28), or Saviour, whose coming meant defeat for all forces of evil. The influence of this idea is seen most clearly in the tenth avatara. It was in the north of India, that is in an area exposed to Persian influence, that the avatara doctrine developed, at a time when Zoroastrian religion was in the ascendant in Persia. Vaishnavism may, however, have derived these beliefs at second-hand through Buddhism, with its doctrine of the coming Buddha, Maitreya, who was to appear at the end of the present age; for Zoroastrian influences possibly shaped this Buddhist doctrine of Maitreya.

The incongruity of the beliefs which were brought into juxtaposition in the Krishna mythology was characteristic of the incongruity of the whole range of the brahmanisation of local cults and mythologies, or what is more accurately described as the process of reciprocal acculturation, which was going on at this time. Kosambi has described the process in some detail (1965; 170), commenting that 'this conglomeration goes on for ever, while all the tales put together form a senseless, inconsistent, chaotic mass.' From the sociologist's point of view this can be seen as the form in which a religious tradition was likely to develop in the social situation provided by a widely extended political empire based on a rural, village economy; or as Kosambi describes it, in economic terms, 'a highly composite society with a relatively primitive level of production' (1965; 115). On the other hand, some other factor beside the social and economic was undoubtedly also present, maintaining the need for such a religious 'superstructure' of beliefs and myths: to put this at the lowest and most general level, an unsatisfied search for the meaning of human existence, with all its injustices, its frailty, its sorrows, its transience; this is a search which men seem to have embarked on whenever the most elementary needs have been met and there is time for reflection. Economic activity may have remained at a primitive agrarian level so far as the villagers were concerned, but it was apparently adequate in terms of food production; the India of the centuries immediately B.C. was considerably better fed than the India of today. Certainly so far as India is concerned some of its most religiously fertile periods have been periods of *economic* adequacy, even though they may also have been periods of psychological or social malaise. Indian religion, that is to say, is not necessarily associated with Indian poverty, as some Westerners tend so easily to assume; for India's present dire poverty is a relatively modern phenomenon.

3.39 *The development of Hindu ethics*

By the beginning of the Christian period our survey has reached a stage in the history of Indian religion when what is known now as Hinduism was recognisably beginning to emerge. Its full emergence is to be seen a few centuries later, in the time of the great Gupta dynasty (320–650 C.E.) (4.26). One feature which remains to be noted in the period with which we are at present concerned, however, is the development of a formal concern with questions of right conduct. A certain number of brāhman manuals dealing with religious matters made their appearance during the centuries immediately before the Christian period. These were, first, the *Śrauta-Sūtras* and the *Gṛhya-Sūtras*, which consisted of explanations of scripture (*śruta*) and rules for household religious rituals and ceremonials. But somewhere between the sixth and the second century B.C. there appeared also a third type of secondary sacred literature called *Dharma-Sūtras*, or discourses on right conduct. Until this time brāhman literature had not shown any great concern with ethical questions; in the Upaniṣads, for example, it was acknowledged that immoral conduct was a serious hindrance to the realisation of brahman *(1.58)*. Whatever aided the meditative life was regarded as morally good, and whatever detracted from it was bad; but beyond this there was no positive teaching on ethical conduct until Buddhism had appeared, with its clear moral obligations for monks and laymen *(2.33)*. From this time Brahmanism also develops a more formal system of ethics, or rather, systems of ethics, for what is very characteristic of the brāhman approach to the subject is the idea that for every man there is an appropriate course of right conduct according to his situation in society (his varṇa, or class) and the stage in life which he has reached. The notion of the four stages of life, or āśramas, also appears in Brahmanism during this period: namely, those of the pupil, the householder, the ascetic, and the homeless one who seeks only for union with Brahman. Every individual's dharma, or right course of conduct, thus has a double reference – what is appropriate to his class (varṇa), and within his class what is appropriate to his age (āśrama). It is therefore properly described as varṇa-āśrama-dharma (usually written as a compound: 'varṇāśramadharma'). It may be significant that this positive concern of the brāhmans with matters of conduct coincides with the ascendancy of Buddhism and the period of its greatest popular appeal as a social philosophy *(3.26)*.

The reciprocal interpenetration of the Buddhist and Brahmanical ways of life was thus well advanced by the beginning of the Christian era, and the major themes of both Mahāyāna Buddhism and of what is properly known as Hinduism (especially in its theistic form) were already in evidence by the time Christianity had possibly made some small initial impact in South India. It is claimed that the apostle Thomas made his way eastwards from Palestine and arrived on the Malabar coast, journeying thence across India to somewhere near Madras. His preaching of a new religion was, according to the tradition, violently resisted, and Thomas himself martyred about 68 C.E. That a Christian apostle should have reached India during this period is not impossible, but nothing at all is known with certainty. That his preaching is likely to have met with such violent opposition is doubtful. We must turn now to a consideration of what it was that he would have preached.

3.4 THE RISE OF CHRISTIANITY, TO 70 C.E.

3.40 Sources for the life of Jesus

The central figure of Christianity is Jesus of Nazareth. Materials for a life of Jesus are virtually non-existent, as T. W. Manson stated:

> Not a single chronological point can be fixed with certainty. The life of Jesus lasted probably between thirty and forty years: concerning at least twenty-eight of them we know precisely nothing at all. What information we have is mostly concerned with the public career of Jesus, that is, with the last period of his life, a period whose length is uncertain, but probably not less than one year nor more than about three. But there is not even enough material for a full account of the Ministry. (Manson, 1943; 323)

The reason for this, as Manson goes on to point out, is paradoxically that the major sources of material are *Christian* sources, namely the documents of the New Testament and the apocryphal gospels; in using the former the modern reader has to ask, 'What allowances must we make for the editorial activities of Evangelists and the compilers of the sources which they used? How has the material been affected – perhaps even created – by the practical needs of the Early Church?' Thus, one is uncertain of the historical value of the material available. With regard to the apocryphal gospels, these consist very often of stories which are bizarre, grotesque, revolting, and inspire only mistrust.

3.41 The non-Christian testimony

Beyond these Christian sources there is material of two kinds: first, Jewish accounts, Talmudic and later, mainly hostile and tendentious, (and it is significant that the later they are the more hostile they become); second, very brief references in the works of the non-Christian historians, Tacitus and Josephus. Tacitus (*c.* 60 to *c.* 120) in his *Annals*

writes, in explanation of the name 'Christians': 'Christus, from whom
their name is derived, was executed at the hands of the procurator
Pontius Pilate in the reign of Tiberius' (Bettenson, 1963; 2). Incidentally,
it is worth noting that the second-century Latin historian, Suetonius,
writing of the Neronian persecution, referred to the Christians simply
as 'a set of men adhering to a novel and mischievous superstition',
without mentioning Christ. The Jewish historian Josephus's work
Antiquities of the Jews includes a passage which runs as follows:

> Now there was about this time Jesus, a wise man, if it be lawful to call
> him a man, for he was a doer of wonderful works – a teacher of such
> men as receive the truth with pleasure. He drew over to him both many
> of the Jews, and many of the Gentiles. He was Christ; and when Pilate,
> at the suggestion of the principal men amongst us had condemned him
> to the cross, those that loved him at the first did not forsake him, for he
> appeared to them alive again the third day, as the divine prophets had
> foretold these and ten thousand other wonderful things concerning him;
> and the tribe of Christians, so named after him, are not extinct at this
> day. (Whiston, n.d.; 379)

It has been suggested that this passage is a later Christian interpolation,
even though, as T. W. Manson points out, it is 'cool, objective,
patronising and faintly contemptuous'. Nevertheless, he agrees that 'it is
quite likely that the passage as it now stands is not what Josephus wrote:
that, in fact, the original was even cooler and more contemptuous than
the existing text, and that the features most objectionable to Christian
piety have been toned down or removed' (Manson, 1943; 329). There
is, however, a small but important common element in these non-
Christian references: they both affirm that Jesus was a *crucified teacher*.

3.42 The New Testament documents

Apart from these brief references, then, the main sources for our
knowledge of Jesus of Nazareth are the Christian Gospels, that is to say,
documents of a missionary character written by Christians for the
furtherance of their movement. The reader who is unacquainted with
the technicalities of theological study, and is disposed to believe that the
writers of the Gospels were honest men who would only have put down
what they knew to be true, may see no reason why these documents
may not be taken at their face value as straightforward historical

testimony. The position is not quite so simple, however, honest and devout though the Gospel writers undoubtedly were. It is not merely that they do not always agree among themselves on matters of fact; but rather that the composition of these narratives took place several decades after the death of Jesus, and after important developments had taken place within the Christian society and in the nature of Christianity. When the Gospels came to be written (after 65 C.E.) it was inevitable that this internal development should affect the way the historical facts were presented. What Edwyn Bevan wrote in 1932 on this subject is still cogent: 'While we have documents to show us the Christianity of the Gentile churches – most notably the letters of Paul himself – we have no document which emanates from the primitive Jerusalem community without having passed through a Gentile-Christian medium' (Bevan, 1932; 24). Nevertheless, as we shall see (3.46) this need not imply that it is entirely impossible to recover anything of the earliest disciples' understanding of the significance of Jesus.

3.43 *The evidence of St Paul's letters*

The oldest evidence we have for the nature of the early Christian society and its beliefs is to be found in the letters of St Paul. These have the advantage, from the point of view of historical inquiry, that (apart from Romans) they are not self-conscious literary productions, shaped by a missionary purpose, but fragments of spontaneous writing called forth largely by the demands of ongoing internal controversies. Of such a character are the undoubtedly Pauline letters – to the Corinthians, Galatians, Thessalonians, and Philippians. The letter to the Romans is more consciously theological in purpose, but even here controversy keeps breaking in. (The letters to the Colossians and Ephesians may or may not be Pauline, or incorporate Pauline thought; the letter to the Hebrews and those to Timothy and Titus, while they were once attributed to Paul, are fairly generally agreed to be non-Pauline.) From the evidence of those documents which are undoubtedly of Pauline authorship it appears that during the first four decades of the Christian movement's history it consisted of two main streams. One was that of Jerusalem; essentially this was the community of those who had been associated with Jesus of Nazareth as his disciples during his lifetime. These were Jews by upbringing, outlook, and belief, who within the

continuing context of traditional Jewish life and worship were committed to proclaiming to their fellow Jews the transformation of the
whole contemporary Jewish view of things which had come to them
through the life, teaching and death of Jesus. The other stream was
made up of the communities outside Palestine, largely Gentile in
composition, which had resulted from the religious preaching and
propaganda carried on by Paul, himself a non-Palestinian Jew who,
after an initial period of hostility towards the Jewish disciples of Jesus,
had experienced a vision of Jesus which led him also to believe in Jesus
as the Messiah.

3.44 Two types of early Christianity

The difference between the two wings of the movement – the Jerusalem
community and the Pauline Gentile communities – was avowedly one
of attitudes to the Jewish Law. The Jerusalem disciples held that the
transformation in their lives which had resulted from belief in Jesus as
the Christ did not mean that they could become indifferent to the
observance of the Law; this for them was still the divine Law and its
importance was by no means diminished but, if anything, enhanced by
the new impetus to faith in the divine ordering of things which their
view of Jesus entailed. To some extent their religious position has to be
a matter of conjecture for the reason already given (3.42); we can infer
it only from the nature of their disagreement with St Paul, together
with the positive quality of their conviction regarding the significance
of Jesus. They remained Jews, in intention and in obedience to the Law
and in their participation in the worship of God in the Temple, but
Jews with a difference, that much is very clear; and it is that difference
which on the one hand set them apart from their fellow Jews who did
not acknowledge the significance of Jesus, and on the other hand led
them to recognise St Paul and his Gentile communities as in some sense
fellow-travellers. It was because of this affinity between them, based on
a common devotion to Jesus, that they found it necessary to be critical
of what in their view was incongruous with such devotion, namely the
Pauline-Gentile attitude of indifference to certain aspects of the Law of
God.

3.45 St Paul's view of the significance of Jesus

An important question still remains to be answered, however: how was it that devotion to Jesus as Messiah should in the case of the Jerusalem community have led to different conclusions about the importance of the Law from those reached by St Paul starting from similar convictions about Jesus. The answer which has suggested itself to some scholars is that St Paul's view of the significance of Jesus was in fact somewhat different from that of the Jerusalem community (Brandon, 1957). It is clear from Paul's letters that he fairly soon began to conceive of Jesus in terms of the central Saviour-figure of Jewish apocalyptic thought (*3.19*). Since his death Jesus had become, according to Paul, an exalted, heavenly being who would before long appear in glory 'from heaven with the angels of his power in flaming fire'. Such a conception is particularly clear in the second letter to the Thessalonians. In Paul's view the power of the Jewish Law was that it was able to bring man under sentence of death, because of man's inability to fulfil the Law. In this view it was virtually a demonic power, and it was this power which had been supernaturally conquered in the death of Jesus, so that for those who had faith in him the heavenly Jesus was their vindicator, their Saviour from the power of death and sin. It is this conception of faith in the heavenly Jesus as the way to deliverance from the penalty for transgression of the Law which is at the root of Paul's attitude to the Law. It was an attitude which was easily misunderstood and apparently led some of his converts to the conclusion which is known as antinomianism. The basic difference between this Pauline view and that of the Jerusalem disciples was that Paul's theology was based on a vision, whereas theirs was based on a knowledge of the historical Jesus. Paul's claim (Gal. 1: 12) was that his theology was by direct revelation, quite independent of the Jerusalem tradition and of equal status with it.

3.46 How did the Jerusalem community think of Jesus?

Since the Jerusalem community differed very strongly from Paul over the status of the Law, it would seem likely that they had not at that time come to share this view of Jesus as the supernatural Saviour who had conquered the demonic power of sin, a view which he had come to 'by revelation'. What then would their view of Jesus have been? This is to ask the question, What was their 'Messiah-doctrine'? or, to use the Greek form of title instead of the Hebrew, What was their Christology? Some scholars take the view that this is a question that can never be answered. We cannot, they say, pierce the layers of Pauline and Hellenistic interpretation and re-presentation of Jesus which now lie very thick over all the New Testament documents, to get at the earlier, pre-Pauline view of Jesus held by the disciples in Jerusalem. To try to discover what really were the Christological ideas of the early disciples is an enterprise whose folly is exceeded only by that of trying to get one stage further back and discover anything about the historical Jesus himself. Noble attempts have been made, it is said, at both of these projects. *The Jesus of History* is the title of a book by T. R. Glover of Cambridge, in which an attempt was made to get behind the Jesus of the Church's preaching to find the real, human, historical Jesus. In the light of New Testament scholarship since then, Glover's work, and the attitude of the Liberal Protestantism which it represented, now looks very naïve and unsophisticated. It was said of the Liberal Protestant who thought he had discovered the Jesus of history that he had seen only his own face at the bottom of a deep well. In 1934 R. H. Lightfoot concluded his Bampton Lectures with some words which have since become notorious. The form of the earthly Jesus is, he said, no less than that of the heavenly Christ, for the most part hidden from us. 'For all the inestimable value of the gospels, they yield us little more than a whisper of his voice; we trace in them but the outskirts of his ways' (Lightfoot, 1934; 225). Interest since then has switched to the possibility of discovering, if not the historical Jesus, at least what the earliest community proclaimed *about* him. The great work in this connection was C. H. Dodd's *The Apostolic Preaching and its Development* (1936). On the basis of an analysis of the speeches in the book of Acts attributed to the early apostles, speeches setting out the early missionary preaching about Jesus, and on the basis of the New Testament epistles, Dodd arrived at what he identified as the primitive *Kerygma* (lit. 'that which is preached'), that is the basic pattern of ideas about Jesus which underlay all the missionary work of the early, apostolic community. This basic pattern was, according to Dodd, that Jesus was the fulfilment of Old Testament prophecy, the events of whose life, death, resurrection and ascension into heaven constituted a call to men to repent, to acknowledge Jesus as Lord and Messiah, and to obtain forgiveness of sins. This view was challenged by the German scholar and form-critic, Martin Dibelius, who argued that the speeches in Acts are not reliable evidence for the pattern or content of the preaching of the early apostles: they represent very largely, he claimed, the kind of preaching that would have been going on at the time the Acts of the Apostles was composed towards the end of the first century; these were typical sermons of about 90 c.e., put into the mouths of the apostles who preached some fifty-five years earlier; they were no proof that that in fact was how the apostles did preach about Jesus in the years just after his death. In general, German New Testament scholarship has tended to develop this line of argument, and to say, in effect: we can only know the Christ who is proclaimed by the Church. What the Church preaches is the 'Christ-event' and how this is relevant for modern man's experience. This, broadly, is the Lutheran existentialist kind of argument which has been developed by Dibelius's colleague, Rudolf Bultmann.

New Testament scholars are not all, however, entirely agreed to leave the matter there, and abandon altogether the quest for the historical Jesus. One group of scholars in England has recently re-examined the possibility of this quest in a volume of essays entitled *Vindications* (Hanson, 1966). Another New Testament scholar has suggested that it is possible to discern certain primitive and genuinely early ideas of the church of Jerusalem about Jesus embedded within the speeches in Acts which are *not* those of the Church in 90 c.e. (J. A. T. Robinson, 1962; 139–53). The argument in this case is based on the speech found in Acts 3: 12–26. This speech, John Robinson points out, possesses certain curious features. There is not the space here to go into the technicalities of Robinson's argument; sufficient to say that he has made a strong case in support of the view that there was an extremely primitive Christology in the community of disciples at Jerusalem, 'whose essence may be summed up in the proclamation: We know who the Messiah *will be*' (present writer's emphasis). This was a view of Jesus as *the* Prophet of God, who appeared among men with the good news of God and with a final call to repentance, in preparation for the final eschatological event which lay in the not too distant future 'which would inaugurate the messianic rule of God and vindicate him as the Christ'. This certainly would accord better with the Messianic ideas of the Old Testament and of the apocalyptic literature (*3.19*), that the

Messiah, as Messiah, would appear once and finally. The later Christian view is that there is a *Second* Coming of the Messiah, based on the assumption that the ministry of Jesus was the First Coming of the Messiah *as Messiah*. This notion 'that the Christ was to come, not only once, but twice' was, as Robinson comments, 'unprecedented in Judaism'. Hence what we may have in Acts 3 (together with Acts 7) is something which may be described as the original Christology of the early community in Jerusalem, the Christology of the Prophet, 'which lies embedded in the book of Acts like the fossil of a by-gone age'.

3.47 *A possible answer*

The question remains whether it is possible, even now, to discover anything of the original historical realities which lie beneath the later theological interpretation of them. Some Christian scholars take the view that this is unnecessary and pointless, since, they say, it is only in the perspective of fuller experience and the development of the Christian community that the historical reality is properly understood. In this view, the modern Christian is nearer to a proper appreciation of Jesus than was the first generation of disciples in Jerusalem. There is, on the other hand, the possibility that the passage of time has the effect of obscuring as well as illuminating earlier insights. The impact of great moments of religious experience can be weakened by the many other forces which intervene to influence individuals and societies, forces which are historical, political, economic and social. Too often orthodox Christian theologians seem to assume that Christian history has taken place in a clear vacuum, so that the farther we move away from the historical Jesus, the fuller and more complete is the view of him that we shall obtain. This is to deny the existence of the intervening factors and forces which may have rolled in like fog to blot out or obscure the distant scene; it is also to deny the value of historical research.

There is, as we have seen, evidence that until the beginning of the activities of one who had had no experience of the original events, the non-Palestinian Jew, Paul, the disciples of Jesus of Nazareth considered themselves to be witnesses to a great Prophet who had brought to men a new and supremely important revelation of God. Like the Hebrew prophets of an earlier period, he had achieved this both by his teaching, and by his personal involvement in the affairs of men and his fate at their hands. There is a stubborn element of the historical material that has survived more strongly in the earlier synoptic Gospels (Mark, Matthew and Luke) than in the later Gospel of St John, where it has been smoothed away by a developing theology, namely the rejection of the notion of *power* as this is commonly understood, especially as it is understood by those who exercise secular power. What the Prophet seemed to be teaching was very hard for even those closest to him to grasp: that the kingship (or kingly rule, or kingdom) of God is no kingship at all as this is generally thought of. Monarchy had corrupted Israel's monotheism; Yahweh had become an oriental potentate: such was the view of God which had come to be accepted; such were the ideas which underlay the Jewish attitude which, even at that time, can be called a kind of Zionism. The reality of which this Prophet spoke, however, was one which was most compellingly encountered in the situation where all the normal criteria of power were most conspicuously absent. It was a form of teaching which vindicated itself to the Prophet's followers most clearly in the Prophet's own suffering and violent death. A humble birth, an upbringing in a particularly despised village (John 1: 46), the patient acceptance of suffering and violence, and finally, a broken human body hanging on a post: here is a very different picture of the divine nature from that held by most of the Jews of the time, and one which has not always been accepted by the Christian Church. This was an overturning of the Near Eastern potentate conception of the divine being, but in spite of it the potentate conception has persisted in Western theology.

3.48 The fusion of the two types of early Christianity

In his book *The Fall of Jerusalem and the Christian Church*, S. G. F. Brandon has shown that there was a period in the early development of Christianity when the two types of thought, the Pauline and that of the Jerusalem church, existed side by side. St Paul, who had not known the historical Jesus, had by virtue of a visionary experience come to believe that Jesus of Nazareth had been the messianic Saviour-God through whom the demonic powers had been conquered and the messianic era inaugurated. On the basis of this belief he had built up communities of Gentile Christians in various cities of the Mediterranean world. Over these communities he exerted considerable personal authority. Their most important devotional practice was 'the Supper of the Lord' which Paul explained as a regular 'showing-forth of the death of the Lord' until his full manifestation, or parousia, which was expected to occur at any time. In the community of disciples at Jerusalem the emphasis was upon the figure of the historical Jesus of Nazareth, prophet of God to the Jewish people. This community originally regarded itself as a challenging and revitalising sect within Judaism, recalling Jews to a true and proper allegiance to God.

For a while these two movements existed side by side, each influencing the other to some extent, but also conscious of serious differences and tensions with regard to the question whether or not Gentiles should be admitted, and with regard to the importance of the Torah. The arrest of Paul and his removal from the scene meant a temporary eclipse of the Pauline Gentile-Christian communities, so that by about 65 C.E., just before the outbreak of Jewish revolt against the Romans in Jerusalem, 'the future of the nascent movement appeared to lie irretrievably in the hands of the Jewish Christians' (Brandon, 1957; 249). The Jewish revolt, however, involving war with the Romans and the destruction of Jerusalem in 70 C.E. 'dynamically changed the whole constitution of the Church, and vitally affected the future development of its organisation' by 'the complete obliteration of the Church of Jerusalem' (Brandon, 1957; 250). The fall of the Jewish state and the destruction of Jerusalem had the effect also among the Christian communities of rehabilitating St Paul's reputation, argues Brandon, and of reviving the influence of his teaching. After 70 C.E., therefore, the Christian movement was reborn: there was a fusion of the Pauline idea of the Saviour-God, and of devotion to the historical person of Jesus which had been characteristic of the Jerusalem Church, a fusion which finds expression in the canonical Gospels. It was this which now transformed the early Christian movement, removing it once and for all from the old context of Judaism, and allowing it to move out unhindered into the Hellenistic-Roman world as a universalist Saviour-God cult.

3.49 The increasing importance of Rome

Even before the fall of Jerusalem in 70 C.E. the Christian movement had its adherents in many of the larger cities of the Graeco-Roman

Mediterranean world: Antioch, Caesarea, Alexandria, Corinth, Ephesus, Philippi and Rome. In all these and other cities and towns small groups of Christians were to be found, mostly from the lower classes of society, meeting together in private houses for prayer, for teaching and discussion, and for participation in the Supper of the Lord. Christianity from this time is a religion which has its greatest appeal to people of urban areas. Especially in Rome, the imperial capital, there seems to have been a community of considerable size, or a group of communities, associated with various households, to judge from the list of greetings which St Paul adds at the end of his letter to the Christians at Rome (Rom. 16: 3–16). Christians had become numerous enough there for the Roman authorities to be aware of their existence. They seemed to be a secret society, which as Tacitus noted (*3.41*) derived its name from a criminal who had been 'executed at the hands of the procurator Pontius Pilate in the reign of Tiberius'. From past experience, the Romans had a horror of religious secret societies. The Christians of Rome therefore provided the emperor Nero with a convenient scapegoat: in 65 C.E. he declared they had tried to set fire to the city, and punished them by having them smeared with pitch and burned at night in his own gardens. The Neronian persecution did not destroy the Christian community at Rome, however, and after the fall of Jerusalem in 70 C.E. the community of Christians in Rome emerged as one of special importance with the removal from the scene of what had until then always been regarded, especially after St Paul's arrest, as the source of authority, namely the mother-church of Jerusalem. The centre of gravity for Christians now shifted, therefore, to the imperial city, a shift with very important consequences for the subsequent development of the Christian religion.

SUMMARY AND COMMENT ON CHAPTER THREE

At the conclusion to Chapter Two (p. 110) it was noted that prophetic breakthrough, the reception by a particular individual of some new insight into the human condition and situation, does not occur universally; that is to say, historically it has occurred in some societies but not in others. We have now to take account of what is a complementary factor, one that makes possible the correcting of the balance of knowledge and insight between one tradition or society and another, namely the fact of *diffusion*. By the diffusion of ideas and new discoveries, what was originally peculiar to one society can come to be shared by all. A great deal of the history of religion is in fact the history of the diffusion of religious ideas beyond the culture in which they originated.

Jewish thought, for example, in the period after the Exile in Babylon (sixth–fifth centuries B.C.) and before the rise of the Christian Church, was considerably influenced, especially during the Persian ascendancy, by Zoroastrian ideas. On the whole, as we have seen, the Jews had good reason to be well disposed towards things Persian, since it was the Emperor Cyrus who had enabled Jews to return from Babylon and set about the rebuilding of their desolated city and Temple. This was at a time when Zoroastrian religion was in its early vigour; the Prophet of Persia had set men's minds thinking in new ways about the spiritual forces that shaped men's lives. Human life was seen within the context of a cosmic struggle between good and evil powers; man's vocation was to take his part in the struggle, resisting the evil powers and aided by the good. It was a struggle which was to culminate in the victory of good at the end of the age; all that was good, including the physical creation, the work of the Lord of Wisdom, and man's physical bodies, would be restored and established and the evil powers banished for ever. Hence we find in Jewish thought during the centuries before the Christian era the emergence of ideas of angels and archangels, including angels of darkness; ideas of a final consummation and resurrection. Not all Jews accepted these new ideas; some accepted the doctrine of physical resurrection, others, the Sadducees, rejected it. Jewish apocalyptic literature was full of the warfare of the spirit powers, and the great eschatological events that were to bring this warfare to an end. It was expressed in Jewish terms, it was developed within the context of characteristically religious ideas concerning God and man; but it was in very large measure a way of thought which had developed first in Persia.

Such diffusion of religious beliefs, of which many other examples are to be found in the history of religion, requires the presence of certain favourable conditions: a predisposition in favour of the culture from which the ideas come, or, at least, the absence of actual antipathy; a situation within the receiving culture that provides a fertile ground for the incoming ideas to take root. One of the most favourable situations is that in which there is a sense of inadequacy of old ways of thinking, or the breakdown of existing moral or social structures, the condition known to sociologists as anomie. But there must also be sufficient strength and coherence and cogency in the new ideas, for sometimes the favourable conditions may be present without any really satisfactory new doctrines; in that case no new development can take place. When it does this is partly at least a tribute to the worth of the imported ideas. The fact that they are welcomed and accepted, as in the case of Zoroastrian ideas in Judaism, indicates that they have a power of appeal beyond the confines of their area of origin, a cogency which is recognised even in alien cultures, providing men with a way of understanding the human situation which they recognise as an advance on earlier ways of thought. This is true, of course, of human knowledge in general. The making of new discoveries and their dissemination and acceptance over a wide area is a large part of the story of civilisation.

In principle, therefore, one cultural area has no sufficient reason to be suspicious of ways of thought that are until now alien to it, *simply because they are alien*. To give a modern illustration of this, the West has no grounds for entertaining suspicion of Buddhist ideas simply because they are Buddhist, rather than Semitic, or Greek, or even modern Western scientific. Buddhist ways of thought are not necessarily in conflict with Western ideas, and may in fact be capable in certain ways of enriching Western thought.

Another important point which must be noticed in connection with the diffusion of doctrines is that such diffusion entails also differentiation. Men become aware of contrasting views of life, or theories of human destiny. An example of this we have seen in Judaism: the influx of Persian ideas in the post-Exilic period brought about a sharp differentiation between those who accepted the doctrine of resurrection, mainly the Pharisees and their sympathisers, and those who did not, mainly the Sadducees. In modern times the knowledge of Buddhist doctrines has spread to the West, just as some knowledge of Western religious ideas has spread to Asia, with the result that there has been a sharpening of the difference between on the one hand the ancient Near Eastern doctrine of an omnipotent creator, and on the other hand agnosticism about such a doctrine. To the Jew and the Muslim, and to many Christians, especially of the more Augustinian type, it seems that human life would be deprived of all ultimate meaning without the basic notion of an omnipotent being who by his own word of authority had brought the universe into existence, and who directs and is responsible for all that happens. To the Buddhist on the other hand, it seems that it is the acceptance of such a doctrine which deprives life of any intelligible meaning and evacuates it of spiritual purpose. In the Pali Buddhist scriptures the argument used is based on the presence of evil in the world; it is a familiar one, apart from its use by Buddhists: if God is really *lord* of the whole world, then why has he ordained misfortune in the world? For what purpose has he made the world full of injustice, deceit, falsehood and conceit? Is not the creator of all things evil in that he has ordained injustice when there could have been justice? (Jayatilleke, 1963; 260f., 410f.) More positively, the objection from the Buddhist point of view is to what may be called 'theistic determinism', that is to say the theism which means accepting unquestionably all that happens in the world as being God's will, whether it be good or evil. ('Does evil befall a city, unless the LORD has done it? Amos 3: 6) This basically Jewish view, the corollary of belief in a god who is an absolute potentate, modified in post-Exilic times by the influence of Zoroastrian dualism, but reappearing later in a more vigorous form in Islam, when it is encountered by Buddhists meets with the objection from them that it is likely 'to stifle the human liberty to investigate, to analyse, to scrutinise, to see what is beyond this naked eye, and so to retard insight' (Piyadassi, 1964; 59). The Buddhist objects to a theism which implies that man is not responsible for his actions. This latter is considered by Buddhists a false proposition, and any theism which depends on it must therefore be rejected.

These, then, are some of the immediate results of diffusion of doctrines – the interplay of criticism among the various points of view which are thus thrown into contact with each other. Another important result is not only the acceptance of new doctrines in the way we have already noticed in connection with post-Exilic Judaism, but also the provision of the conditions for the emergence of wholly new insights – or, to resume the earlier terminology, of a new prophetic breakthrough. Historically this is what appears in the case of emergent early Christian belief. As far as it is possible now to recover the belief of the Jerusalem community this appears to have centred around the conception of Jesus as the Prophet in whom was glimpsed the Messiah *who was to come* (3.47), that is, at the end of the age, at the consummation of human history. In distinction from this was the Pauline conception of the heavenly Jesus, the divine Saviour of man. Now it has to be recalled that there was nothing new in Jewish thought in the idea of God as saviour, nor in human saviours raised up by God as instruments of his purpose. It has been pointed out that this was the message of Israel's religion: 'Its history is the history of saviours, i.e., of organs and instruments of the divine salvation, human all of them . . .' (*E.R.E.*, XI, 115). What was new in the Pauline doctrine was the assertion that Jesus, as saviour, was not merely a human agent, but was himself divine. For the Christians God was no longer a being whose attributes were described by seers and prophets; their primary knowledge of the character of God was derived from what they knew of the victory of this crucified teacher. A new position was established in the realm of theology: the essentials of man's knowledge of the divine are derived from the essentials of men's knowledge of Jesus. It is basically this position which is affirmed by the modern theologian Karl Barth, who strenuously argues against every attempt, such as that of 'natural theology', to establish human knowledge of God other than by what is known of Jesus.

The diffusion of religious ideas had brought together a very rich mixture in Palestine at the time of the emergence of the Christian community. In some senses there was nothing new in the Christian religion – nothing, that is to say, which could not be traced to its roots in some other religious tradition – the ideas of Messiah, Saviour, resurrection from the dead, the ethical teaching of Jesus, the conception of the infinitely loving nature of God – for all of these we need look no further than Judaism itself, as it had developed by that time, enriched to no little degree by the infusion of ideas from elsewhere. Yet there was in another sense a real prophetic breakthrough, and it is this which was the primary reason for the initial expansion of the Christian faith in the Mediterranean world. The conviction that a totally new strain of humanity had appeared in Jesus of Nazareth was held with such intensity that it could only be expressed by speaking of his nature as divine. Moreover, along with this among the earliest disciples there was the conviction that it was this Man who was to be the eschatological figure, the Messiah, whose future appearance would inaugurate the consummation of all things. This future appearance of the Man they had glimpsed in Jesus, the Messiah, would contrast with the brief glimpse they had received, which had been partial, limited to a few people, and of temporary duration; for it would be complete, universal and of an eternal nature. These were the convictions which fused together in the faith of the early Christians, and in their view it was not a new doctrine or set of doctrines, but *Jesus of Nazareth himself* who was the 'prophetic breakthrough'. It was for this reason, they held, that at his name 'every knee should bow in heaven and on earth and under the earth'.

It is important to note the distinction between this faith and the earlier forms of theistic faith. In the latter the conception of deity had been derived in no small measure from the manner in which power was exercised by human potentates, for the historical reasons we have noted. The Christian conception of deity is derived from the strange kind of power exercised by Jesus, the crucified, helpless, yet strangely powerful victim of violence. These two conceptions of deity are by no means reconcilable; but that is not to say that the attempt to reconcile them has not been made. It has frequently been made in the course of European Christian history, as we shall shortly observe.

4 Creeds and Conformity

4.1 CHRISTIANITY: FROM JEWISH SECT TO ROMAN STATE-RELIGION (70–500 C.E.)

4.10 The Jewish basis of the Christian concept of scripture

FOR the reason given in the Introduction (p. xxiii), we shall not at this point attempt to engage in anything like the full study of Christian history that the abundance of material makes possible, or even to provide a complete outline survey. Rather, in accordance with a more limited purpose, we shall merely touch on some of the more important issues in Christian history which are specially appropriate to a comparative historical study of religion.

One of the most important of these, for the period we are now surveying, is the growth of a body of sacred literature, and the movement towards a general consensus on which books were and which were not to be included as canonical. It is important, in the first place, to notice that this is something that the early Christian sect inherited from its parent Judaism. The concept of 'holy scripture' was central to Judaism, with its preoccupation with the books of the Law, and its unceasing study of them, since they were held to provide basic guidance on all affairs of human conduct and relationships. This attitude to scripture is something which originally was peculiar to Judaism, although it passed from Judaism into Christianity and Islam. As Bethune-Baker put it, for the Christian as for the Jew, 'a kind of glamour hung over the written words. They were invested with an importance and impressiveness which did not attach to any spoken words, giving them an existence of their own' (Bethune-Baker, 1903; 49). The reason for this lay in the idea that these writings were divinely inspired down to the last jot and tittle, a view which was fostered by the Jewish scribes from Ezra (3.13) onwards. The Alexandrian Jew, Philo, regarded even the grammatical errors of the Septuagint, the Greek translation of the Jewish scriptures, as divinely inspired, for he

said they provided a basis for religiously valuable allegorical interpretation.

4.11 The development of Christian literature

At first, Christians adhered to the Jewish 'Law and Prophets' as the
definitive form of inspired writing, and sought to prove all controversial
questions on matters of belief and practice by an appeal to these.
Traditions about Jesus were seen in the light of the idea that the events
of his life happened 'in order that it might be fulfilled as it was spoken
by the prophet . . .'. Then, as Christian literature began to accumulate,
the practice of venerating a sacred text began to attach itself to Christian
writings also. The maxim 'All scripture is inspired by God' (2 Tim. 3:
16) used by an early Christian meant originally 'All *Jewish* scripture is
inspired by God' – rather than, for example, the writings of Homer,
though these too were, for the Greeks, invested with the glamour of
divine inspiration. But the application of this maxim by Christians to
certain writings of their own did eventually follow, although the
process of deciding which were and which were not to be so regarded
took some time. Among the earliest to gain this status were the letters
of certain apostles: 'a letter coming from a teacher or a church of great
authority would interest Christians generally, and so get copied and
circulated and read, long after the original occasion of its dispatch had
passed by, in churches other than that to which it had first come'
(Bevan, 1932; 44).

Besides the primary interest in the Pauline supernatural Christ, the
Saviour who had conquered the demonic forces of sin and death, and
the explication of these ideas for Christian believers that the apostolic
letters were concerned to convey (as well as instruction in Christian
conduct), there was also a very natural interest among Christians in the
historical Jesus, that is, in that element which was contributed especially
by the Jerusalem community; this too began to be reflected in the
appearance of a narrative type of literature which, since such books had
as their object the setting forth of the historical basis of the 'good news',
became known by the short title, 'Good News' or 'Gospel'. There were
many of them; some were eventually relegated to the position of
private or 'apocryphal' works; others were accepted as authoritative
and acceptable for public reading in the communities. These were

finally four in number, attributed to Mark, Matthew, Luke and John respectively. The last named, written towards the end of the first Christian century (? 95 C.E.), and differing considerably in outlook from the other three, was only accepted after some hesitation. The process of sacralisation of these books was fairly slow; there was an intermediate stage at which it became necessary simply to make some kind of distinction between accepted and non-accepted books, because of the need to distinguish between authoritative Christian teaching and ideas of teachers who, while claiming to be Christian, were seen by the majority to be subverting the essential historical basis of the Christian faith. We must now consider how this came about.

4.12 The challenge of Gnosticism

At least since the time of the Persian empire of Cyrus (*3.12*), on through the time of the Greek empire of Alexander and his successors (*3.15*), religious ideas and practices from India (mainly Hindu) and Persia (mainly Zoroastrian) had been spreading westwards to mingle with Greek and Minoan elements to form a new religious syncretism which was found throughout the Mediterranean world. One of the most outstanding products of this is the family of cults and doctrines known as Gnosticism. The basic theme of Gnosticism was that of escape from the present material world, which was regarded as basically evil, the creation of a demiurge or inferior god, into another sphere where it would be possible to enjoy the pure life of the spirit, a sphere which was held to be the true home of the divine spark within man. How to attain this higher, spiritual realm was the concern of the various Gnostic cults; in general its attainment was believed to be by knowledge (gnosis) of a divine saviour who alone could effect the soul's release. Such salvation was for the 'spirit' of man; not for the flesh or the body. The flesh is evil, said the Gnostics, and only by breaking free from it can man find the life of the spirit, and return to his true home. He cannot break free himself; a divine saviour must come from above, from the realm of pure spirit down through the increasingly gross emanations which lie between the spiritual realm and the evil world, a saviour who will rescue the soul of man and return it to its home. Knowledge of the saviour was the all-important requirement so far as men were concerned.

To those who thought in these terms, the Christian gospel, especially as preached by St Paul, appeared to be an excellent Gnostic system. In Pauline soteriology men whose thoughts were moulded in this way recognised the gnosis they had been seeking and were strongly attracted to it; not only for its central Saviour-figure, the Christ who had conquered sin and death and all the stoicheia, or elementary spirits of this world, and was able to guarantee man's entry into 'the life of the ages', but also for its strict asceticism, its insistence upon the need to crucify the flesh, and its encouragement of celibacy.

There thus developed by the second Christian century what may be described as a Gnosticised version of Christian belief and practice.

It must be added that the foregoing is the more commonly accepted view of the relationship between Gnosticism and early Christian belief, but another view is that Gnosticism was itself a Christian heresy, produced, that is to say, within the Christian community from an over-emphasis on certain elements of Pauline Christology; it has been suggested that the Gnostic development within Christianity was the work of over-zealous apologists, men who were concerned at all costs to make the Christian faith relevant to men of the second-century Mediterranean world.

Whichever of these views is the more accurate, the fact remains that there had developed by the second century a Gnostic version of Christian belief and practice which was condemned by non-Gnostic Christians as a deviation from the original doctrine. It was in this connection that the use of the word 'heresy' first appeared in Christian usage to describe such deviation, a term which once introduced was to enjoy currency for a long period of Christian history, and even today is still regarded in some Christian circles as a relevant, necessary and very useful concept.

From the perspective of the modern situation, perhaps the most important Christian response to the challenge of Gnosticism can be seen to be that made by St Irenaeus, bishop of Lyons (c. 130–c. 202 C.E.). Man does not live in this world as a prisoner within alien territory, territory which is ruled over by an inferior deity or evil power from which he must be liberated and taken back to his true home, as the Gnostics affirmed; in Irenaeus's view the whole history of human existence is one of progress from immaturity towards perfection, and it is this which explains life's present imperfections: 'by nature we are adapted for virtue; not so as to be possessed of it from our birth, but so as to be adapted for acquiring it.' Man, said Irenaeus, 'was not perfect in his creation, but adapted to the reception of virtue...' (Hick, 1966; 222). It has recently been pointed out that this view of the human situation provides, within Christian theology, a very important alternative to that other view which has largely dominated the thought of the Christian West, namely that of Augustine (*4.18*). 'Instead of the doctrine that man was created finitely perfect and then incomprehensibly destroyed his own perfection and plunged into sin and misery (i.e., the doctrine of Augustine), Irenaeus suggests that man was created as an imperfect, immature creature who was to undergo moral development and growth and finally be brought to the perfection intended for him by his Maker' (Hick, 1966; 220). Irenaeus was the first Christian theologian to work out such a view of man's nature and destiny; it is a view which for various reasons has been obscured in the West by that of Augustine.

4.13 Christian resistance to Gnosticism

It is clear from the anti-Gnostic Christian writings of the second century that Christian leaders were seriously concerned at the threat of a Gnostic take-over. The local communities of believers were often exposed to infiltration by Gnostic teaching; some Christians succumbed to the new trend; others saw that it was a serious distortion of the original tradition. There were three major issues between the latter and the Gnostic Christians. First, the Gnostics identified Yahweh, the God of Israel, with the inferior god, the creator of the evil, physical world, and for this reason Gnosticism was on the whole strongly anti-Jewish. Second, the Christian idea that the divine Saviour had actually suffered and died was rejected by the Gnostics: a divine being could not suffer, and most certainly could not suffer death. They therefore introduced the idea that the Jesus of Christian tradition had been not a real human being but only by outward appearance human. (From the Greek verb dokein 'to seem' this doctrine became known as Docetism.) Another Gnostic idea was that the divine Saviour who had inhabited the body of Jesus had returned to heaven before the Passion so that it was only a 'seeming' death, an illusion to deceive the evil spirit-powers of this world. Third, since it was held by the Gnostics that it was by sexual reproduction that the divine spark imprisoned in man was transmitted to other bodily prisons, their attitude to married life such as Jews and

Christians normally practised was one of hostility: some sought to prevent procreation by taking refuge in celibacy, while others debased the sexual relationship with the aid of some rather disagreeable contraceptive practices (Bevan, 1932; 69).

It is worth noting that the resistance to Gnosticism on these three fronts came pre-eminently from that tradition within the Christian community which owed most to the Jerusalem disciples. Primarily it was by emphasis upon the Jewish idea of the goodness of the created world, on the real humanity and real death of the historical Jesus, and on the moral law, that Christians succeeded in countering the subversive Gnostic influences. It was pointed out that the deliverance man needs is not from his sinful flesh but from his own state of moral discord, his lack of harmony with the life of God, so that salvation is not a release from the physical conditioning of bodily life, but a transforming of this, and a redirection of effort. It was further argued against the Gnostics that in the Christian view the divine life is not far off, remote from this empirical world, and separated from it by countless emanations; this was reinforced by the Christian insistence that Jesus was a real man in the fullest possible sense, who demonstrated the quality of the divine life in his own real death. It is significant that the theology of Rudolf Bultmann with its reliance upon the idea of an existential Christ-event, not dependent on historical verification, has been seen by some as a new form of Gnosticism, to be met in the same way in the twentieth century as in the second, by an insistence upon the reality of the historical Jesus, and on those things concerning him which *can* be known from the testimony of contemporary witnesses.

4.14 *The importance of Origen*

One of the great names in the Christian struggle with Gnosticism – and there are many – was Origines Adamantius, known in the West now simply as Origen. Born in Alexandria about 186 C.E., he died some seventy years later after imprisonment and torture. He has been described as 'the first theologian to put out a full and methodical exposition of the whole intellectual framework of the Christian faith' (Prestige, 1940; 60). If the danger of Gnosticism lay in its uncontrolled emotionalism, its obscurantism, and its wild speculation, the proper response was that which Origen exemplified – a balanced emphasis on the rational, historical and experiential elements in Christian thought and practice. The rational power of the human mind was, Origen maintained, capable of a genuine apprehending of truth. It has been said that the Church owes it first and foremost to Origen that, whenever Christianity is true to itself, it shows itself to be a rational faith. But there were also Christian presuppositions which inevitably rendered Origen's task extremely difficult, if they were accepted. For Origen was faced with the task of reconciling virtually irreconcilable data. These data were: the notion of an absolutely omnipotent Creator God; the notion that this God is one and indivisible (monotheism); the notion that Jesus, a real human person, was also identical with the God who had already been defined in these terms; and, finally, the literal truth of the inspired sacred writings, the Bible. Origen's exposition was successful and coherent in its way, but was based on a modified view of the literal truth of the Bible. Whatever presented historical difficulties or was morally offensive Origen interpreted in an allegorical way. He treated much of the Book of Revelation, for example, in this fashion. In his doctrine of God he distinguished between the Father who alone is God, and unbegotten, and the Son, or Logos who is a second god, the divine Wisdom, subordinate to God. The Logos brought into existence a multitude of souls, who thereafter adhered more or less closely to the author of their being; those who adhered less closely tended to fall away and developed material forms within a physical universe. Such souls are credited by Origen with the ability to rise or fall in the scale in a way that is very closely related to the Indian notion of karma and rebirth (*1.32*). At the highest level are ethereal souls, angels and principalities; then men of varying degrees of goodness; animals; and lowest in the scale, the demons and Satan. All, however, would at last return to a state of communion with the Logos.

For the vast majority of his contemporaries Origen's exposition was too metaphysical. It is perhaps significant that the people of Egypt, and Syria (Origen removed to Caesarea at the age of forty-six and died in Tyre at the age of sixty-nine) did not respond favourably to what was virtually an exposure to Hindu thought; they believed and insisted on believing in a God whom they thought of as an anthropomorphic celestial being. Above all, such philosophising conflicted with many statements in the scriptures about God which they took in a literal sense. This was one of the Christian presuppositions Origen was prepared to dispense with, but the majority were not, and such metaphysical speculation was therefore largely rejected. The Catholic Church does not afford Origen the title of Saint.

4.15 The routinisation of the Christian religion

The Christian struggle against Gnosticism coincided with the process of routinisation of the religious life of Christianity, and to some extent helped to accelerate it. By this is meant the process, observable in various religious systems, whereby after a new breakthrough (*1.26*) of religious thought and practice there follows a settling down to accepted forms of organisations and patterns of thought. In the period represented by the New Testament writings, that is, up to the last decade of the first century, the Christian communities were largely independent local groups, acknowledging, however, that they together formed a single community of believers, the ecclesia, among whom a special authority belonged to those who had experienced the vision of the risen Jesus, the apostles. With the passing away of the apostolic generation, combined with the threat of subversion by Gnosticism, there was a need for some way of safeguarding the essentials of Christian faith, and thus we find in the letters of Ignatius the bishop of Antioch (who was martyred in Rome in 115 c.e.) a new development: the Christian communities were being urged to be loyal to the leadership of their local 'pastors' or 'bishops' and to acknowledge their authority, and so to hold together against the threat of heresy and disintegration. Among the local churches one in particular was singled out by Ignatius as possessing special authority, namely the church in Rome, the church associated especially with one of the foremost of the disciples, St Peter, which was to be regarded by Christians as the guardian of the true faith. Thus, towards the close of the second Christian century St Irenaeus, bishop of Lyons, names the church in Rome as the special bearer of the historical Christian faith, and able to provide guidance and sound teaching in the conflict with Gnosticism. The rudiments of a hierarchical structure now began to appear: the president or 'bishop' of the local community as the authority within that community, to whom its members must rally in loyalty and obedience; and among communities the gradual further emergence. after the fall of Jerusalem, of Rome as the pre-eminently authoritative bearer of the orthodox faith.

Another aspect of the process of routinisation was the trend towards an established consensus on the canon of scripture. By the end of the second Christian century this was virtually complete and most of the books of the New Testament as it now exists had been afforded universal recognition, although a few were still accepted in one place but not in another, notably James, Jude, Hebrews and the Apocalypse. Christianity was thus well on the way to becoming, like Judaism, the religion of a book (or, more exactly, a collection of books).

Yet another development was the routinisation of practice. Certain ways of carrying out the important devotional ceremonies such as baptism and the Supper of the Lord (by this time known as the Eucharist) were prescribed. A document discovered in 1875 at Constantinople, known as the *Didache*, or Teaching (of the Twelve Apostles), sets out in systematic fashion the essential procedure for the rite of baptism, for the celebration of the Eucharist, the correct attitudes to leaders and teachers, and so on.

It was the Eucharist which undoubtedly by the end of the second century, if not earlier, had become the focal point of Christian religion, the specifically Christian rite which drew together the various strands that went to make up the religious life and belief of the Christian. The word 'Eucharist' means thanksgiving, and the fact that this was the central rite characterises the religion of the early Christian community as pre-eminently the religion of thanksgiving: thanks rendered to God for the objective fact of man's salvation which the events of the life and death of Jesus were seen to be; thanks for the new life together into which the followers of Jesus had entered; thanks shown in practical terms by the rendering up of themselves to God's service, and their economic resources for the use of the needy, the sick and the distressed. 'The one word "Eucharist" fitly described the mood and quality of Christian devotion. . . . The Eucharist, whether as the great moment of the cult, or as the chief food of the individual, constituted the essential thing in the regimen of Christian living and conduct, as well as the empowering motive of action . . . at the Eucharistic service the Gospel was expounded, Christian ideals of belief and conduct were explained, exhortation and instruction given.' Nor was this all. 'Succouring the needy, assisting the distressed, caring for the helpless and wronged were not thought of as by-products of Christianity. This type of social activity was of the very stuff not only of the Church's actions but of the Church's worship. "Gifts", "offerings" and "oblations" were carried to the very altar itself' (Gavin, 1932; 109f.). The Church was thus essentially a community, but it was a community within which distinctions had already been made between 'clergy' and 'laity'; the Eucharist was by the end of the second century a formal act of worship which could not take place, as the epistles of Ignatius make clear, 'apart from the bishop' (Srawley, 1947; 27). And it was a community distinguished from the rest of men in that only he could be a member of it, as St Justin said, 'who believes that the things we teach are true, and who has been washed (i.e. baptised) with the washing for the remission of sins, and for regeneration, and who is so living as Christ enjoined' (Gavin, 1932; 93). It was a community, membership of which was already beginning to be controlled by certain external forms, or institutions, namely the Creed, the rite of baptism, and church discipline. These things presupposed the exercise of authority within the Church; the principle is present at this period in embryo only, but from that embryo was to grow the ecclesiastical system of the Augustinian (or Constantinian) and medieval Church. In such ways as these, therefore, the scattered communities of Christians which were to be found in various parts of the Mediterranean world not only resisted disintegration by an alien ideology but also strengthened their position, internally and externally.

4.16 Controversies concerning the nature of Christ

One of the problems which Christians were forced to think out in their controversy with the Gnostics was that of the nature of Jesus, whether human, or divine, or both, and if so, how the natures were related in him. If he was really human, as Christians asserted against Gnostic docetic ideas (4.13), what then was his relation to God? How could the assertion of his real humanity be reconciled with the Christian tendency to regard him as revealing the divine nature? And how were the references in the New Testament writings to Jesus as the 'Son' of God to be interpreted? These are some of the questions considered, for example, by Origen (4.14), questions which continued to exercise the Church from the third century onwards, without fully satisfactory answers being worked out. The controversy in this area of Christian thought became extremely acrimonious at times, to say the least; it has to be noted, however, that the bitterness that was engendered among Christian leaders and pastors frequently had underlying causes other than theological disagreement; diplomatic intrigues, political conflict, and personal prestige can be seen to have been at least as important in the disputes that dragged on over the centuries as was concern for true doctrine. The course of the controversies was long and involved, and of a kind which cannot be summarised. An account which combines eminent readability with realism as to the underlying political issues as well as fair assessment of the religious values at stake was provided by G. L. Prestige in his *Fathers and Heretics* (1940).

Two aspects of these Christological controversies call for comment here. One is that the Christian community inherited a mixed bag of theological data which, if it is all accepted as of equal worth and indispensability, would probably defy indefinitely any fully logical or systematic presentation. From Judaism Christians inherited the idea of the literal truth of the Scriptures. The specifically Christian element was the conviction that Jesus was divine, and, as the Christian Scriptures from the Pauline epistles onwards declare, that he was the son of God. This specifically Christian contribution seemed incompatible with the monotheistic ideas of the Jews. Jews and Muslims therefore reject the idea of the divinity of Jesus, for it seems to them to involve the separate existences of two Gods. To say, on the other hand, that the only knowledge we have of the divine is from what we see in Jesus of Nazareth must involve at least a serious modification of the idea, inherited from the Near East, of God as an arbitrary, all-powerful monarch. The history of Christian thought shows, however, that Christians have tried to combine all these ideas, with the result that one of the great preoccupations of Western theology has been theodicy, the attempt to justify the ways of God to man. The attempt has failed as often as it has succeeded; yet the attempt has to continue, since the sacred tradition stemming from the period of the Hebrew monarchy seems to affirm this kind of potentate deity. And who may challenge anything contained in Scripture? The fact that Jesus of Nazareth did challenge *this* conception in particular has failed to gain full recognition. Among those for whom he is not an authority in religious matters, Jews and Muslims, this is perhaps inevitable. Again, for those Christians who do not accept that he challenged conceptions of God found in Hebrew scripture the potentate conception of deity remains. But for all of these kinds of Western religion the problems connected with belief in deity in terms of sovereign power remain, and will continue to embarrass those who hold this view, and will continue to repel many others to whom religious scepticism is preferable to religious belief of this kind.

In parenthesis it may be added that thoroughly consistent monotheism, that is, one based on the Eastern potentate conception of God, is found more clearly than anywhere else in Western religion in that tradition which rejects the reality of Jesus' crucifixion, namely Islam. In Islamic orthodoxy, one may see perhaps the ultimate form of monotheism of the kind that has its roots in the centralised political power structure of Egypt. The history of Islamic theology shows too that there is an inevitable implication of this kind of belief, namely, the complete and absolute predestination by the sovereign deity of all that happens in the world. Monotheism of this kind, if consistent, leaves no place for human freedom.

The challenging of the potentate concept of deity which is found whenever Christians say of Jesus Christ ('the Lamb that has been slain from the foundation of the world'), '*Here* is deity', or simply 'Jesus is Lord', is something which perhaps needs to be given much greater place in systematic theology than it has received in the past. The old, naturalistic potentate conception of a king has been allowed to invade what is meant by the kingship of Christ. In the latter case, the term 'king' is used, but *almost* in a satirical sense so far as the potentate concept is concerned, though not entirely. For there *is* kingship here, there *is* power; but not the quality of absolute omnipotence which some systematic theology seems to assume is a necessary presupposition about the nature of God.

The second main aspect of the Christological controversies which is important for the student of the history of religion is the depressing effect which all this had on the quality of religious life of Christendom. Here was one of the main factors which by the seventh century had predisposed large areas of the Mediterranean world that were nominally Christian, but weary of Christian theology's apparently endless disputations and feuds, to accept what to them appeared as the simpler, more straightforward and religiously more vital faith of Islam (*5.16*). This was specially true of Asia Minor, Syria and Egypt, where theological disputes were accompanied by public disorder.

Another theological product of these controversies was the doctrine of the Holy Trinity: God as Father, as Son, and as Holy Spirit. This has become an item of orthodox belief for Churches which adhere to the conciliar creeds, although the practical working belief of many theologically unsophisticated Christians more often approximates to a binitarian view, that is, a belief in God the Father, and in Jesus as God, the Second Person, but with a much diminished concern with God the Holy Spirit as a separate person. Belief in the threefold nature of the divine being is, however, not an uncommon phenomenon in ancient religion. The better known parallel cults are those of the Egyptian Isis, Serapis and the divine child Horus, or the Indian trinity of gods, Brahmā, Vishnu and Shiva; when Brahmā became less important the trio changed to Vishnu, Shiva, and Shakti the female deity. Mahāyāna Buddhist doctrine developed a conception of the three bodies of the Buddha, or Tri-kāya (4.34); the Neoplatonic theory of the Good, the Intelligence and the World-Soul is regarded by some as another parallel. It is important to notice that this Christian doctrine of the Trinity is one of the major grounds for Islamic criticism of Christian theology. To the Muslim it seems no better than equivocation to say that this is not a doctrine of three gods, and thus a movement towards polytheism. The Hindu, on the other hand, who is much more ready to affirm the existence of divine being in many forms, asks: If the Christian allows that God may exist as *three* persons, why not more? To Christians who held that the doctrine of the triune God was the ultimate truth Islam had to be rejected as a unitarian heresy.

Historically, the movement or system of thought known as Unitarianism emerged as a feature of the Protestant Reformation of the sixteenth century in many countries of Europe, although its adherents claim for their view an antiquity reaching back to before the age of the creeds. In the sixteenth century Unitarianism was one of the particular forms taken by the revolt against authoritarian and ecclesiastically controlled religion; in this case the emphasis was primarily intellectual.

4.17 The emperor Constantine and Christianity

During the first three centuries the attitude of the Roman imperial authorities towards Christianity had varied from indifference towards a harmless superstition or contempt for its apparent extravagances of thought, to active hostility and persecution when it appeared to be a danger to the state. Under the emperor Decius (249–52), for example, the full resources of the state were used in order to make Christians conform to the state religion. Some were tortured and killed rather than conform, though many others took the easy course. But this was soon over and the Church quickly regained its lost adherents. The last such persecution was in the reign of Diocletian; it began in 303 and lasted for ten years until in 313 the emperor Constantine granted full freedom of worship to Christians by the Edict of Milan.

Constantine is an enigmatic figure in his relation to Christianity. Proclaimed emperor of the western provinces of the Roman empire at York in 306, he granted Christians equality of religious rights in 313; in 324 he succeeded Licinius as emperor of the eastern provinces also and thus became the sole ruler of the whole Roman world. It was in the eastern provinces that disagreements among Christians were particularly fierce (*4.16*). Since the Christian population of the empire was now large and extensive, Constantine, desirous of securing peace in his realm, called a council of bishops from all parts of the empire which met at Nicaea in 325 and over which he presided; the majority of the bishops, however, were from the eastern part of the empire, with only a few from the Latin west. The council succeeded in framing a creed which was intended to provide an agreed statement of universal Christian belief, and thus to secure peace and harmony among the Christians of the empire. In fact, as the subsequent history of disputes shows, it failed to do this for more than a short period.

The question whether Constantine himself was a Christian is capable of various answers. There are broadly three views on the subject. The first is that he had a genuine conversion experience, a view which the story of his vision of the Cross in the sky is intended to support. Certainly the cross now became the symbol of the Church of the empire, but there is a possibility that its associations were with sun-worship as much as with Christianity (the symbol used by the early Christians had been the fish, since the letters of the Greek word *ichthus* (fish) were also the initial letters of the phrase Iesous Christos Theou Uios Soter – Jesus Christ, Son of God, Saviour); there is also the fact that the day for worship was called by its pagan name, in honour of the sun-god, Sunday. Constantine certainly continued to act as pontifex maximus of the pagan state religion; he received Christian baptism on his death-bed, but other Christians used to postpone baptism in this way in order to reduce the possibility of post-baptismal sin, so this in itself is not decisive. A second view is that he was a far-seeing statesman who perceiving that the future lay with the Christian religion rather than the old pagan state religion of Rome decided to gain the support of the everywhere increasing number of Christian citizens for the Roman state by giving Christianity an officially recognised position. A third view is that he remained thoroughly pagan at heart, a superstitious man who had a taste for collecting any new kind of religious talisman (Baynes, 1939).

Among the important results of the official Roman recognition of Christianity were, briefly, on the one hand a considerable improvement in the moral condition of Roman society, and on the other a greater degree of Romanisation of Western Christianity which now took into its system not only a good deal of state ceremonial, the use of Roman vestments at the liturgy, and so on, but also much of the spirit of Roman organisation – its hierarchical structure and its domination by legal principles and procedures. It had also the effect of assisting the growth of the Christian Church throughout the area ruled by Rome. Other results were the increasing use of force by the Church in the suppression of men of unorthodox religious opinions, or heretics; the increasingly enhanced role of the Christian priest so that he became elevated into a privileged position, and more and more distinguished and separated from his 'lay' fellow-Christians. Christianity became a state church, its ministers paid from official funds – some of which came from the old pagan temples – and the bishops important state officials, with the bishop of Rome continuing to grow in importance. Finally, while the empire now called itself Christian, its inhabitants were far from being Christian in any other sense, a fact which in subsequent history has affected the nature of the empirical reality called Christianity, especially as the non-Christian world sees it.

The history of Christianity in Europe is not one of sudden and dramatic conversions of large numbers of the native peoples to the Christian faith. The beginning was more tentative, and the whole story has been that of a gradual process of the Christianising of one area after another. In Britain, for example, during the period of Roman rule there would have been not a few servants of the empire and soldiers from Rome and Gaul who came to settle in this province and who were Christians. These people would have formed a kind of Christian aristocracy in Britain, so that even before Constantine made Christianity the official religion of the empire it would already have been growing in social esteem. But the new religion did not radically displace earlier pagan beliefs and customs; rather these were incorporated and Christianised. Many features of Christian religion as it emerged in the course of European history were adaptations of earlier beliefs and cults. Pagan polytheism found a new outlet in the veneration of the saints. Poseidon-Neptune, the guardian of sailors and boatmen, was succeeded by St Nicholas as their patron saint. The cult of the goddess Diana of Ephesus looks very strongly like a prototype of the cult of the Virgin Mary, who was first honoured as 'the mother of God' in that city. The idea of a virgin mother-goddess was by no means strange to the Roman world. The characteristic features of the Roman festival of Parentalia become transferred to the feast of All Souls, although on a different date in the calendar. Saturnalia, the festival of the promise of the sun's return, just after the shortest day, becomes the Christian festival of the birth of the Light of the World. The spring festival of the return of life, possibly in Britain the feast of the Saxon goddess Oestre, becomes the celebration of the risen life of Christ at Easter, linked with the spring festival of the Jews, Passover, which provided the authentically historical occasion for the remembering of the death of Jesus, even though at first the early Church had confined its celebration to the first day of the week as the day of resurrection, the Lord's Day. In these and many other ways local, national, or regional observances of a pre-Christian religious kind were absorbed and given a Christian aspect. The contribution which the pagan religious beliefs and practices of Europe have made to the actual historical character and shape of Christianity is an important one, one that is sometimes overlooked, and which still provides a rich field for study.

4.18 Monotheism, sin and St Augustine

One of the most notable first-fruits of Constantinian Christianity was St Augustine (354–430 C.E.). Born at Tagaste in North Africa, he is the last in the line of outstanding Fathers of the Church which North Africa produced. In his youth he was strongly attracted to the system of belief known as Manichaeism (from the name of its founder, Manes, born about 216 C.E.). This consisted basically of a dualistic view of the universe, of the kind in which the material world was regarded as the source of evil, and good was to be found only in the realm of spirit. The material, physical world was the realm of Satan; the spiritual world was God's realm; and these two were eternally at war with each other, both within the human individual and in the universe beyond.

The ideas of Manichaeism may have been derived ultimately from Zoroastrian dualism (*2.23; 2.24*), but this non-Zoroastrian, peculiarly pessimistic form of dualism, in which matter was regarded as inherently evil, is more properly regarded as part of the whole complex of Gnosticism (*4.12*). For nine years Augustine was an adherent of Manichaeism, and seems to have absorbed much of its characteristic outlook, especially its view of the fundamentally evil nature of the physical body. He went to Rome at about the age of twenty-nine, as a teacher of rhetoric. After a while his interest in Manichaeism waned in favour of Neoplatonic thought, which increasingly engaged his interest; this, too, subsequently provided an important element in Augustine's theology. In Milan he met and was powerfully influenced by Ambrose, the bishop of that city, and there experienced a dramatic conversion. He was baptised as a Christian in 387 c.e., to the joy of his pious Christian mother, and then returned to North Africa, where in 391 he was ordained priest in the diocese of Hippo. Four years later he succeeded to the bishopric of Hippo, where he remained for most of the remaining thirty-five years of his life.

Through his writings Augustine exercised a profound and long-lasting influence on Roman Christianity. During his lifetime the final collapse of the Roman secular power occurred, and when Rome was sacked by the Visigoth king Alaric in 410, and then North Africa invaded by Vandals in 430, the political empire of Rome was in ruins. But Christianity had been the official religion of the empire long enough to have absorbed its authoritarian spirit. By the time the political empire collapsed, the Church had gained positions of influence throughout the provinces over which Rome had ruled (*6.20*), so that, as H. A. L. Fisher puts it, 'the chaos of Empire was the opportunity of the Church'. Augustine's conception of the Church is, in a sense, an idealised version of the Roman empire: the City of God, embattled against the forces of evil and barbarism, but destined ultimately (unlike the Roman empire which collapsed because of internal corruption) to triumph over its enemies. It is not improper to ask who, in this conception of the Church, held the place corresponding with that of the emperor. In Augustine's view the ruler of the Church was, of course, God, and it can be seen how difficult it would have been for Augustine's conception of God to have escaped being shaped to some extent by the idea of an all-powerful emperor. All other considerations were sacrificed to the principle of 'God's sovereignty, which he maintained unflinchingly'. The Church thus becomes a theocratic state, and it is this idea which looms all-important in Augustinian thought; the secular state was regarded as an auxiliary, which might or might not serve the purposes of the eternal theocracy. Outside the Church there was certainly no salvation, in Augustine's view, and in the last resort physical force was justifiable against rebels or, in theological language, heretics. In keeping with Augustine's monarchical conception of God – for which he could certainly find support in the Scriptures, especially in the Jewish Scriptures, as we have already seen (*2.18*) – was his view of man as the humble subject of this heavenly monarch. Once again, as in the ascendancy of the monarchical idea of God in the time of the Hebrew monarchy (*2.19*), the notion of man's wretchedness and sinfulness was emphasised. By the fall, man lost all power to do anything good; all that he wills and does is evil. Man is the humble, even *base* creature, the subject who deserves only the penalty for his wickedness. God is the all-sufficient potentate, and it is solely by means of the grace which the monarch extends to his subject that there can be any relationship at all between them. The sinfulness of man was identified very closely in Augustine's thought with man's physical nature, and in particular with his sensuous and sexual nature; it was this emphasis which powerfully reinforced Western Christian tendencies to regard sexual activity as wicked, and celibacy as the ideal – in contrast to Jewish and Eastern Orthodox Christian attitudes. The grace of God, by means of which alone man has any freedom worth the name, that is, the state of freedom from any desire for sin, is extended to man in God's own wisdom; it is extended to some, but not to others. God's will alone decides the matter.

It is worth recalling that the tenor of Augustine's extremely authoritarian theology produced a reaction from a British monk, Pelagius. The story of Pelagius's resistance belongs to a more detailed history of Christian doctrine than can be provided here. That Pelagius found others to agree with him in regarding Augustine's theology as shocking and ultimately immoral and degrading is fairly clear; it is also clear that their protest was successfully muffled in a characteristically authoritarian way – by force (Bethune-Baker, 1903; 312–20). In both religious theory and in practical affairs Augustine was the product of Constantinian Christianity, and it was he who was to have the most powerful single influence on Western Christianity for at least a thousand years.

4.19 The beginnings of Christian monasticism

Mention has just been made of the British monk, Pelagius. This serves as a reminder that by the time of Augustine monasticism had become a fairly familiar feature of the Christian religion in Europe, and was to become so increasingly during the medieval period (6.22).

The beginnings of Christian monasticism were in Egypt in the third century. The full significance of this fact becomes apparent only when two other facts are considered together with it. The first of these is that the monastic way of life, by which is meant one of withdrawal from the world to a life of asceticism within a community of fellow ascetics, was alien to the early spirit, principles, and development of Christianity. At the close of the second century Tertullian made it his boast that 'among us are no Brahman or Indian gymnosophists, no forest hermits or anchorites . . . we abjure neither forum nor market-place nor baths nor books nor factories nor inns nor fairs nor the exchange. We sojourn with you in the world . . .' (Kirk, 1931; 179). The other fact to be noted is that there had been ascetic communities in Egypt long before Christians began to withdraw to the Egyptian desert to live the ascetic life. In other words, the monasticism of Egypt was in origin a non-Christian religious phenomenon. The ascetic community was, as Flinders Petrie (1909) showed, foreign to Egypt before the fourth century B.C. It was, however, established in Egypt by about 340 B.C., and it is clear that it had not come to Egypt from Palestine or Greece. Petrie therefore made the suggestion that the most obvious source of this newly appearing phenomenon in the Egypt of the fourth century B.C. was India. 'Figures of Indians have been found in Memphis, certainly dating from 200 B.C., and probably also earlier.' The most obvious period for the influx of Indian religious practices would have been the time when the Persian empire extended from North Africa to north-west India, that is, between 500 and 400 B.C. Moreover, the features of the life of the ascetic communities of Egypt correspond almost exactly with those of Indian asceticism: the celibate community, recruited regularly by converts; the renunciation of family and possessions, the rejection of wealth, the avoidance of bloodshed, and the vegetarian diet; the regular observance of a holy day; 'practically the whole system of life was that of Indian asceticism, planted as an ethical system, as it was preached later by Aśoka . . .' (Petrie, 1909; 83).

All this looks certainly remarkably like Indian Buddhist monasticism of the early period between the decease of the Buddha and the reign of Aśoka (*3.21; 3.26*). In the early years of the first century C.E. there were Egyptian ascetic communities known as the Therapeutae in the region of Alexandria, and the tradition seems to have been continuous up to the time it was taken over by Christianity in the fourth century (Petrie, 1909; 59–84).

For the first three centuries from its birth Christian religion appears to have been non-monastic, as Tertullian asserted. Towards the end of the third century the young Egyptian Christian, Antony, contrasting the life of the apostles with the comfort and superficiality of life in urban Egypt, withdrew to the neighbouring desert to live an ascetic life. While there is some doubt concerning the details of Antony's life there is no doubt that in broad outline the story is authentic, and that there were at that time others like him. By the early fourth century groups of Christian ascetics were living the common life (koinos bios) of asceticism, and hence were called cenobites. The real founder of the cenobitic, organised monastic life is usually held to be a contemporary of Antony, named Pachomius (d. 346 C.E.), who instituted monastic settlements in upper Egypt; these were independent communities linked by the observance of a common rule of life, not unlike that of the Buddhist Vinaya rules (*3.21*) (Kirk, 1931; 258). From the Egyptian desert the practice spread to other parts of the Christian world in the fourth century, and by the end of the century monastic life had become a feature of Christianity from the farthest east to the farthest west and north of the Roman empire, including Britain.

4.2 THE EMERGENCE OF HINDUISM (*70–500* C.E.)

4.20 *The caste system: further ramifications*

We have seen that by the beginning of the Christian era the characteristics of Hinduism as it is known in modern times had begun to be recognisable (*3.39*). One of the most important aspects of the reciprocal acculturation which had been going in the centuries before the Christian era between Brahmanism and the local village cultures was the further development of the caste system. There were various reasons for this.

One was the growth of formalised systems of ethics for particular classes of society (*3.39*); this would have had the effect of emphasising already existing differences among social classes. Another was the bringing within Hindu social structure of formerly non-brahmaniṣed tribes and groups as a result of the brāhman enterprise which was described earlier (*3.33*). In addition to the contribution to the already vast mythology which each of these might make, they would also result in a further multiplication of the number of jati (castes, or sub-castes), since each group, with its special beliefs and observances, would be incorporated bodily as a new sub-caste. A further reasoning for the hardening of caste differences was the continually increasing prosperity of the vaiśya or merchant castes; this would have the effect of making the brāhmans more than ever careful to defend their privileged position and emphasise their social superiority. In all of this it will be seen that there was very little which could be called a religious factor in the growth and elaboration of the caste system – a fact which needs to be borne in mind when the nature of the Indian caste system is being assessed. It was, however, provided with a *general* religious rationale by the doctrine of karma and rebirth, which afforded a convenient explanation of why some men enjoyed membership of a superior caste while others were less privileged: it was all the outworking of men's karma, good and bad. There is also an economic correlation so far as the lowest castes are concerned; the 'untouchables' whose touch is believed to pollute Hindus of other castes, are also the most economically depressed sector of society.

4.21 The growth of Hindu philosophy and literature

In the early years of the Christian era a classification of various Indian religious schools of thought was made from a brāhman point of view. The existing known schools of thought or philosophies of salvation were divided into two classes: those which were affirmed (*astika*), that is, the orthodox schools; and those which were not affirmed (*nāstika*), that is, the heterodox schools, such as the Jain and Buddhist, and the Cārvakas, or materialists. The orthodox schools were held to be six in number and were collectively known as the saḍḍarśana (six-viewpoints). They were set out in three groups of two, as follows. First, *Nyāya* and *Vaiśesika*; Nyāya is a system of logic and barely merits inclusion in a

scheme of salvation-philosophies; its inclusion was defended on the
grounds that clear thinking was necessary to enlightenment; Vaiśesika
is a doctrine of atoms similar in some ways to the Buddhist Abhidhamma
(3.22), in which the whole material universe is held to be composed of
atoms with special characteristics (viśesas) and all of which are subject
to the four non-material realities, namely, the soul, the mind, time, and
space. The second pair of schools is *Sāṇkhya* and *Yoga*. Sāṇkhya is
probably the oldest of the six, and is ascribed to a mythical teacher
named Kapila; its origin is probably to be found at the time of the
Buddha. It is an atheistic philosophy, which regards the universe as
having evolved from a basic given substance, prakṛti, not through any
divine creative activity or direction, but in accordance with its own
inherent nature. Alongside prakṛti there is puruṣa, the soul, an entity
which exists in infinite numbers, independent of prakṛti just as prakṛti
is independent of puruṣa. However, the soul tends to become involved
in the material processes of prakṛti, and salvation consists in being made
aware of its separateness from and independence of the material
universe. The Yoga school of thought, which is paired with Sāṇkhya,
taught that control and discipline of the body enabled the soul (puruṣa) –
which normally fails to distinguish itself from the world of matter
(prakṛti) – to do so, or to 'unveil the essence of the soul'. The main
difference between Sāṇkhya and Yoga is that the former is atheistic,
while the latter is not, but allows the existence of a being called Īśvara
(God) in the contemplation of whom the soul finds its own true nature,
and thus release, mokṣa, or salvation. The third pair of viewpoints are
Mīmāṃsā and *Vedānta*. Mīmāṃsā is based on the view that the Vedas
are eternal and authoritative and that salvation begins from a rigorous
observance of Vedic rules; in other words, Mīmāṃsā is a philosophical
form of Brahmanism. The Vedānta similarly accepts the authority of
the Veda, as its name indicates (veda-anta, the end, or consummation,
of the Veda) and is based particularly on the teaching of the Upaniṣads;
the Upaniṣadic teaching is summed up in the Vedānta basic text, the
Brāhma Sūtras of Bādarāyana, dating probably from the first century
of the Christian era. The Vedānta school is the most influential and
important of the six today, and forms the philosophical basis for most
modern Hindu thought (7.29). Its basic philosophy is that which has
already been described in connection with the Upaniṣads (1.58). The
characteristically popular Hindu sacred literature (if by this we mean
the literature known to the masses of the people either directly or

indirectly) is not the ancient Vedic books (*1.34*) and their appendages in the form of Upaniṣads, (*1.57*) however, but the two great religious epics, the Mahābhārata and the Rāmāyana; which in turn form part of the Purānas, or chronicles of ancient times; there are also the manuals of ethics, the Dharma Sūtras and Dharma Śāstras. Like the inchoate mass of mythology which resulted from the process of reciprocal acculturation between the Great and the Little Traditions (*3.38*), this popular literature is the result of the same process. The two great epics were originally secular sagas, which were taken over by the brāhmans and given a new look, or more precisely, made to serve as literary reinforcements of the priestly point of view. For example, into the Mahābhārata (an immensely long verse saga of some of the heroes of the Indian past) was introduced a lengthy interpolation which we know as the Bhagavad-Gītā, the Song of the Lord (Krishna).

4.22 The Bhagavad-Gītā

This long poem takes the form of a dialogue between the perplexed nobleman, Arjuna, and Krishna, disguised as his charioteer. Arjuna, on the eve of battle, faced with the possibility of doing his duty and yet slaughtering his own kin within the opposing army, is inclined to withdraw from the battle. Krishna's advice to Arjuna, which forms the substance of the book, consists of an amalgam of virtually every point of view within Hinduism; the purport of it is that a man should do his duty, according to his class and his stage of life (*3.39*). R. N. Dandekar has pointed out two ways in which the ethics of the Gītā differs from the Vedic, Upaniṣadic thought. First, the Upaniṣadic attitude to life is fundamentally individualistic, whereas that of the Gītā is that Man has a duty to promote loka-sangraha, the stability and solidarity of society, recognising the necessary part which every caste and occupation plays within the social system. Second, whereas the Upaniṣadic view of life is one in which the phenomenal world is seen as *unreal*, the attitude which the Gītā seeks to foster is that of an acceptance of the world and of active engagement. However, this is an activism tinged with renunciation: one should engage in good actions without interest in personally reaping the fruits of one's actions; above all, this is all to be done in devotion to the Lord, the personal god, Vishnu.

4.23 Varying views of the Bhagavad-Gītā

It is sometimes said that the great virtue of the Gītā is that instead of
endless discussion of the points of disagreement between the various
systems of thought, it emphasises their points of agreement, since the
many different doctrines are enunciated as though from the one divine
source. It is undoubtedly for this reason, and for the quality of its style
and its aesthetic appeal, that it has been the Hindus' best known and
most highly esteemed devotional book. On the other hand there is the
minority of modern Indians who take the view that it is an overrated
work which attempts unsuccessfully to reconcile many irreconcilable
Indian religious points of view. In modern times both B. G. Tilak and
M. K. Gandhi drew from the Gītā totally different conclusions
concerning the course of action for the Indian independence movement
(*7.25; 7.27*). In its perplexing and yet beautiful inconsistency it is a
typical expression of Hinduism as a whole. In the *theological* incongruities
of this long poem, and in the variegated *social* patchwork of the caste
system and its duties, we see the two major features of that tolerant
acculturation inspired by the brāhmans which go to make up Hinduism
as it is known today.

4.24 The Rāmāyana

The other major epic poem of Hinduism is the Rāmāyana. This is only
a quarter of the length of the Mahābhārata (24,000 as against 100,000
verses) but comes a close second to the Gītā in popularity. It is generally
held to have originated during roughly the same period (not earlier
than the second century B.C. nor later than the second C.E.) Unlike the
Mahābhārata it is regarded as having a single author, the poet-sage
Valmiki. The poem consists of the story of Rāma the king (the avatara
of Vishnu), and his wife Sīta; the enmity of Ravana, the demon king;
and the trials and tribulations which this hostility brings upon Rāma
and his queen. Rāma represents the ideal ruler, virtuous, brave,
resourceful; his wife Sīta is the Indian ideal of womanhood, faithful,
devoted and chaste. The virtues which the poem inculcates are those of
ardent piety, patient endurance in adversity, and the proper performance
of duty. The story has become known to Indians, many of whom are

illiterate, through the public recitations of it which are frequently given on great festival occasions, and through dramatic performances. In this way it has constituted one of the major means of communicating the ethics of Hinduism over a wide social area.

4.25 The Hindu Law Books

More prosaic are the ethical teachings contained in the Dharma Sūtras and Gṛhya Sūtras, already mentioned (*3.39*), and in the later expansions of these dating from the first two centuries of the Christian era, known as the Dharma Śāstras. Of these the most outstanding and important is that attributed to Manu, and known as the Manava Dharma Śāstra. Manu is a legendary figure, the first man, the Hindu Adam, of whom it is related in the Mahābhārata that at the beginning of human society Brahmā, the high god, appointed him to control the affairs of men, direct their relationships, rights and so on. The law code attributed to him (translated into English in the *Sacred Books of the East* series, Vol. xxv, 'The Laws of Manu') sets out the duties of the various classes of Hindu society as it was at about the beginning of the Christian era, with the penalties, fines and punishments which are to be inflicted upon offenders; it was this law code which was to remain normative through the subsequent centuries of Hindu history, both in its original form and in the form of subsequent elaborations and commentaries (Basham, 1954; 112 f.).

It is important to notice that a distinction was made by the brāhmans between the Vedic literature down to the Upaniṣads (*1.33; 1.54–1.57*) and this later literature consisting of the Purānas, Epics, Sūtras and Śāstras. The Vedic literature is given a higher status, being classified as *śruti*, or 'heard' (that is, directly revealed), whereas the Purānic literature is described as *smṛti*, or 'remembered' that is, only in a secondary sense revealed.

4.26 The golden age of Hinduism

About the year 320 C.E. a new dynasty arose, which restored the former splendour of the Mauryan rulers. The capital of the Magadhan empire, Pātaliputra (Patna) which had declined almost to a village, now became once again the imperial court. The new rulers were the Guptas, Hindu by religion and adherents of the cult of Vishnu. The early part of the dynasty was the most notable, under Chandragupta I and his successor Samudra Gupta. Towards the end of the three centuries through which it lasted the dynasty grew weaker; but the period of Gupta rule has been regarded by modern Indian historians as the golden age of Hinduism. It was so in the sense that this was the period in which Hindu culture reached its normative form in north India; it has to be remembered, however, that the most prosperous and vigorous period of Hindu culture in the Deccan and in South India came somewhat later.

Vaishnavism, or the cult of Vishnu, had by now come to cover a fairly wide range of originally separate cults, or 'sects' as they are sometimes called – Bhāgavatas; Pañcarātrikas; worshippers of Krishna, or of Vasudeva, of Rāma, Narayana, or of Vishnu. It has to be remembered, however, that these were not sects in the sense of *divisions* of the Vishnu cult; they were in origin separate cults of independent origin which had all by this time begun to be regarded as being cults of the one god Vishnu. The other principal form of deity worshipped by Hindus is *Śiva* (anglicised, Shiva).

4.27 The cult of Shiva

The characteristics of the deity who in classical Hinduism is known as Shiva are, as we have seen (*1.19*), of a kind which are found associated with what seems to be a deity of the Indus valley civilisation. In classical Hinduism, as it is found at the time of the Gūptas (*4.26*), Shiva incorporates a number of features: he is sometimes regarded as a god of love and grace, but he has a darker side to his nature, which he seems to have inherited from the Vedic Indra, the storm god and destroyer; Shiva is the god of destruction also, whose realm is the battlefield, the cemetery and the burning-ghat. It is for this reason that he is sometimes depicted with a garland of skulls. Since he is the 'destroyer' he is thought of as the power which destroys the world at the end of the kalpa (the Hindu 'era', almost immeasurably long by Western standards). But he is thought of also as the great ascetic, who by his yogic meditation keeps the world in existence. He has also the character of a fertility god: he is Lord of the beasts, the patron of procreation, and his symbol by the Gupta period had become the lingam, the symbol of the male organ of reproduction.

4.28 *Shiva, Vishnu and their consorts*

The cult of Shiva is strongest in Kashmir and in southern India (Andhra Pradesh, Mysore, Madras and Kerala); in southern India especially he is worshipped as the compassionate one, the one who is gracious and cares for all life. Clearly we have here another example of the wide variety of features that the brāhmanical process of acculturation has brought together to form, in this case, one outstanding figure in the Sanskritic Great Tradition (*3.33*).

By the Gupta period another of the characteristic features of Hinduism had made its appearance, namely the associating of what were originally mother-goddesses with the *two* principal gods, Vishnu and Shiva, as their consorts. In the case of Vishnu it is the goddess Śri, or Lakṣmi who has now come to be the partner; in the case of Shiva it is Śakti (Shakti), the female personification of the divine energy or power, known also under the names of Parvati, Kālī and Durga (a fact which indicates the great variety of goddess cults which have thus been brought into association with that of Shiva).

4.29 *Brahmanism and South-East Asia*

What the brāhman tolerance of the village cults or little traditions throughout the whole of north India had achieved was the triumph of a form of religion which, while paying lip service to the Vedas and acknowledging the special importance of the brāhman, yet preserved and continued the ancient non-brāhman cults of India under new names, and accepted the social allocation of groups and tribes within the great system of caste over which the brāhman class presided. This meant that the challenge to Brahmanism which the Buddhists and to a lesser extent the Jains (*2.40; 2.41*) represented had been successfully met and overcome. The enduring presence of Brahmanism as a strongly resistant religious and social force had prevented the Buddhist social philosophy (and the religious philosophy which underlay it) from becoming a really determining force in Indian society. Hinduism, its mythology and its caste-structure were now becoming firmly established; the brāhmans were important functionaries in the state, advising the kings, administering the laws, transmitting the sacred texts, and controlling the teaching of the now very prestigious priestly language of Sanskrit. The mechanism by which they achieved this end was, as we have seen, the careful and clever process of reciprocal acculturation. The reasons which underlay this achievement were various; prominent among them were their own determination to maintain their status; the attitude of religious tolerance which comes very easily to brāhman philosophy, rather than any rigid and doctrinaire exclusivism; and finally, at the political level, the fact that the village remained the fundamental unit of Indian society, a feature which Kosambi describes as 'the idiocy of village life' – that is, its isolated, autonomous character.

One further point which remains to be mentioned in connection with the importance which the brāhmans had achieved, especially in the courts of kings, is the brahmanisation of a number of South-East Asian countries during this period. In Burma, Thailand, Cambodia, Java and Sumatra there is evidence of extensive cultural influence from India. This shows itself in various ways: in the Hindu architecture of the massive ruined temples which are still to be found in the jungles of South-East Asia – Angkor Wat in Cambodia or Borobodur in Java for example; in Sanskrit linguistic remains in the languages of these countries; and in the medieval cosmology centred upon the king and the royal palace as the centre of the cosmos, evidence of which is still to be found in popular religious ideas (7.41).

How this Indian influence came into South-East Asia has been a matter of controversy. At one time it was claimed that it was the result of Indian political expansion, that is, empire-building by Hindu kings. Thanks to the research of scholars such as J. C. van Leur (1955) and Georges Coedès (1964; 1966) it is now fairly certain that the Indianised culture of these South-East Asian countries was largely a matter of brahmanisation. The initiative for this lay with the local South-East Asian rulers. Traders from India visited these countries regularly and the fame of Indian culture and especially the prestige of brāhmanic rituals in connection with king-making gradually spread eastwards, with the result that South-East Asian rulers began to summon brāhman priests and architects to their courts, in order that their dynasties might be given the highly prestigious sacral legitimation for which the brāhmans were renowned. What thus came to be imported from India consisted, says Coedès, of: (*a*) a concept of royalty based on Hindu cults; (*b*) a mythology which gave legitimation to royal genealogies which were taken from Sanskrit works and bestowed on the South-East Asian kings; (*c*) the use of Sanskrit language; and (*d*) the use of the Hindu law books, the Dharma Śāstras, particularly that of Manu (*4.25*). The importation of Hindu culture to these areas was thus not due to Indian political expansion or popular missionary activity by Hindus, but was a matter mainly involving native princes and Indian priests. The purpose of these rulers in obtaining Hindu sacral legitimation was that it placed them in a stronger position to assert their superiority over other local rulers who may not have obtained it, and as D. G. E. Hall says, thereby dominate them 'into a state of vassalage' (Hall, 1968; 19).

4.3 THE HINDUISATION OF BUDDHISM
(*70–600* C.E.)

4.30 *The further development of the Mahāyāna*

The growing ascendancy of Brahmanism during the early centuries of the Christian era is also reflected indirectly in some of the developments which took place among the Buddhists during this period, and which eventually produced a separate system of Buddhism, namely the Mahāyāna or 'Great Vehicle'. The name is deceptive, for it suggests that this now became the dominant form of Buddhist life and doctrine. In fact the 'Great Vehicle', so described by its own adherents, remained a minority party in Buddhist India up to at least 500 C.E. The Chinese pilgrim-monk, Hsuan-tsang (*5.25*) who visited India about 640 C.E. records that even then at least half the Buddhist monks belonged to schools which were non-Mahāyānist, and only a fifth at the most were zealous Mahāyānists. So far as the allegiance which this Great Vehicle commanded, therefore, it was in no position to call itself 'Great' on account of its extent within the monastic communities. Nor were its adherents justified on these grounds in applying the derogatory term Hīnayāna, or Lesser Vehicle, to the monks who adhered to the traditional doctrine and monastic rules. The claim to 'greatness' on the part of the Mahāyānists was based on other considerations.

H   L.H.R.

4.31 In what sense was the Mahāyāna 'Great'?

It is necessary at this point to recall in the first place that the Mahāyāna was the continuation of the Mahāsanghikā or Great Sangha party – the faction which had separated itself from the main body of Buddhism after the Council of Vesālī (*3.21*) and which had subsequently continued to criticise the orthodox for their literalism (*3.29*). They claimed to be the Great Vehicle in so far as their appeal was potentially wider and more popular; that is to say, they adopted an attitude which laid *less* emphasis upon the importance of the monastic life and discipline. (This, however, was only relative, for they too maintained the monastic life; the difference between them lay in the greater laxity the Mahāyāna allowed in the interpretation of monastic rules.)

Another sense in which the Mahāyāna was the Great Vehicle was that its doctrines became very much more comprehensive than those of the traditional schools. The two regions in which the Mahāyāna developed most strongly were north-west and southern India. In north-west India there was lively contact with Persian (i.e. Zoroastrian) ideas, and with ideas originating from even further west, from Greece. Gandhāra especially was an area of Greek influence, and here Buddhism absorbed the doctrines of the Asian-Greek *Sophia*, or Wisdom, together with possible elements of Manichaeism and Neoplatonism (Dutt, 1962; 262). In southern India Mahāyāna thought was influenced by the strong mother-goddess cults.

4.32 Mahāyāna and the Great Tradition of Hinduism

Perhaps the most important single factor, however, in the emergence of this 'Greater' Buddhism was the discussion and debate that was going on during this period between brāhmans and Buddhists. Such debates with brāhmans were not confined to Buddhists of the Mahāyāna school, but it was they who were prepared to go further towards meeting the brāhmans in matters of philosophy. It was they who were prepared to make Sanskrit the medium for their new scriptures and commentaries, while the Theravādins stuck to Pali. The Mahāyāna wholeheartedly adopted Sanskrit, the prestige language for intellectual discourse in brāhman India. In their dialogue with the brāhmans the

Mahāyānists learnt several lessons. Like the brāhmans they too began to admit new gods into the pantheon, as subordinate to the Buddha, who was now increasingly regarded by the Mahāyānists as quasi-divine at least. Later the new gods, joined now by goddesses, were identified with bodhisattvas, once this doctrine had been fully developed and the bodhisattvas had come to be regarded by the Mahāyānists as heavenly beings. In the Mahāyāna, though it was still a minority movement, during the first five centuries of the Christian era, Buddhism was developing a form of religious life which was more and more like Brahmanism, and less and less distinctively Buddhist. The final outcome of this process was reached in a later period, when the Buddhism that remained distinctive had grown weak, and Brahmanism finally triumphed throughout most of India (*6.41*).

4.33 *Nāgārjuna and the Mādhyamika school*

We have seen (*3.29*) that one of the earliest developments in Buddhist thought in the Mahāyāna direction was the idea that even dhammas (regarded by the Theravādins as the indivisible ultimate events of which all existence is composed) are in fact substanceless; all things, even dhammas, are void of substance, or śūñya. This idea is first found in a Mahāyāna text which was translated into Chinese at the end of the second century C.E. and which may therefore be regarded as having had its origin somewhere in north-west India in the first century C.E.

Those who assert (vādin) this doctrine of the voidness of substance (śūñya) even in dhammas, are called śūñyavādins. Another name for this school of thought is the Mādhyamika school, or school of the 'middle position' (mādhya is cognate with Latin media). The middle position referred to was not that of the earlier period of Buddhism, when the Buddha's teaching was known as 'the Middle Way', that is, between self-mortification and sensuality, but between the complete *realism* of the Sarvāstivādins (*3.24; 3.26*) who asserted that all dhammas, past, present and future, were real; and the absolute *idealism* of the Yogācārin school (*4.35*).

The Mādhyamika school is generally regarded as having been founded by Nāgārjuna in the second century C.E. It is significant that Nāgārjuna was a brāhman from south central India (Andhra) who had thrown in his lot with Buddhism. The school of thought which he developed certainly has affinities with brāhman philosophical thought; although it was developed in opposition to certain of the orthodox brāhman philosophies (Sānkhya and Vaiśesika) (*4.21*), it was generally more akin to these schools than to the early Abhidhamma of Pali Buddhism. An excellent account of the Mādhyamika school has been provided by T. R. V. Murti (1955). His view of the development of this school is that it may be described in terms of a dialectic. The original thesis was the atma-affirming doctrine of the Upaniṣads; the antithesis to this was the denial of any enduring atta (atma) in early Buddhism, formalised in the Abhidhamma; the synthesis is found in the Mādhyamika. According to Murti it was the inadequacy and inconsistency of the Abhidhamma system, especially the Sarvāstivādin Abhidhamma, which led to the development of the Mādhyamika. The essential concern of the Mādhyamika is with the relation between the empirical world of the senses, which in Buddhist thought generally is known as saṃsāra (the continued round of existence), and the trans-cendental reality nirvāṇa. According to the Mādhyamika, nirvāṇa is present in saṃsāra, but men are prevented from recognising this and entering into it because of the false constructions they put upon the world. The removal of these false constructions (the negation of the negation) and the attainment of nirvāṇa is the religious goal, in the Mādhyamika Buddhist view. The way to do this is by cultivating a view of the substanceless nature of things. To accomplish this, they hold, needs a long course of meditational training.

4.34 Two new Mahāyāna emphases

In addition to the metaphysical analysis developed in the Mahāyāna type of Buddhism two important new emphases were also characteristic of this variety of Buddhism. These were, (1) an emphasis on the virtue of 'great compassion' (mahākaruṇā) towards all living beings, a virtue which every Buddhist monk and householder was enjoined to cultivate; and (2) the bringing into prominence of the doctrine of the Three Bodies (Tri-kāya) of the Buddha. According to this doctrine, it is possible to distinguish three different aspects of the Buddha-nature: there is the eternal dharma (the dharma-kāya); there is the historical manifestation of this in a Buddha, that is, in a human existence (the nirmāna-kāya, or appearance-body); and there is thirdly, beyond this manifestation for the benefit of mortals another manifestation for the benefit of those in the heavens, or those far advanced in spirituality; this is a refined and refulgent body and is known as the bliss-body (sambhoga-kāya). This doctrine indicates the extent to which Buddhism in some of its schools was becoming theological; the doctrine is an example of the kind of purely speculative activity which has often characterised theology, of whatever tradition.

These two doctrines sometimes seem to Christians to indicate an influence of Christian thought on Buddhism. But the conception of karunā, or compassion, as a virtue is found in earlier, Pali Buddhism, and does not need to be explained as being derived from Christianity; the doctrine of the 'three bodies', moreover, though it suggests the idea of the Trinity has very little in common with that doctrine as it was hammered out by Christian theologians in the early centuries, other than the common element 'three'; the roots of this conception of the Tri-kāya are in fact to be found in the earliest form of Buddhism (Conze, 1960; 36).

According to T. R. V. Murti it was the combination of the speculative metaphysic of the Mādhyamika school with the emphasis on 'great compassion' and the doctrine of the 'three bodies' which provided the characteristically Buddhist basis for the culture of a large part of Asia.

4.35 The Yogācāra school

The other of the two main philosophical schools of Mahāyāna Buddhism was the Yogācāra school, or Vijñāna-vādins. The school is generally regarded as having been founded by Maitreyanātha in the third century c.e. but it was his disciple Asaṅga in the fourth century who, with his brother Vāsubandhu, continued and developed the work of the founder, and were the first well-known teachers of this school. The name Yogācāra indicates that there is an emphasis on the practical technique of meditation, and means 'practitioner of Yoga', that is, as a means of the attainment of enlightenment. The additional name Vijñāna-vāda was used by the second of the two brothers, Vāsubandhu, to emphasise the view of this school that consciousness (vijñāna) alone is real: nothing in the way of external 'objects' has any reality; they are real only within the consciousness of the subject. This contention was directed against both the Abhidhamma school, for whom dhammas were external, real entities, and also against the Mādhyamika school, for whom both subject *and* object were unreal, substanceless, śūñya. This kind of philosophy may therefore be described as a form of idealism: ideas alone are real; according to this school the basic perversion consists of mistaking what is an idea for a real object having external existence. Ordinary sense-perception is illusory; 'the yogācāra sees what is, as it really is'. That is to say, according to this view, a man engaged in deep meditation is nearer to the truth than one who is distracted by concern with external 'objects'. It has been pointed out that whereas the Mādhyamika critique of the Abhidhamma position was based on logic (the pressing of the Abhidhamma method of analysis to its logical conclusion), the Yogācāra or Vijñānavādin critique was based on a certain kind of psychology.

It was this development of thought in the Mahāyāna, with its strong emphasis on the necessity for purging the consciousness, which led to the development of the later Vajrayāna, or Tantric Buddhism (*5.26*).

4.36 The spread of Buddhism to China

The geographical expansion of the Buddhist Sangha had been fairly continuous throughout the Mauryan period and after. By the second century B.C. it was well established in the Indo-Greek Bactrian kingdom in the north-west of India, and from there passed easily into Central Asia. Another considerable advance took place from the second century of the Christian era, when Buddhism began to enter China from Central Asia. The circumstance which assisted its initial entry was the very considerable trade between north-west India, Central Asia and China. Merchants from this cosmopolitan area to the north of India moved back and forth with ease along the trade route into western China. It is notable, however, that of the various religious traditions of India at the beginning of the Christian era, Buddhism alone succeeded in establishing itself in China. Various factors combined to make this possible from about the middle of the second century C.E. onwards. First, China was passing through a period of cultural unrest, or anomie, as the Han dynasty declined and old traditional moral and social structures were weakened. Many in China at this time were seeking for some more satisfactory way of life, such as would enable them to see meaning and significance in human existence. Second, Buddhist

religion met just this need in a way that no other Indian religion could –
particularly because it was not rooted in local cults in the way that
brāhmanical Hinduism was, and was more flexible and adaptable
socially. Third, the Buddhist monks were the inheritors of a missionary
tradition; the obligation to spread the Dhamma was integral to all the
schools of Buddhism. It is this which throughout the history of
Buddhism has frequently impelled its monks to travel beyond the
confines of their own territory whenever the opportunity has arisen,
even although there have also been long periods when the missionary
spirit has sunk to a low ebb. But the second century of the Christian era
and the immediately succeeding centuries were a period of opportunity,
and of readiness to meet the opportunity on the part of the Buddhist
monks, who now began to travel the long mountainous routes through
Central Asia and into China; first a few pioneers, and then, as the
Chinese people welcomed this new faith, in increasing numbers in
response to beckoning opportunity.

4.37 Establishment and growth of Buddhism in China up to 600 C.E.

Although, as we have seen (4.36), certain general conditions favoured
the spread of Buddhism to China, there were also severe difficulties
attending its introduction. Of all the countries outside India into which
Buddhism has spread China was notable for having already, before the
entry of Buddhism, an ancient and well-established culture and its own
indigenous philosophy and national religion. Confucian scholars, who
constituted the most influential sector of society, were inclined to look
askance on this foreign (and therefore in Chinese eyes barbarian)
religion. But it was precisely because of its religious character that
Buddhism appealed to the Chinese masses other than the Confucian
literati and governing classes; for Confucianism was by its nature
incapable of being invested with a popular religious quality. On the
other hand, China's own popular religion, Taoism (2.47), had not the
rational and philosophical basis which characterised Buddhism and
gave it greater prestige. Another point in Buddhism's favour was the
standard of morality which it inculcated and which was exemplified in
its Indian missionary monks.

The process by which Buddhism gained acceptance in China, and
eventually came to be regarded as almost an indigenous religion,

continued over many centuries, but an important early step was the translation into Chinese of numerous Buddhist texts. These were from various schools, but predominantly from the Mahāyāna wing. Most notable in this connection was the work of Kumārajiva (344–413 C.E.) during the early years of the fifth century. The son of an Indian, he was originally a Sarvāstivādin who had later accepted the doctrines of Nāgārjuna (*4.33*). He is credited with having translated about a hundred Buddhist works into Chinese; other Indian monks in China were engaged in the same work throughout the early centuries. Towards the end of the fourth century C.E. the Chinese were allowed (by their rulers) to become Buddhist monks, and Buddhism had thus become a genuinely Chinese religion. During the sixth century the popular Chinese Buddhist cults such as the 'Pure land' began to develop, but these will be dealt with in later sections (*5.22; 5.23*).

4.38 Mahāyāna Buddhist influence in Ceylon

During the second, third, and fourth centuries of the Christian era, Buddhism in Ceylon passed through a period of upheaval and turmoil. The kings of Ceylon, the monks, and the people are the three factors in the situation, and the religious history of the period is one of shifting alliances among these three. So far as the monks are concerned there are the two factions, those of the Great Monastery (Mahā-vihāra), and those of the rival Abhayagiri Monastery. The former, as we have seen, was broadly orthodox Theravādin, while the latter tended to follow the Mahāyāna form of Buddhism, which continued to make its way into Ceylon from India throughout these three centuries. Successive kings of Ceylon favoured first one, then the other of these two monastic centres; some supported both. In the second century C.E., it was the Abhayagiri Monastery which received special royal support and was considerably enlarged. In the early part of the third century, however, a form of teaching which claimed to be Buddhist, and which is known in Ceylon as Vaitulya, appears to have been introduced. Exactly what this teaching was is unclear. It seems to have had some affinities with Indian Brahmanism, and its sacred texts were probably in Sanskrit (Rahula, 1956; 89). The term 'vaitulya', or 'vetulla', is still used in Ceylon of ideas which are contrary to accepted beliefs, and means literally 'dissenting'. It is highly probable, therefore, that this was some form of

Mahāyāna doctrine which had recently arisen in India, possibly that of Nāgārjuna (*4.33*). The king of Ceylon at the time, Voharika Tissa, gave his authority for the suppression of the Vaitulya. Towards the end of the third century and the beginning of the fourth, exponents of Vaitulya again began to assert their views in Ceylon; the king held an enquiry, the Vaitulya texts were burnt, and sixty monks who upheld this doctrine were banished. An Indian monk named Sanghamitra, hearing of this, came to Ceylon with the intention of winning the king's support for Mahāyāna Buddhism; his learning impressed the king and he was favourably received. He made the Abhayagiri Monastery his centre, and became tutor to the prince, Mahāsena. When the latter became king Sanghamitra's influence over his former pupil enabled him to persuade the king to forbid the giving of alms by the people to the monks of the Great Monastery, whom Sanghamitra had failed to convert to his Mahāyānist views. The monks were therefore forced to abandon the Great Monastery and take refuge in an area somewhat removed from Anuradhapura the capital, where the lay people were prepared to disregard the royal command and to continue to support the Theravādins. For a period of nine years the Great Monastery was deserted, and during that time was despoiled by the king to benefit the Abhayagiri Monastery. Popular support for the Theravādin monks was so great, however, and resentment at the king's action so strong, that the king was eventually forced to admit that he had acted wrongly, and to promise to restore the Great Monastery and allow its monks to return. Reaction against Sanghamitra welled up, and he was murdered by a carpenter, at the instigation of the queen. An elder monk who had been honoured by the king was disrobed and expelled from the Order by one of the king's chief ministers. That this could be done is an indication of the weight of public opinion against the king's religious policy. Mahāsena's son, who succeeded him during the fourth century c.e., went to considerable lengths to make amends for his father's action, and established what he decreed was to be a great annual festival and procession in honour of Mahinda (*3.27*) the missionary monk who had first brought Theravāda Buddhism to Ceylon (Rahula, 1956; 96).

The lesson which the monks of the Great Monastery learnt from these events was that some more positive development in Theravāda learning and scholarship was necessary if the Theravāda was to hold its own against further infiltration of Mahāyāna Buddhism from India.

The medium in which Mahāyāna doctrines were taught was Sanskrit, a language whose prestige was now internationally higher than that of Pali, the language of the Theravāda texts. Moreover, even the use of Pali had fallen into neglect in Ceylon for purposes of teaching, Sinhalese being used instead. As Nyāṇamoli points out, 'Theravāda centres of learning on the mainland (i.e. India) were also much interested and themselves anxious for help in a repristinisation (i.e. of Pali)' (Nyāṇamoli, 1964; xiv). It was at this time, the early part of the fifth century C.E., and in such a situation that the great Buddhaghosa came from India to Ceylon to embark on his monumental work of Pali Buddhist scholarship.

4.39 The work of Buddhaghosa

Buddhaghosa's name is best known for his great compendium of Theravāda Buddhist thought and practice entitled Visuddhimagga – 'The Path of Purification'. This is not so much a theological treatise as a manual of Theravāda spirituality, based on the whole of the Pali Tipitaka and, as he himself says, 'on the teaching of the dwellers in the Great Monastery' (*Vishuddhimagga*. I.1.4.). It is a work of considerable size, amounting to 838 pages in its English translation by Bhikkhu Nyāṇamoli (1964). The material is arranged in three main sections, Morality, Meditation and Wisdom, the bulk of the work being devoted to the latter two subjects. By virtue of its principles and method it belongs broadly to the Abhidhamma type of literature, although of course it is not included among the canonical Abhidhamma books, and in some respects it goes beyond the Abhidhamma-pitaka. In a sense it is the *summa* of Theravāda Buddhism, and is to the Pali Buddhist Tipitaka as Shankara's work (*6.12*) is to the Upaniṣads (*1.57; 1.58*). Certainly Buddhaghosa's name is held in as great esteem in all the lands of Theravāda Buddhism today as those of Aquinas (*6.24*) and Shankara are in the Catholic and Hindu communities respectively. Since this is so, even a rapid survey of the contents of the Visuddhimagga will enable us to see what were, and have remained, the central concerns of the Theravāda.

The work is divided into twenty-three chapters. Of these, the first two deal with Morality, as the indispensable basis of the holy life. The twenty-one chapters which form the bulk of the work are divided fairly evenly between Meditation, eleven chapters (3 to 13), and Wisdom, ten chapters (14 to 23). The eleven chapters on Meditation are taken up largely with a description of the process and method of meditation. After some general introductory observations on the subject, preliminary matters are dealt with: impediments to meditation; meditation subjects; the suiting of meditation subject to the temperament of the one who meditates, the necessity for sincerity of purpose, and an attitude of goodwill. What is said on this last-named topic will perhaps be surprising to those who think of the Theravāda monastic ideal as somehow 'selfish':

> When a monk takes up a meditation subject, he should first develop loving-kindness towards the Community of monks within the boundary (that is, approximately, 'within the parish of his monastery') limiting it at first to 'all monks in this monastery', in this way: 'May they be happy and free from affliction'. Then he should develop it towards all deities within the boundary. Then to all the principal people in the village that is his alms-resort; then to all human beings there, and to all living beings dependent on human beings. (*Visuddhimagga* III. 58)

Detailed instructions concerning the development of concentration are given, the stages of increasing absorption, and so on. The last two chapters of these eleven remind the monk of the spiritual rewards of meditation.

The ten chapters on Wisdom consist, first, of four chapters setting forth the truths which constitute spiritual wisdom, and then a further four chapters (18 to 21) in which these truths are related to the individual experience of the one who meditates. Chapter 22 describes the stage where nibbāna begins to be 'seen' for the first time, at a distance as it were, having until then been known intellectually only, that is, by hearsay. Finally chapter 23 sets forth the rewards of spiritual wisdom, of which the ultimate is the attainment of nibbāna.

The Visuddhimagga is thus an explication of the Buddhist life, and therefore essentially a manual of Buddhist meditation. Theravāda Buddhist thought and practice has found in the subject matter of this great work enough and more than enough to occupy its attention, and has not felt the need for further speculation, logical analysis, or metaphysical enquiry. Since its goals are still well ahead of the achievement of the vast mass of mortals, the Theravādin maintains that it is more appropriate to undertake the spiritual enterprise that is indicated here, than to engage in ever more subtle theorising.

Besides his original work, the Visuddhimagga, Buddhaghosa produced numerous commentaries on the Pali canonical books. His works were preserved more completely in Burma than in Ceylon, and from there were transmitted to Cambodia and Thailand. So highly is Buddhaghosa's work valued in Burma that he is claimed as a man of Burmese origin. The Pali historical chronicles of Ceylon say he came from Magadha, the Buddha's own homeland, but in fact the evidence points more clearly to somewhere in southern India as the place of his origin, probably the east coastal region of Andhra (Dutt, 1962; 255 f.).

SUMMARY AND COMMENT ON CHAPTER FOUR

The period we have just surveyed is one in which two of the world's major religious systems, Christianity and Hinduism, reached an important stage of their development. Both were in the ascendancy in their respective areas, and both were developing the normative features that were to continue to characterise them throughout the medieval and early modern periods. Both received the support of the secular imperial power in the early years of the fourth century: Christianity, under the emperor Constantine from 313; Hinduism under the Gupta emperors from 320. The favoured position into which the two religions thus moved involved in both cases more than patronage: it entailed something more like an invasion of religious belief and practice by the norms and standards of political power. It was more blatant in the case of Christianity, with the emperor presiding over councils of bishops and church leaders, urging them to produce creedal formulas that would put an end to dissension and division within the empire; more subtle in the case of Hinduism, where it resulted in the enhancement of the value of the Hindu law books (*4.25*) and of that work of supreme religious compromise, the Bhagavad-Gītā (*4.22*), in which everyone could find his views approved, and all good Hindus were encouraged to fight for the state as their sacred duty. In India and South-East Asia emperors and brāhman priests engaged in reciprocal support and validation of each other's status and office; in the Mediterranean world and Europe the political ruler, whether emperor or king, became a

Christian leader, while the bishop became a state official, and each took into his system something from the other side of the partnership.

In particular, this meant for Christianity that the accepted norm was assent to certain propositions: he is a Christian 'who believes the things we teach are true' (*4.15*), and as the inhabitants of new territories were led by their kings into the Christian fold it was assumed that they would accept as true the things they were taught by those who baptised them into their new faith. Thus Christianity in the course of its routinisation moved still further in the direction of giving prior place to certain *external* authorities, a process which had already begun in the special status given by the Church to the canon of sacred writings. In theory the Christian Church adheres also to the idea of an *internally* experienced authority, that of the Holy Spirit, but for long periods of its history the appeal to this internal authority was labelled enthusiasm and looked on with disfavour. More usually it has been the external authority to which appeal has been made: Bible, or Creed, or bishop; and sometimes all three. The orthodox view has been that the internal testimony of the Holy Spirit could not possibly be in conflict with these: these, it is held, are the channels through which God speaks to men. Those who disagree and who consider that this is tantamount to laying down the conditions under which the Holy Spirit can operate have to be content to accept that they are unorthodox from the point of view of the institutional Church. In medieval times their lot was less happy than it is today.

In the case of Hinduism conformity was achieved with somewhat more subtlety, and with less show of the outward persuasion of force. For here the conformity required was not so much to standards of belief as to standards of social conduct. The Hindu was required to conform very much more to the requirements of caste and custom. So long as he did not overstep these bounds, but performed the duties and rituals required of him as a Hindu, it mattered much less what intellectual speculations he might engage in, if any. We see why, therefore, in this period of Hindu ascendancy, Buddhism developed as it did. The essential nature of Buddhism, as constituting *both* a social philosophy *and* a religious discipline, was denied fulfilment so far as the first part was concerned. For the Buddhist doctrine of society was incompatible with a caste system, and it was the caste system which the brāhmans had succeeded in establishing. Hence Buddhism retreated to the side-lines and concerned itself more and more with intellectual speculation of the Mahāyāna variety. There were periods and places where exceptions to this general trend occurred, but by and large it was the partnership of brāhman and king which increasingly dominated the medieval scene in India. It was the strength of this alliance, once established, which in principle had already sealed the fate of Buddhism throughout most of India.

5 Religion and Civilisation

5.10 Arabia at the beginning of the seventh century C.E.

ATTENTION must now be turned to the Arabian peninsula, the birthplace of the religious tradition of Islam, today found in countries as diverse as Turkey, Pakistan, Indonesia, Malaya, India, Persia, China, the U.S.S.R., the older Mediterranean countries of North Africa, and in the newly emerging states of Africa south of the Sahara; a tradition which has left its mark on the culture and history of Europe, notably, though by no means exclusively, in Spain and the Balkans.

The Arabian peninsula about the year 600 C.E., was not, as it is sometimes imagined, a desert area remote from the mainstreams of civilisation. The south of Arabia, known generally as Arabia Felix, and especially that south-western region of mountain and valley called the Yemen, had already attracted the attention of neighbouring powers, notably Persia and Christian Abyssinia, by the end of the sixth century. Both of these had been responsible for introducing Zoroastrian and Christian influences into south Arabia; Persia, moreover, was Arabia's neighbour on the north-east and Persian religious ideas at least would not have been unknown in the north of the peninsula. Jews also had been moving into Arabia for some centuries and settling to form Jewish communities. And on the north-western frontier of Arabia was Christian Egypt, one of the great centres of Greek Christianity. In many and subtle ways the ancient religion of Arabia had thus by about the beginning of the seventh century been subjected to outside influences: Zoroastrian, Jewish and Christian. The ancient religion, often described as a form of paganism, consisted of the worship of various numinous entities of the earth and the sky, together with a strong element of what has been called tribal humanism, a way of life in which there was a strong sense of brotherhood and a high valuation of such virtues as courage, manliness and generosity. By the end of the

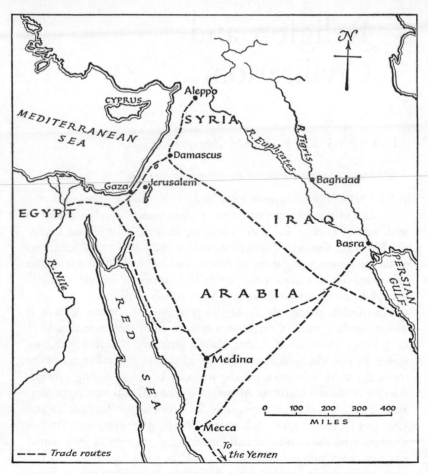

The Near East in early Islamic Times

sixth century this was already permeated by a belief in a powerful deity, Allah, who was the creator of all things. Moreover, throughout Arabia both Judaism and Christianity, in various forms, were being practised. What room was there, or what need, for a new form of religion, and wherein lay the secret of its success, soon to be manifested not only throughout Arabia, but through the whole of the Near East and beyond?

5.11 The social situation in Mecca

In order to find the answer to this question we have to consider the social situation in Arabia at this time, and in Mecca in particular. On this subject there is a mass of information in the traditions (hadith) of Islam, which preserve many sayings of Muhammad and stories about the prophet and the early Islamic community in Arabia. Next to the Qur'an itself (*5.12*) this is the most important of Islamic source materials. These traditions have throughout the years been subjected to a process of sifting and testing by European as well as by Muslim scholars, and a fairly coherent account of the social situation in Mecca at the beginning of the seventh century has been produced (Watt, 1953).

Mecca was an ancient centre of pilgrimage for the inhabitants of Arabia. In its shrine, the Ka'ba, was the Black Stone, an object of veneration which later tradition associated with Adam who, it was said, had brought this sacred object with him from Paradise. Probably the stone was a burnt-out comet and was regarded with awe because it had fallen from the sky. The importance of Mecca had increased by about 600 C.E. for other reasons, however, namely as a town favourably situated for the control of the caravan trade route which ran north and south along the western edge of the Arabian peninsula and along which the commodities of south Arabia, and also goods brought to the south Arabian coast by sea from Abyssinia and India, were carried overland to the Mediterranean world. Another route which led north-westwards from the Persian Gulf was closed by the conflict between Persia and the Byzantine empire during the latter part of the sixth century, and the route that passed through Mecca thus increased correspondingly in importance, largely because Mecca remained neutral in the Greek-Persian conflict. The result was that Mecca became a commercial centre, a place where considerable financial transactions were under-

taken by increasingly wealthy Arabian merchants. These were a new
phenomenon in Arabian society. Previously a man's prosperity consisted in the camels he possessed. But there was a limit to the number
of camels a man could own, since camels need caring for and even if
this is deputed to others, there is a limit to the number of camel-
keepers that one man can effectively supervise, and over whom he can
exert the kind of control that must be largely of a personal kind. The
merchants of Mecca, however, dealt in luxury goods of small bulk –
such as spices, incense and silk, and this made it possible for one man to
operate on a much larger financial scale. Hence there was a great
increase in personal wealth among a relatively small number of merchants who were able to benefit from the concentration of trade on the
Meccan route, organising the caravans to their own convenience.

With this increase of personal wealth went, apparently, a disregard
for traditional ties of family and clan. Men who had become rich by
their individual efforts were less and less inclined to take kinship
responsibilities seriously, and the number of kinsmen who thus lost
their natural protectors, according to tribal tradition, increased. Watt
has shown that this situation constituted a crisis for Arab society. The
new individualism based on money undermined the old cultural
structure, and resulted in a growing sense of social malaise, disharmony
and personal insecurity. Metaphysical questions were raised by the
breaking down of the traditional idea of immortality within the life of
the clan and in the memory of one's clan descendants; ethical questions
were raised as ideals of manliness and generosity were eclipsed by the
growing status of money as an indicator of social importance. In short,
this was a situation of anomie, and it resulted in the formation of a new
religious movement led by a native of Mecca named Muhammad.

5.12 Muhammad, the prophet of Mecca

Muhammad, a member of the Quraysh tribe in Mecca, born about the
year 570 c.e., was an orphan; that is to say, his father Abd Allah died
before he was born and his mother died when he was six years of age.
He was thus one of the 'weak', or relatively exposed and unprotected
members of Meccan society. In his youth he was poor and without
influence. However, he found employment with a wealthy widow
named Khadija, a woman some years older than he, who had already

had two husbands. Eventually, at the age of twenty-five, Muhammad married Khadija, and there thus opened up for him new possibilities for leisure and reflection. He appears to have spent long periods in meditating, perhaps upon the unhappy condition of Meccan society, during the ensuing fifteen years, until the experience which he underwent at the age of forty which he interpreted as a call to prophethood.

The message of the prophet was delivered by him in the form of Arabic verses or suras, which, gathered together, form the Qur'an (*5.16*). The suras which belong to the early Meccan period show that Muhammad was concerned to proclaim the reality of one who has created all things, and before whom every individual must at the last appear, and before whom in that day of judgment personal wealth will count for nothing. The prophet's mission was at first to warn the men of Mecca of this. The first person to recognise his prophethood was his wife. Another early convert was Abu Bakr, a small-scale businessman who became one of the pillars of the early community and eventually succeeded Muhammad in the leadership.

Watt has examined the composition of the congregation of followers which eventually gathered round the prophet in Mecca in response to his preaching (Watt, 1961). Some were young men of the leading clans of Mecca, but who were not themselves within the circle of the merchant monopolists. The second and largest group were leading men from less influential clans, clans which had failed to make the grade in the jostle for power and position in Mecca. The third group, amounting to less than ten per cent of the whole congregation, were people of the 'weak' or unprotected type. From this analysis it is clear that Muhammad's role in Mecca was certainly not that of the leader of a proletariat rising against capitalists.

5.13 The religious ideas of the Meccan period

It is important to realise that the religious ideas which Muhammad was most concerned to proclaim during the Meccan period do not extend to the full range of Islamic religious ideas that developed later, some of them after the prophet's death. If Western scholars are correct in the broad measure of agreement they have reached in identifying certain suras of the Qur'an as Meccan and others as Medinan, it is possible to reconstruct the pattern of Muhammad's preaching in

Mecca. Certain major emphases have been discerned (Watt, 1961), and they are as follows: God is the creator of the world and of man, and is its active controller; He will also bring the world to an end, and all men will be raised to appear before him to be judged according to the lives they have lived, and on that day wealth and power will count for nothing. Hence men must live with this end in view, desist from unscrupulous money-making, and instead practise generosity. Of all this Muhammad is sent to warn the men of Mecca, especially those whose profiteering was responsible for the disintegration of Meccan society and the resultant loss of a sense of meaning and purpose in human life.

About this pattern of religious ideas that was produced by Muhammad in Mecca two observations need to be made. The first is that there is little that is novel – little, that is to say, that had not already been proclaimed by the Hebrew prophets and by Zoroaster in areas adjacent to Arabia. The second is that Muhammad himself appears to have recognised that it was not novel, that he stood in the tradition of the earlier prophets; the essential feature of his mission was that it was now necessary that these truths should be proclaimed in Arabia by an Arab. He was conscious of speaking these truths to men to whom no prophet had as yet been sent. This can be seen very clearly from the words of Sura 93, 'Thus unto thee (i.e. Muhammad) as unto those who preceded thee doth God, the Mighty, the Wise reveal himself. . . . Thus have we revealed to thee an Arabian Qur'an, that thou mayest warn the mother city [i.e. Mecca] and all those around it.'

It should be noted that the adherence of Meccans to either of the already existing systems of monotheistic belief, Jewish and Christian, even though it had been urged as the answer to the ills of the Meccan society (and there are indications that both of these courses were urged), would have been seen by Meccans as politically unwise. Mecca's prosperity as a trading centre depended on her neutrality in the conflict between Persia and Byzantium. For Meccans to have turned in large numbers to the Jewish faith would have meant becoming associated with the strongly Jewish element in Persia; on the other hand, if Meccans had turned to the Christian faith they would immediately have identified themselves with Christian Byzantium. In either case Meccan neutrality would have been lost, Mecca drawn into the conflict between Persia and Byzantium on one side or the other, and her privileged economic position overthrown.

From the content of his preaching in the early, Meccan, period therefore, Muhammad appears as a man profoundly disturbed by the irreligious quality of the contemporary life of Mecca; a man who finds this intolerable, and who feels himself constrained to appeal to men on the basis of religious ideas already received – certainly in other places, if not in their fullness in Arabia – ideas which had to be drawn together and combined in a way that was relevant and meaningful for the Arabian situation. He accepted, though not without the reluctance and even fear characteristically felt by prophets, the task of speaking to men of his day and his country, of the things of religion; that is of the necessity to see their lives in other than a purely materialistic context.

The view that he was challenging was, as we have noted, one which saw the course of human events as controlled entirely by wealth and irresponsible individual power, a view characteristic of the merchant princes in particular, but from them spreading into and corrupting society as a whole. Over against this he believed that men should acknowledge that there is a greater power who controls events and by whom man is ultimately confronted and judged. His prophetic mission was directed primarily against the unscrupulous and irresponsible pursuers of wealth. These he seems to have believed had to be opposed and resisted by every means possible because of the harm they were doing. So far as the rest of Meccan society was concerned, their acceptance of what he was urging, their acknowledgement of the power of God as the real power, would in itself be a denial of the omni-competence of wealth and personal privilege.

Individualism as such, as it had now emerged in seventh-century Mecca, was not challenged by Muhammad. Nor was the possession of wealth denounced. Individualism was accepted, but it was placed firmly within a *theocratic* instead of a materialistic context. Each human individual must at the last, Muhammad proclaimed, stand alone before God to be judged entirely on the moral record of his life. In this sense there is no religious tradition that is more individualistic than Islam, for this element of belief persists to the present day. But primarily it was to his own day and to the needs of his own generation that Muhammad spoke in his Meccan preaching, re-expressing known religious ideas in terms relevant to local conditions, and in this most characteristically he is a prophet.

5.14 Muhammad, the statesman-prophet of Medina

The response to Muhammad's preaching in Mecca was, on the one
hand, the growth of a congregation of followers, the Muslims, i.e.
those who were 'surrendered' to God, and on the other the hardening
of the attitude of the mercantile monopolists. These latter not only
rejected Muhammad's idea that man's life must be seen within the
context of the divine rule of the universe, with the assertion that 'there
is nothing but this life of ours', but they also rejected the claim implicit
in such preaching – namely that Muhammad was a man of greater
insight than they, whose advice on the conduct of human affairs should
be listened to with respect. Their operations, they claimed, brought
them wealth and success, and that in itself was a guarantee of the
superiority of their attitude to life. There appears also to have been
some resistance to Muhammad from upholders of the worship of the
pagan deities of Mecca, and perhaps this was closely connected with the
resistance of the monopolists. In response to this opposition two new
emphases appeared in Muhammad's preaching, namely, that God will
vindicate his prophet, as he has always done, against the prophet's
opponents, and that pagan deities or idols can avail nothing, since
'there is no god but God'. This emphasis upon the unity of God becomes one of the two main assertions of Muslim belief, but it had not
at this time assumed its later well-known creedal form.

Although the opposition became serious, it did not deter other
Meccans from joining Muhammad, and for some years the prophet
enjoyed the firm protection which his uncle Abu Talib now afforded
him. But when both Abu Talib and Muhammad's wife and faithful
supporter Khadija died within the same year, things became more
difficult for the prophet. There are indications that these events
deepened his religious feelings, but on the other hand, the new head of
Abu Talib's clan withdrew support for Muhammad and the prophet
was eventually forced to leave Mecca. It was a dark period in the
prophet's life, but encouragement came in the form of an appeal from
the men of the neighbouring town of Medina, to the north of Mecca,
who were impressed by his sagacity, and who invited him to come and
help them with the affairs of their town. So in the year 622 Muhammad
and his followers in Mecca migrated to Medina, and there established
what was to be known as the new community of Islam, the *umma*. It

is this year of the migration, or Hijra, 622 c.e., that marks the beginning of the Muslim chronology and from which all subsequent dates in the Muslim era are reckoned.

In Medina the situation which confronted Muhammad was one of conflict between the two major Arab groups which he had been called upon to deal with. His task was virtually the integration of Medinan society (Watt, 1961; 59); there was also a considerable Jewish population which might have come within the scope of his integrating work. His qualifications for the task in the eyes of the Medinan Arabs lay in his religious charisma, and in the wisdom, impartiality, and powers of conciliation that he seemed to them to possess.

The basic feature in Muhammad's programme of action was the formal establishment of the umma.

5.15 The Islamic theocracy

The principles governing the life of the new community were set out in a document drawn up by Muhammad known as the Constitution of Medina (Watt, 1956; Levy, 1957). In its own words it is 'a charter of Muhammad the prophet (applicable) amongst the believers and the Muslims of the Quraysh and of Yathrib (Medina), and amongst those who follow them and attach themselves to them and fight along with them. They are one umma [community] over against mankind.' What had formerly not been given conscious expression was now made explicit, namely that men were divided into two kinds, those who accepted the prophethood of Muhammad and responded to his message, shaping their lives according to the prophetic revelations which he delivered from time to time, and those who did not. The charter is largely concerned with the collective security which membership of the Islamic umma affords to those who acknowledge the overlordship of God and the apostleship of Muhammad. The idea of an 'overlord' was one which was foreign to the Arabs, among whom leaders emerged by virtue of their possession of a special measure of courage or whatever other quality was regarded as the tribe's characteristic *par excellence*; such men were *leaders*, rather than overlords. The fact that in the new umma political power was exercised by the prophet meant, moreover, that there was no separation of the religious and political realms. It was a political community whose ruler derived his authority from his prestige as a prophet. It was thus similar in character to the amphictyony in ancient Israel, the political confederation whose centre was the Yahweh cultus and whose authoritative figures were men inspired by the spirit of Yahweh (*1.40, 1.42*). In this case it was certainly the charismatic personality of Muhammad which provided the cohesion.

An important aspect of the response of those who thus became Muslims was the adoption of certain specifically Islamic practices, namely the recitation of the simple formula 'There is no god but God, Muhammad is His Apostle'; prayer at certain set times every day; fasting; the contribution of money to a fund for the use of the community; and, later, pilgrimage to the shrine at Mecca. In this way the special religious ideas (*5.13*) which had been combined in the preaching of Muhammad were given regular outward expression in practical ways that would have the effect of strengthening an attitude of assent to these ideas.

The extent to which Medinan society was thus integrated within the life of the umma was, however, limited in one important direction: that of the Jews. Contrary to Muhammad's hopes that the Jewish groups in Medina would be included within the new unity of Medinan society, they formed a dissident element. They did not accept Muhammad's self-assessment as a prophet in the true line of Abraham, Moses, and the prophets of Israel. From their own greater familiarity with this tradition they pointed out the discrepancies between Muhammad's revelations on the subject of the earlier prophets and their own scriptures. This constituted another severe disappointment and setback for the prophet, and his grappling with this challenge led him to the view that such discrepancies must be due to the Jewish scriptures having been tampered with or corrupted in some way. From this point onwards, in the second year of the settlement in Medina, the centre towards which Muslims turned in devotion was no longer Jerusalem as hitherto, but the shrine of the Ka'ba in Mecca.

On the other hand the new community did extend to include other Arabian tribes in the vicinity of Medina. Impressed by Muhammad's achievements especially in the unification of Medina, and possibly to a lesser degree by his charismatic qualities, they sought entry into the umma and were admitted upon their acceptance of the duties of Islam which were enumerated above. In this way the umma developed into a federation of Arabian tribes, and again, this was very similar to the pattern of the Yahwistic federation of tribes in ancient Israel (*1.42*). As a further expression of Muhammad's opposition to the merchant monopolists of Mecca, raids were organised from Medina upon the Meccan trade caravans travelling in the vicinity. It is possible to see that in doing this Muhammad was still prompted by his original conviction that the Meccan merchant princes who were responsible for the ills of the society of his day had to be opposed and resisted by every means possible. That he should also at this time have made the shrine at Mecca the focal point for Islamic devotions (its direction indicated by a mark known as the qibla on the wall of the mosque from this time on) indicates that his concern was with *Arabian* society. Formerly Arabians had converged upon a pagan Mecca; this practice was now to be Islamised, in that devotions expressive of a new Arabian religious system were directed towards Arabia's ancient shrine, and also in that actual pilgrimage to Mecca was to become a practice of the new religion. The true centre for the monotheism that began with Abraham was now to be found within Arabia.

It was during this Medinan period also that the vigorous pursuit of Islamic goals by every means possible, including armed warfare, was given formal recognition in the idea of jihad, a word which means 'striving' or 'effort'. In the course of Islamic history the term acquired the connotation of 'holy war' and it is in this sense that it is better known to non-Muslim readers. How it came to have this specialised meaning can be seen by reference to pre-Islamic Arabia. The practice of making raids (razzias) on neighbouring tribes was a common feature of Arab life; apart from any economic gains these raids provided an outlet for the energy of the Arab men. This practice was now harnessed to the needs of the Islamic community; frequently the phrase used in this connection in the Qur'an is 'striving in the way of God', that is, in furtherance of the theocratic ideals of Islam. ('Islam' means submission; to become Muslim meant the decision not to struggle *against* the power of God and his community, and instead to exert one's effort in harmony with them.)

Another aspect of this matter is that such tribal raids or attacks were forbidden within the confederation of the Islamic umma, and among the tribes which now began, if not to become fully part of the umma, at least to enter into treaty relations with Muhammad, as its leader. This meant that the old predilection for raiding needed a new outlet, so far as Islamic Arabian tribes and their allies were concerned. This they began to find by directing their efforts northwards and thus expanding the range of the influence and authority of the theocratic confederation. On one occasion during the later Medinan period Muhammad, accompanied by a thousand men, is said to have made an expedition to a place as far as four hundred miles north of Medina. In this way more and more tribes came to submit to Muhammad, and became nominally Islamic. The results of this nominal Islamisation were soon to be seen at the prophet's death in 632 C.E. But two years before that event one further notable victory was gained for the prophet which demands mention here, and that was the submission of Mecca in 630 C.E. This made possible the reconstitution of the ancient shrine of the Ka'ba as an Islamic shrine, to which in future pilgrimage was to be made by Muslims, at first from all parts of Arabia, and later from all the regions into which Islam spread.

5.16 The four 'rightly guided' caliphs of Medina (632–661)

European historians of religion are agreed that the death of Muhammad in the year 632 C.E. constituted a major crisis for Islam. Often this is said to be due to the fact that the Prophet had no surviving son, and had made no arrangement for anyone to succeed him in the leadership of the community, and what went with this, the command of the army. But it was equally a crisis in another sense, that there was no one with the same charismatic endowment as he, and this was possibly even more ominous for the future of Islam. It was not to be expected that there should be, of course, for it is the nature of charisma that apparently it cannot be controlled or arranged to suit human convenience. However, since it was the prophetic charisma of Muhammad that had been decisive in winning first the Meccans and then the Medinans and after that many other Arabian tribes to the new theocratic community, it was the withdrawal of this element which now resulted in the immediate defection of some of the tribes, and later on, in the next few decades, various other rebellious or dissenting groups.

The question of leadership of the community was eventually, after some difficulty, decided in favour of Abu Bakr, one of Muhammad's earliest supporters in Mecca and his faithful friend throughout. As 'successor' or 'representative' of the prophet he was known as khalifa (caliph), a title which for the next six centuries and a quarter was to be given to the acknowledged leader of the Islamic community. His caliphate lasted only two years, however, and the time between the Prophet's death in 632 and his own death in 634 was spent largely in seeking to regain the allegiance of Arab tribes who considered their allegiance to the umma was at an end when Muhammad died. So well did he succeed in putting down apostasy that at the end of his caliphate Arabia was even more firmly united than ever before, at least in a political sense. It might have seemed that the crisis had been successfully overcome.

Moreover, during the rule of the next two caliphs, namely Umar for ten years and then Uthman for twelve years, the Islamic state went from strength to strength. During these twenty-two years the extent of Islamic territory (dar-al-Islam) was increased in a spectacular manner.

The expansion of the Islamic community beyond Arabia into the richer lands of Egypt to the north-west, Syria to the north, and Mesopotamia to the north-east can be explained in a number of ways. Economic historians have tended to see the process as a further example of population overspill from the Arabian peninsula of the kind that is a characteristic feature of the history of the Near East. The dry and infertile nature of most of Arabia severely limits the number of humans it can support. By the time of the Arab caliphs Umar and Uthman two other factors due to Islam had been seen to operate in a way that exacerbated the problem: internecine conflict between tribes in the days before the Islamic unification had reduced the number of the male population from time to time, while the practice of female infanticide by exposure had kept the balance fairly even. But Islam meant the cessation of the former and the prohibition of the latter. An already overstrained territory thus became further over-populated. Hence, inevitably, the Arab breakthrough into the neighbouring more fertile lands. On the other hand Christian writers with an antipathy towards Islam have fastened on the fact that large numbers of the formerly Christian population of Egypt and Syria became Muslims in this period, and connecting this with the military methods of the Arabs have concluded that the expansion of Islam is to be understood primarily as a religious campaign carried out by means of the sword.

The truth probably lies somewhere between these two explanations. As we have already noted, jihad, or 'striving in the way of God' was an important motive in the northward thrust of the Islamic state.

Religious sanction was given to the well-established Arab practice of raiding, and the Islamic unity of the tribes generated a massive force and gave this force its only possible geographical direction. And under the new umbrella of Islamic jihad there were no doubt many Bedouin tribes, men whose motive was self-interest rather than the God-fearing zeal which characterised the prophet and his companions (B. Thomas, 1937). Another fact, not always very clearly perceived or recognised by Christian writers, is that the Christian population of Syria and Egypt turned to Islam not by coercion but by choice (Arnold, 1913). Islam is a missionary religion, and as Arnold pointed out in his classic work, the Qur'an enjoins preaching and persuasion, and discountenances force in the conversion of non-Muslims, and for this reason the history of the expansion of Islam is in fact very much more a history of missions than a history of violence or persecutions.

During the caliphate of Uthman (644–56 C.E.), however, internal conflicts within the Islamic community reached serious proportions. Uthman was of the Umayyad clan, one of the more powerful and influential in pagan Mecca, and which in the early days had been among the foremost of the Prophet's opponents. Later, in the days of his success, they had become Muslims, still retaining their aristocratic and influential position. Uthman appears to have been a rather insignificant member of this clan and perhaps for this reason the more zealous Muslims agreed to his election to the caliphate in the hope that he would be an easier representative of this clan to deal with. But in fact his rule was that of his Umayyad kinsmen; and the more religious members of the community, especially Ali the Prophet's nephew and son-in-law, soon found themselves in opposition to the irreligious and worldly character of Uthman's caliphate. They looked for charismatic leadership of the kind they had known in the Prophet's day, and Uthman seems to have been totally lacking in prophetic charisma. Insurrection led to Uthman's murder in June 656 C.E. in his own house, while he was at prayer. A detail of the incident was that his blood is said to have flowed out over a copy of the Qur'an which was by his side – a reminder to us of the fact that it was during his caliphate that the text of the Qur'an (5.12) was, at his command, fixed by a committee of men from the Quraysh tribe, and the new official recension sent from Medina to all the main Islamic cities. (This at least is the orthodox view of the finalising of the text, although it has been questioned in modern times at some points.)

On the day of Uthmàn's murder Ali received an oath of allegiance as caliph from his supporters in Medina. But Uthman's brother Mu'awiya, who held the post of governor of Damascus, contested Ali's claim to the caliphate; the struggle between them continued for the next five years until in January 661 Ali was assassinated in the mosque at Kufah in Iraq. Mu'awiya had already been acclaimed caliph by his troops; he now became the uncontested leader of the Islamic state, which from 661 onwards for the next ninety years was ruled from Damascus. Thus began a new chapter in Islamic history, but before we turn to that it is important to review briefly the development of religious ideas in Islam since the Prophet's death.

5.17 Muslim religious ideas during the Medinan caliphate

At the death of Muhammad the dominant religious ideas in the Islamic community were the omnipotence of God and the unity of God. To put this another way, it was monotheism in one of its purest and most consistent forms. Emphasis upon the unity of God was not so marked in the earliest preaching at Mecca, according to Watt, but developed very quickly in Muhammad's early controversy with the alliance of merchant princes and religious conservatives – that is, the upholders of the traditional Arabian polytheism. If, as Robertson Smith argued (1927), monotheism among the Semites has usually emerged from an association of religion and monarchy, it is not difficult to see that in Medina Muhammad's role was perhaps nearer to that of a monarch than was the role of the traditional Arabian tribal head. Watt has suggested that one of the reasons that attracted the men of southern Arabia to Muhammad was that in the south there was a strong tradition of 'large political units with a high degree of civilisation' owing to the occupation of this region by both Persians and Abyssinians, and that associated with this was a tradition of the king as a superhuman, semi-divine, charismatic figure; hence the men of the southern part of the peninsula would readily have turned to this new charismatic leader, Muhammad, bringing such conceptions with them into the Islamic umma (Watt, 1961; 105 f.). There is at least an interesting correlation here between the increased degree of overlordship exercised by Muhammad compared with the absence of the idea of overlordship among the Bedouin, and the great emphasis which now came to be placed on the doctrine of the unity of the divine being. Such correlation is not, however, the only factor to be taken into account; at least equally important is the positive rejection of polytheism by Muhammad, both on account of its social consequences and because of the common cause of the monopolists and the polytheists.

Allied to this emphasis upon the unity of God is the emergence of 'shirk' as the great sin, that is, the associating of any other being with the single unique divine being. No sin was so serious as this; no virtue was so great as the confession of God's unity. This was Islamic faith *par excellence*.

A further important idea to emerge during the Medinan period was, as we have seen (*5.15*) that of jihad, or holy striving. Such striving came to mean vigorous prosecution of the task of extending the dar-al-Islam, the area of society surrendered to God. This could be both by preaching and controversy and also by military means. Next to the confession of God's unity came the virtue of fighting for the community of this faith.

These notions of what was the great sin and what were the great virtues underlie a good deal of the development of Islam during the rule of the first four, or 'rightly guided', caliphs who ruled from Medina. For such emphasis led to a correspondingly more lenient attitude to moral shortcomings which by comparison could be regarded as 'venial' sins (to use a Catholic term), compared with the 'mortal' sin of shirk. Among the hadith, or traditions, is one related by Abu Dharr, a Muslim who laid stress upon the importance of a wider range of moral virtues as essential to Islam. Abu Dharr narrates the tradition as follows:

> I came to the Prophet and found him sleeping in a white garment. I came a second time and found him still sleeping. The third time I found him awake. When I sat down near him, he said to me: Whosoever sayeth: There is no God but God and dieth in this belief, will enter Paradise. I replied: Even if he should have fornicated and stolen? He answered: Even if he should have fornicated and stolen. [The question and answer are repeated three times.] The fourth time Muhammad added: Even though Abu Dharr should turn up his nose. (Wensinck, 1932; 46)

The tradition is intended to combat a puritan strain within early Islam which before long manifested itself in one of the first sectarian movements, that of the Kharijites.

The Kharijites were the 'Seceders' or Separatists. One of the first groups thus to secede from the main body of the community 'went out' during the caliphate of Ali (656–61 C.E.). The roots of their discontent lay in the preceding caliphate of Uthman, who was regarded with disapproval for his unfairness, favouritism, and worldliness. These Kharijites claimed that leadership of the Umma had fallen into the hands of those among the Meccan aristocrats who in the early days had opposed the Prophet. In the rapid expansion of Islam to neighbouring lands under Umar and Uthman orthodoxy had come to mean primarily *faith*, (sc., the confession of God's unity) and secondly *jihad*; with less emphasis on *works*, that is of moral righteousness. According to the Kharijites the true Umma was not to be found where such formalism was the rule; the true Umma consisted of those whose conduct went beyond the avoidance of the primary sin of polytheism. The conception is in some ways similar to one emphasised at certain periods of Christian history, under Oliver Cromwell for example – the community of the saints. The basis of the Kharijite position is to be seen in a tradition which lists not one mortal sin (shirk) but seven, namely: polytheism, magic, unlawful manslaughter, spending the money of orphans, usury, desertion from battle, and slandering chaste but heedless women who are faithful (Wensinck, 1932; 39). Among the majority, however, the emphasis remained upon the *one* mortal sin of shirk.

A contributory factor in the emergence of the Kharijites may also possibly be found in the growing sense of dissatisfaction and insecurity felt by former nomadic tribesmen who had now become absorbed in a vast authoritarian organisation, whose officials had, inevitably perhaps, become preoccupied with financial and administrative affairs. If we remind ourselves of the extent of the territory controlled by Islam at this time – most of Egypt, Syria and Iraq, as well as Arabia – it will be realised that such a feeling would be by no means unlikely.

For these reasons, then, an extreme puritan strain begins to show itself towards the end of the period of the Medinan caliphate, a strain which continues to be seen at various times in the subsequent history of Islam. It is one of two opposite tendencies within the Islamic world, namely emphasis upon the *charismatic community* on the one hand, and on the other emphasis upon the *charismatic leader* (Watt, 1960). The tendency to emphasise the importance of the charismatic leader is represented principally by the Shi'ites. For them charismatic leadership of the Islamic community was found only in Muhammad, in his surviving male relative Ali, and after the murder of Ali, in his descen-

dants. That is to say they rejected the claim to the caliphate made by
Mu'awiya and his Umayyad descendants. The Shi'ites' high valuation
of the charisma of the Prophet and of Ali may possibly have been to
some extent due to their having been predominantly South Arabian in
origin (Watt, 1961; 105f.), for in that region, as we have seen, the
conception of the superhuman, semi-divine king was fairly well
established. Whereas the Kharijites with their emphasis on the charismatic community distrusted the rule of the individual, the Shi'ites took
the view that *only* the inspired leader could safely be entrusted with the
guidance of the community. It will be noticed, however, that theirs
was a view of charisma as something hereditary; the Prophet, in this
understanding of the matter, is the founder of a charismatic dynasty, a
conception which lies very close to Kingship. Associated with this is
the Shi'ite idea of the infallibility of Ali's leadership; he had 'the guidance of heaven'; this infallibility was attributed by the Shi'ites to Ali's
descendants, the Imams.

5.18 Islam under the Umayyad caliphs (661–750)

With the seizure of power by Mu'awiya, governor of Damascus, on
the assassination of Ali in 661, the centre of activity of the Islamic state
now shifts to Damascus. Islam was already developing that dual aspect
which has characterised so much of its subsequent history. There is, on
the one hand, the religious factor in Islam. This has its roots in the
prophetic mission of Muhammad at Mecca (5.13), the recalling of men
to a dimension in human life other than that to be found in immediate
material interests and concerns. And there is, on the other hand, the
political factor in Islam, which has its roots in the reorganisation of
Medinan society by Muhammad and the creation of a new super-tribe
as the context in which Muslim religious life and practice were to be set
(5.15). Inevitably this creation by Muhammad of a political reality, the
Islamic state, attracted those whose principal interest lay in the
political power of this increasingly strong and increasingly pan-
Arabian community. In any society religious belief and practice will
inevitably tend to influence and be influenced by the economic and
political structure of that society. But here we have a case in which the
two are *deliberately* brought into conscious relationship with each other:
a religious system which is internationally organised as a political

entity, a state. It is this dual aspect of Islam that has to be borne in mind when one studies its history. For in this case, a marriage had been *arranged* between religion and politics; and fairly soon the two partners began to show signs of disagreement.

The Umayyads ruled from Damascus the Islamic empire, an empire then consisting of Arabia, Egypt, Syria, Iraq and much of Persia, but it was not a case of political power in Damascus in conflict with religious interests in Medina and Mecca. Rather, the two elements, religious and political, were present throughout the empire. In Arabia just as much as in Damascus there were Arabs who had become Muslims out of largely political or secular considerations, and what the more pious Muslims considered worldliness was to be found just as easily in Medina as in Damascus. Under the Umayyads Arabs everywhere fell in with the hedonism of the caliphs; the development of Arab love poetry celebrating the joys of flirtation was a notable feature of the caliphate of Abdal Malik (685–705 C.E.); and even drinking songs emerged during the last decade of Umayyad rule – an indication that the Prophet's prohibition of the drinking of wine was largely disregarded, especially in Iraq. On the other hand, there were the faithful, whether Arabs or non-Arabs, who had been attracted to Islam for religious reasons, those who had turned to this sytem of belief and practice from paganism or from a superficial or formal adherence to Christianity or Zoroastrianism or even Judaism. With the kind of protests that the faithful raised we shall be concerned later (*5.19, 6.36*).

Some eleven Umayyad caliphs ruled from Damascus and among these the most important reigns are those of Mu'awiya (661–80 C.E.), Abdal Malik (685–705 C.E.) and Walid I (705–15 C.E.). It is proper to peak of their 'reigns' for they were in all but name autocratic kings from Abdal Malik onwards. During the caliphate of Walid I Islamic political control was extended in the West to include most of Spain, and in the East to the area of north-west India known as Sind.

In the case of Spain, the crossing of the Muslim Arab army from the north coast of Africa in 711 C.E. under a general named Tariq and their victorious landing at the Rock (which was thereupon named Jabal Tariq, hence Gibraltar), was seen in religious terms as a fulfilment of the Muslim duty of jihad – vigorous striving on behalf of God and Islam. The Muslim occupation of Spain was very rapid and was largely complete by 714 C.E., it was followed by the accession to Islam of large numbers of the population of Spain, both during these

I

and the succeeding years. Those who became Muslims did not do so, however, out of fear or threat of violence. There was a considerable Jewish population who had been subjected to severe discrimination and disability under Christian rule; there were many Spaniards whose adherence to Christianity was, at the most, formal; and there were not a few slaves – brought to Spain by a flourishing trade in captives taken in wars elsewhere in Europe – whose condition was, to say the least, not too happy. The Jews openly co-operated with the advancing Muslim armies; some embraced Islam, as did numbers of the formal Christians and slaves; while some non-Muslims became known as 'near-Arabs' or Mozarabs, that is to say, they continued to adhere to their former faith, which they were allowed to practise, while becoming loyal subjects of the Muslim ruler. Forced conversion to Islam or persecution of non-Muslims is not a feature of the Arabs' occupation of Spain, and in T. W. Arnold's view 'it was probably in a great measure their tolerant attitude towards the Christian religion that facilitated their rapid acquisition of the country' (Arnold, 1913; 136).

The entry of Islam into the Indian subcontinent was rich in consequences which have continued down to the most recent times, and are seen, for example, in the partition of India and the creation of Pakistan in 1947. In the case of India Islam entered sometimes peacefully, sometimes violently: five important phases can be distinguished:

1. In the first Islamic century the settlement of Muslim Arab traders in the coastal regions of South India
2. The campaign in Sind under Muhammad ibn Qasim in the eighth century C.E.
3. The violent invasion under Muhammad of Ghazni at the beginning of the eleventh century
4. The missionary work of the Sufis, spread over a fairly long period
5. The invasion by Muslim Turks which resulted ·in the setting up of the Mughal empire in the early sixteenth century.

In all of these cases except the first Islam entered by land routes via the north-western region of India. The first two of these phases come within the period of the Umayyad caliphate, and in these two instances the bearers of Islam were Arabs.

Before the time of Muhammad Arabs had traded with the countries of the East, notably India and China, to bring to South Arabia for transhipment overland the spices, gems and silk which were highly valued in the Mediterranean world. In the course of their trading activities the Arabs formed settlements on the coasts of South India. One reason for this was that timber for shipbuilding was scarce in Arabia whereas a plentiful supply was to be had from the Indian tropical forests. Thus at the time Arabia became Muslim there were already established natural bridgeheads in South India for the entry of Islam. Arabs now came as Muslims. Their settlements constituted only a small minority of the population and the new religion seemed to offer no threat to a resurgent Brahmanism which was now making inroads into South Indian Buddhism and Jainism. Moreover, the Arabs were seen to be making a contribution to the prosperity of the land, and they were consequently treated with considerable honour. During the first three centuries of the Islamic era there was a steady growth of the Arab settlements, a growth which Muslim historians have seen to be a result of the 'quickening of the constructive spirit among the Arabs after their conversion to Islam' (Qureshi, 1962; 12). They now built mosques in their settlements and were by the Hindu rulers allowed the right to manage their own civil and personal legal affairs. They were allowed also to take wives from among the local high-caste Nāir women, and in this way the Muslim population grew, and there gradually came into being the strongly established Muslim community of Malabar.

Meanwhile the Arabs had experienced a different kind of encounter with Hindus in north India. On the whole Hindus had an aversion to travelling to foreign countries because of the caste taboos and the ritual impurity such travel incurred, and this is why it was the Arabs who carried on the sea trade between India and Arabia. In the north, in the region of the lower Indus valley known as Sind, there appears to have been among the Hindus less disinclination to seafaring, at least to the extent that some of the men of Sind had taken to piracy. Hence it came about that when some Arab vessels sailing westwards from Ceylon, carrying gifts from the king of Ceylon to the Arab viceroy of the eastern Umayyad empire, and carrying also the widows and families of some Arab mariners who had died in Ceylon, were blown off course towards the coast of Sind, they fell into the hands of some of these Indian pirates who plundered the gifts and carried off the women and children. The caliph Walīd I was persuaded to take strong action against the Hindu rāja of Sind, who had refused to reply to a protest from the Arab viceroy. A special expedition of Arab troops was sent under the command of the youthful and extremely able young general, Muhammad ibn Qasim. In spite of strong resistance the well-fortified town of Debul fell to the Arabs in 711, and then, after a long siege followed by a vigorous battle, the capital of Sind, Brahmanabad, in 712 C.E. The rāja was killed, Muhammad ibn Qasim married the rani, the dead king's widow, and himself became the ruler of lower Sind. After a while he turned his attention to upper Sind, and in 713 extended his rule there, and over part of the Punjab. The rāja of Kashmir became alarmed and appealed for help to the emperor of China. No help came from that quarter, but in 715 the caliph Walid I died, and was succeeded by Sulaiman, a bitter enemy of Muhammad ibn Qasim's family. The latter was therefore recalled, and imprisoned in Iraq; there he died, and this brought to a halt for a while the Muslim invasion of India.

The success of ibn Qasim was due partly to his spirited generalship and the ability and enthusiasm of his troops, and partly to his considerate treatment of the local population which was still predominantly Buddhist, and who welcomed relief from the rule of a Hindu rāja. Qasim did not discriminate between Hindus and Buddhists, and learning that they had their own sacred scriptures is said to have treated them as dhimmis or 'protected peoples', that is, as 'people of a book', just as Jews and Christians had been treated in other parts of the empire. It is possible to see in Muhammad ibn Qasim a representative of Islam at its best during the Umayyad period; vigorous, resourceful, hardy, possibly aggressive, but also tolerant of the religious attitudes of other worshippers of God. However, it is also possible that his tolerance of Buddhist and Hindu practices, which appeared to later Muslim invaders as idolatrous, may have been due to religious indifference. This certainly would be more in line with the prevailing attitude of the Umayyad rulers. We know that the caliph Abdal Malik had trouble with some of the more pious Muslims of Medina; his son Walid I whom ibn Qasim served was a man of similar disposition. Subsequent phases of the Muslim conquest of India belong to a later period and will be dealt with in Chapter six (*6.38*).

5.19 Muslim religious ideas during the Umayyad period (661–750)

The seizure of power by the Umayyads had a notable effect in the realm of Muslim religious ideas, namely the questioning of the orthodox doctrine of the predestination of good and evil by God. The references in the Qur'an upon which this doctrine is built, when they are set out in full and with nothing that is relevant ignored, leave no doubt that the Qur'an is overwhelmingly in favour of the idea that all that happens in the world, whether it appears to man to be good or evil, is the direct activity of God (Sweetman, 1947; 157ff.). A characteristic saying occurring in a number of suras is: 'God leads astray whom He pleases and guides whom He pleases.' A. Jeffery comments that Muhammad seems in the course of his prophetic mission to have expressed more and more definitely this doctrine of predetermination of all things by God (Jeffery, 1958). There is an irresistible logic in this orthodox Islamic doctrine, granted the premise: that God is all-dominant power. Clearly God cannot be subject to the action of any other being, and nothing can be incumbent upon him (Sweetman, 1947; 167). As a modern Muslim writer has put it, whatever man does God is doing; and, moreover, God's ordering of events is not based on benevolence or goodwill (Sweetman, 1947; 168).

Such a doctrine was very congenial to the Umayyad caliphs at Damascus. Mu'awiya, the first of these Umayyads, who had resisted and overthrown Ali, was far from being a man of pious life, nor apparently did he care very much one way or the other about orthodoxy, but *he ruled the community of God*. What could the faithful say in criticism, for according to orthodox doctrine he could only hold such a position by the will of God?

However, Muslim opposition to the Umayyads did arise: not in Mecca, certainly, nor in Medina, still less in Damascus, but in Basra, an Islamic military town on the lower Euphrates. This opposition took the form of a questioning of the orthodox doctrine of divine predestination and the asserting of the possibility of human free-will. According to traditions quoted by Wensinck discussions on human freedom of action were initiated by a man named Ma'bad who had discussed these matters with a Christian from Mesopotamia who had become a Muslim, and who later returned to Christianity. But it was not enough to assent to the possibility of human free-will; it had to be justified from the Qur'an. Recourse to the Qur'an showed that there were *some* passages which were capable of being interpreted in a sense that allowed man some real freedom of action and choice (Watt, 1948; 14). Man, it was asserted, on the basis of such passages as could be collected, *had* the power (qadar) of free action. Those who taught this view came to be known as Qadarites.

To the majority of the orthodox, however, such views were anathema. To say that men had power to act freely was tantamount to ascribing to men a power to initiate, to create: it was virtually to give man a place alongside the Creator himself, and this was shirk, the first (and, for many, the only) deadly sin. Yet the Qadarites maintained their view, against great odds; in so doing they initiated one of the most important theological controversies in Islam; and they suffered for their views. Ma'bad, according to one report, was killed by order of the caliph, Abdal Malik, in 705 c.e. Nevertheless, the controversy went on, and we shall return to it in a later chapter (6.35).

5.2 THE EXPANSION OF BUDDHISM (*600–1100* c.e.)

5.20 Buddhism in China, 600–1000

During the century and a half from 600 to 750 c.e., the period during which Islam arose in Arabia and was carried by Arab armies, colonisers and missionaries to an area extending from Spain to India, Buddhism was in decline in the Indian subcontinent, but was still increasing in influence in China and was establishing itself in Japan. It is significant that a good deal of useful information about the condition of Buddhism in India during this period is derived from the accounts of their travels given by Chinese Buddhist pilgrims such as Hsuan-tsang and I-Tsing (*5.25*).

In China Buddhism had, by about 600 c.e., been known for some five centuries (*4.36*). In 618 c.e. began one of the most notable Chinese dynasties, the T'ang, which lasted until 907 c.e. In terms of art, literature and intellectual activity it was one of the great periods in China's history. The capital of the empire, Ch'ang-an (Sian), had a very cosmopolitan character, and is said to have been probably the most civilised city in the world at that time. It was also a time of continued growth and prosperity for Buddhism, both monastic and lay, and this in spite of two outstanding disadvantages from which Buddhism suffered in China: first, the strongly Confucian tradition of China's rulers, which from time to time resulted in their active hostility towards this foreign religion from India; and second, the conflict between the traditional Chinese social pattern with its emphasis on the family on the one hand, and the Buddhist celibate and economically non-productive monastic life on the other. As far as China's rulers were concerned, however, Buddhism commended itself to them by its encouragement of peace among their subjects; this was a valuable adjunct to effective government. As far as the peasants and artisans were concerned, it offered them comfort and hope within a convincing and coherent view of human life and the human situation. Buddhism was, moreover, able to accommodate itself to indigenous Chinese religious customs to some extent. In the latter half of the eighth century, for example, Buddhist monks began to give official recognition to the ceremonies in honour of the dead (sometimes referred to as the Chinese 'All Souls' Day') which remained a feature of popular Chinese religion up to modern times. On the other hand, as more and more of the Chinese people turned to Buddhism and sought refuge in the Buddha, the Dhamma and the Sangha, so the Buddhist monasteries became more numerous, with the eventual result that more and more men and women were drawn into these places of contemplation and study to become monks and nuns, and more and more of China's resources were devoted to building and extending the monasteries and temples, and making them more elaborate and ornate.

The process brought its nemesis in the form of government disapproval of the way things were going. This became severest in the middle of the ninth century C.E. under the emperor Wu Tsung (841–7). The Muslim Arabs, by their conquest of western Turkestan in the middle of the eighth century, had cut off China's contact with western and southern Asia. Moreover, the decline of Buddhism's vitality in India meant that there was now less impetus for the flow of Buddhist scholars and ideas from India. Added to these things there was rebellion within China, led by An Lu-Shan; this had weakened central control in the T'ang empire and led to the growth of provincial centres of power. China became turned in upon herself and 'the cosmopolitanism of the great days of the dynasty gave way to a cultural defensiveness which occasionally turned into xenophobia' (Wright, 1959; 83). Hence it was that at the instigation of Taoist priests the emperor Wu Tsung launched campaigns against both Manichaeism in 843 and Buddhism in 845. His hostility to Buddhism as a 'foreign superstition' was proclaimed in an edict which spoke of the dangers to the country of the vast numbers of monks and nuns needing economic support; it spoke also of the innumerable crowds of lay people who helped to perpetuate this state of affairs as they thronged the great temples which had absorbed so much of the national resources. Four thousand of the larger temples and forty thousand smaller rural temples were to be demolished, and a quarter of a million monks and nuns were to be returned to secular occupations. The figures may be exaggerated but they are an indication of the wide support Buddhism was receiving from the Chinese people, and of the extent to which it had been welcomed by them. Wu Tsung himself, however, was of Taoist inclination, and like other Chinese emperors sought to perpetuate his rule by drinking the Taoist elixir of immortality (2.47). It appears, as in most other cases, to have had a deleterious effect upon his health, and shortly after the promulgation of his edict he lost the power of speech and was deposed in favour of his uncle Hsuan Tsung, who immediately reversed the anti-Buddhist enactment and punished the Taoist priests who had instigated the persecution, but not before thousands of monasteries and temples had been destroyed. The new emperor did, however, take measures to control the numbers of men and women entering the Buddhist Sangha. No further large-scale persecution of Buddhism took place during the remainder of the period of the T'ang dynasty. Just over a century later, in 960 c.e., as a result of the increasingly ineffective rule of its later emperors, the dynasty collapsed and the Chinese empire fell into disorder.

From 960, however, the fortunes of the empire improved once again under the Sung dynasty which was to last for just over three centuries, until the growing strength of the Mongols brought it to an end in 1280 with the establishment by Kublai Khan of Mongol rule. The Sung dynasty is notable for further tributes to the prestige of Buddhism; particularly for instance the printing in 972 c.e. by the newly developed technique of printing blocks, of the Buddhist scriptures, the Tripitaka, to which the first Sung emperor, Tai Tsu, himself contributed a foreword; and the building by the second Sung emperor at very great expense, of a magnificent Buddhist stupa, 360 feet in height, in his capital city. During the Sung dynasty, moreover, the Ch'an school of Buddhism, a peculiarly Chinese development, succeeded in making its way and becoming accepted among the upper classes of Chinese society. This is another indication of the ability of Buddhism to establish itself within Chinese culture, and to adapt itself to Chinese conditions. However, before a brief account of the Ch'an system is given, it will be convenient to note two other characteristically Chinese developments in Buddhism under the T'ang dynasty.

Within any given society in which it becomes influential Buddhism tends to manifest itself in two main forms, monastic and lay. In the period under review Buddhism developed its characteristically Chinese variants in both the monastic sphere, in the Vinaya school, and in the lay sphere, in Amida or Pure Land Buddhism, and finally in a form which in a sense is a peculiarly Chinese attempt to abolish the distinction between monastic and lay, in the Ch'an system. We shall deal with each of these in turn.

5.21 *The Vinaya school*

In the purely monastic sphere the Lü-tsung school, founded by Tao Hsüan (595–667 C.E.), laid great emphasis upon the Vinaya (*3.21*), the canonical collection of rules governing the life of the Sangha. Against a growing laxity in monastic life, Tao Hsüan urged a more faithful adherence to ascetic discipline and morality as the essential condition for the Buddhist life. In Indian Buddhism there was no Vinaya school as such, although this kind of emphasis on the importance of monastic morality and discipline is very characteristic of the Theravāda. The fact that in China such an emphasis emerged as a special school indicates how liberal and possibly how lax Buddhist monastic life in China had become. Whether monastic laxity was due to the swollen size of the Buddhist Sangha by this time, or whether the large numbers who entered the monasteries were a result of lowered standards of discipline and morality it would be difficult to decide. The existence of the Lü-tsung, virtually as a protest movement, is at any rate an indication there was some correlation between hypertrophy of the Sangha and laxity of discipline. The Sangha is essential to Buddhism, and essential to the Sangha is ascetic discipline. It is difficult to see that the emphasis of the Lü-tsung was anything other than wholly proper, except in so far as *excessive* emphasis upon discipline might detract from that other equally essential feature of the Sangha's life, namely, meditation. Eliot sees some evidence that Tao Hsüan was not much inclined to the mystical life but was a man of practical temperament for whom asceticism was by itself a sufficient concern (Eliot, 1921; iii,

316). But there was a connection, which we shall note later (*5.23*), between the Lü-tsung and the Ch'an with its emphasis on inward enlightenment, and this also may be significant.

5.22 The Pure Land school

In the purely lay sphere, on the other hand, the proper emphasis for a Buddhist must be on achieving a good rebirth hereafter. In early Buddhism this meant rebirth of the kind that would make possible a life of contemplation as a monk and so, ultimately, lead to nirvāna. But in Chinese Buddhism a more immediate religious goal appears – rebirth in Paradise, or more precisely in one of several possible paradises. Common to most forms of lay Buddhism is the idea of rebirth in the world of the coming Buddha (*3.29*), Meitreya, a kind of messianic age. But added to this in China were two yet more immediate paradises – those of the bodhisattvas (*3.29*) known as Akshobhya and Amitābha (or Amida). The second of these hopes became very widespread among lay Buddhists in China during the T'ang dynasty. The idea of a paradise or 'Pure Land' to which the bodhisattva can bring men at death is to be found in China before the T'ang period; it was, for example, taught by Hui-yüan in the fourth century: its emergence as the doctrine of a school, however, is usually connected with a man named Tao-ch'o (562–645 C.E.). Even more prominent a 'patriarch' of this school was Shan-tao (613–81 C.E.). There is a striking similarity between the Islamic idea of the bridge a hairsbreadth wide over the gulf of Hell across which men must pass in the Last Day and which only believers will traverse successfully, and the idea taught by Shan-tao (who was born at about the time Muhammad began his preaching in Mecca) that there is a 'White Way' or bridge which leads to the Pure Land, or Paradise, over which the faithful will be guided by Amida. The school of Shan-tao is sometimes spoken of as the school of the 'Short Cut', that is, the short cut to Paradise. So far as the lay Buddhist was concerned it was required of him only that he should have faith in Amida and call upon Amida by name.

What was being affirmed was the power of a supremely holy and enlightened being (a bodhisattva) to create by virtue of his own merit and holiness a realm, or an environment, or a 'field' of blessedness – a doctrine which was wholly characteristic of the Mahāyāna. In addition it was now being affirmed that the bodhisattva's merit was such that he was able to introduce into this realm of blessedness all who had faith in him. In other words, what had developed in China was a doctrine of salvation by heavenly grace, through faith in Amida.

It is not necessary to suppose that this doctrine of the heavenly saviour must have been borrowed from Christianity. True, Nestorians were to be found in China early in the seventh century, and they received a certain degree of patronage from some of the T'ang emperors. But an account of the doctrines of the Nestorian church given in the inscription dating from 781 C.E. found at Hsian-fu, while it deals with the life of Christ, omits all reference to the crucifixion and explains the Christian symbol, the cross, as a representation of the four cardinal points of the created world. Eliot suggests that the Christian doctrine of the atonement was probably felt to be unacceptable in Buddhist China, and was for that reason suppressed by the Nestorians (Eliot, 1935; 149).

Certainly, however, the doctrine of salvation by faith in Amida, once formulated in China, appealed very strongly, especially to the poor and unsophisticated, among whom it met with widespread acceptance. It was never even in the early days of its development wholly confined to one sect, and after the ninth century C.E. Amidism ceased to be a separate school and became an all-pervasive mood in the popular lay Buddhism of China, and subsequently of Japan.

5.23 The Ch'an school

The Ch'an (Japanese, Zen) school of Buddhism is in Chinese tradition regarded as having been founded by an Indian named Bodhidharma who arrived in Canton about the year 520 C.E. There is little evidence about Bodhidharma outside the Chinese sources, and there is much in these that appears to be legendary. There seems to be no certainty that his teaching was Buddhist; it may well have been Indian Vedantist, from what accounts there are of it. Certainly the period of the most characteristic and vigorous development of the Ch'an was during the T'ang dynasty. As it then developed this school showed itself to be a very *Chinese* form of Buddhism, though not necessarily any the less *Buddhist* on that account.

Its peculiarly Chinese character is revealed in several ways. There was a feeling of impatience with the elaborate Indian system of scholasticism which required a Buddhist monk to spend years and years poring over scriptural texts, commentaries and sub-commentaries, and impatience also with the equally elaborate systematisation of the long slow processes of meditation, possibly (it was assumed) through a succession of rebirths. Over against this there developed a conviction that enlightenment could be gained here and now in this life, by concentrating on one or two Sutras at the most, and giving even these a place subordinate to the essential activity, namely the earnest seeking of enlightenment. The word used for this in Indian Buddhism is bodhi; literally, the state of being 'awakened'. The Chinese word used by the Ch'an School was wu, that is, awareness (in Japanese, Satori). It was with this kind of emphasis that Ch'an developed from the time of *Hui-neng* (638–713 C.E.), who is virtually the patriarch of this school, although it was claimed that he received the Ch'an method by an esoteric transmission 'from mind to mind' going back to the Buddha Shakyamuni himself.

An even more characteristically Chinese aspect of Ch'an was introduced by Po-chang (720–814 C.E.). In reaction to the overgrown system of scholasticism of the monasteries, he taught that the Buddhist monk should engage in some economically useful occupation; his slogan was: 'a day without work is a day without food'. This was possible if the monk was not tied to the study of scripture and the long routine of monastic meditation and if he could instead concentrate on a single sutra so far as the Buddha-word was concerned, and on a form of mental discipline which left his hands free to work. The mental discipline was provided by the use of the koan – a statement or proposition presented to the aspirant for enlightenment by his Ch'an master, usually a statement of the kind which affronted the reason. In wrestling with this, and possibly with further such koans (which would progressively undermine the assumptions of worldly 'commonsense') the aspirant would suddenly, so it was held, experience illumination. Meanwhile his feet and hands could be at work, ploughing any number of fields. The possibility of the monk thus becoming economically productive once more represents no less characteristically Chinese an interest than does the impatience with the over-elaborate systematisation of monastic thought.

Great importance still attached, however, to the moral discipline which was part of the necessary preparation for enlightenment, and it is interesting to note that during the earlier period of the development of Ch'an, its monks were to be found in the monasteries of the Lü-tsung, the Vinaya-emphasising school (*5.21*). On the other hand Ch'an stands in contrast to the Pure Land school in two ways. First, it is much more clearly dependent on the master-pupil relationship, and in this sense more obviously a religious *order*, with an important place for the Sangha, whereas the Pure Land school is a form of devotion open to all without the necessity for a spiritual master; second, in the Ch'an system much greater emphasis is laid upon the spiritual effort of the aspirant after enlightenment,whereas the Pure Land makes salvation possible on what looks like easier terms – simply the repetition of the name of Amida, and the cultivation of an attitude of devotion.

5.24 Buddhism in Japan, 600–800

Buddhism arrived in Japan about the middle of the sixth century C.E. from Korea. Prince Shōtoku (574–621) who became the ruler of Japan in 593 C.E. and reigned for nearly thirty years, was the son of Buddhist parents, and is remembered not only for his statesmanship but also for his energetic furtherance of Buddhist ideals and policies. Anesaki (1963) describes him as 'the founder of Japanese civilisation as well as of a united Japanese nation'. One of his first acts as a ruler was to proclaim Buddhism the state religion, and to found a great Buddhist institution consisting of a religious centre, an orphanage and old people's home, a hospital, and a dispensary. This was on the west coast, on the shore of the inland sea which separates Japan from the Asian continent; it was thus conveniently situated for the reception of Buddhist immigrants and monks from Korea and China, and for the despatch of Japanese monks and pilgrims to the continent, where they went to study and to acquire and bring back to Japan the civilised arts and sciences of Buddhist China.

Buddhism in Japan during the reign of Shōtoku was primarily a religion of the aristocracy. The Lotus Sutra provided its scriptural basis and motivation, and it was characterised by a strong social consciousness, which received expression in the kind of welfare institution we have just mentioned. The Buddhist Order became virtually a state church, with the ruler protecting, encouraging and supporting the work of the monks, and the monks willingly giving their allegiance and support to the ruler. The actions and attitudes of Shōtoku were those of the sincere Buddhist ruler; for instance, he was criticised for not taking revenge upon the murderers of his uncle (as the old tribal morality of Japan would have required); for him such action would only be to perpetuate evil karma, and would remedy nothing.

In the early eighth century a new capital, Nara, was established, and it is as 'the Nara period' that the years from 710–84 c.e. are known. During this time Buddhism in Japan began to develop a more popular character, alongside the official, aristocratic state church. This took two main forms: (1) the Pure Land cult of devotion to Amida and reliance upon his saving grace was gradually introduced from China, where it had by this time been flourishing for about a century (*5.22*); and (2) from about 750 onwards, a gradual growth in numbers of lay Buddhist ascetics known as the Ubasoku-zenji, that is, the upāsaka- (or layman-) ascetics. These were men often of humble social origin who by private ascetic discipline aimed at achieving superhuman powers. Later on they came to be known as hijiri, or 'holy-men' (Hori, 1958).

Alongside these developments during the latter part of the Nara period one more must be mentioned: the gradual adaptation of the indigenous tribal religion of Japan to Buddhist forms and names. Until the introduction of Buddhism there was no need for a special designation for the peculiarly Japanese corpus of beliefs, myths and ritual practices, but now, in order to distinguish it from the Buddhist way, it came to be known as 'the way of the kami'. The kami were, as we have seen (*2.48*), the gods; or more exactly the exalted or superior beings, or heavenly beings. The Chinese character for 'heavenly beings' was shin, and for 'way' tao, and so the native Japanese religion became known as *Shin-to*. (It is tautologous to add the ending 'ism' although it is not uncommon among Western writers.) Among the mass of the Japanese people this system of belief and practice retained its hold in spite of the introduction of Buddhism, and indeed it has persisted right up to modern times. The reason why it survived the period of Buddhist ascendancy was that its guardians and officials, the priests of the local shrines, did not resist the Buddhist invasion, but bowed to it, came to terms with it, agreed with it, adopted its names and even some of its ideas – and thus avoided open conflict. In all this Shinto was aided, of course, by the tolerant attitudes of Buddhists. Indeed, the process may even be seen as an example, of which there are others, notably in

South-East Asia (*6.45; 6.46*) and in the Tantra (*5.26*), of the Buddhist readiness to admit pre-Buddhist elements into Buddhist ideas and attitudes. This process had certainly begun in the Nara period; it was in the next, the Heian period, to be dealt with later (*5.28*), that it is most clearly recognisable.

5.25 Buddhism in India, 600–1100

Some of the most important sources of information about the condition of Buddhism in India during this period are the accounts provided by Chinese Buddhist monk-pilgrims of their travels in India, notably those of Hsuan-tsang and I-Tsing.

These, and many other Chinese monks like them, made the long and hazardous journey from China westwards through the mountainous regions of central Asia and thence into India by the north-western passes into Kashmir and the Punjab. Some made the long sea voyage from China southwards, round Malaya to the east coast of India. They went to what was for them the Holy Land, in search of deeper knowledge of Buddhist truth and of Buddhist texts. Hsuan-tsang left China about 629 c.e., and returned there in 645 after having travelled round most of the Indian subcontinent. I-Tsing was in India from about 671 to 695 c.e. (An earlier pilgrim-monk, whose record of his travels was somewhat briefer, was Fa-hsien, who was in India and Ceylon from 399 to 414 c.e.) I-Tsing in the epilogue to his account tells of the difficulties of the expedition: 'It is an extremely difficult and perilous undertaking . . . only with the help of elephants can the desert be crossed. Nothing can be seen there except the sun. . . . Many days I have passed without food and even without a drop of water. . . . When I left China I had fifty companions with me, but when I reached the Western Country [India] only two or three were left' (Dutt, 1962, 311f.).

India itself, however, both Hsuan-tsang and I-Tsing found to be a pleasant and prosperous country. Their accounts are particularly valuable for the information they give us concerning the number and size of Buddhist monasteries in India in the seventh century. This is one of the reasons why our picture of Indian Buddhism is clearer for the seventh century c.e. than for the immediately preceding or following centuries. The first half of the century was the time of the emperor of northern India Harsha-vardhana (606–646), who is said to have written some Buddhist poems and, even in the midst of a busy life of campaigning and governing, three plays, the third of which is of a religious character, largely Buddhist but with some elements of Shaivism also. The Buddhism of the emperor was, like that of many of his subjects, of an eclectic and tolerant nature; in fact it was only in the latter part of his life that he became markedly Buddhist, and modelled his activities on those of his predecessor Aśoka. Hsuan-tsang devotes a good deal of space to the city of Kanauj, on the upper Ganges, which Harshavardhana had made his capital (rather than Patna, which had been the earlier capital of the north Indian empire). Hsuan-tsang records that under Harsha's patronage the number of Buddhist monasteries there had increased to about one hundred, housing ten thousand monks of both the Hīnayāna and the Mahāyāna. (In Fa-hsien's time there had been only two monasteries with a few Hīnayāna monks.) But this was exceptional; in some places Hsuan-tsang found only deserted and ruined monasteries. What was perhaps typical was the growth of the Mahāyāna at the expense of the Hīnayāna. At Shrāvastī, one of the famous names in Buddhist history, where the Buddha had spent much of his time and where many of his discourses had been delivered, were now to be seen only the ruins of once large and important monasteries. Even in Fa-hsien's time there had been a few monks there who had received him courteously, but now the place seems to have been deserted by the Buddhists; on the other hand, Brahmanic temples abounded. Kapilavastu, the birthplace of the Buddha, Hsuan-tsang found desolate, its former buildings almost completely ruined, and only a very few monks still surviving.

One notable exception to this general decline of Buddhist monastic centres in India in the seventh century was Nālanda. Here, on the Ganges plain a few miles south of Patna (Pātaliputra), a monastery had been founded in the fifth century C.E. by a Gupta king (probably Kumāra Gupta I, who reigned from 415 to 455 C.E.). Other Gupta kings added further monasteries adjoining the first one, and had also endowed these monastic corporations with considerable lands and villages. S. Dutt points out the probable reason for this generous royal munificence, namely that Nālanda and possibly some other Buddhist monasteries like it were by this time developing as seats of higher learning (Dutt, 1962; 331). That is to say a process of what amounts almost to the secularisation of the Buddhist monastery in India had begun. They were turning away from the earlier ideal, of being centres of 'study for faith', to that of being centres of 'study for knowledge', away from monastic life proper to that of institutions of secular learning in many ways similar to universities. Certainly this is what Nālanda, the greatest monastic centre in India at this time, had become. Two other monastic universities of this kind were Vikramasīla and Odantapura, also in eastern Bihar. The grouping of several neighbouring monasteries into a single organisation called a Mahāvihāra had begun some time in the Gupta period, and with this process of enlargement went another, namely enlargement of the scope and content of learning. The master–pupil relationship of the cloister, which had originally a spiritual end in view, was now adapted to the acquisition of a wider range of scholarship by much larger numbers of students. Thus while Buddhist culture and general education flourished Buddhist spirituality declined. The former, more even distribution of Buddhist centres of influence, certainly throughout northern India, gave way to a pattern of opulence in a few places and desolation in many others. While he was staying at Nālanda Hsuan-tsang dreamt that he saw its magnificent courts deserted and become the haunt of wild animals; in a vision he saw too the state of confusion in north India that would follow the emperor Harsha-vardhana's death. 'The dream and the vision,' comments S. Dutt, 'must have been prompted by Hsuan-tsang's own haunting thoughts of a dark future – a time when Buddhism would fall into eclipse and Buddhist culture into neglect.'

The change which had begun to come over the monastic life by the seventh century is only one aspect of the process of the decline of Buddhism in India. Another was the growing strength of pagan practices and ideas which by this time were beginning to find their way into Buddhism, and were bringing about its destruction as surely as the jungle that overwhelmed its neglected monasteries. Just how this triumph of paganism came about is still not fully understood; we can only try to trace some of the factors involved, and to this we now turn.

5.26 The growth of Tantric ritual

From the sixth to the ninth century of the Christian era Nālanda grew in size, prestige and influence as a centre of Mahāyāna philosophy and secular learning. It was the strongly Mahāyānist emphasis which made possible the development within Buddhism of a cult known as the

Tantra. In its earlier form this is known as *Mantrayāna*, that is, the use of mantras (sacred chants that were invested with a mysterious quality and efficacy of their own) as a yāna, or 'vehicle' of salvation. The Tantra's later form is *Vajrayāna*, which is an attempt to systematise the vast number of mantrayāna ritual practices and relate them to five principal Bodhisattvas.

The Vajrayāna had affinities with one of the principal Mahāyānist school, the Yogācāra (*4.35*). The yogic practices which were a feature of the latter led to great importance being attached to mystic devices and diagrams of a geometrical kind. Such symbols, or maṇḍalas, were made use of especially in the setting forth of the inter-relationships of the principal bodhisattvas. A basic type of diagram, according to Snellgrove (1957), consists of the Buddha Vairocana as the central figure, with four others round him at the main points of the compass, each with attendant bodhisattvas. With each of the four surrounding buddha-figures are two goddesses, and together these eight goddesses symbolise the act of worship. This is reflected in their names: Vajra-Gaiety, Vajra-Garland, -Song, -Dance, -Flower, -Incense, -Lamp, -Perfume. Each of the four groups has also its own special mantra, or magical chant, and mudra (hand-gestures), which were used in the performance of the Tantric ritual.

While this systematisation is indebted to the yogic maṇḍala-symbols, the materials which are thus subjected to a systematic arrangement, the magical chants and the gestures, are derived from Indian folk-religion. One of the important aspects of Tantra is that it belongs to the lay-Buddhist tradition, in which as we have noted before (*5.22*) the main emphasis until now was upon the achievement of a good rebirth. But the Tantra provides a parallel with the Ch'an system of China, in that the purpose of the Tantric ritual was the achievement not simply of a good rebirth, but, by the inducing of yogic trance, possible enlightenment here and now in this life, and in this the Tantra cuts across the distinction between lay and monastic spirituality with their lower and higher religious goals respectively. The Tantra has its own three grades of human beings: non-adepts, adepts and super-adepts.

Yogic trance, and possibly enlightenment, were only the highest aims of Tantric ritual. There were others. Many of the magical spells which were included in Tantra had less exalted purposes in view. 'The acquisition of buddhahood was merely a special application of a general magical practice, for there were maṇḍalas of all sorts and sizes.

The tantras refer to rites of all kinds: petrifying, subduing, exorcising, causing hatred amongst one's enemies, mesmerising, slaying, propitiating, causing prosperity, bringing rain, winning a woman, finding a thing which was lost and so on (Snellgrove, 1957; 76). There is much in this kind of list that reminds one of the Atharva-veda (*1.59*); we are here in the same world of magical incantations and charms. In other words, Tantra represents a frontier between on the one hand Buddhist belief and practice, and on the other the ancient magical practices of the Indian peasantry. It is another example of the kind of Buddhist bridge-building, between the Dharma and local indigenous culture, that has been noted already in other connections (*5.22; 5.24*).

To put the matter another way, we have here an example of the strong affinity which exists between the peasant class and magic (or forms of religion that have a large admixture of magic), an affinity which was discussed earlier, in connection with the Atharva-veda (*1.59*). This is the form which lay Buddhism very understandably assumes in a predominantly agricultural economy and a peasant society. But north-eastern India (Bihar and Bengal), where the Tantra developed most notably, had not recently *become* agricultural. It had been so for centuries. Yet in the accounts of Indian Buddhism given by the Chinese travellers Fa-hsien in the fifth century, and Hsuan-tsang and I-Tsing in the seventh, there is no evidence of the development of Tantra. The question which thus arises is: why do we not hear of the Tantric form of Buddhism until about the middle of the eighth century? This is when the earliest available Tantric texts are dated (Dutt, 1962; 349). One possible answer is that this form of Buddhist practice tended to be esoteric, and disclosed only to the properly initiated. So behind the earliest texts there may be a period of hidden, or at least undocumented, development. Another possible factor in the Tantra's emerging when it did is that by the middle of the eighth century the process of secularisation of the Buddhist monasteries had been going on for about three hundred years – Nālanda was founded in the middle of the fifth century (*5.25*). That is to say, during the earlier period of Buddhist history in India the frontier between Buddhist truth and the magical folk-lore of the Indian peasant had been effectively controlled by the Sanghas, by monks whose religious life and practice had been centred in the Dharma, whose study of it had been 'study for faith', and whose goal had been nirvāna. This is not to say that popular folk-lore and magical practices were not associated with lay Buddhism in the earlier period;

almost certainly they were from the earliest days, but they were held in check, and allowed only a subordinate position. Now with the decline of the monastic life the check was removed, and these popular magical practices came flooding in, and produced this late form of Indian Buddhism we know as the Tantra.

Besides the spells and charms and incantations which were one of its most prominent features was the importance given to the feminine partners of the buddhas, to which brief reference was made above. Female deities are a persistent feature of the religious traditions of east India, as of southern India also (1.31). Just as in the Hindu bhakti cults the god has his consort, so now the buddhas began to be represented as having female partners, who were usually some form of Prajñā pāramitā, the Transcendental Wisdom. This partnership between the masculine Buddha and the feminine Transcendental Wisdom introduced an element of sexual symbolism into Tantric Buddhism, and permitted the development of certain aspects of Tantric practice which have filled early European commentators with horror, and which have also probably been highly exaggerated. Sexual symbolism was used to convey what was held to be the characteristic feature of existence: unity in apparent duality. This was worked out in various ways. For example, combining of consonants and vowels gives birth to the mystic syllables of the mantra and hence affects the intentions of the user of these sacred sounds. So too the buddha and the bodhisattva were represented together in the ecstasy of union, a reminder to the devotee that oneness in the state of enlightenment is the highest bliss (mahāsukha). In some cases these ideas may have led to the performance of erotic rituals culminating in the intercourse of the yogin and his female partner, but in fact very little is known of such rituals in Buddhist contexts.

The whole question of sexual symbolism within religion is a vast and complicated one, but it is worth remembering (especially for those whose cultural environment is that of European Protestantism) that sexual forces are too real and powerful simply to be dismissed as having no part in religion; that there is perhaps an excessively masculine quality about much of Western monotheism; that there is on the other hand a persistent strain in other religious traditions which links holy Wisdom, as an aspect of deity, with feminine qualities – notably, both motherhood and virginity; that while the complete repression and denial of sexual activity may possibly, in some cases, lead to sublimation, it can also lead in less desirable directions; and, finally, that there is a good deal of undisguised sexual symbolism in mystical experience and writing in all traditions. All this suggests that the place given to the two principles, the feminine and the masculine, in Tantric Buddhism, is neither entirely unusual in the history of religion, nor necessarily surprising.

In conclusion certain general observations need to be made concerning Tantric Buddhism. The first is that the so-called 'immoral practices' over which some early European writers professed their disgust were probably not typical or representative of Tantra as a whole, and that where they existed they may be seen as an example of antinomianism, the idea that out of the whole-hearted embracing of moral evil will come redemption from it (an idea found elsewhere in the history of religion). The second point to be made is that while the use of Tantric forms and rituals undoubtedly increased from the eighth century onwards, such usage was by no means universal among Buddhists in India. The Tantra implies a recognition of the principle which is widespread in Indian religion, that there are different types of human beings, and that the forms of religious life and practice which suit one will not suit another. Finally, Tantric Buddhism was associated with certain regions of India rather than others, and most prominent among these was that area of eastern India which we call West Bengal and Bihar.

5.27 Buddhism in Tibet and South-East Asia, 600–1000

Buddhism was by the beginning of the seventh century well established in Central Asia, i.e. in the region to the north-west of India through which it had passed to China. But it had as yet not been received in Tibet. The first efforts to introduce it there are associated with the Tibetan king, Sron-btsan-sgam-po (b. 617 C.E.). By his military success he had considerably increased the prestige of his kingdom among neighbouring rulers, so that the king of Nepal and the emperor of China each considered it prudent to effect an alliance with him by offering him a daughter in marriage. These two princesses brought with them to the capital at Llasa Buddha-rupas (or 'images') and their knowledge of Buddhist belief and devotion. It became the Tibetan king's desire to introduce the spiritual and cultural benefits of Buddhism to his own country, and this he tried to do, but in spite of its royal patronage the new faith encountered strong opposition from the priests of the indigenous Bon religion of Tibet. A visiting Indian Buddhist teacher from Nālanda (5.25) realised that for people such as the Tibetans, whose culture was so deeply engrained with magical practices, the form of Buddhism which was most likely to meet with success was the Tantra. Hence it was that Padma-Sambhava, a well known exponent and teacher of Tantric Buddhism, was invited from Uḍḍiyāna, a region to the west of Tibet. Padma-Sambhava met with much greater success, and his name continued for many centuries to be highly venerated among Tibetans. The form of Buddhism which he introduced in the middle of the eighth century, the Vajrayāna (5.26), gave Tibetan Buddhism two of its characteristic features, its non-celibate monks and its magical rituals. Buddhism was no means permanently established in Tibet however, and after Padma-Sambhava's death there was a period of fierce persecution and a Tibetan king who was a royal patron of the Sangha was murdered by a rival for the throne. After a time of internal confusion, during which Buddhism virtually disappeared, peace returned, and by the beginning of the eleventh century scholar-missionaries were arriving in Tibet from the Pala kingdom of Bihar and Bengal, to reintroduce and re-establish Buddhism in the Tantric form that flourished in north-east India at that time. Outstanding among them was Dīpankara Srījnāna, (980–1053) or Atīsha (the venerable Lord) as he later came to be known by the Tibetans. Atīsha was a Bengali monk who had been head of the monastic university of Vikramasīla in eastern Bihar and who is said to have studied earlier at Thaton, in Burma (or possibly at a Buddhist centre in Indonesia; there is some uncertainty). Influential in persuading Atīsha to go and live in Tibet was a member of the Tibetan royal family who had renounced his claim to the throne in order to become a monk. Thus the Tantric Buddhism which at that time flourished in the Pala Kingdom of Bihar and Bengal in the eleventh century became the predominant religion of Tibet; it is in the Buddhism of Tibet, as it is known to modern scholars, that perhaps we come nearest to popular Buddhism as it existed in India before its virtual disappearance there (6.41).

In connection with Tibet, it will be appropriate at this point to turn to that area of continental South-East Asia which now forms the Union of Burma. Into this area had been moving during the early centuries of the Christian era a branch of the Tibetan peoples known today as the

Burmese. They came southwards from the mountainous Himālayan region of the north, into the river valley of the Irrawaddy where, possibly in the second century of the Christian era, their capital city of Pagan was founded on the east bank of the Irrawaddy just below its confluence with the Chindwin. Ahead of these immigrants into Burma by land was another group, the Pyus, whose capital had been established at Prome, in the lower Irrawaddy valley. Before the coming of the Pyus the whole of lower Burma had been occupied by another ethnic group, the Mons, whose territory also extended east into what is now Thailand. Possibly the Mons were the first of the peoples of the Indo-China subcontinent to receive Buddhism. (There is a legend that the emperor Aśoka of India in the third century B.C. (*3.27*) sent two Buddhist monks, Sona and Uttara, to 'Suvanna-bhumi', the Golden Land, which *may* have been Burma, but there is no other evidence apart from this story, which is found in the Ceylonese Buddhist chronicles.) Burma would not have been too difficult to reach by sea from Southern India, and possibly by land and sea from north-east India. Throughout the period up to about 1000 C.E. then, it seems that Buddhists from various places on the eastern side of India found their way to Burma: first of all Theravādins from the south of India and Ceylon; then as the Mahayāna developed, Buddhism was introduced into Burma in this form also; and finally, from about the eighth century, in the Tantric form. The Mons, the earlier occupants of the deltaic region of lower Burma, appear to have accepted the Theravādin form. Their capital, Sudhammavati (modern Thaton, on the eastern side of the Gulf of Martaban) was a centre of Theravāda Buddhism until the eleventh century. At Hmawza, five miles east of Prome in the Irrawaddy valley, the earliest archaeological evidence of Buddhism in Burma has been found, in the form of fragments of (Theravāda) Pali canonical scriptures dating from the fifth century C.E. There is evidence that among the Pyus both the Theravādin and the Sarvāstivādin (*3.24*) schools of Buddhism had their adherents. Architectural remains and statues exhibit the style of north-east India and the Orissa coast of the late Gupta age (Coedès, 1966). Early ninth-century Chinese accounts record that there were at this time in the Pyu kingdom over a hundred Buddhist monasteries at which education was given to young people, both boys and girls, up to the age of twenty.

Although the Burmese chronicles claim a date as early as the second century for the founding of the Burmese capital, Pagan, in the upper

Irrawaddy valley, the generally accepted date is 849 C.E. By this time it was the Mahāyāna form of Buddhism which was coming to Burma from north-east India, and from this time more particularly the Tantric form. The Buddhism of central Burma practised by these Tibeto-Burmese immigrants from the ninth to the middle of the eleventh century C.E. seems to have been very strongly Tantric; associated with it was a class of religious functionaries about whom not a great deal is known, but who seem to have combined something of the roles of guru, lama and priest, and who were known as 'aris' (a corruption of the word 'arya', in the sense of holy man). The region now known as Thailand was also one which, lying on the western side of the Indo-China peninsula, was open to Indian influences from an early period, but particularly during the time of the Guptas onwards. Archaeological discoveries in the area west of modern Bangkok indicate that Buddhist forms of devotion were practised here from the first or second century C.E. Sanctuaries, Buddha-rupas, and the characteristically Buddhist symbol of the Dharma-cakra (the 'wheel of the law'), and a number of fine pieces of sculpture of the Gupta period have been discovered both here and in the neighbouring areas now known as Laos and Cambodia. Possibly the greatest centre of Buddhist learning and culture in South-East Asia between the seventh and the eleventh centuries C.E. was in the islands of Sumatra and Java, where the influence of eastern India (especially Bengal) was also fairly strong. The Chinese pilgrim I-Tsing, who visited this area as well as India towards the end of the seventh century, records that its rulers favoured Buddhism, and that it was the Hīnayāna form which flourished there. A later dynasty, the Sailendras, who ruled over Malaya and a large part of what is now Indonesia, were patrons of the Mahāyāna form, and maintained close connections with eastern India, especially with the great centre at Nālanda. From that area of north-east India came also to Indonesia the Tantric form of Buddhist belief and practice which eventually became predominant in Indonesia and, as in India, preceded the gradual disappearance of Buddhism within a form of religion that was dominated by brāhman priests and Hindu cults (*6.41*).

5.28 Buddhism in Japan in the Heian period (794–1185)

In the period up to 794 C.E. Nara had been the centre of Japan's life, political and religious. In that year the political capital was moved to

Miyako, the modern Kyōto, the poetical name of which was Heian. This remained the capital of Japan until 1868, the beginning of the Meiji period (*7.43*). The period to which Heian gives its name is remembered as one of 'peace and ease' (Anesaki, 1930), and as the classical age of Japanese art, literature and religion.

During this period the 'catholic' school of Buddhism, the Tientai, introduced from China into Japan (where it was known as Tendai), was the most influential form of Buddhist religion. The Hossō, the most influential school in the previous (Nara) period, was a religion for the spiritually *élite* only, whereas the characteristic feature of the Tendai was its universalism; it emphasised that all sentient beings were capable of attaining salvation. A Buddhist monk named Saicho (posthumously known by the honorific title Dengyo Daishi, i.e. 'The Propagator of the True Religion') was largely responsible for introducing the Tendai and for its rapid spread. Of Chinese immigrant stock, Saicho was born in 767 near Mount Hiei, and in 785 at the age of eighteen was ordained into the Buddhist monkhood. There followed ten 'hidden years' during which Saicho lived a life of solitude and contemplation. When in 794 the capital was moved to Heian, Saicho identified himself with the new political regime and began to develop a monastic institution close to the new capital; at the end of a further ten years this had become a thriving centre of Buddhist religious life and was officially designated 'Chief Seat of the Buddhist Religion for Ensuring the Security of the Country'. Saicho was a remarkable combination of saint, philosopher and organiser, and after a visit to China in 803 in search of deeper understanding of Buddhist truth this remarkable man introduced the broad and very catholic synthesis of doctrine and practice which became for the next five centuries the main stream of Buddhism in Japan.

A notable younger contemporary was Kukai, born seven years after Saicho, in 774. Schooled in Confucianism, he turned to Taoism (*2.47*) in his youth in search of spiritual satisfaction; not finding it he passed through a period of mental struggle until at the age of twenty-two his conversion to Buddhism occurred, as the result of a vision he had of a certain great Buddhist saint. Like Saicho he too went to China in search of deeper understanding. There he was introduced to the Chinese form of Mantrayāna (*5.26*), which in China was known as the Chen-yen, and it was this combination of the practical, the popular and the mystical that after his return to Japan he began to teach, with great success. The Japanese name for Chen-yen is Shingon, and from the time of Kukai's return from China its centre was the monastery which he founded on Mount Koya (fifty miles south of the new capital), and where for thirty years he trained disciples in this new mystical syncretism, the great strength of which lay in its blend of contemplative, undogmatic thought, and ritual practice. Kukai was successful too in reconciling Buddhist and Shinto groups. A notable feature of this bringing together of Buddhist with Shinto traditions was the identification of the old gods of Japanese Shinto with the bodhisattvas of Buddhism. Another feature of the synthesis was the provision of an inner, Buddhist sanctum within the shrines where the Shinto gods were worshipped. This system whereby the Japanese people accepted Buddhist names for Shinto deities and incorporated Buddhist devotion into the Shinto ritual system is known as Ryōbu (or Dual Aspect) Shinto. At his death in 835, in the monastery at Mount Koya, Kukai had achieved such spiritual prestige that he is regarded even now in Japan as a kind of saviour, who could come forth from the deep trance (rather than death) into which he is believed to have passed to exercise miraculous powers. He too, like Saicho, is known by a posthumous name – Kobo Daishi, 'The Propagator of the Law'. By many he is regarded as a manifestation of the bodhisattva Vairocana.

The Shingon in Japan, like the Mantrayāna in India from which its principles were ultimately derived, was a form of religious practice for laymen as well as for monks. Alongside it, and not always entirely distinct from it, there further developed during this period devotion to Amida. It was mainly during the tenth century, however, that this popular system of salvation by faith in the Lord of the Western Paradise really began to gain ground, and the story of its full flowering in Japan belongs properly to the next period (6.48). It is clear that the credit for the gain in the popularity of Buddhism in Japan belongs initially to the monks of the Tendai and the Shingon during the period we have been reviewing. It was they who by their efforts adapted Buddhist ideas and practice to the Japanese environment.

5.29 Buddhism in Ceylon, 600–1000

Similar developments to those already noted in South-East Asia and Japan are evident in Ceylon during this period. After Buddhaghosa (4.39) there are no great figures in the Buddhist literature of Ceylon until Anuruddha (6.43) in the eleventh or twelfth century, nor were there in this period any notable developments in Buddhist thought in Ceylon. But during these four centuries there was the same growth of Mahāyānist and Tantric influence that was going on elsewhere. One of the most important factors in the situation was the relationship between the Sinhalese rulers and those of South India. Towards the end of the seventh century, after some decades of instability, a ruler named Manavamma succeeded, with the help of troops provided by a South Indian ally, in establishing himself in power and initiating a period of internal peace for Ceylon which lasted for about two centuries. After this, from the end of the ninth century onwards, Ceylon was very closely involved in the inter-state rivalries of South India and had a keen interest in the political balance of power between these various states. This meant an increasing exposure to South Indian influences, not only political but also cultural and religious.

Hence we find that the Abhayagiri monastery, the rival to the Great Monastery (Mahāvihāra) of Anuradhapura, and stronghold of the Theravādin tradition (4.38), became increasingly influential as a centre of the Mahāyāna, and throughout these centuries of the political involvement of Ceylon with South India, tended to enjoy the favour of the Sinhalese rulers. During the ninth century an Indian monk residing there introduced elements of the Vajrayāna (5.26). This had the patronage of the Sinhalese king and also met with ready acceptance among the Sinhalese peasants for whom it provided, as elsewhere, a means of holding together Buddhist doctrine and their own popular cults, which were strongly intermixed with magic. It is during these centuries that the recital of paritta, or charms against evil powers, becomes overt in Sinhalese Buddhism.

Involvement in the politics of South India led eventually, during the tenth century, to the disturbed period in which invasions of South India led to counter-invasions of Ceylon and finally to the retreat of the Sinhalese rulers from their capital at Anuradhapura, south-eastwards to a new capital at Polonnaruwa, and to the domination of northern Ceylon by the Tamils. Anuradhapura continued for a while to be a Buddhist centre and a place of pilgrimage. But it could not maintain itself indefinitely, once the centre of the state had shifted to Polonnaruwa, and so the great shrines and monasteries of Anuradhapura were abandoned and for many centuries engulfed by the tropical jungle.

What is clear from our survey of Buddhism in Tibet, South-East

Asia and Ceylon during these centuries is the continuing influence of
India. Developments in India in Mahāyāna, and especially Mantrayāna
and Vajrayāna, are faithfully reflected in these surrounding countries.
Sometimes, however, the newer developments met with resistance,
notably in the case of Ceylon, where the Great Monastery of Anuradhapura remained predominantly Theravādin, and where in the mid-
seventh century its monks protested against the royal patronage of
their Mahāyānist rival, the Abhayagiri monastery, by taking the drastic
step of 'turning down the alms-bowl' to the king, the most extreme
sanction open to them. The spread of Vajrayāna among the lay people
of Ceylon was also deplored by the Theravādin chronicler who
recorded that it had become prevalent 'among the foolish and
ignorant people of this country' and his attitude is undoubtedly
representative of the Theravādin monks of Ceylon of that period.

SUMMARY AND COMMENT ON CHAPTER FIVE

During the period we have been reviewing both Islam and Buddhism,
which in some ways are so unlike each other, succeeded in gaining the
adherence of large numbers of the population of those new areas into
which they expanded: the Near East, Middle East, North Africa and
Spain in the case of Islam; China, Japan, Tibet and South-East Asia in
the case of Buddhism. For the more partisan Christian church-historian
the successes of Islam in areas which had for some centuries been
regarded as Christian is disconcerting, and is explained away as the
achievement of military conquerors who forced their religion on the
inhabitants of the regions they conquered. This is a view which, as
T. W. Arnold has shown, does not bear prolonged examination. The
reasons for the successes both of Islam outside Arabia and of Buddhism
outside India are to be found in the readiness of the peoples of the areas
into which these faiths penetrated to receive and embrace new systems
of belief and practice because of the superior appeal and attraction
which the new faiths possessed, compared with the systems to which
nominal recognition was being given. The appeal of the new faiths in
both cases lay, first, in the simple standard of morality which was
inculcated and exemplified, especially by their humbler rank and file
representatives (Indian Buddhist monks or Arab traders and settlers);

and second, in the convincing, rational, and coherent view of human life and its meaning which each of these systems offered. One of the lessons of this chapter of religious history is that a system of religious thought and practice emanating from a foreign source is capable of being received and naturalised given two major conditions: a situation in the receiving area of social, intellectual, or moral disturbance, unease, or discontent; and a sufficiently dynamic, intellectually self-consistent, morally and emotionally satisfying system of religion capable of being transmitted, by reason both of openness of access, and of resources of personnel prepared to act as its bearers or transmitters.

It is noteworthy also that in the cases of Islam and Buddhism the effect of the influx of these faiths into the new areas was in each case the emergence of a new chapter in the civilisation of those countries. With Islamic civilisation and learning in the Mediterranean area and the Middle East we shall deal in the next chapter (6.32). In the case of China, Buddhism entered a country which already possessed an ancient and well-established civilisation, but even there Buddhism made some significant contributions, especially to the popular art and culture. It was, writes C. P. Fitzgerald 'until modern times the major, almost the only strong foreign influence affecting the Chinese culture, and the only one which left a permanent mark'. This influence was, however, as he adds, confined in China to art and religious thought, and did not extend to social and political thought (Fitzgerald, 1964; 10). In this latter respect Buddhism was, in China as in Japan, prevented from being altogether true to itself, for it is essentially, as we have seen (2.38), a social doctrine as well as a religious discipline (6.44). So far as Japan was concerned, D. C. Holtom's testimony regarding the general effect of Buddhism's entry into that country is impressive:

> Buddhism brought with it literature, art, astronomy, medicine, education and more definite and humane social and political institutions. It stimulated compassion through its central teaching of *Jihi*, or benevolence, and deepened the sense of human equality. . . . It established monasteries and alms houses and brought relief to famine and pestilence. . . . It introduced Japan to a noble ethical code and heightened the expectation of life beyond death. No other influence, with the single exception of the modern scientific-industrial revolution has so modified Japanese civilisation. (Holtom, 1938; 32 f.)

Something very similar was true in parts of Christian Europe, especially those areas which, unlike the Hellenistic world, had been

relatively barbarous. Here too Christian religion had a civilising effect'
mainly through the spread of the monastic system (*6.22*). Greece and
Rome already had rich civilisations of their own to which Christianity
made an additional contribution, but in northern Europe especially it
was the abbeys and monasteries which were the centres from which
learning and literature, arts and sciences of all kinds were communicated
to the surrounding areas. And, as we shall see in the next chapter, the
Hindu mathas or monasteries, adapted from earlier Buddhist models,
similarly served as medical and educational and cultural centres in
medieval India (*6.12; 6.13*).

This aspect of the history of religion is one which serves as a valuable
corrective to the modern, reduced view of religion as a mainly private,
individual affair between a man and his God, a view which has been
particularly characteristic of Christianity in the period since the
sixteenth century. In Islam and Buddhism especially it is possible to see
what a genuinely popular, religiously inspired culture could be; a broad
fair river, providing for the surrounding area a means of communication,
fertility, and vitality; in contrast with this was the severely confined
and sterile culvert which religion had become in Europe by the
nineteenth century. It is possible that the two destructive deluges called
communism and secularism were partly due to the fact that the channel
of religion had in Europe become so artificially narrow.

6 Theologians, Poets and Mystics

6.1 MEDIEVAL HINDUISM (500–1500 C.E.)

6.10 Medieval Hinduism: major factors and features

THE period in the history of Hinduism which we are now to consider (500–1500 C.E.) may be described broadly as the medieval period, although it includes also the beginnings of the modern period. During this thousand years the Indian subcontinent consisted, politically, of a number of independent monarchies. Most of these were Hindu, though from the twelfth century onwards there was also the Muslim kingdom or sultanate in north India, which was growing in extent and influence throughout the centuries. It would be difficult to summarise the political history of India during this period; it is however important to note some of the more outstanding dynasties. With the decline of the Gupta dynasty (4.26), north India was divided between a number of independent kingdoms, some large, some small, one of the most important of which during this period was that of the religiously eclectic ruler Harsha-vardhana (606–46 C.E.), whose capital was Kanauj, a city on the upper Ganges which had superseded Pātaliputra (Patna) as the most important city of the Gangetic plains (5.25). In the lower Ganges plain, in the area covered approximately by modern Bihar and Bengal, the Pala dynasty was important and influential during the eighth and ninth centuries. The Pala kings seem to have been adherents of the cult of Chandi, a goddess who was now regarded as the consort of Shiva. The Pala kingdom had trading connections with South-East Asia from a port near the modern Calcutta, and in this way exerted a religious and cultural influence in South-East Asia during this period.

In South India the dominant kingdom from the seventh to the tenth century was that of the Pallavas, a Hindu dynasty established by Mahendra-Varman I (600–30 C.E.), whose capital was at Kanchipuram (about seventy miles south-west of modern Madras) in the Tamil region. Mahendra-Varman I was thus a South-Indian contemporary of Harsha, of north India, and is noteworthy in that he was originally an adherent of the Jains, but later became a Shaivite, ostensibly under the influence of the Shaiva saint Appar *(6.11)*. His conversion could also be taken as an indicator of the religious trends of the times: Jainism, like Buddhism, was beginning to lose influence at the expense of the bhakti cults of Vishnu and Shiva. In the south the Pallava dynasty was succeeded by that of the Cholas, who were the dominant power in peninsular India from the tenth to the twelfth century C.E. This, too, was a Tamil dynasty, and during this period Tamil culture and religion was at the height of its vigour, with an influence extending beyond India to South-East Asia and Ceylon *(5.29)*. One further dynasty demands mention for its great importance in the history of Hinduism, namely that of Vijayanagar, which began in the early fourteenth century and lasted until the middle of the seventeenth. The role of Vijayanagar in the defence of Hinduism belongs properly, however, to a slightly later period, and will be dealt with in that connection *(6.53)*.

The mention of these outstanding dynasties serves as a reminder that medieval India was a land of monarchies and that this was the important background to the religious situation during those centuries. Two other major elements in the picture were (1) the brāhmans, who were closely associated with kings as their advisers; and (2) the popular bhakti cults. These tended increasingly to be favoured and supported by the kings, with the result that the brāhmans found it necessary to make large concessions to the cults religiously, while seeking to preserve their own status socially. The essential point of issue between the adherents and exponents of the bhakti cults on the one hand and the brāhmans on the other was that of caste; brāhmanic orthodoxy upheld the caste structure, while many of the Vaishnavite and Shaivite teachers and cult-leaders tended wherever possible to adopt a liberal attitude to caste differences.

6.11 The songs of the Tamil saints of the seventh century

From the seventh century onward the most vigorous religious activity occurred in the Tamil region of South India. This centred upon the ardent devotionalism of a class of religious virtuosi known among the Vaishnavites as *alvars*, or 'divers' (that is, into the divine depths), and among the Shaivites as *nāyanārs*, or 'leaders'. The wave of theistic devotion connected with these 'saints', as they are often called, was in southern India to some extent an expression of a reaction against the theological radicalism of the Buddhists and the Jains, and to some extent due to the peculiarly fervent form which the bhakti type of Hinduism assumed as it spread into the south from north India.

The literature of this Tamil devotionalism is contained in collections of hymns composed by the Tamil saints of the seventh century. As well as the expression of the most ardent devotion to God they contain a good deal of animosity against the Buddhists. This was expressed also in public debates, a frequent condition of which was that the one who was worsted in the debate should transfer his allegiance to the religion of his opponent. There appear also to have been public competitions in the performance of miracles, and trials of doctrine by means of ordeals (Sastri, 1963; 40). The collections of hymns composed by the various bhakti saints now form the major part of the Vaishnavite and Shaivite canons of scripture. The composers were men of all castes, including the lowest; sometimes they were people of doubtful parentage, and in one or two cases, women. In some respects they resemble the ecstatic prophets of the Near East; they are described as dancing, laughing, weeping and singing 'like people who had lost their senses' (*Cultural Heritage of India,* 1958–62; vol. iv, p. 166). They were greatly venerated, and their compositions are accorded by Vaishnavites and Shaivites the same status as those of the Vedic ṛṣi or seers (*1.35*), the entire collection of hymns sometimes being referred to as 'the Vaishnava (or Shaiva) Veda'. For the people of medieval India one of the attractive features of this kind of religious devotion was that it was open to all: to those of the lowest castes, to women or to men, and to the fallen and sinful. The leaders of the movement, the great alvars of Tamil Vaishnavism, are traditionally twelve in number; among the nāyanārs, or adiyars, of the Shaivite movement three are regarded with special veneration, namely Sambandha, Appar who is said to have converted Mahendra-Varman to Shaivism (*6.10*), and Sundara. Of these three Sambandha, a brāhman of the seventh century, is afforded very high honour: his image is to be found in Shaiva temples, and subsequent Tamil writers frequently begin their work with an ascription of homage to him. He is said to have been a strong opponent of the Buddhists and Jains, and included in his hymns frequent imprecations against them. His victory in debate with the Jains is said to have resulted in the punishment of 8,000 of them; this, according to the story, took the form of death by impalement, an event which is said to be commemorated still in an annual festival in the temple at Madurai. A modern Hindu, however, finds this 'a shocking legend', and 'can hardly believe' such 'intolerance of heresy'; it must be, he claims, 'the product of orthodox imagination of a later time animated by a false scale of values' (Sastri, 1963; 43).

6.12 The philosopher Shankara (788–820 C.E.)

Seldom does a single personality affect the subsequent course of religious development so powerfully as Shankara has done. A Shaivite brāhman from Kerala, his great achievement was the reinstatement of Upaniṣadic ideas in opposition both to Buddhism on the one hand, and the excessive devotionalism of the popular cults on the other. It is significant that he came of a Shaivite family, for the Shiva cult, having its roots in the pre-Aryan proto-Shiva of the Harappā culture (1.19), had always somewhat more affinity with the method of yoga than with that of bhakti. That is to say, the emphasis in Shaivism is placed more upon asceticism and yogic self-realisation than upon devotional fervour towards God, as is the case in the Vaishnavite cults, although Shaivism did assimilate some of this Vaishnavite fervour, especially in the seventh century. Shankara's teacher, or guru, is said to have been Govinda Yogin. Certainly Shankara's own doctrine lays stress on the importance of asceticism, and yogic realisation of the individual self as brahman. This doctrine he expounded in the manner which has become almost de rigueur for Hindu philosophers and theologians, namely, that of an exposition of the famous Brāhma Sūtras of Bādarāyana (4.21). What prevents men from realising that reality is one and indivisible, namely, brahman (the impersonal absolute), and that nothing else exists but brahman, is the factor which Shankara identifies as maya – the quality of illusion which makes the One appear as many separate, independent entities. It is maya which is the cause of all man's futile strivings after so-called pleasures, and of all his sufferings and troubles. The senses are deceived by maya, and only by ascetic practice and contemplation can brahman be realised. This doctrine has strong affinities with that of the Yogācārin and Mādhyamika schools of Mahāyāna Buddhism (4.33; 4.35), and Shankara was in fact accused by his religious opponents of being a Crypto-Buddhist. He seems to have learnt some practical lessons also from the Buddhists, for he established a number of mathas or monastic settlements which became centres for the propagation of his characteristic teaching, with its strong emphasis upon asceticism and yogic practice rather than on devotionalism or ritual. These mathas were situated strategically at certain great centres of religious pilgrimage – Badrinath in the Himālayan region; Dwārakā on the west coast; Puri on the east coast; and Shringeri and Kancipuram in the south. At the last-named of these he is said to have spent some years teaching his doctrine of Advaita (non-dual) Vedānta.

In this way Brahmanism, in the person of Shankara, once again showed its perennial ability to survive by assimilating the ideas and practices of a rival system and making them its own. In this case Buddhism was the victim, and the work of Shankara marks more clearly perhaps than any other single factor the beginning of the decline of Buddhism's status in India.

6.13 Medieval Hindu temples and monasteries

In borrowing from the Buddhists the idea of the monastic settlement and incorporating it into his organisation, Shankara was responsible for inaugurating what became a characteristic feature of medieval Hinduism. Hindu monasteries, or mathas, were religious centres which served a number of purposes. They were at first located near famous shrines, and provided places where pilgrims could rest, and find food; they were also centres of education, and helped to propagate the doctrines of the religious sects which maintained them. From the tenth century onwards it was regarded as a meritorious use of capital on the part of the wealthier classes to endow a matha, so that by the thirteenth century almost every important place of pilgrimage was provided with an adjacent religious settlement of this kind. In some cases Buddhist monasteries were actually turned into Hindu mathas as Buddhism declined; since the Hindu ascetics who inhabited them devoted themselves to very much the same kind of social programme as the Buddhist monks had done (giving medical aid, feeding the very poor, and educating the young), the local community would scarcely notice the transition (Sastri, 1963; 118).

The other major religious institution which was developing during this period was the temple. Little is known of the early history of Hindu temples, for up to the Gupta period (4.26) they were built of wood or clay, materials which do not survive easily in India. The classical stone-built Hindu temple appears to date from about the sixth century C.E. An earlier preliminary form was that of the cave-temple, hewn out of solid rock; this was a type of shrine which Hindus had adopted from the Buddhist prototype. As in Europe so in India the medieval period was one of vast temple-building, once the technique of building free-standing structures had been developed. An example of a transitional stage between the rock-hewn and the free-standing types is the Kailashanatha temple at Ellora in western India (about 200 miles north-east of Bombay), a temple hewn from the surrounding rock, but open to the sky, and partly free-standing. The cost of building it must have been very great, and indicates resources such as only a king could have commanded (Thapar, 1966; 192).

The subject of the style and architecture of Hindu temples is a large one, and the reader must be referred to specialist works for an adequate account of what is a fascinating aspect of Indian culture (Basham, 1954; 355–64; Sastri, 1963; 97–112). The central feature within the shrine-room (which may be vast in size) is the vigraha, or image – the *symbol* of the deity, rather than a representation. That this instead of an altar was the central feature, indicates where the prime emphasis in popular Hinduism now lay: not in sacrifice, but in devotional ceremonial, or bhakti. The larger temples had an important economic function as well as a religious one; the temple at Tanjore during the Chola period, for example, is said to have had attached to it and economically dependent on it, a staff of various class of attendants, musicians, dancers, readers and so on totalling about 570; in addition to these there were hundreds of priests, also living off the income of the temple. Not all temples were of this size; but by the ninth or tenth century there were Vaishnava or Shaiva temples in almost every small town or village; the cost of building them was usually borne by rich merchants or merchant-guilds, the furnishing of them with images, lamps and so on was the responsibility of less wealthy local people. The existence of temples in such large numbers in northern India, often the repositories of a great deal of wealth in the form of jewels which adorned the images, provided one of the major incentives to frequent Turkish Muslim raids from the north-west, beginning from about the end of the tenth century C.E. (*6.38*).

6.14 The development of Hindu theology: Rāmānuja

Before the time of Shankara is the pre-theological period in the history of the bhakti cults. From the time of Shankara onwards, bhakti was forced to develop a theological defence and exposition of its principles, for Shankara's teaching was seen to be a threat to the devotional cults and the principle of bhakti, no less than to Buddhism. The reply from the upholders of devotionalism took some time to develop, and its first clear formulation is associated with Rāmānuja, who lived some two and a half centuries after Shankara, and died in 1137 c.e. approximately. The hymns of the alvars (*6.11*), which were known collectively as the Prabandham, had by this time had ascribed to them the authority of sacred scripture, and in this connection there had emerged the office of ācārya, or teacher, whose expositions of the sacred text and whose rulings in matters of worship were regarded as authoritative for adherents of the Vaishnava cult. The great ācāryas were also the rulers of the temple at Srirangam, the most important of the south Indian Vaishnava shrines. One of these was Yāmunācarya. He was succeeded in his office by Rāmānuja, to whom one of his last injunctions before his death was that Rāmānuja should compose a commentary on the Brāhma Sūtras (*4.21*). Yāmunācarya was conscious of the need for this because of the difficulty of maintaining the doctrine and practice of bhakti, of love and devotion for the deity, in the face of Shankara's absolute monism. Since, in Shankara's teaching, there exists one reality alone, and the true self within man is identical with this reality, there can be no place for the exercise of love and piety towards God on the part of a worshipper, nor any consciousness of the separate being of God and man.

The work of Rāmānuja, and of the Hindu theologians who succeeded him, was to work out a reconciliation of the Upanisadic doctrine (basically that ātman equals brahman), with the bhakti doctrine that man gains release, or salvation (moksạ), through devotion to God, and by God's grace.

Rāmānuja, born probably in the middle of the eleventh century, lived in Kanchipuram and was himself the pupil of an Advaita Vedānta (*4.21*) teacher. He became dissatisfied with the doctrine of monism, however, and turned towards Vaishnavism. Eventually he separated from his teacher and concentrated all his attention on the songs of the alvars (*6.11*), absorbing their spirit of ardent devotion. He settled at Srīrangam, and there spent the major part of his life, occasionally making a pilgrimage to some of the shrines of north India.

The doctrine which Rāmānuja developed was one which he learnt from his Vaishnava teacher Yāmunācarya, whom he succeeded as ruler of the Srīrangam temple. This doctrine is described as viśiṣṭa-advaita (anglicised, Vishishtadvaita), that is to say, the a–dvaita (non-dualism) of qualities (viśiṣṭa). Basically, it affirms a monistic view of the universe: there is only one reality, brahman. But within this reality, three principles or qualities may be distinguished. These are, the individual soul, the insensate world, and the Supreme Soul (or Ishvara). The Supreme Soul is the controller of the individual soul and of the insensate world, which are regarded also as attributes of the Supreme Soul. They are the body of the Supreme Soul, and together the three constitute all that is, or brahman. Salvation consists in the individual soul's seeing itself as distinct from matter and as an attribute of the Supreme Soul. The way to salvation was not only, as in Shankara's system, by knowledge (jñāna) but also by karma, which in this context meant the actions of worship: temple-devotion (pūjā), austerities, pilgrimage, almsgiving and so on. It is this, as the basis of the religious life, which leads to knowledge, and hence to bhakti, understood as contemplation of the Supreme Soul.

It is interesting to notice the convergence of various streams in Rāmānuja's system. The alvars (*6.11*) had emphasised only pure bhakti, adoration of God; the ācāryas had added to this the practice of karma, or religious duties and ceremonies; now, in the system worked out by Rāmānuja, to the combination of bhakti and karma is added jñāna, the way of salvation emphasised by Shankara and the Upaniṣads, that of special *knowledge*. The comprehensiveness of Rāmānuja's doctrine, with its combination of philosophical ·monism and popular devotion, justifies the description of it as an amplified form of the teaching of the Bhagavad-Gītā (*4.22*), upon which Rāmānuja wrote a lengthy commentary.

A further point of interest in Rāmānuja's teaching is his emphasis on the necessity of complete self-surrender; such self-surrender is to a spiritual preceptor, who is trusted by the devotee as able to do all that is necessary for his salvation, that is, to bring him to moksa, or release. R. G. Bhāndārkar considers that if we could be sure of the extent of the influence of Christianity in the country about Madras during the eleventh century, this emphasis might possibly be traced to Christian salvation ideas (Bhāndārkar, 1913; 57).

6.15 The continuing influence of Rāmānuja

Rāmānuja has become as venerable a figure in Vaishnavism as is any of the great saints within the Christian tradition. A modern Hindu (V. Rangacarya, Professor of the History of Economics in the University of Trivandrum) writes: 'No Vaishnava temple is considered perfect without his image, no festival proper without the celebration of his greatness, and no ceremonial occasion adequately solemn without the invocation of his blessing and favour' (*Cultural History of India*, vol. iv, p. 177).

Most of his followers have been, or are, found in the south of India. They fairly early divided into two main schools, the *Vadagalai* and the *Tengalai*. The principal difference between them was, originally, in their respective conceptions of how divine grace operates. The difference between the two conceptions was illustrated by reference to the differing ways a cat and a monkey carry their young. The Vadagalai believe that the process of salvation must be initiated by the man who seeks salvation; he must first take hold of God's grace, as a young monkey takes hold with his hands around his mother's neck, and is then carried by her. The Tengalai believe that the process is initiated by God himself, in his grace, taking hold of man; man can only be ready to be possessed by God, like the kitten who is taken up by the mother cat and carried by her.

A further important distinction relates to caste. The Vadagalai uphold the position that only the three upper classes (brāhmans, kṣatriyas, and vaiṣyas) can become devotees and live the holy life. The Tengalai took the view that there could be no difference in this matter between one man and another whatever his caste-status. Rāmānuja, while accepting that there were some privileges proper to the three upper classes, had tried to end the exclusion of the sudras (the fourth, or lowest class) from temple worship, but without success. A further distinction which indicates the slightly more popular, peasant affiliation of the Tengalai, is that they use the Tamil language to a much greater extent than the Vadagalai, who tend to use Sanskrit Itinerant Vaishnava mendicants known as dāsas were generally Tengalais (Sastri, 1963; 116f.).

6.16 Brāhmans and caste in medieval south India

It is important at this point to notice that the four classes or varna of Aryan society were much less marked a feature of south India. What was more characteristic were the divisions between brāhmans and non-brāhmans, and between clean sudras and unclean sudras. In other words, the distinction was much more clearly between *caste*-groups than between the theoretical and Vedic-scriptural four *classes*. This is a further indication that the caste (jati) system was not an elaboration of the Vedic four classes, but another system, with origins elsewhere. The essential difference between clean and unclean sudras is a matter of pollution. The touch of an unclean sudra was regarded as polluting to one of a higher caste, especially a brāhman; the touch of a clean sudra was not. This distinction was itself closely connected with occupation. So far as the castes other than brāhman and sudra were concerned there seems to have been much less rigidity about their statuses and their intermixing. Strictness about caste-distinction is associated primarily with the brāhmans, who regarded themselves as the upholders and enforcers of the caste system; others, however, were inclined to take a less rigorous view, especially in the middle ranges of the system. As A. L. Basham points out, early Tamil literature gives no evidence of caste in that region; it was the growth of Aryan influence, that is, the influence of the brāhman and his sacred Vedic texts, which resulted in the rigid distinctions which had developed by the period we are now concerned with (eleventh and twelfth centuries c.e.).

6.17 Further developments in Hindu theology: Madhva and Rāmānanda

Rāmānuja's harmonisation of philosophical monism with theistic devotion appears to have gone too far in the direction of monism to be acceptable to some devotees of the bhakti cult. Evidence of this is to be found in the system worked out by a thirteenth-century Vaishnavite from Kanara. He is usually known as Madhva, though he wrote under the name of Ānanda Tīrtha. Trained in his youth in the philosophy of Shankara (*6.12*), he reacted against this and became a fervent devotee of Krishna. He came under the influence of the Tengalai wing of Rāmānuja's followers and in his own teaching laid great emphasis upon the idea that Vishnu by his grace alone saves those who lead pure lives. Evil souls are regarded as eternally damned. Madhva questioned Rāmānuja's doctrine that God has for his body the individual souls of men and the inanimate world. This, he considered, tended to blur the essential otherness of God, and detract from his independent greatness and majesty. A curious feature of Madhva's conception of God is that he deals with the world through his agent Vāyu, the wind-god. Madhva regarded himself as an avatara of Vāyu. The very striking resemblance between the theology worked out by Madhva and certain Christian ideas has led some to suggest a direct Christian influence through the Syrian community of Malabar (Basham, 1954; 333). It is equally possible, however, that the similarities are due to developmental parallels. The followers of Madhva constitute a Vaishnavite sect (the Mādhvas) found in fairly large numbers around Bombay and the west coast.

In the north a new chapter in the history of Vaishnavism began in the fifteenth century with the religious activity of Rāmānanda. Born towards the end of the fourteenth century (his dates are possibly 1370–1440) he was sent to Banaras to be educated as a brāhman, and for a time was a teacher of the doctrine of Rāmānuja (6.14). He was, however, more critical of distinctions of caste than Rāmānuja had been, and gave up the restrictive practices with regard to commensality, or table-fellowship (that is, who may eat with whom). He insisted also on admitting members of the sudra class as his disciples. The exponents of Vaishnavism had always shown a general sympathy for the lower classes, but in so far as they had not permitted the study of Vedic literature by these classes they had to that extent excluded them from the full scope of the methods by which moksa or salvation was to be attained. Rāmānanda, moreover, gave a great impetus to the use of Hindi, the vernacular language, by his own example in using it rather than Sanskrit in his teaching. Another important aspect of the movement he founded was the replacement of the erotic cult of Krishna's consort Rādhā with that of the more chaste Sīta, the consort of Rāma. The Vaishnava religion taught and practised by Rāmānanda was a movement away from the older orthodoxy in the direction of mystical devotion.

6.18 The Lingāyata: a Shaiva sect

Among the Shaivites the most important development during this
period was the emergence, in the twelfth century, of the Lingāyata or
Virashaiva sect, which remained until the present day an important
religious movement in south India, especially in Mysore. Nilakanta
Sastri sums up their position neatly in describing them as 'a peaceable
race of Hindu puritans who deny the supremacy of the Brahmins'
(Sastri, 1963; 64). With their rejection of the authority of the brāhmans
went a high regard for precisely those features of bhakti faith which are
most un-Aryan. They worshipped Shiva alone, whom they regarded as
the sole supreme deity, they practised strict vegetarianism and were
total abstainers from alcohol, and they greatly venerated their own
religious functionaries, their gurus or preceptors. Every Lingāyata was
connected with a local matha (6.13), there being one of these in every
Lingāyata village. The religious symbol most characteristic of the sect
was the lingam or phallus, a small version of which was worn round
the neck by every member of the sect. Caste distinctions were not
important among them. The founder of the sect is generally held to be
a Shaivite of the twelfth century named Basava, who founded a
religious centre from which this reformed Shaivism spread to various
parts of India, but mainly to Karnataka. The five features of the
religious discipline of the sect as it exists today are: daily worship; a
virtuous life of abstinence, hard work and thrift; responsibility for
feeding and clothing the gurus of the sect; the disregard of caste
distinctions within the Lingāyata community; the cultivation of habits
of humility and kindness; and finally continual defence of the faith,
both in its doctrines and its human representatives. It is possible that
the rise of this reformed Shaivism may have been at least partly due to
the influence of Islam in India, and the impression made by its monotheism, its spirit of brotherhood, and its puritan ethic.

6.19 The Shākta cult

A feature of late medieval Hinduism is the coming into somewhat
greater prominence of the cult of Shiva's consort. She is known by the
general term Shakti, that is, the active principle within the divine

partnership. She is known also by a number of personal names, such as Kālī, Durga, Parvati, Chandī, Kumārī and others. The consort of a god was, of course, honoured by those who worshipped one of the male deities; the special nature of the cult of the Shāktas was that they honoured the goddess as the principal form of deity. The coming into prominence of such a cult can be seen as the resurgence of the Dravidian or non-Aryan element in Indian religion, in which the mother-goddess had always been the central figure (*1.30*). In the Shākta cult the qualities associated with Shiva are transferred to Shakti. The goddess represents the force of Nature, upon which the life of man was seen to depend. As the goddess of Nature, she creates only in order to destroy, and she creates because she destroys. The goddess is thus thought of by the Shāktas as fierce and hungry and violent, needing to be appeased by offerings of some form of life, animal or human.

It is in this connection that human sacrifices were a feature of the Shākta cult. The Chinese pilgrim Hsuan-tsang travelling in seventh-century India records how he narrowly escaped being sacrificed to Durga by Ganges river pirates. The notorious Thugs of north India were devotees of Kālī, who dedicated their victims to her in sacrifice. The earliest known reference to the Thugs is in the twelfth century. In sixteenth-century Bengal the invading Muslims discovered that human sacrifice to the goddess was not uncommon. The practice was made illegal in 1835, and survives only in the form of animal sacrifices, as at the Kālī Ghat at Calcutta.

The other major feature for which the Shākta cult is known is a form of Tantric practice, possibly derived from late Mahāyāna Buddhism in India (*5.26*). Among Shāktas this was called Chakra-pūjā (circle-worship) and consisted of a closely guarded esoteric rite based on the supposedly magical qualities of the maṇḍala or circular diagram developed in Buddhist Tantra. The initiates were men and women of various castes, the idea of ritual pollution being rejected by the Shāktas. The purpose of the rite was apparently the achievement of spiritual exaltation and moral purification through ritual indulgence in 'the five Ms': *madya* (intoxicating drink), *māmsa* (meat), *matsya* (fish), *mudra* (stylised hand gestures), and *maithuna* (copulation). The principle underlying the ritual was held to be that of destroying poison by the use of poison as antidote.

Europeans have tended to dismiss the Shākta cult in disgust. E. A. Payne sums up his important survey of the whole subject (Payne, 1933)

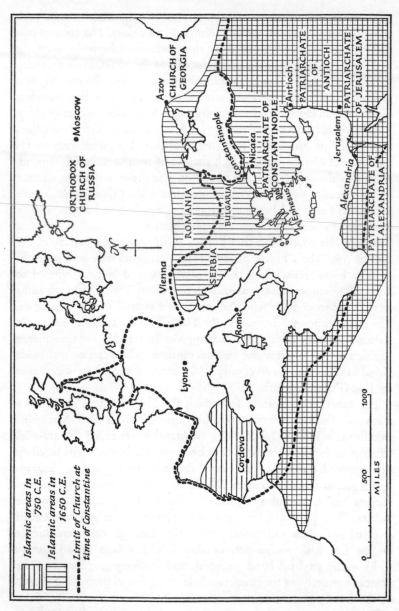

Christianity and Islam in Europe and North Africa

Islamic areas in
750 C.E.

Islamic areas in
1650 C.E.

Limit of Church at
time of Constantine

ORTHODOX
CHURCH OF
RUSSIA

●Moscow

CHURCH OF
GEORGIA

Azov

Constantinople

Nicaea

PATRIARCHATE OF
CONSTANTINOPLE

Ephesus

Antioch

PATRIARCHATE
OF
ANTIOCH

Jerusalem

PATRIARCHATE
OF JERUSALEM

Alexandria

PATRIARCHATE OF
ALEXANDRIA

BULGARIA

ROMANIA

SERBIA

Vienna

Rome●

Lyons●

Cordova●

MILES

0   500   1000

by pointing out that the Shakta cult has certain affinities with similar religious phenomena elsewhere; it is in essence the worship of the *numinous*, here seen as the forces of Nature; it has parallels in the mother-goddess worship of the Mediterranean and Near East; it has parallels also with the mystery religions of the Hellenistic world, with their emphasis upon divine grace; and it has a certain parallel within the Christian tradition in the Roman Catholic cult of the Virgin Mary.

6.2. THE RISE AND FALL OF MEDIEVAL CHRISTENDOM (500–1500 C.E.)

6.20 The primacy of Rome

The barbarian invasion of Rome, and the collapse of the Empire, had an important result in the history of European religion. 'As the emperor vanished from the West, the empty place was taken by the descendant of St Peter' (Fisher, 1936; 172). The primacy of the bishop of Rome was not easily established, was not fully accepted outside the churches of the West. However, there were certain strong reasons for the assertion of this primacy. There was the tradition that the apostle St Peter who died in Rome had commissioned his successor in the office of bishop, and that from him there had continued an unbroken line of bishops of Rome. And as in other religious traditions, so here too the presence of the bones of holy men – in particular of St Peter and St Paul – made Rome a very holy place. Above all, there was the fact that the Christian Church of the West, after the collapse of the Roman empire, was the only unifying force left in Western Europe.

> Modelled on the lines of the Imperial administration, with its dioceses and provinces, corresponding to Roman divisions, it was able to maintain its cohesion while the Empire crumbled. It was therefore the main bastion of order and administration, able to take charge of cities and regions. This ability, together with its unique spiritual authority, was to make the Church the most influential power in preserving the past and refashioning the future. (Leff, 1958; 25 f.)

It was this which both enhanced the power of the bishop of Rome and ensured the predominantly Roman character of medieval Western Christianity (*6.23*).

6.21 The political importance of the Roman Church in medieval Europe

Two of the most important factors determining the course of the development of religion in Europe during the medieval period were enhancement of the status of the Church which followed the collapse of Rome, on the one hand, and on the other, the rise of Islam in the seventh century (*5.1*) and the growth of Muslim political power and cultural influence in the Mediterranean region. During the early medieval period the focus of European culture was no longer in Greece and Italy, but the north-west, especially in France; during the latter part of the period from the twelfth century onwards, with the decline of Islamic influence in the western Mediterranean, Italy regained some of its former cultural importance.

By the time the Muslim armies had occupied most of Spain (*5.18*) the emergence of the Carolingian empire in France had at least to some extent filled the gap left by the disappearance of Roman power in the West; the king of the Franks, Charles Martel, was able to halt the advance of Islam at the battle of Poitiers in 732. The power of the Franks commended this empire of the north-west to the Pope, who recognised in it a possible successor to the empire of the Caesars. There happened also to be very strong reasons for this recognition of the Carolingians by the Pope. In the east, the emperor Leo the Isaurian, whose capital was Constantinople, had successfully resisted the attack of the Muslim Arab armies; he had, however, also become convinced that Islam was a scourge sent by God to punish the idolatrous use of images in the Christian Church. He thereupon embarked on a campaign of iconoclasm, which he extended to the Church in Italy also. This was not well received by the Italians, especially of Lombardy, whose kings had now become the chief contestants for political power in Italy. There are certain ethnic links between the Mediterranean people and the Dravidians of India (*1.30*). Nowhere does this show itself more plainly than in the deeply-rooted polytheism of both Italy and India, the 'ineradicable polytheism of Mediterranean man' as H. A. L. Fisher called it (1936; 152f.). 'The pagan genius became the Christian angel, the pagan Isis the Christian Madonna, the pagan hero became the Christian saint, the pagan festival the Christian feast.' Not surprisingly, therefore, the Lombards vigorously repudiated this attempt of a Greek tyrant to interfere with their religion; those iconoclasts in Italy who had co-operated with the eastern emperor were excommunicated, and in 731 Pope Gregory III anathematised the emperor himself. This was a diplomatic move, designed to avoid any immediate trouble with the Lombards. As a long-term policy, however the Pope preferred for various reasons to look elsewhere than to the Lombards for political support; having turned his back on Constantinople, he turned to the new power in north-west Europe, the empire of the Franks. In 739 Gregory III invited Charles Martel to assume the title of emperor. This invitation was declined, but eleven years later Charles Martel's son Pippin agreed to be crowned king by authority of the Pope; and finally, at Mass on Christmas Day 800, his son Charlemagne was crowned emperor of the 'Holy Roman Empire' by the Pope in St Peter's at Rome, The idea of a Roman empire had thus been revived; it was, however, beyond the ability of Charlemagne's successors to give it political reality in the highly fragmented condition of feudal Europe. The result was that although the *theory* of an empire persisted for the next five hundred years, there was no effective emperor, unless it was the Pope. 'Only an international body like the Church could effectively transcend local boundaries, and the Pope alone was able to make his voice heard throughout Christendom' (Leff, 1958; 30). It is this fact which lies at the root of the predominantly Roman character of Western European Christianity during the medieval period.

6.22 The growth of Christian monasticism

Papal Christianity, dominant in Europe from the fifth century for the reasons which have just been outlined, was territorial, authoritarian and priestly. In the situation of the sixth and seventh centuries in which the Church was an effective agency of social control, it attracted into its service as bishops and senior dignitaries considerable numbers of noblemen and others of high social standing. But during the sixth century, and indeed throughout the succeeding centuries of the medieval period, monastic organisation also continued to increase and constituted an element in the religious life of Europe which was not always entirely compatible with the Papal and episcopal authoritarian system.

The monastic life was essentially the pursuit of contemplative religion; the inmates of the monastery were not necessarily priests, and were therefore not subject to episcopal discipline in the same way as the priest. For many who, in the unsettled and difficult conditions of social life in the early medieval period, wished to live a religious life, the monastic centres provided havens of peace and light and order. At the same time it became a work of merit on the part of princes and wealthy rulers to endow an abbey or a monastery, and their number multiplied. Various reforms and reorganisations of the monastic life, notably that of St Benedict (480–540 C.E.), were aimed among other things at a close co-ordination of monastic life with that of the episcopal, secular system. The doctrinal clash between Augustine and Pelagius (*4.18*) was in a sense a manifestation of the disagreement between the authoritarian and sacramental priestly system of Papal Christianity, and the more independent, individualistic, almost lay character of the monastic life. The principle which underlay Augustinian religion was that man was utterly incapable of any good, apart from the grace of God mediated to him through the sacramental system of the Church. The principle which underlay monastic life was that man had it in him to achieve moral and spiritual perfection and attain to the vision of God through the exercise of asceticism and contemplation. In two outstanding respects the monasteries were a benefit to medieval Christianity: they were centres of learning and culture, and their function in keeping scholarship alive during the Dark Ages is well known; they were also centres of missionary activity, from which monks went forth into new areas, to establish new monasteries and to Christianise the surrounding territories. But the medieval monasteries were always to some extent, because of the above mentioned differences of principle, a potential source of what in a later age would be called nonconformity, but which, because of the special associations of that term, it is better to describe as alternative religious attitudes to that of authoritarian Papal and priestly religion, the main features of which it will be convenient at this point to summarise.

6.23 Medieval Roman Christian orthodoxy

We have now reached a point where it is possible to understand how a man born during the medieval period in Europe (rather than in, say, India or Persia) unless he were a Jew would find himself, so far as his religious life was concerned, required to believe certain propositions about the world in which he lived. These were: that it was ruled by a single, absolutely powerful divine being who had created all things *ex nihilo*; that the human race was in a chronic condition of rebellion against this omnipotent deity, and was deserving of eternal torment therefore; that the deity, in compassion for the weakness of the creatures he had made, was prepared to give men a second chance, if they responded favourably to the declaration of forgiveness which had been made in the words and in the death, resurrection and ascension of the man Jesus, who was also God incarnate; that this second chance, this recovery of good standing with God, man's 'justification', which was also the earnest of his eternal salvation, could be received through the sacraments of the institutional Church, and in no other way at all; and that as a result of men's reception, or alternatively refusal, of the Grace available through the sacerdotal ministry of the Church, they would be destined after death to enjoy the eternal bliss of heaven, or to suffer the everlasting torments of hell (with a third alternative – purgatory – in which there was still some hope of heaven). We have seen that some of this doctrine was bequeathed to the medieval Church by the Jews (especially through the elevation to canonical status of the Jewish scriptures, wherein the doctrine of the omnipotent creator deity was dominant), some by St Paul and some by St Augustine. We have seen (*4.18*) that the doctrines of the latter, especially, were very influential in the development of this predominantly authoritarian, institutional and sacramental form of religion which has just been outlined.

A question which arises in this connection is how far these were the universally accepted religious beliefs of the men of medieval Europe. It is easy to assume that they were, but there are indications that even in those times Augustinian orthodoxy had to contend with scepticism, intellectual unrest, and outright disregard by those whose spirit would not allow them to be forced into this particular religious mould, however strongly it might be asserted by the theologians that this and no other was the eternal divine truth. Some of the evidence for this dissent is oblique (*6.24*); some is direct (*6.25; 6.26*).

6.24 The significance of medieval catholic theology

The oblique evidence of religious dissent from medieval Roman orthodoxy is to be found in the preoccupation of theologians themselves. A brief reference to two of these, St Anselm and St Thomas Aquinas, will serve to illustrate the point.

Anselm (1033–1109) was born in north Italy, became a Benedictine monk, and was successively prior of the abbey of Bec in Normandy, its abbot, and finally Archbishop of Canterbury from 1093 onwards. The theological position which he set out to defend was broadly that of Augustinian orthodoxy (*6.23*). The existence of dissentient religious views in Anselm's time can be inferred from the special areas of emphasis in his teaching. In general he made use of reason only to explicate what had already been accepted in faith. First of all believe as a Christian, and then use the method of reason to show how coherent and self-consistent is the Christian creed: this was Anselm's position. 'If you do not believe, you will not understand', he said. Another maxim for which he is remembered is his *credo ut intelligam* – 'I believe in order that I may understand'. Evidently faith in the Augustinian God was not without its difficulties for some of Anselm's contemporaries. It is for his attempt to use rational argument in proof of the existence of God that he is best remembered. The type of argument used by Anselm, set out in one of his major works, the *Proslogion*, is known as the ontological argument, that is, an argument from the nature of being itself. He begins by affirming 'That God really exists, even if the foolish man said in his heart "There is no God"' (an admission of contemporary scepticism as much as a quotation from scripture). His argument for the existence of God was on the grounds that God must exist, since he is 'that than which no greater can be conceived' (*id quo nihil maius cogitari potest*). Something than which no greater can be conceived can exist in the understanding, i.e. it is conceivable, as all will agree, he argued. Now if it exists not only in the understanding, but in being, then this is even greater than mere conceivability. The God who *is*, the existent God, is the one than whom no greater can be conceived. In this way Anselm believed he had proved that the God of Augustinian orthodoxy must really exist. The criticisms which have been levelled at Anselm's argument do not concern us here (but see, for example, Smart, 1962; 57f. and 1964(1), 89ff.); what is important is the implication, from the great emphasis which Anselm laid on this point, that it was a belief that was felt by his contemporaries to require some rational support.

Some two centuries later another Italian, St Thomas of Aquino, (1225–74) went considerably beyond Anselm in seeking to establish the preliminaries of Christian belief by rational argument based upon empirical evidence. Like Anselm he too was a monk, of the Dominican Order, and like Anselm he held that the most characteristically Christian doctrines, such as those of the Trinity, the Incarnation and the Last Judgment, came to men by revelation alone (although they could be demonstrated to be reasonable); but he held also that it was possible to arrive at a theistic prolegomena to Christian belief by a process of observation and reason. The existence of God could, he held, be demonstrated in five ways (Smart, 1962; 61–70). This was the kind of truth about God which human reason *could* investigate (other truths about God it could not, but had to accept in faith). In this way, by what is referred to as 'natural theology', he demonstrated the existence of one who is the prime mover of all things; the first efficient cause of all things, the ground of all necessary being (as distinct from contingent being); the source of all perfection; and the director of all that happens. These arguments of Aquinas, like those of Anselm, have been criticised by both Christians and non-Christians (Smart, 1964(1); 94 ff.); it is worth recalling the general criticism levelled by the modern German theologian Karl Barth, namely that although Aquinas may have been justified in claiming that he had demonstrated the existence of a prime mover, a first cause, etc., he was *not* justified in making the leap involved in identifying this prime mover, etc., with the God revealed by Jesus Christ. However, what is important for our present concern is the fact that Aquinas *did* thus labour to establish the reasonable nature of Augustinian orthodoxy, both in his *Summa contra Gentiles* (1259–64) and in his *Summa Theologica* (1272–3). Who the 'Gentiles' were whom he was attempting to convince of the intellectual respectability of catholic orthodoxy is not altogether clear, but in view of the dominant position which Muslim Aristotelian philosophers had held in the medieval intellectual world until then it is more than likely that if anyone was the 'cultured despiser' of the Christian religion in those days it was the Muslim philosopher, especially in connection with such characteristically Christian doctrines as those of the Trinity and the Incarnation, which to the Muslim monotheist looked too much like the ideas of pagan polytheism.

It was not only Anselm and Aquinas who were engaged so strenuously in trying to demonstrate that orthodox catholic belief was intellectually respectable; other theologians of the medieval period also took part in what was obviously a very important and necessary task. Their efforts are significant simply because they were necessary, even in the so-called ages of faith. For men do not commonly expend great effort in seeking to prove what is generally accepted as true. Catholic orthodox bishops and priests might *demand* that all Europeans should believe in the God of Augustine, but evidently even they could not procure such universal belief.

It is important to notice that there is a parallel to this enterprise within Judaism. Maimonides (1135–1204), a Jewish rabbi, Talmudic scholar, and philosopher, was similarly concerned to work out a harmonisation of empirical human knowledge and faith in an omnipotent deity, by the use of rational arguments. His *Guide to the Perplexed* was, he said in the preface to it, intended for the reader who had some acquaintance with philosophy and was concerned to reconcile this with monotheistic faith. Maimonides anticipates Aquinas in holding that reason can uphold monotheism, but that there are also certain aspects of the faith which have come to men by revelation alone and are inaccessible to reason. Here again is evidence that the theology of the omnipotent creator deity, in its Jewish context as well as in the Augustinian form which was derived from it, was among educated Jews of the twelfth century presenting intellectual difficulties, and was not easy to accept. Another indication, in the case of medieval Judaism as well as in that of Christianity, was the appeal of the alternative form of belief provided by mysticism, to which reference will be made later (6.27).

6.25 Religious alternatives: anti-sacerdotal

Evidence of a direct kind, that not all men in medieval Europe held to the Papal pattern of religious belief and practice, is to be found in a number of movements of dissent which occurred from time to time and in various places, but most characteristically in the *cities*. In view of the power of the Church and the very harsh penalties for religious deviation it is not to be expected that there would be any widespread expression of alternative religious ideas and practices; the wonder is that there were so many. Such, for example, were the Waldenses, a sect whose founder Peter Waldo, a merchant of the French city of Lyons, in 1173 underwent a religious experience of a profound kind which resulted in his adoption of a life of simple piety and spirituality.

He gathered others who were attracted by the character of his life, and they too adopted his way of simple piety and joined him in preaching and ministering to the people of the city. By the time the archbishop expelled them from Lyons they were a community of some thousands. The points on which they differed from the official religion included their refusal of obedience to the Pope and to bishops; their insistence that religious exhortation and teaching was open to all to undertake who were fit to do so, including women; that masses, prayers and alms for the dead were of no avail; and that prayer outside church is as efficacious as prayer within church. Official sentence was pronounced on them in 1184: 'these are eternally anathema' and with them all others 'not having the authority of the Apostolic See or of the Bishop of the diocese.' It is worth noting that the notion of 'authority' here is one that is primarily institutional. The view of the Waldenses was that spiritual power is not conferred by ordination at the hands of a bishop, but was bestowed by Christ directly upon an individual. Their quality of life is well attested, and it became the common practice of orthodox catholic priests to apply to a man of good moral character the smear, 'He is a Waldensian' (Jones, 1923; 142, 144). Various other forms of anti-sacerdotalism appeared in the thirteenth century. 'The priestly monopoly in sacramental grace, coupled with its sordid financial operations, provoked a full-blown storm of protest, at the very time when the papacy was advancing to the climax of its earthly power' (Walker, 1961; 143).

6.26 Religious alternatives: mystical

Another kind of religious practice which earned the displeasure of the ecclesiastical authorities was that of the Brotherhood groups, the Beguines (women) and the Beghards (men). They emerged in the early thirteenth century in northern France. The Beguines were women who lived a kind of monastic life, and devoted themselves to works of charity and religion. The Beghards, similarly, formed an independent order, living in communities, vowed to poverty and good works. More serious from the official point of view even than the fact that they took no vows of obedience to authority was that their communities were hot-beds of heresy. Mystical ideas had begun to provide a real alternative to Roman institutional religion, and in a popular form were penetrating everywhere; 'every time we get a glimpse of the doctrine the *central idea* is the same. God is all. . . . In this universe of multiplicity everything *real* is divine. The end of all things is a return to the *divine unity*. Man has within himself the possibility of such return – he can become like Christ, like God. He can even become God. . . . The Church therefore is unnecessary. Heaven and hell are allegories . . .' (Jones, 1923; 206). Another popular religious society of this kind in the early thirteenth century was one which a university professor in Paris named Amaury had brought into being by means of his teaching. The official condemnation of Amaury was on the grounds that he had declared 'that God is called the End of all things, because all things are to return into Him and to remain unchangeable in Him. . . . He holds that God is the essence of every creature, and the ultimate reality of everything that is. . . .' The society which was formed of his disciples, many of them university students, believed that the highest spiritual experience was that of realising the divine life within one's own being, and in pursuit of this goal practised silence and contemplation. Another teacher of a similar popular doctrine was David Dinant, also of the early thirteenth century, who according to Aquinas held that 'God, intelligence and matter are identical in essence', and that 'individual qualities which distinguish beings are only *appearances* due to an illusion of sense' (Jones, 1923; 184). This is remarkably similar to the monistic doctrine of Shankara, the great brāhman philosopher of India of the ninth and tenth centuries (*6.12*). In spite of the official persecution of such mysticism, in spite of the Papal denunciations, the Inquisition, the burning of books and of men, it continued to provide a powerful and attractive alternative religious system to the authoritarian Augustinian orthodoxy.

By the fourteenth century it is this view of spiritual reality which attracted the Dominican monk, Heinrich Eckhart. Creatures share in real being, according to Eckhart, only as they share in the nature of God. In order to reach God man has to turn inward, realising the divine reality within himself, and renouncing all desire. It is easy to see how such views led to a devaluation of sacraments, the official channels of grace, and consequently the challenge to priestly authority which this ascetic, contemplative system implied. Eckhart's mysticism was condemned by Papal Bull in 1329. It was not thereby destroyed, however, as the mysticism of at least two of the more famous of his immediate disciples shows – John Tauler (1300–61) and John Ruysbreck (1293–

1381). The mystical tradition continued to attract many men and women in various countries of Europe throughout the fourteenth and fifteenth centuries, many of whom will remain unknown by name, like the author of the mystical treatise, *The Cloud of Unknowing*; those whose names are known include Thomas à Kempis, Henry Suso, Margaret and Christina Ebner, and in England, Richard Rolle of Yorkshire, Walter Hilton of Nottinghamshire, and Julian of Norwich.

6.27 Jewish medieval mysticism

It is one of the characteristics of mysticism, of the kind described above (6.26), that it cuts across traditional, institutional boundaries. In the medieval period the mystical tradition within Jewish religion is known as the Kabbalah. The word means 'tradition', and its use in this connection refers to the claim that this was an element of religious life which had been handed down orally from earlier times. In the eleventh century Jewish mystical ideas and practices had something of an esoteric quality, but by the fourteenth century they had become 'the manifest pursuit of the many' (Epstein, 1959; 223).

In so far as the historical transmission of mystical ideas can be traced, Jewish mysticism appears to have developed first in Iraq and from there to have been carried in the ninth century C.E. to Italy and thence in the tenth century to Germany. Another form coming from Iraq appears to have reached Provence in the twelfth century and from there to have spread to Spain where it became prominent in the fourteenth century. In Germany, owing to the persecution the Jews suffered, and to their more socially withdrawn and inward-looking condition, mysticism developed in a predominantly practical, ecstatic and sometimes magical direction. In Provence and Spain, where the Jews enjoyed relatively more favourable conditions (especially in Muslim Spain) mysticism developed in a more metaphysical and speculative direction. Influential in this development were Isaac the Blind of Provence in the middle of the twelfth century, and his disciple Azriel (c. 1160–1238 C.E.) who in turn numbered among his disciples Moses Nachmanides, who in the thirteenth century was responsible for spreading among the Jews of Spain the mystical doctrines which, he declared, were the real essence of Judaism. Most influential of all, however, was the compilation which appeared about 1300, known as the *Zohar*, made by Leon of Granada; this was a work which 'very soon became the textbook of Jewish mystics, and after the Talmud has exercised the profoundest influence in Judaism' (Epstein, 1959; 234), especially after 1492, when, the Jews being expelled from Spain as a result of the Catholic Inquisition, they spread abroad into other countries of the Mediterranean region and of northern Europe, carrying with them into these countries the mysticism of the Zohar, by which they had been fortified to bear persecution and to view their sufferings in a wide perspective.

6.28 *The disintegration of the Christian medieval pattern*

It is possibly significant that the period of greatest intellectual influence of Augustinian theology, the theology of the omnipotent deity, coincided with the period of greatest political influence of the Papacy. There is not the space to do more than note this fact, beyond remarking that the decline of the one also accompanied the decline of the other. The Church was the *City of God*, of God the omnipotent ruler; the Church was also, in the period which began towards the end of Augustine's own lifetime, the undisputed successor to the Roman empire, and its earthly ruler was Caesar's heir during the centuries when there was virtually no single secular power strong enough to resist ecclesiastical control. The two realms, the theological and the political, manifest some striking parallels. By the fourteenth century challenges to the supremacy both of the theology and Papal secular control had begun to appear. Since the days of Augustine a new intellectual force had entered the European arena in the shape of Aristotelian thought – preserved and transmitted to Western Europe by Islamic philosophers. In Anselm's day reason was very clearly subordinate to revelation; it was a useful tool for explicating what was known by revelation. By the time of Aquinas, two centuries later, we see reason admitted to something approaching a partnership with revelation (*6.24*). By the following century faith based on revelation, and knowledge based on reason, were beginning to be regarded as separate and distinct from each other. Aquinas's system of philosophical theology may be seen as a valiant attempt to stave off the day of the divorce of reason and faith. Nevertheless in the thought-systems of men such as William of Ockham (1300–49) and his disciples it is axiomatic that reason and faith operate in entirely different realms, and are independent of each other. William of Ockham (the name of his birthplace in Surrey) was a member of the Franciscan Order, who at the age of twenty-four was charged by the Papal court at Avignon with unorthodoxy. Two years later his writings were condemned, and two years later still he fled from Avignon to Germany, to spend the remaining twenty-one years of his life in controversy with orthodox theology and in assisting the temporal ruler to resist Papal political claims.

Ockham's position with regard to the natural world was that of the empiricist; observation of individual objects, their properties, and their relation with other individual objects was the only method to be followed. The metaphysical idea of universals, of which individual objects were particular expressions, he rejected. Such an empirical approach to the natural world ruled out the possibility of natural theology such as Aquinas had believed possible, that is, the demonstration of the existence of God from the rational use of evidence derived from that natural order. So far as knowledge of God was concerned, this was, according to Ockham, entirely a matter of faith. The elaborate schemes of medieval theology, which analysed God's being and his attributes, were ruled out. The only affirmation to be made about God was that he is absolute power (*potentia absoluta*) and this for Ockham was a matter of faith alone. God was otherwise utterly unknowable and unpredictable; he could do whatever pleased him at any time. 'Where reason ended, God's *potentia absoluta* began, taking charge of what was not subject to verification and showing how uncertain and unknown it was. It removed all effective standards of judgment. In that sense the God of scepticism ceased to be the God of tradition: He was so unknowable that His attributes melted in the blaze of His omnipotence, leaving no certainty' (Leff, 1958; 290). It is important to notice the one positive note that remains in this late medieval scepticism about the nature of God, when all else has been dissolved away – God as absolute power. Ockham did not cease to believe in God; faith had still its object, and for a medieval man the one enduring characteristic possessed by this object of faith was omnipotence. This is interesting confirmation of where the emphasis ultimately lay in medieval Christian theology; when all other characteristics of God had gone, this one remained, not to be surrendered; and even this could only be affirmed by faith.

The religious scepticism which Ockham represented had certain

affinities with the mysticism which, as we have seen, was also a feature
of the times, and which also provided an alternative to the Augustinian
and Thomist schemes of theology. The opponents of this scepticism,
such as Thomas Bradwardine (1290–1349), Archbishop of Canterbury,
denounced it as Pelagianism (*4.18*). The reason for this lay in the
similarity of practical effect – the Ockhamists denied any certainty or
regularity about the working of God in relation to man, and hence
virtually denied the whole scheme of institutional grace. In this, as in
the mood of agnosticism about the nature of God, there is a connection
between the Ockhamists and those who were inclined to mysticism as
an alternative to orthodoxy, for as Josiah Royce put it, 'The mystic is
a thorough-going empiricist' (Jones, 1923; xx).

The denial of a metaphysical hierarchy ranging from truths of
revelation down through truths of reason, and the establishing of a
divorce between them, had its parallels in other directions; for instance,
there was a tendency to pay less attention to the established hierarchical
structure which had until now characterised medieval society. The
political authority of the Popes began to be challenged by various
secular rulers. Towards the end of the fourteenth century there were
signs of social unrest; the fixed order of society (which, justified as a
divinely ordained structure, was in some ways curiously like the caste-
system of India) was beginning to be challenged in such movements as
the Peasants' Revolt in England, and by similar movements in France
and Flanders. As we have seen, those who took part in the rebellion
against theological and sacramental authority were not infrequently
involved also in the rejection of the social and political authority of the
Papal Church.

6.29 Eastern and Western Christianity

One important point remains to be touched upon in connection with
the religion of medieval Europe, and that is the alienation which
occurred during this period between the Church of the Latin West and
that of the Greek East. This is a handy distinction, but should not be
pressed too far, for the East had absorbed elements of Latin culture,
just as the West had inherited much that was Greek. The rift between
Rome and Byzantium which occurred in 731 has already been noted
(*6.21*); it continued to grow, and was aggravated both by political

factors and by certain differences of culture and outlook. The East criticised the Papal Church for a number of what it considered to be departures from Christian principles – the notion of Purgatory, the compulsory celibacy of the clergy, and the denial of the right of the priest to confirm the baptised, for example. The final separation occurred when the Eastern Church objected to the Pope's having, as they held, taken upon himself to add the word *Filioque* to the Nicene Creed, to indicate that the Holy Spirit proceeds from (God) the Father, *and the Son*. The repudiation of this idea by the East enabled the Western Church, whose political strength lay with Charlemagne and his successors, to accuse the East of heresy in response to the Eastern Church's criticisms of Papal religion. The traditional date for the schism is 1054, when the Papal legate to Constantinople, Cardinal Humbert, laid on the altar of St Sophia a letter of excommunication of the Patriarch of Constantinople and his associates. Four centuries later when Constantinople was threatened by Turkish Muslim armies, negotiations with Rome were entered upon in the hope of gaining Western help, and it is to be noted that the four major points which were declared to be at issue between the two Churches were the Papal claim to supremacy, the *Filioque* clause, the doctrine of Purgatory, and the question of the use of leavened or unleavened bread in the Eucharist.

The differences between the two Churches, apart from these matters, are differences of emphasis within Christian religion; some of these, however, are matters of such primary importance that these two wings of Christendom have developed into almost separate types of religion. The differences have been summarised as follows (Zaehner, 1959, 76–9). In the West the essential feature of the Christian life is man's *justification*, whereas in the East it is his *divinisation* ('God became man in order that man might become God'). Connected with this is the Western Christian view of man which lays stress on his *original guilt*, whereas the Eastern Church emphasises man's *potential goodness*. Western theology tends towards a dualism of matter and spirit (as in Augustine), whereas the East holds to the idea of the unity of matter and spirit, or at least their interdependence. In the West it is most important that the right dogmas are held, whereas in the East it is in worshipping aright and in the true experience of worship that orthodoxy (literally, 'right-praise') consists. In keeping with the West's emphasis on the guilt of man and his prime need being for justification it is the idea of Christ as *the victim*, the sacrifice to God which cancels man's sin, which is emphasised;

whereas in the East it is the idea of Christ as Victor over the forces of evil, which is more strongly emphasised. Finally, there is a contrast in ecclesiastical structure. The Western Church is characterised by a monarchical authoritarian system, that is, authority with a recognised *focus*, namely the Papacy; whereas in the East authority is vested in the whole congregation of the faithful, and there is no one visible head, no authoritarian individual who is regarded as Christ's vicar. This shows itself in another way in the strong sense of identification with the community which is characteristic of the Eastern Church, whereas Western Christendom has tended to emphasise the individual.

6.3 ISLAM COMES OF AGE (750–1500 C.E.)

6.30 The social basis of Islamic civilisation

An account of the orthodox beliefs and practices of Islam, such as will be given later (*6.34*) would show us only the bare bones of what was in fact a living religious culture, and certainly from the period of the Abbasid caliphate in Baghdad, a vigorous and distinctive Islamic civilisation. The Arabs had brought to Iraq and Persia a new religion, a language, and a social system: a religion whose creed had the attraction of simplicity and rationality; a language which, as B. Thomas says, was by reason of its richness and flexibility well fitted for becoming 'the scientific and classical as well as the religious idiom of an empire in much the same way as Latin served for medieval Europe' (1937; 124); and a social system which was in essence democratic, based upon a strong sense of brotherhood, and able to reach across national loyalties. The religion of Islam is unfavourable to discrimination between men on the grounds either of social class, or of race and colour. This is not to say that Islam has never been affected by such kinds of discrimination, but more often than not its coming has meant to the people of the territory into which it came a sense of social release. This wide humanity is undoubtedly one of the principal factors in the success of the Islamic community in absorbing peoples of diverse types from Spain to Indonesia, and from Mongolia to equatorial Africa.

6.31 Islam in Iraq

We have seen (5.11–5.13) that Islam arose as a specifically *religious* response to the condition of Meccan society at the beginning of the seventh century C.E. Muhammad's religious experience had as its background his awareness of the irreligious and materialistic trends of the time in Arabia. His prophetic role consisted initially of his proclaiming to his contemporaries the reality of a transcendent being to whom all men were responsible and whose judgment ultimately they must encounter. We saw also that the initially *religious* movement which he inaugurated very soon assumed a *political* character, in the new integration of Medinan society which Muhammad saw to be his task. A new religio-political state developed, consciously organised as a theocracy. The success which this achieved in integrating the Arab tribes of Medina soon attracted neighbouring Arab tribes, and the process of growth was considerably stimulated by the idea of jihad, or striving in the way of God (*5.15*). Arab tribesmen began to be drawn into the new community for reasons that were primarily political rather than religious. What had begun as a prophetic religious movement became thus at a very early stage a community combining both religious and political interests and aims. Before long these two elements had their recognisable representatives: those who were attracted on religious grounds and regarded this as the essential element in Islam; and those who, when they saw how things were going, had jumped on to the pan-Arab political bandwagon which Islam appeared to them to be.

By the time of the Umayyad caliphs this duality had become obvious to all; the protest of the Qadarites and the puritan Kharijites at the blatant secularism of the Umayyad rulers and their party was an expression of this awareness. What we now have to consider during the period of the Abbasid caliphs (750–1258) is the growth of interaction between the political and the religious elements, and how this affected, in particular, the religious development of Islam.

The caliph transferred his capital from Damascus to Baghdad in 762 C.E., and from then onwards for the next two and a half centuries it was in Iraq and Persia that some of the most important developments in Islam took place. The scene is that of the former Sassanid Persian empire, conquered by the Muslim Arabs and progressively occupied

and brought under their rule during the caliphate of Umar (634–44
c.e.) (5.18). Up to this point our study of Islam has been concerned
mainly with its Arabian origin and with Arabs as its bearers. We have
now to take account of the fact that it soon came to be embraced by
peoples of non-Arab stock, a fact which is significant for two reasons:
first, it reminds us of the ability of this Arabian system of religious
belief and practice to appeal to men outside the culture in which it
originated – a further example of the principle of *diffusion* and a
demonstration of Islam's character as a missionary religion; and second,
the obverse side, the effect upon the nature of Islam as a religion of this
spread into other cultural regions. Not only have we to note the impact
of Islam on Persia and Iraq, but also their impact on Islam.

At the time of the Muslim military occupation of this area four classes
in Persian, or Persianised, society may be distinguished: the Zoroastrian clergy; the army; the secretaries or civil servants; and the mass
of the people, both artisans and peasants. Zoroastrianism had been the
established religion; its clergy had the support of, and themselves
supported the secular power and because of this alliance were able to
oppress dissident religious minorities, such as Christians and Jews;
these therefore were by no means sorry to see Sassanid Persian-
Zoroastrian rule replaced by that of Arab Muslims, who here as elsewhere showed a very tolerant attitude towards these minority religious
groups, 'peoples of the book' as they were. Moreover there was
apparently no great respect among the common people for state
Zoroastrianism; many of the artisans by reason of their occupation
were regarded with disfavour by religious officials, and these too were
inclined to welcome their new Muslim masters. The army and the
Zoroastrian clergy were now dispossessed of power and hence receded
in importance; the crucial case among these various social classes was
that of the secretaries. Those were the public administrators upon whose
knowledge and skill the functioning of the Persian state had depended;
they were the real bearers of Persian culture, the literati; to a large
extent they correspond with that class in modern western society called
'the professionals', 'the salariat' or 'the pace-makers'. Their attitude
towards Islam was more complicated. Previously many of them had
been formally Zoroastrian, since that had been the established form of
religion. Some of these when they saw it was in their interest to do so,
became Muslims. Others, however, resisted Islamisation. To them the
Arabs were their cultural inferiors and this new religion of the Arabs a

matter for contempt. Their rejection of Muslim belief and practice was mostly, however, not from a Zoroastrian position, but rather from that of Manichaeism, the dualistic religious system which had its origin in third-century Babylon and which had a strong appeal for these Persian literati; in some cases it was from the position of intellectuals who had now turned to Hellenistic philosophy. Among those of the secretary class who were thus critical of Muslim religion there was a further reason which sharpened their criticism: a class of religious specialists, the ulama, had emerged within Islam and these men were now succeeding to the place in Persian society formerly held by the Zoroastrian clergy, and some also were being appointed to administrative posts in the Muslim state. Intellectual controversy thus developed between the Muslim religious institution and the Persian secretaries, and it was in the course of this, and also to some extent in controversy with Christians and Jews, that the Muslims were forced to engage in the study of Greek philosophy, and especially in the art of logical disputation.

6.32 Islamic civilisation and learning

There were, however, other reasons for the growth of Islamic learning, one of the most important of which was the openness of Islamic society (6.30). Islamic civilisation under the Abbasids was a compound in which three elements can be distinguished: the ancient culture of Persia, the philosophy and science of the Greeks, and the stimulus to both of these within the Persian environment provided by the spirit of Islam and the new degree of socialisation of knowledge that became possible within the relatively free society of the Islamic cities, especially in Baghdad. It is to the credit of the Muslim Arabs, moreover, that when they came into contact with other systems of thought and men of keen intellect they did not evade the challenge to their Arab culture which this presented, for fear that alien philosophies should upset revealed truth. On the contrary their leaders, particularly the early caliphs of Baghdad, gave positive encouragement to the pursuit of classical Persian and Hellenistic learning. In particular, possibly through the Nestorian Christians of Persia, the Arabs discovered the philosophy of Aristotle, whose works now began to be translated into Arabic. This led to the discovery of other fields of classical Greek learning and literature. Islamic cities in Persia became free meeting places for wandering scholars from Greece, Persia and India. We are told that 'philosophers, mathematicians, astronomers, medical scientists' and other scholars of wide reputation in the Greek sciences moved freely into this area throughout the ninth, tenth and eleventh centuries of the Christian era. Great libraries of learned works were built up at centres of scholarship throughout the Muslim world, such as Baghdad, Cairo and Cordova, and to a lesser degree in many of the mosques.

6.33 Islamic thought in Iraq

It thus came about that the rising class of Muslim ulama acquired a considerable knowledge of Greek philosophical concepts at a time when their own religious ideas needed to be restated and possibly reinterpreted in the interests of religious apologetic, and it was in this situation that a new school of Islamic doctrine arose from about 800 C.E. onwards, known as the Mutazila. The meaning of this name is uncertain and various explanations have been offered, none of which commands universal acceptance. What is known of the Mutazilites, however, is that they made use of Greek philosophical concepts in the exposition of Islamic dogma, partly in debate with other Muslims, and partly in the dialogue with other faiths; it is known also that in the course of this dialogue they were concerned above all to uphold (a) the unity of God, and (b) the justice of God.

With regard to the first of these, the Mutazilites were in controversy with other Muslims. The point at issue is one which illustrates the kind of difficulty which religious thought gets into when a prophet's words have become canonised as sacred scripture and the original situation to which they were addressed has passed away, leaving only the words themselves which, while they had an immediate relevance and vitality in that original situation, have now lost it, but have gained an independent existence and are being cogitated upon, and systematised, and shaped into dogmas. This is what had happened to a number of the ways in which the Prophet had spoken of the divine being.

In the Qur'an God is sometimes described in highly anthropomorphic terms: he hears, and sees, and speaks, he comes down and seats himself upon his throne, and so on. The Mutazilites maintained that such descriptions should be interpreted allegorically. One of the most important points in this connection is that seven names for God (out of a very much larger number of what were called 'the beautiful names of God') had been fastened upon: the Knowing, the Powerful, the Willing, the Living, the Seeing, the Hearing, the Speaking. From the fact that these names were used of God in the Qur'an it was deduced that God must be thought of as possessing the 'attributes' indicated by these names: Knowledge, Power, Will, and so on. The seventh attribute of God was thus that of Speech, or Word. This 'Word' of God was then identified as being, in fact, the Qur'an. But since God is eternal and uncreated, His attributes must also be eternal, and uncreated; so it was argued. Hence the Qur'an was eternal and uncreated. To some Muslims, possibly to those who were conversant with Greek thought and especially Greek Christian thought, there was a danger here. Such Muslims would know that Christians believed in a Logos or divine Word, and that such belief appeared to imply a second God. This multiplicity of attributes might well seem to them to endanger the doctrine of the unity of God, especially when one of the attributes was identified with an entity known to men as the Qur'an. The Mutazilites therefore denied that the Qur'an was eternal and uncreated; it had appeared, they said, at a certain point in time, and was not identical with the 'speech' of God, which had to be understood as part of God himself, not a separate attribute.

It so happened that this assertion by the Mutazilites suited very well the purposes of the Abbasid caliph at the time; for reasons of governmental policy he was concerned to reduce the supreme status of the Qur'an. From about 830 C.E., therefore, Mutazilites seem to have been very much in favour with the Abbasid caliph, and were appointed to important administrative posts in the state; all officials were required to make an assertion to the effect that the Qur'an was created and not eternal; those who refused to do so were imprisoned.

As the second main point in their doctrine, they emphasised the *justice* of God. This, perhaps more than the first point, was for apologetic reasons in connection with their disputations with Manichaeans and Christians. They were concerned to refute the charge that the omnipotent God of the Qur'an was unjust in his dealings with men; God, they said, could will only what was for man's good. In support of their view they, like the Qadarites (with whom they had a close connection) asserted the freedom of the human will. Man's destiny, they argued, depended on his actions; God has shown man how to live

L

so as to gain Paradise; it was therefore for man to heed God's word and live accordingly. Their orthodox Muslim opponents had also learnt the use of logic in doctrinal disputes, and they began to raise awkward questions concerning the fate of children who died before they could be held responsible for their actions. The story of the three brothers is an example of the kind of argument used by the orthodox against the Mutazilites. There were three brothers, one good, one wicked, and one who died as a child; the good one went to Paradise when he died, the wicked one to Hell, and the one who died as a child to Limbo. According to the story, the third brother complained that God had been less than fair to him, in making him die as a child and thus be unable to gain Paradise. The reply he received was that God knew that had he lived he would have grown up to be wicked and would in fact have gone to Hell. At this, the second brother complained that God had dealt less than fairly with him, since he had not caused him to die in infancy like his brother but had allowed him to grow up, become wicked, and be sent to Hell. Why had God seen fit to deal so unfairly with him? To this there was no answer, and the Mutazilite doctrine, that God must deal with men for their good, was shown to involve God in a charge of injustice, a charge to which it appeared God would have to plead guilty. The orthodox opponents of the Mutazilites were also beginning to learn to use the methods of rational argument in defence of their orthodoxy; for them the important truth to be defended was that nothing is incumbent on an omnipotent God and no charge of injustice can therefore be made against Him.

The favour of the caliph which the Mutazilites had enjoyed came to an end after about 848 C.E., when the caliphs were no longer concerned, as they had been previously, with lowering the status of the Qur'an, and the Mutazilites' views were no longer of importance to them. After about 850 C.E. they therefore ceased to have much popular influence, but one lasting result of the controversies they had stirred up was the use of philosophical methods, and in particular logic, in the exposition of orthodox doctrine. It was the excessive use of philosophy which later, as we shall see, resulted in a reaction towards mysticism (*6.36; 6.37*).

6.34 The emergence of normative Islam

By the second century after the Hijra (5.14) or the ninth century of the Christian era, Islam may be said to have reached the fully developed form in which it was to persist down to modern times. This full development was reached when the major items of belief and practice had been settled and an agreed body of authoritative sources had emerged. For in addition to the Qur'an, orthodox Islam accepts also certain collections of the Hadith *(5.11)* or traditions about the Prophet Muhammad which are regarded as genuine and authentic, namely those compiled by al-Bukhari, who died in 870 c.e. and those compiled by Muslim, who died in 889. These constitute a canonical authority secondary to the Qur'an, and are the source for ascertaining the Sunna, or customs, of the Prophet and the forefathers. The orthodox Muslim, in questions of theology and of law, appeals to the Qur'an *and* the Sunna, and it is from the latter term that the orthodox community of Islam is named the Sunni.

It will be convenient at this point to summarise the main items of belief and practice in orthodox Islam as they had by this time developed. The major items of belief are seven in number:

1. *God*; above all the Muslim believes in the *unity* of God, the creator of all things, who in his omnipotence overrules all things.
2. *Angels*; who are God's servants and messengers, the chief of whom is Gabriel; this is in contrast to Judaism, where Michael is regarded as the chief of the angels. A. I. Katsh (1954) has suggested that the reason for the primacy of Gabriel in Islam is that he is traditionally the guardian angel of Abraham, who is regarded by Muslims as 'the father of Islam'.
3. *The prophets*; a large number of whom are recognised but seven of whom are given special prominence, namely, Adam, Seth, Enoch, Abraham, Moses, David and Jesus, with Muhammad as the final prophet, after whom there are no more.
4. *The holy books*, containing the words of the prophets, again culminating in the Qur'an, delivered through Muhammad and regarded as either abrogating or superseding the previous prophetic books, some of which, however, are regarded as having been already either 'withdrawn' by God, since they are not known to exist (e.g. a book written by Adam) or corrupted in the course of transmission and no longer trustworthy (those concerning Jesus, for example).
5. The doctrine of the *predestination* by God of good and evil.
6. The doctrine of the Last Day, the *Day of Judgment*.
7. The doctrine of *bodily resurrection* of all men at the Last Day.

The main items of religious practice, the 'Five Pillars of Islam', are:

1. The confession of faith, or shahāda: 'There is no god but God, and Muhammad is his apostle'.
2. Prayer, at the five set times daily.
3. Almsgiving.
4. Fasting, especially during the daylight hours of the month of Ramadan, when it is compulsory for all but certain exempted individuals, such as pregnant women, and the sick, who must make it up later.
5. Pilgrimage, if possible at least once in life, to the holy city and shrine at Mecca.

6.35   The work of Al Ashari (873–935)

The Mutazilites, in their attempt to expound the Qur'anic revelation by the use of reason, raised as many difficulties as they solved – as, for example, in the case of the story of the three brothers, where their efforts to uphold the idea that God is just and can will only what is good for man appeared to involve them in the end in demonstrating God's unfairness (6.33). It was dissatisfaction with this method of interpretation of the Qur'an which led Al Ashari, one of the most brilliant pupils of the leading Mutazilite teacher in Basra, to abandon this kind of approach. This happened about the year 912 c.e., when Al Ashari was nearly forty. By this time the Mutazilites had ceased to enjoy the favour of the caliph, and between their philosophical ideas and the religious beliefs of the ordinary Muslims there was a wide gulf. Nor was the Mutazilite philosophical position sufficiently philosophical for the minority who were inclined towards Greek ideas. Al Ashari's 'conversion' to orthodoxy and his rejection of the philosophising methods of the Mutazilites is connected with a series of dreams in which Muhammad is said to have appeared and spoken to him. He became convinced that the Qur'anic revelation must be restored to its proper place in Islamic religion: it must be held to be the uncreated Word of God; it must be given absolute priority; and it must be understood not metaphorically or as allegory but literally. One of the most important implications of this was that the Mutazilite doctrine of human free will had to be rejected. As we have seen (5.19) the Qur'an is overwhelmingly in favour of the doctrine of divine predestination of all the actions of men. In the view of the orthodox, the Mutazilite doctrine of free will endangered the supremely important Islamic idea of the absolute omnipotence of God. Nevertheless, some way had to be found to explain the apparent freedom of choice man has, and a certain degree of human moral responsibility postulated by the injunctions to man contained in the Qur'an. Al Ashari's reconciliation of the Qur'anic data shows that he did not in fact altogether reject the use of rational methods of exposition; they were however assigned a completely subordinate position to the Word, that is the Qur'an itself. His view was that God provides all the attendant circumstances for a man's action; man then enters into those circumstances and 'acquires' the acts which God has made possible for him. Thus man does not create his actions, and God's sole Creatorship is safeguarded. God allows man room within which to act, but since it *is* God who does this, God's omnipotence is maintained. On the other hand, in Al Ashari's view man has a certain degree of accountability for his actions (whether he does willingly act as God has made it possible for him to act or not), and this is sufficient to form the criterion for man's punishment or reward at the Last Judgment. This view of the matter expounded by Al Ashari was, says Wensinck, one which 'determined the direction in which dogmatic Islam was to move for centuries' (Wensinck, 1932; 86f.). Orthodox Islam was committed to a *literal* interpretation of words spoken in an Arabian situation by an Arab prophet. Within the limits of the literal acceptance of these words Muslim theologians were free to engage in philosophical argument and reasoned exposition of the data. With such theological orthodoxy many, apparently, were satisfied; but not all, as we shall see.

6.36 The Sufis

The division between the religious and the political elements in Islam, which was mentioned earlier (*6.31*), becomes particularly noticeable in the Sufi movement. The Sufis are sometimes described as the mystics of Islam but this is perhaps too restrictive a description. Their origins are to be found in the ascetic religious tradition of early Islam, and in the growing dissatisfaction which the more faithful Muslims felt in a situation where the rulers of the Islamic community were becoming increasingly secular and irreligious. Discontent of this kind began, as we have seen, with the Umayyad caliphs. The faithful were very unhappy with the turn events had taken; a few minorities such as the Shia, the Qadarites, and the Kharijites expressed their discontent during the Umayyad period; others may have hoped for better days. When the Umayyads in their Damascus capital were succeeded in the leadership of the Islamic community by the Abbasids in their new capital of Baghdad these hopes sank very low. Power, wealth, luxury and ostentation were now the most characteristic features of the life of the men who had seized control of the Muslim community. 'I will tell a tale of long ago,' wrote Ahmad ben Asim of Antioch (757–830 C.E.), 'how first the Faith began, and how it grew to full perfection; yea, and I will tell how next it withered, till it hath become e'en as a faded garment.' He goes on to tell how he lived in 'an age become exceeding strange, cruel and terrible'. Men might eulogise Islam, but it was 'as mourners praise the dear, departed dead!' (Arberry, 1950; 31).

Out of such dissatisfaction and protest, out of a desire for the recovery of the religious dimension to life, out of a situation, that is to say, not unlike that in which the Prophet himself had been inspired to embark on his mission, there emerged a new emphasis on the virtues of abstinence and self-denial, on simplicity of life and the disciplines of prayer and fasting. Men recalled that though the first caliph Abu Bakr had been a great ruler, he had worn only a simple garment held together by two pins; the caliph Umar, who had ruled even greater territory, had lived on the simplest food and had worn patched clothes; these had been in the tradition of the prophets of God before them who had practised austerities and cared only for the service of God. The men who recalled these things did so in explanation of their own austere practice, undertaken in the first instance as a protest against the stifling atmosphere of worldliness and more formal adherence to Islam. To this ascetic, and to some extent negative attitude of protest there came to be added a more positive fervour, a desire 'to know God' in some way more direct and real than that set forth by the theologians and lawyers. The ascetic protest began in Iraq in the towns of Basra and Kufa during the eighth century, whence it spread to Syria and Persia, especially to the region of Khorasan. The devotional, or mystical, development of the movement had its centre in Baghdad whence originated much of the early devotional literature of the *Sufis*, as these men had now come to be called. This positive emphasis on direct, inner knowledge of God developed a theory of union with God which had strong affinities with the idea of theosis, or the divinisation of man, that is emphasised in the Christian East (*6.29*). It led some of the Sufis to express their position in terms that sounded to the majority of Muslims like blasphemy. Thus, al-Hallāj, who expressed his inner experience by saying 'I am the Truth' was crucified in 922 C.E. Others were similarly executed for heresy. However, Sufi holy men continued to teach their doctrine and their practice to groups of disciples, and by the eleventh century C.E. a number of Sufi schools were in existence, in which the teaching of the Sufi masters was transmitted. This led to the development of established Orders by the twelfth century; these were religious communities or brotherhoods (though not celibate) with their own distinctive mode of initiation, and a common discipline and doctrine. Four such great Orders emerged in the twelfth and thirteenth centuries:

1. The Quādirīs, owing their original inspiration to the life and preaching of a Persian Muslim, al-Quādir (1078–1166 C.E.).
2. The Suhrawardīya, named after another Persian, al-Suhrawadī (1144–1234 C.E.).
3. The Shādhiliyā, founded by al-Shādhili (1196–1258 C.E.), who gained a large following in Tunis, fled to Alexandria and there was even more successful in the number of disciples he gained.
4. The Order whose founder was the great Jalāl al-Dīn Rūmī, perhaps the greatest of all the mystical poets of Persia, who died in 1273 C.E.; this was the Order known as the Maulawīya.

The first two of these subsequently became important in India, the third in Egypt and North Africa, and the fourth in Turkey.

The man who more than any other perhaps was responsible for Sufism gaining a firm footing within Islam was the great teacher and mystic Al Ghazali and to a brief account of this man's religious experience we now turn.

6.37 Al Ghazali and the philosophers

It is sometimes said that if anyone in Islamic history was to be held a prophet after Muhammad it would have to be Al Ghazali (1058–1111 C.E.). He is usually regarded as the greatest and most original of the scholars in the orthodox tradition of Al Ashari (*6.35*) and the highest authority of the Sunni school. In order to understand the characteristic ideas and emphases which Ghazali succeeded in establishing within

Islam it is necessary to know something of his own history and personal religious experience. The five hundred years which separate Muhammad and Al Ghazali were a period in which the relationship of reason and faith was being constantly explored. Some of this exploration we have already reviewed in connection with the Mutazilites (*6.33*). More especially, however, under the influence of Greek thought mediated through the translations of Aristotle and Plato that became available to the Arabs during this period, a tradition of Islamic philosophy developed. The great figures in this tradition were concerned not only with the theological problem of relating reason and faith, but also with the nature of the world, its phenomena and its laws, their approach to the subject being entirely empirical and rational.

The outstanding names in this tradition are, in the ninth century, Al Kindi; in the early tenth century Al Farabi; in the eleventh Ibn Sina (Avicenna) and in the twelfth Ibn Rushd (Averroës). Al Ghazali, born twenty years after the death of Ibn Sina, began by being keenly interested in philosophical problems, and became perplexed and unhappy as the result of his study of contemporary philosophy at Baghdad, so that he came to doubt even the evidence of his senses and the workings of his own mind. 'My sickness was too much for me', he wrote. 'It lasted for almost two months during which I was a sceptic. . . . In the end God cured me of my sickness. . . . But this did not happen through systematic processes of proof or through the weight of arguments but through a light which God (to Whom be Praise) cast into my breast . . .' (Hottinger, 1963; 92). He came to the conclusion that the philosophers were basically unbelievers. They denied the resurrection of the body, they denied that God concerns himself with individual happenings and they affirmed that the world was eternal, without beginning and without end, all of which was, said Ghazali, in the light of the Qur'an sheer unbelief. He wrote a critical attack on the position represented by Ibn Sina in particular, which he entitled *The Incoherence of the Philosophers*. A reply to this was produced somewhat later by the philosopher Ibn Rushd, entitled *The Incoherence of the Incoherence*.

From the philosophers Ghazali turned to the mystics. He gave up his post as lecturer in Baghdad, and went to Mecca where for ten years he lived the life of the ascetic. 'I realised with certainty', he wrote, 'that it is the mystics above all others who are on God's Path. Their life is the best life, their methods the best methods and their character the purest character. Were the intelligence of all intellectuals, the wisdom of all scholars and the scholarship of all professors who are experienced in the profundities of the Revealed Truth brought together in an effort to improve the mystics' conduct and character they would achieve nothing, for all movement and all rest, both external and internal, illuminate the mystic with light from the Lamp of Prophetic Revelation and there is no light on the face of this earth which illuminates more than this Light of Prophetic Revelation.

How must one follow this mystic path? Purity, the first condition, means complete purification of the heart from everything but God (to Whom be praise). The key thereto, and also the password of the ritual prayer, is to sink one's heart in the contemplation of God; its goal is complete identification with God' (Hottinger, 1963; 94).

Later, Ghazali endeavoured to popularise the subject-matter and methods of philosophy; he tried to make it intelligible to ordinary people in order that they should understand its inherent weaknesses. His great influence was, however, in the direction away from philosophy, to a renewed study of the Qur'an and the Hadith. He brought into prominence again an element which had been neglected, at least among the educated, namely the healthy sensation of fear, as he regarded it: the fear and horror of hell as a motive force to a moral life. Above all his influence helped a great deal in establishing the position of Sufism within orthodox Islam. In the tension created by the attempt to reconcile a monistic philosophy with belief in the God of the Qur'an, Creator, Almighty, Determiner of all that happens, mysticism provided a great release to others like Ghazali, vexed by the same problems. Different types of religious thought have found different ways of resolving this tension; some have accommodated a popular devotional cult to a basically monistic philosophy; this was the method followed by Rāmānuja, for example (*6.14*); others have categorically rejected the idea of a unitive principle and have affirmed various forms of absolute dualism; others again have found a *modus vivendi* in mysticism, affirming what they regard as unchallengeable truths of revelation about an omnipotent God on the one hand, and the idea of the unity of all things on the other. It is in this last direction that a good deal of Islamic thought has moved, especially from the time of Ghazali.

6.38 The Muslim Turks in north India

About the year 1000 C.E. the plains of the Punjab began once again as so often before in the history of India to be the scene of violent raids carried out from the mountains to the west, this time from the Muslim Turkish kingdom of Ghazni in what is now Afghanistan. The purpose of Mahmud, the ruler of Ghazni, in carrying out these raids was to seize the treasure that was known to be available in the form of gold and jewels in the Hindu temples of the Punjab (6.13). It so happened that the Islamic concept of jihad (5.15), now interpreted as 'holy war', provided a religious motivation for the raids; for as Mahmud's own account of his activities makes clear, he regarded himself as engaged in a war against infidels and idolaters. The nature of his operations has earned him the title of 'Mahmud the idol-smasher'. He is said also to have ordered the slaughter of many brāhman priests. The part which he played in the coming of the Muslim Turks to north India is of the kind which has too often been taken to be typical of the advance of Islam everywhere – by the sword. It was against this view that T. W. Arnold's account of the expansion of Islam (1913) provided so valuable a corrective.

Success in his operations against the Hindu rājas of the Punjab led Mahmud to extend his activities further into India, and by the time he died in 1030 C.E. he had established a Muslim governor at Lahore and incorporated all this area into the Ghaznavid kingdom. For a century and a half after this there were no more Turkish attacks and Hindu India enjoyed a respite from invasion. A Muslim writer of that period, Al Biruni, who spent some time in the Punjab, has left a useful account of Indian customs and manners in the eleventh century. While he is ready to praise whatever in Hindu culture seems to be praiseworthy – their philosophy, mathematics, astrology, and even their art – he does not hesitate to point out their shortcomings. In a frequently quoted passage Al Biruni says of the Hindus: 'They are haughty, foolishly vain, self-conceited and stolid. They are by nature niggardly in communicating that which they know, and they take the greatest possible care to withhold it from men of another caste among their own people, still much more of course, from any foreigner' (Ikram, 1964; 28). This is a verdict worth pondering. Why, when Indian skill in logic and mathematics was so great, did not natural science develop in India?

One possible reason may lie in this lack of social openness among Hindus, the lack of the facility for the socialisation of knowledge. It is on this score that Islamic civilisation was at an advantage compared with Hindu society in that it was an open society, prepared to adopt ideas and practices from a variety of sources (Ikram, 1964; 28).

Towards the end of the twelfth century C.E. a new wave of invasions by the Turks began. North India at this time was divided between numerous Hindu kingdoms of varying size. They seem to have been incapable of making common cause against the Muslim invaders, who now once again began to come in increasing numbers. As P. Hardy points out, the Turkish raids began as a financial enterprise, continued as a profitable outdoor occupation for Muslim adventurers, and ended with the colonisation of the north of India and the eventual provision of a home for large numbers of Muslim refugees from Persia at the time of the fall of Baghdad to the Mongols in 1285 (de Bary, 1958; 378). By the beginning of the thirteenth century most of north India, from Sind to Bengal, had passed into the control of Muslim soldier-rulers. The reasons for their success were various. They were aided by the peasantry, many of whom in north-west India and in Bengal were nominally Buddhist lay followers, but who also heartily disliked their Hindu rulers and were glad to see them worsted; the Muslims had certain physical advantages – their horses had greater mobility than Hindu elephants and they had the advantage of the offensive; and added to this was their religious-military ardour. In 1206 C.E., a Muslim general named Aibak established his rule in the defeated Hindu city of Delhi and thus began the Sultanate, the rule of Turkish Muslim soldiers and noblemen over a vast indigenous population of Hindus and Buddhists with whom they began to intermarry and many of whom also they converted to the faith of Islam, so that the numbers of indigenous Muslims now began to grow, and continued to do so throughout the succeeding centuries of Muslim rule. There thus came into being a new kind of Muslim – the Indian Muslim, some of whose descendants were to be the citizens of the modern state of Pakistan.

A further factor in the growth of the Islamic community in India was the deliberate missionary activity undertaken during the period by the Sufis. These often began by identifying themselves with the beliefs and practices of the Vaishnavites and Shaivites, and then, having persuaded the Hindus that they were sincere religious teachers, they went on to tell of a new name for the supreme God, namely Allah, of a new avatara named Muhammad, and of his law and way of life.

6.39 The diversification of Islamic culture

By the end of the eleventh century C.E. the unity of the Arab Muslim empire was beginning to crumble. Since the Islam of the early centuries was both a religion and a political community, this meant that Islam henceforth began to exhibit that variety of regional and cultural forms which have continued to the present day. In the far west the invasions of Spain by the Berber Muslim tribesmen from north Africa gave to Spanish Islam a new, fiercer and more intolerant character. It was this which forced Jews such as the philosopher Maimonides out of Spain to seek refuge in another part of the Islamic empire, more congenial to the Jew, namely Egypt. In the Near East Islam now confronted a new enemy from the West, in the form of the Crusaders, Christian soldiers who were inspired by a determination to drive Islam out of Palestine at least, and remove the hindrances which at that time stood in the way of Christian pilgrimages to the holy places. In accordance with the medieval penitential system, Pope Urban II promised a plenary indulgence to all who enlisted for the Crusade, a declaration of freedom from debt and the maintenance of their wives and families. The Crusades thus attracted a motley collection, including not a few debtors and criminals who seized the opportunity with which a man was thus provided, as Ernest Barker has commented, 'to indulge the bellicose side of his nature . . . at the bidding of the Church' – in much the same way that the Muslim Turks of Ghazni had descended on the Hindu temples of the Punjab (6.38). The Franks constituted the predominant element among the Crusaders so that *Ferenghi* came to be the common Arabic term for any European foreigner. Whatever importance these expeditions may have had for Christian Europe, they were, so far as Islam was concerned, however, only one of a number of contestants for power and territory within the Islamic world.

An enduring result of the Crusades was the embittering of relations between Christians and Muslims for many generations and a vast amount of misrepresentation and misunderstanding on both sides.

More damaging to the unity of Islam was the wave of Mongol invasion under Genghiz Khan which swept into Persia in the mid-thirteenth century. The Arab historian Al Athir said of the Mongols that their coming was the greatest calamity to civilisation that he knew. The whole of Persia was laid waste; Baghdad was destroyed, and the caliph was executed together with many of his kinsmen. So long as the caliphate lasted, some semblance of an undivided Islam remained, but now the commonwealth of Islam was seen to be shattered. Many Persian Muslims fled eastward into India, to find a home within the sultanate of Delhi, and to enrich Indian Islam by their coming. From that time onwards Delhi grew in importance as the cultural and religious centre of Islam in Asia. Many of those who took refuge there were accomplished scholars and artists. The Muslim historian Barani tells at length of 'the scholars, poets, preachers, philosophers, physicians, astronomers and historians who thronged Delhi' as a result of the sack of Baghdad (Ikram, 1964; 112). The Muslim community in Asia now looked to the sultan of Delhi as its head, in place of the caliph. To him were ascribed those functions which formerly had been performed by the caliph, namely 'the defence and maintenance of true religion and the Holy Law (Sharia), the dispensing of justice and the appointing of the godfearing to office' (de Bary, 1958; 465). From this development there was to follow, in due course the emergence of a new variant of Islam, an Indian variant, for no more than any other of the invaders of India did the Muslims remain unaffected by the many subtle influences at work upon their faith and their culture.

In the Middle East, the centre of Islamic affairs now moved to Cairo, and the cities of Syria and Iraq which had formerly been the great centres now became provincial towns on the outskirts of Egyptian Islamic civilisation. Here now were to be found large numbers of schools and colleges which were strongholds of Sunni orthodoxy, and religious houses where Sufi communities lived and prayed. The architecture of old Cairo dating from this time suggests something of the mood Egyptian Islam was experiencing: 'The domes and walls of Mameluke buildings have something overwhelmingly repressive and blocklike about them . . . they are citadels, refuges of the spirit, richly decorated cells of ascetics, places of segregation. As such they are signs of a narrowing world. Life is approached defensively; a spirit of uncertainty and suspicion prevails; confronted with it, people tend to withdraw to a circumscribed realm which they adorn and furnish for themselves' (Hottinger, 1963; 112).

6.4 BUDDHIST CIVILISATION IN ASIA BEYOND INDIA (*1000–1800* C.E.)

6.40 *The further development of Buddhism in South-East Asia*

Buddhists sometimes adopt a division of their history into periods of five hundred years. In each of the first three periods, namely 500 B.C. to 0, 0 to 500 C.E., and 500 to 1000 C.E., a new form of Buddhism appeared. The Theravāda, represented most strongly in the continuous tradition of Ceylon where it was planted in the third century B.C. (*3.26*), is the product of the first period. The second period saw the rise of the major Mahāyāna schools (*4.3*). In the third period there was the development of two extreme forms of Mahāyāna: Ch'an (*5.23*) or Zen in Japan, and the Tantra or Vajrayāna (*5.26*). The last thousand years up to the present day, however, are sometimes regarded as blank, that is to say, it is held that in these two periods of five hundred years no new development took place. This may be true so far as the appearance of radically new ideas is concerned, but on the other hand there was development in the pattern of Buddhist cultural and social structure during the period 1000–1500 C.E., especially in South-East Asia; and, from about 1800 C.E. onwards, there was in some places the forging of a new and more committed form of what might be called lay Buddhism, in the face of the disruption of the old political and social patterns which was brought about by the coming of the Europeans to Asia.

Before we turn to these aspects of Buddhist history, however, we have to take account of the fact that the period 1000–1500 witnessed the virtual disappearance of Buddhism from India.

6.41 *The disappearance of Buddhism from India*

Buddhism as an institutional religion had ceased to be a feature of the Indian scene by about 1200 C.E. The reasons for this are various and complex. It is sometimes held that the Muslim Turkish invasions of India (*6.38*) were largely responsible, and that Buddhist religious institutions, centred upon the monasteries, were more vulnerable than other religious systems to the pillaging and plundering of what the

Turks regarded as pagan shrines. There is some truth in this, and it may go a long way towards explaining why Buddhism disappeared while Hinduism and Jainism, which were subject to the same violent attack, survived. Another reason which has been suggested (Thapar, 1966; 260) is that the militaristic values which the feudal system of medieval Indian society required were not supported by Buddhism, and that it was thus at a severe disadvantage compared with Hinduism whose ethic, as set forth in the Bhagavad-Gītā for example (4.22), is by no means unfavourable to militaristic activities. The same argument would not, however, apply to Jainism, where the doctrine of non-violence (ahimsa) is basic; yet Jainism survived in India. Perhaps more important was the extent of the assimilation to Hindu popular devotional cults and magical practices which had occurred in Buddhism in its Mahāyāna form. With this growing emphasis on the use of magical mantras and rituals there went a corresponding decline in the importance of the Buddhist ethic; this too was a trend which the Mahāyāna obsession with metaphysics did little to check (3.21; 4.33–4.35). Another possible reason that has been seen for the Buddhist decline is that so long as the Buddhist religion had the patronage or support of Indian kings it prospered, and when it was deprived of this it languished. Thus, it is pointed out that the Pala kings of eastern India (6.10) tended to support Buddhism and kept it going in that region when it had disappeared elsewhere. It cannot be concluded from this, however, that Buddhism has *never* survived loss of royal patronage – indeed it is precisely the ability to maintain itself in the face of a government alien to it which characterised Buddhism in Ceylon during the period of British imperial rule (7.40). But in India in the eleventh and twelfth centuries Buddhism had not developed this capacity and the circumstances were against such a development. Most important of its disabilities was the concentration of the monastic life in certain great centres such as Nālanda, together with the decline of the local 'parish' monastery devoted to 'study for faith' (5.25). This had the result that over large areas there was no local centre of Buddhist life to act as a focus, to stimulate Buddhist piety, and to maintain a community of lay adherents. It was this development which made Buddhism so vulnerable to the Muslim Turkish attack, concentrated as it had become in large wealthy centres whose riches provided an irresistible temptation to plunderers. One final point which has to be mentioned is that once the situation had become so difficult because of the Muslim invasions, those Buddhist monks who were left and who maintained their serious resolve to pursue the Buddhist way had only one course open to them – to leave India and settle in some other region where the practice of Buddhist monasticism was still possible. Since there was nothing in the nature of their faith to attach them to one area of the world rather than another it was in the natural course of things that they made their way north and east, beyond the borders of India, to Nepal and Tibet, to China and to Burma. A few remained in those border areas of India such as the parts of East Bengal and Assam where the monastic life had survived; in some of these places a small Buddhist population has persisted, and in the modern period (*7.41*) has begun to grow again.

6.42 The growing influence of Theravāda Buddhism in South-East Asia

While Buddhism had thus virtually disappeared from India by the beginning of the thirteenth century c.e. it persisted elsewhere, and in fact increased in the extent of its influence upon the culture and societies of Tibet and those parts of South-East Asia which are now known as Burma, Thailand, and Cambodia. In these countries the period from about 1000 c.e. onwards was, so far as Buddhism was concerned, one of consolidation. The traditions of Buddhist moral discipline, doctrine and meditation were preserved and transmitted from generation to generation, and continued to influence the culture and social structure of these regions. The history of the growing influence of Theravāda Buddhism upon the countries of South-East Asia during this period is particularly instructive as an example of the way a Great Tradition enters into relationship with local Little Traditions (*3.31*). There are thus two important aspects of the history of Theravāda Buddhism during this period: one is the preservation and transmission of the central ideas of the Theravāda, in the form known as Abhidhamma; the other is the way in which the Theravāda entered into the cultural situations of these different countries in such a way as to produce local variants of the Theravādin Great Tradition, variants which are sufficiently distinct from each other and sufficiently dependent on the local cultures to be known severally as 'Burmese Buddhism', 'Thai Buddhism', 'Sinhalese Buddhism', and so on. First, however, we must note the fact that in all areas there was a single common Great Tradition of the monasteries, namely the Abhidhamma.

6.43 The continuance of the Abhidhamma tradition in Ceylon and Burma

One of the outstanding features of Buddhist monastic life in Ceylon and Burma throughout the medieval period (and indeed during the modern period also), is the study of the Abhidhamma (*3.22; 3.24; 4.39*). It is known from the accounts of Chinese pilgrims' travels in India (*5.25*) that at that time (fifth to seventh centuries C.E.) the Abhidhamma was regarded very highly in certain monasteries and certain areas. In central India the monks who specialised in the Abhidhamma even had stupas built to the glory of the Abhidhamma, and on fast days they performed special devotions at the stupas in its honour (Goonesekere, 1961; 54). In Ceylon the continuance of the Abhidhamma tradition is attested by the text-book for monks called the Abhidhammattha-Sangaha which came into use there from the twelfth century C.E. onwards. This is a digest or summary of the whole of the subject matter contained in the seven books of the Abhidhamma-pitaka (the third section of the Buddhist Pali canon) (*3.24*). The work is ascribed to an elder (*thera*) named Anuruddha, a senior monk in Ceylon, and it seems from its introduction to have superseded the only manual on the subject in existence until then, a similar summary called 'A descent into the Abhidhamma' (Abhidhammāvatāra), attributed to a contemporary of the great Buddhaghosa (*4.39*) named Buddhadatta. This new digest (it can scarcely be called literature) has continued for eight centuries to be the generally recognised introduction to the Abhidhamma, especially in Ceylon and Burma, and has produced a rich crop of commentaries and interpretations. It is briefer and much more concise than Buddhaghosa's Visuddhimagga (*4.39*), although of course the two works have the same purpose, that of teaching the way to enlightenment through the proper understanding of psychological processes, through the pursuit of a moral life, and through meditational practices. The Abhidhammattha-Sangaha (translated into English by the Burmese scholar Shwe Zan Aung as *Compendium of Philosophy*) is a tabulation or digest of the contents of the Abhidhamma-pitaka books. It is thus excessively condensed, and can only be studied under the supervision of a tutor, and this is how it has been used, and still is used, in the Theravāda Buddhist countries, where it is held in the highest possible esteem. The method which it follows is to list the four categories of dharmas, or ultimately real factors of existence: (1) consciousness, (2) mental properties, (3) material qualities, and (4) the one unconditioned and uncaused factor, nibbāna. After the exhaustive listing of all these classes of consciousness, and mental and material qualities, it is shown how they interact, their various possible combinations, how the good combinations are to be encouraged, and so on. This kind of analysis demands good memorising ability; hence the existence of this manual, with its frequent mnemonic summaries in doggerel verse – the nearest approach it makes to literature. What must not be forgotten is that this sort of study has been one of the principal preoccupations of Buddhist monks in Ceylon and Burma; this is not because they were so devoid of imagination that they could think of nothing better to do, but rather because it was an important discipline of the religious life. A modern Ceylonese writer puts it thus: 'what is essential for the seeker after ethical and spiritual perfection is to understand the nature and functions of psychological processes. In the view of the Abhidhamma, the study of ethics and psychology is not an academic pursuit but something that is essentially relevant to the progress and harmony of individual and social life' (Karunaratne, 1961; 48). It is only in the light of these considerations, and when the study of Abhidhamma is seen as an occupation of the monastery, that we are able to understand what was being pursued by these monks of Ceylon and Burma, namely the full integration of ethics, psychology and religion. Those monks who were specially proficient in such study were known as Abhidhammikas, and as such were highly honoured, especially in Burma, a country particularly renowned in Buddhist Asia for its Abhidhamma studies.

6.44 The religious role of the Buddhist kings of South-East Asia

As in India, so also in Ceylon and South-East Asia, an important factor in the maintenance of Buddhist religion was the adherence of the ruler to the Buddhist faith. The reason for this was that Buddhism in Asia has always in its periods of greatest vigour and prosperity shown itself to be a social ethic as well as a religious faith. More precisely, one should say that the Buddhist social ethic is a *desideratum* of healthy Buddhist religion. This is one of the points which earlier European observers failed to appreciate. Max Weber, from what he knew of Buddhist ideas, assumed that a social ethic could not possibly be derived from them. He failed to see that the maintenance of a well-ordered and stable society, in which there were no great extremes of economic and social privilege, and in which every member could count on social justice and a sufficient livelihood, was adumbrated in the teaching of the Buddha, and that it was the responsibility of any ruler who was a devout Buddhist to seek to ensure these things for his subjects (Sarkisyanz, 1965; 37ff., 43ff., 56ff.). The social ethic was not derived *from* the Buddhist way proclaimed by the Buddha; it was regarded by him as a highly desirable condition, if not a prerequisite for its proper pursuit. It is for this reason that in the history of Buddhist South-East Asia great importance attaches to the names of the more devout of its kings, especially those whose Buddhist devotion was undergirded by their establishment and maintenance of social harmony, good order and public welfare.

6.45 *The medieval Buddhist rulers of Ceylon*

In Ceylon, such a king was Parakkama Bahu (Bahu = the Great), who in the twelfth century restored independence and peace to the island after a long period of invasion by and subjection to the Chola kings of South India (*6.10*). He restored the ruined capital of Polonnaruwa, revived agriculture by the construction of extensive irrigation works, and thus alleviated famine. The account of his many undertakings for the reform of the Sangha, the rebuilding of monasteries, the establishment of almshouses and hospitals and provision for medical care of the sick, the restoration of temples and villages, and rest-houses for travellers, fill seven chapters of the Pali chronicles of Ceylon entitled Culavaṃsa (one hundred and twenty pages in English translation); the account concludes: 'Thus Parakkama Bahu, the Ruler of men, by whom were performed divers and numerous kinds of meritorious works, who continually found the highest satisfaction in the teaching of the Master [that is, the Buddha], who was endowed with extraordinary energy and discernment, carried on the government for thirty-three years' (*Culavamsa*; lxxix, 86). Other kings of Ceylon were remembered similarly, although none with greater respect from monks and laymen alike than Parakkama. Some, inevitably, were bad rulers; a few were wicked; but others were remembered for their devout lives, their scholarly achievements, and their support and maintenance of the Sangha. There were times during this period when the vitality of

Buddhist religion in Ceylon sank to a low ebb, but these were followed by times of recovery, and more than once Ceylon provided the resources for the infusion of new life into the Buddhism of South-East Asia.

Superficially the religious culture of Ceylon appears to be one in which the honours are shared between the Buddha and various local Sinhalese deities. Besides the respect which the villager pays to the Buddha at the Buddhist shrine, in the form of the offering of flowers and lights and incense, and in meditation, or the chanting of Pali verses, there is the same villager's worshipful approach to what he regards as the deities of Ceylon, from whom he expects certain well-defined temporal benefits; this kind of worship he will offer at a shrine close to or adjoining the Buddhist one. One interpretation of this which is sometimes suggested is that because as a Buddhist he has no omnipotent deity to worship he has to turn elsewhere in search of deity. But to take this view of the matter is to lose sight of the actual historical development of religious practices in Ceylon. From an initial complete adherence to the deities of Ceylon the Buddhist layman has moved at least as far as a recognition of the absolute superiority of the way of the Buddha. Buddhist values have gradually permeated the entire cultural system and now provide the moral framework and the ultimate religious goals; meanwhile, some temporal benefits are still sought by the use of non-Buddhist (and therefore in this context virtually secular) means, that is, in the approach to local deities. In a similar way many Christians who believe in God nevertheless also visit the doctor from time to time. The latter may or may not be a Christian; he may be an atheist or a Marxist, but Christians see nothing religiously incongruous in thus seeking a temporal benefit from a non-Christian source. Nor does the villager of Ceylon in following a similar procedure.

6.46 Buddhist values and the South-East Asian state

In Burma, a Buddhist king of the kind already described (*6.44*) was Anawratha (Pali, Anuruddha), who lived in the century before Parakkama of Ceylon (and was roughly contemporary with William the Conqueror, of England). Until that time a debased form of Mahāyāna existed in upper Burma (*5.27*), the practitioners of which were called 'Aris'. Anawratha was converted by a Theravādin monk from the Mon kingdom of Thaton (5.27), and thereupon set about the religious reformation of his kingdom, discouraging the Tantric practices of the Aris and establishing the Theravādin order, bringing copies of the Pali sacred scriptures from Thaton, which he now absorbed into the Burmese kingdom which he ruled from Pagan. The effect of his conversion upon Burma is likened by Burmese Buddhist chroniclers to that of Aśoka upon India. Anawratha and his successors in Pagan formed a dynasty (1044–1287) which for its activity in the building of great and impressive pagodas has been compared with the Gothic period in medieval Europe. The dynasty accepted the notion of kingship set out in the early Buddhist texts, according to which a king rules by contractual agreement between the ruler and the people (Sarkisyanz, 1965; 15). In one respect the king enjoyed an extremely exalted status as the central figure of the Indo-Burmese cosmology (4.29), but so far as the Sangha was concerned the king had the inferior status of a layman and, as Buddhist laymen, kings were required to accept the moral guidance of the monks, and frequently did. When a king was disposed to rule despotically and violently the monks of Burma would intervene to promote justice and save life. E. Sarkisyanz, who has made an intensive and authoritative study of medieval Buddhism in Burma, on the basis of extensive evidence considers that 'Burma's Buddhist monkhood went further in the protection of human life than did the historical Churches of Christendom who have hardly resisted and on the whole tacitly recognised the claims of temporal powers to inflict death' (Sarkisyanz, 1965; 76). The Roman Catholic missionary Sangermano, who was in Burma at the end of the eighteenth and beginning of the nineteenth century, comments on the curious behaviour of the monks in saving even 'the lives of criminals'.

The pattern of Buddhist development in Thailand and Cambodia was similar to that in Burma. The Theravādin form was introduced from Ceylon into Thailand in the fourteenth century, to replace a Mahāyāna form; as a result of Thai influence the same thing happened also in Cambodia, where a form of Tantric Buddhism had been known since the eleventh century.

In all these countries, throughout the period when the Theravāda was more and more thoroughly permeating the fabric of society, the monks were the public educators. Almost every village had its monastery, however small, and to it the village children went for their lessons, with the result that these countries are among the most highly literate in Asia. The village monasteries have been the agents of a two-way process of cultural interpenetration between Buddhism and local indigenous beliefs, similar to that which has been noted in connection with Ceylon (*6.45*), a process whose result has been not the corruption of Buddhist values but rather the civilising by the Buddhist presence of what was formerly barbaric (Ling, 1966; 57 f.).

6.47 *The decline of Buddhism in China*

Whereas the Theravādin countries of South-East Asia looked to Ceylon as the source of Buddhist learning and the homeland of their religion, Chinese Buddhists had always looked to India for inspiration, as the place of pilgrimage and the source of Buddhist scripture and commentary. The consequence was that with the virtual disappearance of Buddhism from India Chinese Buddhism was deprived of what had been an important factor in the continuance of a live tradition, and from the thirteenth century onwards began to show signs of decline and decay.

Other factors were involved in this process. The political condition of the Chinese empire had become more stable with the establishment of the Sung dynasty (960–1279 C.E.), and throughout this period Buddhism enjoyed a certain modest prestige, even among the upper classes (*5.20*). The favoured condition of Buddhism under this dynasty had, however, something in the nature of a sunset glow about it: K. K. S. Ch'en characterises this period of Chinese Buddhism as one of 'Memories of a Great Tradition' (Ch'en, 1964; 389 ff.), and it was the prelude to periods of more serious recession and decline. The very recognition which Buddhism had gained for itself in official quarters had to some extent prepared the way for its decline. This is illustrated by the practice which was adopted during the Sung dynasty of selling ordination certificates for monks. Previously these had been gained by the candidate's passing an examination on the Buddhist scriptures. This was now replaced by the payment of a sum of money to the government for the privilege of holding an ordination certificate. The certificates had an economic value, since they exempted the possessor from tax and from a spell of national labour service. Increasingly ordination came to be regarded as something economically advantageous; the fact that a man could now become a Buddhist monk without knowing anything of the Buddhist faith or practice had the result of allowing easy entry into the Order of any number of criminals and vagabonds (Ch'en, 1964; 391 f.).

There was an important difference in the relationship of Buddhism and the state in China during this period compared with that which existed in the South-East Asian countries. In the latter, as we have seen, the ruler was usually himself a Buddhist and as often as not a devoutly practising one; as a layman, moreover, he was required to and usually did acknowledge the superior status of the monks. In China on the other hand what was developing throughout this period was what C. K. Yang has described as the stabilisation of government control over religion (Yang, 1961; 106). There was, moreover, during this period a general reassertion of the superiority of what was Chinese over what was foreign. This tendency is seen in relation to Buddhism in China in two ways: (1) all the religions became increasingly eclectic as Confucian ideas came again into prominence and the classical belief in the emperor as the Son of Heaven dominated religio-political life; (2) within Buddhist circles there was a tendency towards those forms of the religion which were more Chinese than Indian in origin, namely Ch'an (5.23) and Amidism (5.22). Even the latter was no longer the popular mass movement it had once been, but was beginning to decline in importance. A curious feature of Amidism during this period was the transformation of the coming Buddha, Maitreya, into the figure of the Laughing Buddha, or Hemp-bag Bonze (monk). This was a legendary figure who was said to have been the Maitreya Buddha and who had appeared wandering about China as the laughing, pot-bellied fool Mi-lo, surrounded by hordes of children, and who thus symbolised the values upheld by Chinese society: his hemp-bag full of miscellaneous objects symbolising wealth, his fat stomach the sign of contentment, and the crowd of children surrounding him the high value placed on a large family (Ch'en, 1964; 405–8). This provides an illustration of the way Buddhism was now becoming more and more assimilated to Taoism and Confucianism just as in India in its later years it had been to Hinduism.

The Sangha in so far as it retained its original nature and purpose became increasingly marginal, a refuge for those who had become social or economic casualties; it served also to preserve and transmit some Buddhist tradition, albeit feebly. Its one remaining positive function during this period was from time to time to foster rebellions and harbour secret organisations (Yang, 1961; 126). Ch'an (Zen) alone really flourished in China during the Sung period. That is to say the practice of it became more widespread, but it also became more mechanical, with less emphasis upon the meditation necessary to prepare the mind for enlightenment, and more upon the use of riddles, known as kōans, and the use by the master of such techniques as shouting and beating the disciple with a stick. It was during this period of its history in China that Ch'an was successfully introduced into Japan by Japanese monks who had been visiting China for study (*6.48*). Ch'an had great prestige in China at that time, but 'inner impoverishment accompanied outer splendour' (Dumoulin, 1963; 124).

6.48 Buddhism in Japan, 1200–1868

The six centuries with which we are here concerned, the thirteenth to the nineteenth, were in Japanese history a period first of great upheaval, feudal strife, and social disintegration, which reached a climax in the fifteenth century; and then a period of peace and order during the Tokugawa regime from 1600 to 1868. The major religious developments occurred during the first period; under the Tokugawa regime Buddhist religious life was severely controlled by the state and tended to become over-refined and degenerate.

In the earlier more stormy period Buddhism developed the three major forms in which it is found in modern Japan. These may be characterised as intuitionist (Zen), pietist (Pure Land), and revivalist (Nichiren). The practices of Ch'an (*5.23*) were introduced from China by Eisai (1141–1215 C.E.) in 1191 on his return from a period of study; he is regarded as the founder of Zen Buddhism in Japan, although there had been some attempts to introduce it before that time. But this was a period of much warfare, and among the Shoguns the Rinzai form of Zen introduced by Eisai had considerable success. One of these, Tokimune (1251–84) successfully defended his country against the attack of the Mongols in the strength of mind and calmness that the practice of Zen is said to have enabled him to cultivate (Dumoulin, 1963; 142f.). Zen has continued to have a great appeal for the military class in Japan. Another form of Zen was introduced by Dogen (1200–1253), on his return from China in 1228. Unlike Eisai he deliberately avoided contacts with Japanese of the ruling and military class, and it is traditionally to farmers rather than soldiers that the Soto type of Zen which he founded makes its appeal. Dogen disliked also any sectarian emphasis within Buddhism; he regarded Zen simply as the essence of Buddhism – 'the great way of the Buddha and the patriarchs' – and was critical of some of the deviant features of Ch'an as it had developed in China in the Sung period; but in spite of this Soto Zen has, ironically, become strongly sectarian in Japan.

Meanwhile it was the pietism of the Pure Land School that made the greatest appeal to the peasants and lower classes of Japanese society during this period of internal strife and uncertainty. We saw earlier (5.28) that faith in Amida, the bodhisattva Lord of the Pure Land, or Western Paradise, had been gaining ground from the tenth century c.e. Now, after 1200, it began to have the appeal of a messianic religion, the one hope for men in disturbed and dark days: 'The fateful days have arrived; we, the weak and vicious people of the latter days could not be saved but by invoking the name of the Lord Amita', said Genshin (Anesaki, 1963; 170). This was a simple way of salvation that differed very considerably from the severe disciplines of Zen. It was a simple gospel, the assurance of salvation by calling upon the name of Amida in faith; and in the view of its many preachers and adherents this was the only way of salvation from the troubles of the present life: man could achieve nothing by his own efforts, and only Amida could save. The German theologian Karl Barth in his *Church Dogmatics* has noted the striking resemblance between this development in Japanese religion and evangelical piety of the Christian kind. Both Amidism and Zen are more correctly described as Japanese religions; they can hardly be called Buddhist except in so far as historically their roots were in a Buddhist tradition. Amidism is about as much an authentic form of Buddhism as the sect of Jehovah's Witnesses is an authentic form of Christianity. Amidism's great exponent was Honen (1133–1212), a man whose spirit was disgusted with the warlike temper of his times and who saw no hope for men but in turning with simple love to the saviour and trusting in his free gift of salvation in the Western Paradise. This gave him great peace of mind; his own personal serenity attracted many to his teaching and to faith in Amida (Anesaki, 1963; 175). His gospel was taken up by disciples and was preached over a wide area of Japan, with great success. Differences of opinion on matters of doctrine appeared before long, however, and an independent form known as *Shinshu* (the True Doctrine) emerged in opposition to *Jodo* (Pure Land) as Honen's

gospel of pietism was called. Shinshu was founded by Shinran (1173–
1263), a disciple of Honen who emphasised even more strongly the
necessity for utter reliance on the grace of the Lord, to the extent of
rejecting celibacy as a sign of trust in one's own powers and lack of trust
in the Lord's grace, and thus gave doctrinal justification to married life
for priests, which was in practice not altogether unknown. Shinran
himself married and his descendants continued as teachers of the Jodo
Shinshu, down to modern times.

Both Zen intuitionism and Jodo pietism were attacked by the founder
of another Japanese religious tradition, Nichiren (1222–83). Owing to
the imminent threat of Mongol invasion patriotism was very strong in
Japan at that time. Nichiren, who was a combination of prophet,
scholar and reformer, also lived a very adventurous life in the course of
propounding his new doctrine of patriotism. He declared that the
contemporary religions of Japan were leading the nation to the verge of
disaster. He rejected both the ritualism of the old priestly religion and
the sentimentalism of the Pure Land pietists. His was a gospel of struggle
and aggression – the struggle of the 'pure' community of Japan against
all foes. Violent and aggressive methods continued to characterise the
Nichiren sect long after his death. All other denominations were 'hell
... devils ... ruin ... traitors'. The Nichiren sect drew its followers
from the warriors, the more independent of the peasants, and the
tougher kinds of women, for all of whom Nichiren's combative and
exclusive patriotism had a powerful appeal. A modern Mahāyāna
scholar, Edward Conze, comments sadly that all this is very un-
Buddhistic. One scripture alone was venerated by Nichiren, the Lotus
of the Good Law Sūtra, and the slogan of the sect is 'Homage to the
Lotus of the Good Law!' The sect continued to grow, especially during
the period of violence and war which Japan suffered in the latter half of
the fifteenth century and most of the sixteenth, up to the establishment
of the Tokugawa regime, although they were subjected to great
persecution and even torture at the hand of the Pure Land Buddhists.
As in religious wars elsewhere (*6.50*) 'many died on either side, each
believing that the fight was for the glory of Buddha and that death
secured his birth in paradise' (Anesaki, 1963; 230). The most famous of
the modern sects of Japan is the Nichirenite Soka Gakkai (*7.48*).

6.49 Buddhist Tibet, 1000–1800

It was not until the time of Atiśa, in the eleventh century C.E., that Buddhism could claim to be fully established in Tibet (5.27). The form of Buddhism which Tibet then adopted was, as we have seen, the Tantric variety practised in the Pala kingdom and eastern India at that time; based on the Yogācāra (4.35) type of teaching favoured by Atiśa. After Atiśa's time a number of schools of Tibetan Buddhism developed; only two of these need concern us. The tradition which derives from the work of Padma-Sambhava (5.27) is called the Old School, and its followers were known as the 'red-hats'. The school of Atiśa, known as the 'yellow-hats', discouraged the magical practices which were a feature of the old school, and incorporated teachings of the Hīnayāna into their doctrine. It is this school, the Gelugpa (virtuous ones), which dominated Tibet down to modern times, having the Dalai Lama as its spiritual head.

Tibetan Buddhism provides another illustration of the principle which underlay the relationship between religion and secular power in South-East Asian Buddhist countries (6.44). Even in those countries the king's activity in creating within his realm the proper conditions for the pursuit of the Buddhist by his subjects was based on the idea of the king as a bodhisattva (3.29), one who desired the welfare of all beings and bent all his efforts to this end. In Tibet, however, this conception was developed further. The ruler of the country *must* be a bodhisattva; it was therefore necessary to discover in which individual Tibetan the bodhisattva had been re-born, and when he had been discovered, prepare him to be the ruler and eventually install him as such. This is the theory which underlay the search for a new Dalai Lama, or spiritual-temporal head of the Tibetan state, which took place whenever the previous ruler's life came to an end. Succession to the rulership was not hereditary; a Dalai Lama did not rule because his father had ruled, but because he was considered by the spiritual leaders of the country to possess the necessary qualifications – the marks of bodhisattvahood. There was a recognised procedure for establishing the presence or otherwise of these qualities when a new Dalai Lama was being sought, a procedure which was carried out with great care.

The culture of Tibet through the centuries since Atiśa has been in essence Buddhist, although it has incorporated elements of the indigenous pre-Buddhist culture also, just as happened in the South-East Asian countries (6.46). Thus, in its origins and in its characteristic structure Tibetan Buddhism is derived, like the Buddhism of South-East Asia, from the Indian model seen at its clearest in Aśoka (3.26). It has made of the mountain tribes of the Himalayan plateau whose ancestors were exceedingly warlike a people whom European travellers agree in describing as kindly, cheerful and contented (Richardson, 1962; 27). The monk-rulers of Tibet have through the centuries, writes André Migot, 'used their power wisely and humanely'. In his view the social harmony and peace which have characterised the life of the Tibetan people deserve the recognition that Buddhist Tibet was 'one of the best governed countries in the world' (Migot, 1955; 104). The attempt in modern times of a powerful neighbour, China, to destroy such a culture and such a society raises important questions about the values entertained and upheld by the massive states of the modern world, and is itself a powerful indictment of modern secularism.

6.5 RELIGIOUS CONTRASTS AND CONFLICTS
(1500–1800 C.E.)

6.50 Conflict within Christendom in the sixteenth century

The medieval pattern of Christendom was, as we have seen, exclusive and authoritarian. The Church was the ark outside which there was no salvation. Truth was what the Church taught, on the basis of its traditions and its holy scriptures. Man was entirely sinful and could be saved only by the grace of an omnipotent deity. Such grace was mediated to men through the sacraments of the Church, seven in number: baptism, confirmation, the Mass, penance, ordination to the priesthood, matrimony, and unction or anointing. The mediation of grace through the sacramental system was by the agency of the duly and properly ordained priest who owed obedience to his bishop and to the head of the hierarchy, the Pope. At the Council of Florence in 1439 it was declared that 'the Roman Pontiff holds the primacy in the whole world . . . is the true Vicar of Christ and head of the Church, father and teacher of all Christians, and . . . to him in the blessed Peter has been given by our Lord Jesus Christ the full power of shepherding, ruling and governing the whole Church' (Bullough, 1963; 195 f.). The making of this declaration reflected the fact that there were some who disagreed with such a view. For some centuries before Martin Luther (1483–1546) made his famous protest there had been, as we have seen, signs of dissatisfaction with this monopolistic orthodoxy (*6.25*; *6.26*). Secular rulers had already for some time been rejecting Papal ecclesiastical influence in the affairs of government. Such rejection of the authority of Rome increased during the sixteenth century in various parts of Europe, and constituted one of the main features of the disintegration of the Roman authoritarian system. An accompanying feature was the establishment of national churches, independent of Rome, such as the Church of England. Alongside this kind of rejection of Papal claims went another. This was the expression of protest against the system of salvation by sacramental grace as it was by then being practised. The tendency during the fourteenth and fifteenth centuries, represented by such philosophers as William of Ockham (*6.28*), to drive a wedge between faith and reason had the effect of leaving the religious practice of the Roman Church open to invasion by superstition; this in turn led only too easily to commercial exploitation of the priestly craft and the development of such practices as the sale of indulgences which brought the whole sacramental system into disrepute. Men of sincerity and religious integrity now found it impossible to regard such a racketeering enterprise as the one and only channel of divine grace. Such was the basis of Luther's protest, and it soon found a response in many other places. Those who sought to reform religious practice, however, saw no reason to depart from the Augustinian doctrine of the salvation of man by God's grace alone. It was because they seriously affirmed this doctrine that they were concerned at its prostitution by the Roman Church. It has been pointed out that what is called the Reformation can be considered as 'the ultimate triumph of Augustine's doctrine of grace over Augustine's doctrine of the Church' (Warfield, 1909; 224). On its theological side the Protestant revival of the sixteenth century was a revival of the Augustinian emphasis that man, who is entirely sinful, depends wholly on the free grace of an omnipotent and inscrutable God. Calvin, in his *Institutes*, quotes copiously from Augustine. But Protestants such as Luther and Calvin insisted that the grace of God was appropriated by man not primarily through the institutional Church, but by the individual's own response of faith. This placing of the prime responsibility upon the individual was criticised by Keble in the nineteenth century as a doctrine of 'Everyman his own absolver'. The Roman Church, on the other hand, re-emphasised Augustine's doctrine of the Church as the City of God, outside of which there was no salvation, and following Augustine's precedent used every means available, including physical force, to put down heretical attacks upon the Church of Rome's nature as *the* divine institution. Forced by ecclesiastical authority to justify their views, Protestants appealed to the canon of scripture, since this was an authority accepted by both sides. Protestantism thus became character-ised by the appeal to *scripture alone*, over against the Roman Church which appealed both to scripture and the tradition of the fathers. Both sides thus accepted the principle of an external objective authority which could be invoked as the last word on any subject relating to religion. To any question relating to religion the ultimate answer which a Protestant will give is that 'this is what the Bible says'; similarly the ultimate answer of a Roman Catholic has tended to be that 'this is what the Pope says'. However, it was on the authority of the Church that the authority of *this particular collection* of writings called the Bible rested, a point recognised by Augustine when he said, 'I should not believe the gospel did not the authority of the Catholic Church move me thereto.' The Protestants were therefore compelled eventually to seek some other authority than that of the Church for accepting the authority of the Bible, and this they found in the 'internal testimony of the Holy Spirit', convincing them of the divine inspiration of these writings. This is an argument which is not without its difficulties when other large communities in the world are equally convinced that another set of writings, the Qur'an for example, is the final, and truly divinely inspired book. However, the assurance with which an infallible book provided Protestants concerning the rightness of their position, and the assurance with which an infallible Church *and* an in-fallible book provided Catholics concerning the rightness of theirs, led to many bloody battles and burning of men as heretics. One of the last of these was Servetus, burned in Calvinist Geneva for suggesting in his scholarly works that the doctrine of the Trinity, three Persons in one God, was a corruption of authentic Christianity. This serves as a reminder that in addition to the two great parties in the religious conflicts of Reformation Europe there were others, both individuals and minority groups such as the Anabaptists, and in the seventeenth century the Quakers, who belonged to neither camp, but whose emergence was a feature of the final falling apart of the Augustinian system of authoritarian orthodoxy.

6.51 The Catholic Counter-Reformation

One thing which the protest of men like Luther and Calvin made clear to the Roman ecclesiastical hierarchy, even though Rome did not accept what it regarded as the heresies they had propounded, was that the Catholic Church was in need of reform. A general council of the Church was called, to seek remedies for its troubles, the Council of Trent, which met at intervals from 1545 onwards. Among the matters it dealt with were abuses in the Church, and the orthodox doctrines of the Church. Another event of some importance in Catholicism's recovery was the founding in 1540 of the Society of Jesus. Its founder, a Spanish nobleman known by the Latin name Ignatius de Loyola (1491–1556), was a soldier. Convalescing from wounds received in battle he turned to religious matters. The society, originally of ten members meeting in the University of Paris, was organised on military lines, and was dedicated to a warfare against the powers of evil in the name of Christ, the great captain of the powers of good. The discipline of the Society was laid down in the *Spiritual Exercises* of Ignatius, a system of will-training, study, prayer and meditation, centring especially on the example of Christ. The Society met a great need of the time within Catholicism and eventually became a powerful force in the educational and intellectual spheres. One of its most famous early members was Francis Xavier, who in 1542 was sent by Ignatius de Loyola to Asia. The Portuguese had begun to establish settlements on the west coast of India, and beginning from Goa Xavier carried out his missionary activities down the west coast, and then beyond India to Malacca and Indo-China and eventually to Japan, establishing the Society both in India and Japan; in the latter country the work of its missionaries was brought to an end by the Tokugawa regime (*6.48*; *6.59*). Other Jesuits who followed Francis Xavier in seeking to establish Christianity in Asia include Matteo Ricci, who in the sixteenth century had considerable initial success in propagating Christian ideas in terms of Confucian thought and practice, and Roberto de Nobili, who in the seventeenth century went to India and adopted the life of a brāhman (Cronin, 1955; 1959).

By the eighteenth century, however, a new anti-ecclesiastical spirit was making itself felt in Europe; the Jesuits were the target for special attack, and in 1773 the Pope was forced to suppress the Society.

6.52 *The sectarian religion of the disinherited*

The Protestant movement led by Luther, Calvin and Zwingli left the lowest classes of society largely untouched. Both Lutheranism and Calvinism quickly showed themselves to be primarily middle-class religions. The religious movements of protest which were able to appeal to what are described as the 'disinherited classes' of their time (that is, peasants, labourers, lower-paid craftsmen, and casual workers in the towns), were the Anabaptists in the sixteenth century and the Quakers in the seventeenth. But the movement of the disinherited of one century became the middle-class church of the next; the Quakers provide an example of that upward social mobility which was the inevitable consequence of hard work, thrift and a sober life. By the eighteenth century the Protestant churches, Presbyterian, Independent and Quaker, consisted very largely of men of trade and business, not a few of whom were moderately prosperous. Respectability, sobriety, caution, and good sense were the Protestant virtues; whereas passion, extravagance or excess of any kind, and above all enthusiasm, were to be avoided at all costs. England had increased in prosperity, but this increase was not shared by all. 'The wage system and uncertainty of employment, rising capitalism and the competitive order, the growth of the cities and the increase of poverty widened the cleft between the classes' (Niebuhr, 1929; 59). A large section of society existed for whom the churches of the time had no appeal; they had nothing to offer that would meet an emotional need for a religion of salvation. It was this need which early Methodism met. Although John Wesley (1703–91) was an ordained clergyman of the Church of England his work was done mainly outside the normal life of the English Church. Nevertheless, as Niebuhr has pointed out, while the Methodist revival was a movement among the disinherited, it was not a popular movement in the sense of having its origins within this class. Its leaders were middle-class, and this fact helped to ensure that Methodism became socially respectable even more quickly than had earlier movements. It was a revolution so far as the *religious* life and ethos of eighteenth-century England were concerned: instead of the cold, rationalistic tone which dominated most English religion in the eighteenth century it offered men a warm, emotional religion of salvation, a salvation which was freely available to all. What gave Wesleyan Methodism its subsequent quick rise to social respectability was perhaps more than anything the view which Wesley had of the evil from which men needed to be saved. In this connection Niebuhr's words are of importance for the student of religion: 'The primary question to be asked for the understanding of a Fox, a Paul, a Luther, a Wesley, as well as of Old Testament prophets and of the founders of non-Christian religions, such as Buddha, Zoroaster, Mohammed, is this: what did they mean by sin or evil? from what did they want to save men? Now it is evident in Wesley's case that he envisaged sin as individual vice and laxity, not as greed, oppression or social maladjust-ment. Sin meant sensuality rather than selfishness to him and from Wesley the entire Methodist movement took its ethical character' (Niebuhr, 1929; 67) (see also 7.12). Nevertheless, it was the reality of *salvation* which was emphasised by John and Charles Wesley, both in their preaching and in the vast number of hymns which they composed for the use of Methodists. It was both the reality of the salvation accomplished for men by Christ as an *objective* fact which was empha-sised, and also (and this is an important characteristic of Methodism) the possibility of receiving *subjective* or personal assurance of this, especially through the emotions. Men were not invited to participate in a religion of sheer emotion as such (which Wesley called 'wanting the end without the means'); emotional assurance was second in order of importance to the establishing of the external, objective fact of salvation, and the convincing of men of this primary fact (Kent, 1959; 123 f.). It was in this respect especially that Methodism helped to revitalise the older, Calvinistic bodies.

6.53 The nature of the sixteenth-century Hindu revival in South India

As in Europe so also in India, the sixteenth century was a period which saw the rise of movements of religious revival and reform. These were mainly movements within Hindu society, rather than Islamic, but they cannot properly be said to constitute a self-generated revival of Hinduism; rather they should be seen as the result of the impact upon

Hindus of Islamic religion and culture. The important names are those of Kabīr, born in Banaras in 1440, Nānak, a man of the Punjab, born in 1469, and Chaitanya, of Bengal, born in 1485. (The work of Chaitanya bears interesting comparison with that of Wesley.) In the case of Kabīr the connection with Islam is indicated by the confusion about whether he was in fact a Muslim or a Hindu. It will be noticed that all of these, (to whom further reference will be made – 6.54) were men of north India, that is to say of the region under the political rule and cultural influence of the Muslim sultanate of Delhi (6.38). It is sometimes asserted that it was the south of India which was the scene of a consciously Hindu revival, during the period of the Vijayanagar kingdom (1336–1565). The assertion is that the kings of Vijayanagar consciously saw themselves in the role of defenders of Hinduism against the encroachment of Islam. In fact their policy seems to have been one of religious tolerance, even though they themselves were either Shaivites or Vaishnavites. One of the Shaiva rulers, Krishnadeva Rāya (1509–30) was noted for his liberal attitude: 'The king allows such freedom that every man may come and go, and live according to his own creed without suffering any annoyance and without injury, whether he is a Christian, Jew, Moor (i.e. Muslim) or Heathen (i.e. Hindu)', recorded Duarte Barbosa (Sastri, 1963; 127). Krishnadeva's son-in-law, Rāma Rāya, even refused to follow the suggestion of Hindu advisers that Muslims should be forbidden to slaughter cows in their own precincts. Barbosa's words, quoted above, are a reminder that the south contained some of the oldest Christian and Muslim communities in India: the Syrian Christians claiming a tradition going back to the apostle Thomas (3.39), and the Arab Muslims who had been in Malabar since the earliest days of Islam (5.18). The relations between them and the Hindu rulers were generally those of tolerance and respect. The kings of Vijayanagar were more concerned with preserving unity and peace among their subjects in order the more easily to defend their northern frontier against the aggressive Muslim kings of the Deccan. If Shaivism and Vaishnavism seem to have received special patronage from the kings of Vijayanagar this was most probably because they, more than other Hindu monarchs, had the funds at their disposal to endow shrines and temples (Stein, 1960), and to commission and support a syndicate of scholars to compose a full-scale commentary on the entire Vedic literature (4.21). Certainly during this period there was a great expansion of temple-building and restoration. Worship became more elaborate, and increasing numbers of people of all kinds entered the employment of the temples – musicians, dancers, florists, goldsmiths, and jewellers, as well as priests. But endowments were made to Muslim shrines also (Sastri, 1963; 127), and the whole of this upsurge of religious activity in the Vijayanagar kingdom is probably best seen as an aspect of the revitalisation of Hindu theistic cults under the stimulus of Islam, especially through such sects as the Lingayata *(6.18)*. It was not an exclusive or intolerant Hinduism; the sixteenth century saw also the arrival of the Portuguese, and with them their Catholic priests, who were encouraged by the South Indian rulers to take part in public debates with Hindu religious leaders. It was to Madura, in South India, that Roberto de Nobili *(6.51)* came in the seventeenth century, to live among brāhmans as a Christian missionary 'brāhman'.

6.54 *The proliferation of devotional cults in North India*

The sixteenth century was a period in north Indian history which saw the rise of a multitude of sects which combined devotional fervour with social protest. These sects generally consisted of the followers of some religious reformer and mystic who was frequently also a poet. There is not the space to mention more than a few of these by name. The best known are perhaps Kabīr (1440–1518), Namdev (b. 1470), Vallabhā (dates uncertain), Nānak (1469–1538), Chaitanya (1485–1533), Tulasī Dāsa (1532–1620), Rai Dāsa (dates uncertain) and Dādu (1544–1603). Most of these were sudras, men of the urban artisan class; Kābir was a weaver of Banaras, Namdev was of a family of cloth-dealers and tailors in Ahmadabad, Dādu was a Muslim cotton-carder, and Rai Dāsa a leatherworker (a very low-class occupation in Hindu society). With these may be included also Tukā Rāma (1598–1649), a trader born in a small town near Poona, whose devotional songs in Marāthī (a language of western India) exist in two collections printed in Bombay, one containing over four thousand and the other over eight thousand songs. These songs, like those of Dādu and Namdev, are characterised by great devotional fervour, single-minded piety, and a desire to serve one's fellow men.

Extreme displays of emotion were a characteristic of Chaitanya's sect in Bengal. The occasion for this was the kīrtana, or song-session. The fervour displayed is said to have been so intense, and the singing of such vigour that the participants would sometimes swoon and fall to the ground; such phenomena link Chaitanya's sect on the one hand with the ancient Hebrew guilds of ecstatic prophets and on the other with modern Pentecostal sects within the Christian tradition. The deity to whom the devotion is expressed is usually either Rāma or Krishna, but these are understood as names for the one divine being. 'He is one, but fills and encompasses many; wherever you look, you find him there' (Namdev). 'O God, whether Allah or Rāma, I live by thy name' (Kabīr). 'There is but one God, whose name is true . . . God the great and bountiful' (Nānak). 'O Rāma! Thou dwellest in the hearts of those who have no lust, anger, infatuation, pride, delusion . . . who are dear to all, benevolent to all . . . who have no other resort but Thyself; in their minds O Rāma, dost Thou dwell' (Tulasī Dāsa). Kabīr was a disciple of the fifteenth-century teacher and mystic Rāmānda, and he and these other sixteenth-century religious leaders used the vernacular languages of their regions, Hindi and Marāthī especially, instead of Sanskrit, the language of the brāhmans and of orthodoxy. Tulasī Dāsa is remembered for his Hindi translation of the Rāmāyana (*4.24*). This use of the vernacular is in keeping with the popular character of these devotional sects, and so also is the opposition which they all show to ceremonial and ritual practices, and especially the use of idols. It is hard to avoid seeing the influence of Islam, and especially that of the Sufis, at work here; Muslim rule had now for several centuries been established in the north and west of India (*6.38*). Many of the sects founded in this way in the sixteenth century have continued in existence to the present day.

6.55 The Sikhs

Of special importance among these sects founded in the sixteenth century is the community of the Sikhs, which developed from the sect of Nānak's disciples. Both Kabīr's and Nānak's lives provide abundant evidence of the interpenetration of the Hindu and Muslim communities in the Punjab (de Bary, 1958; 360ff. 531ff.). The Sikhs, however, while combining elements from both Hinduism and Islam, have become a separate community, cut off from both of these other traditions, and have now their own sacred book, form of worship and succession of prophets, gurus, or leaders; these are regarded as ten in number, the last of whom, Guru Gobind Singh, born in 1666, transformed the Sikhs into a quasi-military sect. This was a result of the opposition of the Mughal rulers to the emergence of the Sikhs as an organised community. Sikhism is a brotherhood in which there is no caste distinction, and whose members, distinguished from both Hindus and Muslims by the uncut beard and hair, have held that to die fighting in the Sikh cause is to gain Paradise. Predominant in the Punjab, they form a community of some seven millions, found now in many parts of India and elsewhere. They take pride in the fact that 'one of the central points of the Sikh faith is the ideal of service to be given freely and disinterestedly to one's fellow men, no matter to what religion, race, political group, sex or sect they may belong', as one of their own publications expresses it (*Sikh Courier*, London, Spring 1967), although it is admitted that this is an ideal not easily realised.

6.56 The interaction of Hinduism and Islam in India

Much of this bhakti sectarian fervour which has just been described can no doubt be attributed to the influence of Islam upon north Indian Hinduism, especially through the agency of the Sufis. The general effect of Islam in India at this time was to make Hindus sensitive to any suggestion of idolatry, and even to lead the more educated among them to reject the idea of any human representation or incarnation of the divine – even the avatara (*3.37*). There was thus a tendency to affirm the doctrine of an impersonal absolute, the philosophical monism whose Indian name is Advaita Vedānta (*4.21*). There was also, however, a Hindu impact upon Islam. Converts to Islam from among the Hindu peasantry and urban lower classes and intermarriage of Muslim men and Hindu women were not uncommon during the period of Muslim rule. These, on becoming Muslim, did not always leave behind their old ways of life. This applied not only to matters of belief, but even more strongly to social practices and social structure. It is this which explains something approaching distinctions of caste among Indian Muslims. However, it never became a rigid caste system, and there was always a measure of openness and the possibility of social mobility, given a few good harvests or a run of success in business. Another important effect of Hinduism upon the Muslims was the gradual softening of the originally intolerant spirit of the Turkish conquerors, especially in the matter of the encounter of religions. It is this which enables us to see the controversial figure, Akbar, in proper perspective, and to this we now turn.

6.57 The heterodoxy of Akbar (1543–1605), and the orthodox Muslim reaction

Modern Indian history may conveniently be regarded as beginning with the establishment of Mughal rule in 1526. Like the sultanate of Delhi which preceded it, the Mughal empire (1526–1858) was Muslim. The most immediate major difference was that there was a new dynastic line, founded by Babur, the Turkish ruler of a kingdom to the north-west of India, who had attacked and overthrown the sultanate, even though the sultan was his co-religionist. One of the most basic factors in human affairs is the desire for the control of territory, a desire which may very easily, in this as in many other cases, prove stronger than a shared ideology.

The third Mughal emperor was the grandson of Babur, the famous Akbar (1556–1605). At his accession in 1556 he was thirteen years of age. He seems to have been a deeply religious Muslim, so far as the practice of his faith was concerned: he was meticulous about the five daily prayers, and sometimes swept out the palace mosque, an act of great piety. He was engaged regularly in devotions at the tombs of great Muslim saints. Yet he was to be charged later by Abdulla Khan Uzbek, ruler of Transoxania, with being a renegade from Islam. His contemporary Badauni, accused by Akbar of narrow-mindedness, declared he was an apostate. Jesuit priests found him religiously interesting, but perplexing; often they thought he was about to become a Catholic, but were always disappointed. European historians (Vincent Smith, for example) have been inclined to support the apostasy charge. Hindu historians have regarded him as a liberal, open-minded Muslim. Probably they are nearest the truth.

The grounds for these charges were the religious innovations which Akbar appears to have introduced in his attempt to be a worthy spiritual leader of his people. In this connection he issued a decree in 1579 sometimes referred to as the 'Infallibility' decree. This was aimed at giving more religious authority to Akbar and less to some of the orthodox theologians. In fact it did not claim any infallibility for Akbar but appealed to the established Islamic principle that when there is uncertainty about how to apply the words of the Qur'an and the Hadith to a given situation, a 'just sultan' has the right to accept any one of the interpretations offered him by the theologians. The crucial question is whether he deliberately planned to establish a new religion other than Islam, a religion of his own concocting. His projected Din-i-Ilahi or 'Divine Faith', about which the evidence is very uncertain, may have been an attempt to provide religion with a new look, but neither Akbar nor the few members of the new Order appear to have taken it very seriously. It is fairly clear, however, that on the whole he acted in ways which frequently offended the more orthodox Muslim theologians. Three mitigating circumstances can be mentioned in this connection.

1. It was not, as has been suggested, that religious laxity had become general among the Muslims of India by this time; rather, there was a genuine desire for better Hindu-Muslim relations, evidence of which is seen in the rise of the sects (6.54).

2. Akbar, because of the unsettled conditions of the time when he was a youth, had received no formal education and had an ill-disciplined mind.

3. He had married a Hindu princess who, together with her relatives living in the palace, continued to practise the Hindu religion, and would *appear* to pious Muslims to be an undesirable alien influence, whether in fact she was or not.

On balance it seems that there is sufficient evidence of Akbar's loyalty to Islam to the last, but it was an open-minded loyalty, and it was thrown under suspicion by his indiscretion and lack of good judgment. He certainly succeeded in giving great offence to an influential and determined section of the Muslim population, and after his death this resulted in a reaction which destroyed much of the good Akbar had done in the improvement of Hindu-Muslim-Christian relations in India.

Revived orthodoxy showed itself in the religious policies of the succeeding Mughal emperors: Jahangir (1605–27), Shah Jahan (1627–1658), and Aurangzeb (1658–1707). Together these three reigns covered the seventeenth century. In many ways it is a fascinating period of Indian history and has been acclaimed as the 'great age' of the Mughals. But the liberalism represented by Akbar was not dead, and between this and the orthodoxy of these three rather puritanical emperors there existed a state of considerable tension. It reached its climax with Aurangzeb, whose extremely orthodox Islamic puritanism alienated the large Hindu population over which he ruled and was one of the contributory factors in the disintegration of the Mughal empire.

6.58 Islam and Christianity in Eastern Europe, 1500–1800

In an introductory study of the present kind it is not possible to do more than mention some of the main points of the geographical expansion of Islam during the medieval and early modern periods. A concise but fairly detailed account of this expansion will be found in the introduction to Levy's *The Social Structure of Islam*. The story is given in greater detail in the classic work *The Preaching of Islam*, by T. W. Arnold (*5.16*). For the present purpose it may be recorded that from India Islam had spread to Malaya and Indonesia by the fourteenth century, with a further expansion there in the seventeenth and eighteenth centuries as a result of the missionary activity of Arab traders. From central Asia Islam spread into the west and north of China from the time of Kublai Khan in the thirteenth century; from the Middle East into East Africa from the tenth century onwards, and into the northern part of Nigeria and other parts of West Africa from the fifteenth century. This process of expansion has usually been effected in one of two ways; either (1) by Muslim traders and merchants who, as in the case of the modern growth of Islam in Africa, have commended their faith to others in the course of their business activities and have married local women who, with their children, have then become Muslims; or (2) by the political control of new territory by Muslim rulers and the subsequent adherence to Islam of the inhabitants of the region. In neither case has conversion to the Islamic religion usually been the result of persecution or force; where there have been occasional exceptions to this rule the conversions have not lasted and those forcibly converted ceased to be Muslims at the earliest opportunity. The present extent of the Muslim population of the world is due almost entirely to missionary activity, persuasion, and the attraction which Islam has exerted, for one reason or another.

The case of eastern Europe serves as an interesting example. The first factor in the growth of Islam there during the early modern period was the extending of the political power of the Ottoman Turks, especially from the early fifteenth century. From the north-west of Turkey the Ottoman Sultans extended their territory by the conquest in 1453 of Constantinople, and thereafter of much of the Balkan peninsula. The conquests of the famous Sultan Sulayman the Magnificent (1520–66) extended the kingdom further into the Balkans. By the middle of the seventeenth century Turkish territory reached from Azov (on the north-east coast of the Black Sea) almost to Venice and Vienna in the west. It was in the first instance a military occupation, the primary purpose of which was the enlargement of Ottoman political power, an imperialist drive like any other, but certainly no worse than most in its effects on the inhabitants of the conquered areas. If there was also something of the spirit of the jihad, the specifically Muslim holy war, it did not show itself in violent conversions to Islam in the manner which Europeans sometimes imagine to be wholly characteristic of the working of jihad. The Ottoman rulers secured the allegiance of Christians in the conquered area by proclaiming themselves protectors of the Greek Church. Macarious, the Orthodox Patriarch of Antioch in the seventeenth century, compared the harsh treatment received by the Russians of the Orthodox Church at the hands of the Roman Catholic Poles with the tolerant attitude towards Orthodox Christians shown by the Sultan. 'God perpetuate the empire of the Turks for ever and ever! For they take their impost and enter into no account of religion, be their subjects Christians or Nazarenes, Jews or Samaritans: whereas these accursed Poles were not content with taxes and tithes from the brethren of Christ, though willing to serve them . . .' for 'thousands of martyrs were killed by those impious wretches . . .' (Arnold, 1913; 158f.). If many of the Christian inhabitants of the Balkans turned to Islam and became eventually fanatical devotees it was certainly not because they were compelled to renounce their former faith. A German traveller in the Ottoman empire in the middle of the seventeenth century asks in connection with the Christians – what has become of them? He provides the answer: 'They are not expelled from the country, neither are they forced to embrace the Turkish faith; then they must of themselves have been converted into Turks' (Arnold, 1913; 160) A modern member of the Eastern Orthodox Church has recently written with genuinely scholarly fairness towards the Muslims, of a kind not frequently found among Christian writers, who are more often given to emphasising the cunning or the wickedness of the 'infidel Turk'. After the capture of Constantinople, the Turks, he writes, 'treated their Christian subjects with remarkable generosity. The Mohammedans in the fifteenth century were far more tolerant towards Christianity than Western Christians were towards one another during the Reformation and the seventeenth century' (Ware, 1963; 96).

One important point which needs to be carefully weighed in the consideration of the expansion of Islam in eastern Europe is that Islam may have provided for Eastern Orthodox Christians a substitute for a Protestant reformation. For the Orthodox Church had in some ways absorbed the spirit of the Roman Church in becoming hierarchical in structure; it had also developed to major proportions in its religious life the worship of images, relics and saints; intellectual life was oppressed by the dogmatism of the ecclesiastical authorities, and superstition had largely taken its place. Movements to purge the Church's life of its excessive attachment to ikons arose from time to time; one of these, initiated by Leo the Isaurian in the eighth century, we have already noted (*6.21*). There were sects in the Balkan countries, as in the West, who rejected the religion of priest and pontiff, and to whom the Protestant doctrine that man was saved through faith in God's prevenient grace, rather than by his own works and merit, had a strong appeal. Cyril Lucaris, who was Patriarch of Constantinople between 1621 and 1638, had as a young man studied in the universities of Wittenberg and Geneva, and was greatly attracted to the doctrine of John Calvin (*6.50*). He sought to introduce into the Greek Church the doctrines of predestination and salvation by faith alone, and to repudiate the authoritarian view of the Church which had by now been accepted in the East also. But the attempt failed: the Greek Church had in its thought and practice become remote from anything like a Calvinist position. A few weeks after his death a synod of Orthodox clergy pronounced Cyril's Calvinistic doctrines anathema. There is evidence, however, that he had a considerable following, for they, too, were subsequently anathematised by the Orthodox hierarchy. Any potential Protestantism in the East was thus effectively stifled. Yet it cannot be assumed that such a potential thereby ceased to exist. It is perhaps pertinent to mention that the Calvinists of Europe, especially of Hungary and Silesia, were inclined to prefer the prospect of living under Islamic than under Roman Catholic rule (Arnold, 1913; 157f.). It is not altogether surprising, then, that there were considerable numbers among the population of the Balkan countries who, when

Muslim rule overtook them, found themselves turning away from a priestly religion, a religion which had become so excessively one of outward forms, a religion of salvation by endless works, a religion made wearisome by the interminable controversies of its leaders on minute matters of doctrine – away from this to a normally attractive, simple and intelligible religion which bade men have faith in an almighty God whose will predestined all things and by whose mercy alone a man could be saved. If it is one of the curious and possibly momentous facts of Christian history that no Protestant Reformation occurred in the Eastern Church, it is also not altogether impossible to see at least part of the reason for this – in the substitute-Calvinism from Arabia that was more readily available to the men of south-eastern Europe.

6.59 The early interaction of European Christianity and Asian religions

The early years of the sixteenth century saw the arrival of the Portuguese in India, Ceylon and South-East Asia. They came as traders, empire-builders, and missionaries of Catholicism, and were the forerunners of various other European powers, Dutch, French and British, who in the next two or three centuries were to oust them and also to continue what the Portuguese had begun – the exposure, for good or ill, of Asian cultures to early modern European civilisation. In Akbar's day (6.57) India was relatively prosperous; Asia possessed much that Europe wanted in the way of merchandise – cotton cloth, indigo, spices, precious stones, silk and many other commodities. Stuart England sent an ambassador, Sir Thomas Roe, to the court of the Mughal emperor Jahangir in 1615 to try for a favourable commercial treaty, since so much gold and silver was leaving Europe to pay for Indian goods. 'Europe bleedeth to enrich Asia', Sir Thomas complained. If at the end of the European occupation of Asian countries, they were no longer prosperous but sadly impoverished, the reason for this modern state of affairs is fairly clear. It is an aspect of human relationships which concerns the student of religion, in so far as religion embraces ethics. On this fact of international economic affairs was based a good deal of the increasing prosperity of England, for example, by the time of the high noon of imperialism in the late nineteenth century. England was now visibly stronger than and superior to Asian countries, and it was easy to assume that the Christian ideals which had, it was believed, made England what she was, should be imparted to poor, inferior Muslim and Hindu 'natives'.

The religious cultures of Asia, Muslim, Hindu and Buddhist, all without exception suffered disintegration from the European presence. In Ceylon and Burma, for example, the structure of the Buddhist Sangha and its sensitive relationship with the kings meant that the overthrow by the British of these monarchs (for resisting British invasion) seriously upset the traditional functioning of the Sangha within Sinhalese and Burmese society. Moreover, the cultural accommodation which was a feature of the gradual, peaceful penetration of Sinhalese and Burmese indigenous religion (*6.46*) gave Buddhism the appearance, to Europeans, of unalloyed idolatry; a very few of the more discerning appreciated the nature of the situation, but by and large the religious life of Burma and Ceylon was dismissed as simply a case of the heathen in his blindness bowing down to wood and stone.

Japan's rulers, however, saw the danger and took action. When Francis Xavier (*6.51*) with his missionary companions arrived at Satsuma in Japan in 1549, they were received 'as men from India preaching a Tenjiku-shu, the religion of India' (Anesaki, 1963; 241). Towards the end of the sixteenth century the arrival of Spanish friars, Dominican and Franciscan, resulted in dissension among Christians on Japanese soil. The Jesuits were critical of the friars' policy of working among the poorest classes; added to this was the general antipathy between Portuguese and Spaniards. The Spanish friars criticised the Portuguese Jesuits for their worldliness, and both sides thereupon engaged in a campaign of innuendo. It was hinted that Spanish friars were frequently the forerunners of Spanish imperialism. In 1597 many of the Spaniards and their converts were arrested, and some were executed. Dutch and English Protestant traders and sailors visiting Japan were only too willing to enlighten the Japanese ruler on the fact that both Spaniards and Portuguese Catholics were regarded in Europe as dangerous imperialists. In 1637 a popular insurrection at Shimabara was identified as Portuguese-inspired. Spaniards had already been expelled from Japan; now it was the turn of the Portuguese. After this the Tokugawa rulers resolved to have no further dealings with the outside world. Christianity was prohibited and Japan was declared to be 'the land of the kami (*2.48*) and of the Buddha'. The entire religious life of Japan was 'frozen'; all had to keep to their own faith and all foreign influences were henceforth excluded. In the course of time this policy had the effect of stifling Japanese religion, notably Buddhism, which was 'protected' as virtually the official religion, but which, under this kind of protection, sank into a condition of torpor.

The effect of British rule in India upon Hindu and Islamic religion is seen more clearly after 1800, and will be dealt with in that connection (7.20; 7.30).

Summary and comment on Chapter Six

The period which has been surveyed in this chapter is one in which some striking resemblances are to be seen between most of the major religious traditions we have studied. An excessive sophistication in the intellectual formulation of religious ideas (coupled, in the case of Christianity at least, with an excessively authoritarian control of religious institutions) provoked, as a reaction, a turning towards mysticism, which was sometimes linked with a defiantly literalist view of religious texts (scriptures), and sometimes with a proliferation of devotional sects.

In the case of Hinduism it was largely the sophistication of religious thought begun by Shankara which produced the reaction. The awareness that Shankara's intellectually refined monism was inimical to devotional practice of the bhakti kind led first to the fairly mild protest of Rāmānuja (6.14), and later on to the more critical attitude adopted by Madhva and Rāmānanda (6.17) and the latter's movement away from the position of the older orthodoxy of karma and caste towards a more mystical and socially uninhibited devotionalism. The Shākta cult may also be seen as to some extent deriving its vitality from a reaction to an excessively rationalistic type of religion.

In Islam the sophistication of theology under the influence of Greek, especially Aristotelian modes of thought produced, by way of reaction, first, the conversion of Al Ashari to a literalist orthodoxy (6.35), and then in the case of Al Ghazali (whose crisis of personal experience represents a crisis within Islam itself) a turning away from philosophical theology to the pursuit of mystical experience, where he believed the true heart of religion was to be found.

In Christianity the acute necessity laid upon Aquinas (by the intellectual sophistication of Islamic thought) to demonstrate the reasonableness of Christian theology gave rise to a massive and monumental scholasticism. It may be only a legend, as modern Catholic scholars are inclined to assert that it is, that Aquinas, when his *Summa Theologica* was nearing completion, had an overwhelming spiritual experience one day while he was at Mass, and commanded his scribe to abandon the work, saying that all that he had written was but as straw compared with what he had now seen in the experience which had come to him. Legend it may be, but it may also be a parable of the condition of late medieval Christian theology. For after Aquinas came William of Ockham, and the divorce of faith from reason, a divorce which was conducive to the development of mystical tendencies (*6.28*), tendencies which were nourished by reaction, conscious or unconscious, against the straitjacket of the authoritarian dogmatic system. Associated with this fourteenth-century development of mysticism in the Christian tradition was the similar movement in Judaism, which had its focus in the Zohar (*6.27*), and which followed upon the excessively intellectual preoccupations of the thirteenth century with which Maimonides (*6.24*) had endeavoured to deal.

These parallel developments within Hinduism, Islam, Christianity and Judaism during roughly the same period cannot fail to provoke some interpretative comment. To some extent no doubt the movements were interdependent; especially this is true of the three traditions that were in fairly close contact in Europe – Islam, Christianity and Judaism. The influx into European Judaism of mystical thought from Babylon may have stimulated mystical thought among Christians, for example. The situation is complex, and presents a fruitful field for further study. But certain general observations concerning the sources from which religious traditions are nourished may also be offered. It will be seen that the doctrines which are affirmed in any religion are derived from one or more of the following sources:

1. The direct first-hand religious *experience* of individuals.
2. *Received traditions*, consisting of the accumulated deposit of such experiences, which may be embodied in some agreed corpus of sacred writings (the Veda, the Torah, the Tipitaka, the New Testament, the Qur'an, etc.) or may be transmitted from person to person in an oral tradition or in some institutional form such as the traditions of the scribes in Judaism, or the tradition of the Church in Christianity.
3. The exercise of *reason* upon the data of human existence.

In one type of religion one of these sources of religious knowledge may be predominant. In Judaism, for instance, it is the Torah, rather than inner personal experience or the use of reason, but nevertheless those other two potential sources of knowledge still have some contribution to make, the extent of which will vary from time to time; in one period the exercise of reason may be allowed a greater place in the interpretation of the tradition (the Torah) than in another period. In another type of religion the relative importance of the three sources may be quite different. Most of the major religions have, in the course of their histories, allowed some place for all three.

Some religions, however, rely almost exclusively on the authority of the *received tradition*, represented either by scriptures, or institutional tradition, or both. Of such a kind, in the main, have been Judaism, Christianity, and Islam. During the period we have been reviewing all of these had, however, passed through a phase when the dominant preoccupation of their major exponents was with the *rational* exposition of the faith. The reaction against this excessively speculative, intellectual mood was in some cases to reaffirm the scriptural tradition in its literal form; in other cases it showed itself in a turning towards personal, mystical experience as the ultimate and only sure source of religious knowledge. The latter kind of reaction against the authoritarian dogmatism of scripture and against its authorised, official exponents, whether bishops or brāhmans, is closely associated with the rise of sectarian groups especially among socially subordinate or disinherited classes; examples of this are the Waldenses (*6.25*) the Brotherhood groups (*6.26*), the Sufis (*6.36*) the Hindu devotional sects of north India (*6.54*) and the Quakers (*6.52*).

No mention has been made in all this of the Buddhists. This is because in their case no *absolute* canon of authority was ever held to be necessary or desirable. Even among the Theravādins, who are sometimes wrongly accused of resembling fundamentalist Protestants in their attitude to scripture, it is clearly acknowledged and accepted that even the words of the Buddha contained in the Vinaya and the Suttas are to be accepted as authentic only in so far as a man is prepared to go on to investigate and prove their truth for himself in his own religious experience, and by the use of his own reason.

What was 'revealed' to the Buddha is not given uncritical acceptance; it is held to be important that the greatest attention should be paid to his teaching, for it is clearly acknowledged that few individuals can gain such insight unaided and alone; on the other hand the teaching is neither to be accepted nor rejected on any external authority, but it is to be put to the test experientially, that is, in the living of the Buddhist life. It is clearly acknowledged also that by the use of reason alone man cannot discover the most important truths; this is why in the first instance men need to hear the teaching of the Buddha, but to hear it as the word of a guide which is to be verified personally in the only way that such knowledge can be verified – in religious experience. An excellent account of the Buddhist position in these matters has recently been made available by K.N. Jayatilleke in his *Early Buddhist Theory of Knowledge*, especially in chapter viii, 'Authority and Reason within Buddhism'.

In Hinduism, Judaism, Christianity and Islam, however, the situation is rendered more complicated by the very great veneration which has been afforded to the canonical scriptures in each case. The complication is increased by the fact that each of these bodies of sacred scriptures is not a homogeneous whole, but embodies elements of an ancient and sometimes religiously incompatible kind. Even the Qur'an, homogeneous as it is in the sense of having been produced by one man within a short period of time, lacks real homogeneity in the sense that it too embodies a great deal that is derived from a variety of earlier traditions, and is therefore not the expression of a completely unified radical religious insight.

For this reason these faiths have all in the modern period been faced with the necessity of making a drastic reappraisal of the status of their sacred scriptures. In every tradition there have been the literalists, Hindu, Jewish, Christian and Muslim, who have thought that the only reliable course is to affirm piously all that is contained in sacred scripture, and adopt a piecemeal defence of inconsistencies where this is forced upon them. Others have been prepared to acknowledge in the light of historical research that some elements in the sacred tradition are to be given greater importance than others, and that ultimately the criteria for doing this must be religious insight coupled with human reason. Among the literalists of the various religions there can be little common ground; among those who follow a more discriminating policy there is, as the adherents of these various faiths encounter one another in the modern world, at least some possibility of dialogue and exploration.

7 Religion and Industrial Society

7.1 RELIGION IN THE WEST: 1800 TO THE PRESENT

7.10 Protestantism and Capitalism

FOR the Christian religion the nineteenth century was perhaps the period of its greatest success, if by that we mean the growth of its institutions and outward observances, its spread in Asia and Africa, and the respect generally accorded to it. After the religious lethargy of the early eighteenth century in northern Europe a new mood had characterised the close of that century. Some would say that in England, at least, this was due in part to the Methodist movement, and in part to the shock produced by the French Revolution of 1789. The upper classes in England saw the writing on the wall; it seemed that atheism went hand in hand with loss of respect for the hallowed institutions of society, and that religious indifference and moral laxity among the upper classes encouraged revolutionary tendencies among the common people. There was a turning to more serious ways of life and thought: Calvinism came into its own. For here was a doctrine that was serious in its view of man's situation, simple and rational in its principles, and challenging in its implications for everyday life. In its simplest form, that men exist for the sake of God, that some are saved and others are damned, and that assurance of salvation can be found in the success which attends application to one's secular calling, it had the effect of encouraging the serious use of time and resources, and of discouraging expenditure of either of these on worldly pleasures. This Puritan doctrine, which had its adherents in one section of society in the sixteenth and seventeenth centuries, from the beginning of the nineteenth century gained wide acceptance in certain countries of northern Europe. Associated fairly closely with the acceptance of such a doctrine was an economic phenomenon: the growth of private capital. By the 1840s, when Karl Marx was pondering these facts, it seemed to him that the religious ideas of Protestantism were nothing more than the spiritual rationalisation of the brute facts of economic existence: the capitalist economy meant an alienation within humanity, the alienation of the capitalist master from the servant who had only his labour to sell; this, said Marx, was given an epiphenomenal religious form in the idea of a god to whom man owed everything, on whom he was completely dependent, before whom he was but a servile, sinful wretch, and from whom he might expect such scraps of comfort as the god by sheer virtue of his grace might bestow on man. Protestantism, Marx maintained, was precisely the form of religion one might expect to find associated with a capitalist system. A critique of Protestant religion was the way to understand the whole social and economic situation: 'The criticism of religion is the beginning of all (i.e. social) criticism'.

A somewhat different view was suggested by Max Weber (1930). The emergence of the capitalist could be seen, he said, as the result of the outworking of Protestant ideas stemming in the first instance from Calvin. Weber left open the question of *how far* the ideas of the Reformation might themselves be shown to be due to economic and social factors (Bendix, 1959; 69). Instead of religious ideas being regarded as epiphenomenal upon economic realities, Weber argued, they could justly be regarded as themselves constituting a real factor in the European situation.

Certainly an outstanding feature of Protestantism, especially in the nineteenth century, was its strongly individualistic spirit. Some see this today as a good feature, a guarantee against the possible evils of mass society and dictatorships; others see it as a regrettable feature, leading to social irresponsibility and a cover for selfishness. In nineteenth-century Protestant countries there was certainly a tendency to explain the inequalities of rich and poor in terms of individual merit. The rich, so it was argued, had become rich by their serious devotion to duty, hard work, sobriety and thrift, while the poor had become poor by reason of fecklessness, laziness, moral corruption, drunkenness and other vices. Such moralistic individualism, widespread as it was, seriously hindered a more realistic analysis of the ills of nineteenth-century society and the working out of measures to deal with them.

One other feature of nineteenth-century Protestantism which is too important in its social effects not to be mentioned was the impetus it gave to the attitude which Matthew Arnold characterised as 'Philistine'. For men whose principal concern was unremitting devotion to business affairs, in an age increasingly conscious of the marvels of machinery, there was little or no place in life for art or beauty, especially since the ascetic Puritan tradition of religion was positively hostile to anything remotely likely to constitute an indulgence of the senses, a glorifying of the flesh rather than of God. Preoccupation with 'the rational pursuit of economic gain', together with suspicion of all aesthetic interests, combined to produce on the one hand the ugliness of the industrial cities which grew up in nineteenth-century Britain, especially in the midlands and the north, and on the other hand an insensitiveness to the place which art may have in the life of religion. That Protestantism thus succeeded in alienating men of artistic sensibility from the Christian religion would in no way dismay such Philistines, confident as they were of their own election, and of the idolatry and folly of using the arts as an aid to the religious life. A great deal is often made of the intellectual conflicts of the nineteenth century, while this aspect of Protestantism too often goes unremarked; nevertheless such aesthetic insensitivity continues to alienate the sons and daughters of Protestantism, some of whom turn to Catholicism, while others drift away from the life of religion altogether.

7.11 *Evangelicalism, Agnosticism and American revivalism*

One of the important features of Christian religious history during the first half of the nineteenth century, both on the continent of Europe and in Britain, was a movement which is known as Evangelicalism. This had certain widely recognisable characteristics: a strongly lay rather than clerical emphasis (although clergymen were of course affected by the movement and in certain notable cases such as that of Charles Simeon of Cambridge took a leading part in it); a concern for the righting of social injustice such as slavery, and with education; and, above all, the respect given to the Christian Bible as the inspired word of God and the criterion of all truth. Evangelicalism's most characteristic rite was Family Prayers, including reading aloud from the Bible; its most characteristic social location was in the middle and upper classes. Thus it was Evangelicalism which moulded the characters of many of Britain's nineteenth-century administrators, army officers, public school masters and philanthropic aristocrats. In its social function as the religious cult of a privileged *élite* the movement bore a certain resemblance to early Arab Islam during the period of the four rightly guided caliphs (*5.16*). This is seen most clearly perhaps in the dependence on a Book which was held to contain the *ipsissima verba* of God. And as in the case of Islam, in this lay both its strength and its weakness.

The extent to which Evangelicalism succeeded in inculcating the idea of the central and exclusive importance of a verbally inspired, literally true corpus of sacred literature is also a measure of the extent to which nineteenth-century Protestant Christianity was rendered unfit to give a fair hearing to the scientific theories put forward in England by Charles Darwin in his *Origin of Species*, published in 1859. Having committed itself to belief in the literal inerrancy of the Christian Bible, Protestantism (like Roman Catholicism, from whom the doctrine was received) was forced to see Darwin's theory of evolution as a direct attack on the historical accuracy of the early chapters of Genesis (which it was) and therefore as an attack on the very foundations of Christianity (which it was not).

Here then was one of the principal reasons why the Protestant Churches reacted so sharply to new theories concerning the natural world that were being put forward by scientists, and why Christians found it necessary to defend with such passion positions which they have now come to see were by no means so crucial as was then believed. It is also one of the reasons for the opposition to traditional religious ideas shown by serious writers such as Hardy, Meredith, Stevenson and Housman.

Evangelicalism found strongest expression in America, where it took a socially lower-class form commonly known as 'revivalism'. This was generated in frontier situations, as pioneers pushed westwards across the American continent. Various factors combined to produce this type of American Christianity: the personal qualities of the pioneers, partly their independence and self-reliance, partly perhaps their discontent and frustration and disappointments born of the difficulties of frontier life; the easy informality of the camp-fire where the only portable religious equipment necessary was a Bible; the Methodist belief that all men might be saved, which implied the necessity of preaching forgiveness of sins and the cultivation of holiness of life. Great emphasis came thus to be laid on conversion experience or on 'getting religion'; and on emotional fervour in the expression of such religion once obtained.

Later, in the more settled conditions of urban life, revivalism was deliberately organised on a large scale and became formalised in its non-ritualistic rituals in the campaigns and revival meetings of such men as D. L. Moody and his partner Ira Sankey, Billy Sunday, and in the twentieth-century Billy Graham. Such campaigns succeeded to some extent in attracting those of the masses who in Britain and America were largely beyond the reach of more conventional church life; they also had a strong influence on the ethos and methods of Nonconformist Protestant bodies such as the Baptists.

7.12 Methodism and Socialism

It has been said that 'the coincidence in time of Wesley and the Industrial Revolution had profound effects upon England for generations to come' (Trevelyan, 1946; 362). It might be added that the effects were certainly not confined to England. The movement which had begun with such remarkable vitality in the eighteenth century (6.52) continued to grow throughout the nineteenth. The impact made by Methodism, great though it was in Britain, was even greater in the United States. In Britain Methodism reached out, as the Established Church could not, to affect the condition of the working classes both in the newly industrialised areas and in rural areas. It continued to grow in strength throughout the nineteenth century. Between 1800 and 1860 its numbers increased four hundred per cent. Not only did it succeed in providing philanthropic care for the poor, the sick, and the unfortunate; it succeeded also in bringing about a change in the moral and social condition of its largely working-class members, by instilling into them its attitude of religious seriousness, and inspiring them with the notion of holiness as a realisable religious goal. Methodism succeeded where the Established Church in nineteenth-century England largely failed. The alienation of the working classes from the Church was well advanced by mid-century. This was a period of great social unrest in many parts of Europe; in England such unrest was to some extent mitigated by the influence of Methodism.

Methodism had a notable influence also on the older Nonconformist bodies, such as the Baptists and Congregationalists, both in Europe and America, who shared in the wave of 'chapel' life which Methodism had set in motion, a particular feature of nineteenth-century Britain which had visible embodiment in the many Nonconformist chapels built during the period, especially in the midlands and the north. The predominantly lay character of Evangelicalism (*7.11*) even among Anglicans, with the emphasis on family worship and house prayer-meetings, was also due to the influence of Methodism. The movement contributed in an important way also to the revivalism of the newly developing American continent (*7.11*). Finally out of the Methodist milieu came in 1865 the Salvation Army, characterised by its street preaching, its emphasis on hymn-singing and music, and its social relief work among the poorest classes. Founded by William Booth (1829–1912) in Nottingham, the Salvation Army has since spread into other English-speaking countries, to the continent of Europe and through missionary activity, into Asia.

About the year 1835 a new word had entered the English vocabulary, the word 'socialism'. The ideas and principles of the socialists developed first on the continent of Europe, where they had a strong association with movements of violent revolution. In their Marxian form these ideas became known to some extent in England through Karl Marx's presence in London as a writer from 1849 to his death in 1883, but by the time this had happened the most critical years were past, that is the years from about 1847 to 1850 when revolutionary movements were active in various countries of Europe. The blunting of the force of this revolutionary mood so far as England was concerned may have been in large measure due to the hold of Nonconformity and especially Methodism upon many of the working classes. The Church of England threw up its Christian Socialists, notably Frederick Denison Maurice (1805–72) and Charles Kingsley (1819–75), but their effect upon the situation was marginal compared with the role of Methodism.

One effect of Methodism upon its working-class members which had been remarked upon by John Wesley himself was a strong tendency towards the erection of a new petty bourgeoisie: 'For the Methodists in every place grow diligent and frugal; consequently they increase in goods. Hence they proportionately increase in pride, in anger, in the desire of the flesh, the desire of the eyes and the pride of life. So although the form of religion remains, the spirit is swiftly vanishing away.'

Finally, it may be noted that the associational experience which laymen gained in their Methodist societies was also an important factor in the development of the trade unions in Britain.

7.13 Catholicism in the nineteenth and twentieth centuries

The close of the eighteenth century had been marked by the 'Terror' which in France followed the Revolution, when many Catholic priests were expelled from the country or executed, religious orders were destroyed and, in 1793, the Goddess of Reason was exalted on the altar of Notre-Dame in Paris and religion declared to be abolished. One faint light in what for Catholics was a dark period was the publication in 1802 of an important work by Chateaubriand (1768–1848), *Le Génie du Christianisme*, which sought to show the reasonableness of Christianity, presenting it as a civilising power, the inspiration of poets and artists, and the basis of European culture. Nevertheless the political subjection of the Catholic Church continued. Although Napoleon had been crowned emperor by the Pope in 1804 (since Catholicism was still the religion of the majority of his subjects), in the course of his territorial aggression into Italy in 1808–9 he found the Pope a sufficient inconvenience to make it necessary for him to imprison the Holy Father, who remained in prison until 1815, when on Napoleon's abdication he was released. The Jesuit Order, which an earlier Pope had been forced to suppress in 1773, was now reinstated. The effect of Napoleon's action against the Pope was to make many of the French clergy look to the Pope as their protector, the one to whom they owed supreme obedience, and whose authority they honoured above all. This looking beyond France, 'beyond the mountains' (Ultramontanism), i.e. to Italy, became a characteristic attitude in the French Catholic Church of the nineteenth century.

In England the Catholic Emancipation Act of 1829 restored to Catholics some of their lost rights and began an improvement of their social position. Within the Anglican Church a movement arose in 1833 under the leadership first of Richard Hurrell Froude, Fellow of Oriel College, Oxford, and then of certain other Oxford dons, notably John Henry Newman and John Keble, which became known as the Oxford Movement. It was in origin a movement of protest against the interference of the state in the affairs of the Church, and the Assize Sermon preached by Keble in St Mary's, Oxford, in 1833, may be regarded as its charter (Bettenson, 1963; 445ff.). The leaders of the movement were prompted also by a desire to see the Church of England aroused from its lethargy and restored to its place as the divine society of Christ, governed by its bishops, and providing men with what they had found 'the best road to the preservation of purity of life in the services and sacraments, the round of fasts and festivals that formed the daily routine of the Church' (Wand, 1952; 212). To this end they published a series of tracts which gained them and their movement the name 'Tractarian'. The publication of these tracts came to an end in 1841 with Tract 90 (Bettenson, 1963; 448ff.), an interpretation of the Anglican Thirty-Nine Articles in a sense which to many seemed clearly Roman, and was certainly offensive to some Evangelical members of parliament. The Bishop of Oxford intervened, and the movement suffered the loss of Newman, who resigned his living in 1843 and then entered the Roman Catholic Church in 1845. His *Essay on the Development of Christian Doctrine*, written in 1844 before he actually made his submission to Rome, had a considerable influence on Catholic thought in the latter part of the nineteenth century. Newman's activities as a Roman Catholic, together with those of Manning, were an important factor in stimulating the growth of the Roman confession in England, a growth which was aided also throughout the nineteenth century by the influx of Irish immigrants.

The latter half of the century was characterised by what can be seen as a long process of interaction between traditional Roman Catholic orthodoxy and various aspects of modern, and increasingly industrialised, European life. A group of writers of whom de Lammenais (1782–1854) is the best known had attempted to work out a synthesis of Catholic and liberal ideas; de Lammenais, however, was condemned and excommunicated by Pope Gregory XVI (1831–46). In 1854 the Pope declared the doctrine of the Immaculate Conception of the Blessed Virgin Mary an article of faith. Catholics maintain that nothing new was being introduced into the doctrine of their Church, but that the Church's growth in understanding the implications of Christian doctrine was receiving full and official recognition. The growth of Rome's confidence is seen also in the publication in 1864 of a 'Syllabus of Errors', denouncing such contemporary liberal ideas as the separation of Church and State, primary education on a common secular basis, and the recognition of value in non-Catholic religion. What does appear in the declaration of 1864, and even more clearly in the decisions of the Vatican Council of 1869–70, is the growing strength of the Pope's position in Europe, after the events with which the eighteenth century closed. The Council of 1869–70 discussed matters of the Faith, and of the Church and its powers, and in 1870 affirmed the infallibility of statements uttered by the Pope *ex cathedra*. This was carried almost unanimously, but with some opposition from German Catholics. In this way Roman Catholic doctrine gained an authoritativeness which has proved to have a considerable appeal to modern men unable to bear the uncertainties and perplexities of contemporary currents of thought; many of these have been intellectuals – for they more than most have been aware of the full extent of the uncertainties of secularism.

Matters of social justice in an industrial society were dealt with by Pope Leo XIII's famous encyclical *Rerum Novarum* of 1891, which condemned the tendency of modern states to usurp the rights of the individual but in which the state's protection of the interests of the wage-earning class was urged and trade unionism was commended. On the other hand, a movement to interpret Catholic ideas in terms of contemporary thought, generally known as Catholic Modernism, a movement which had exponents and adherents in Germany, France, Italy and Spain, was condemned by Pope Pius X in 1907 in his encyclical *Pascendi*.

Meanwhile the Roman Catholic community continued to grow in numbers, especially in the United States and Britain. In the former, Catholics now comprise about a fifth of the total population and Catholicism is recognised as one of the three principal faiths of modern America (together with those of the Jews and the Protestants), a fact which Catholics claim as an indication that Catholicism can flourish in a genuinely democratic country as well as anywhere.

7.14 Religion in Russia, 1721–1917

If any country can be said to be the bridge between East and West it is Russia. The vastness of Russian territory is such that its frontier is with Protestant and Catholic Europe in the west, with Buddhist Japan and Korea in the east, and with the Muslim lands of Persia, Afghanistan and Pakistan to the south. Russia's peoples include, or have included in the past, Buddhists and Muslims as well as Jews and Christians. These facts need to be borne in mind when one is considering the religious history of this very important area of the world's surface.

Predominantly, religion in Russia has meant Christianity of the

Eastern Orthodox tradition. Here again the meeting of East and West may be discerned. Two features of Eastern Orthodoxy in Russia may possibly help one to understand its tortuous and often troubled history; these are, first the Church concept, which has been a very strong factor in Russian religious history, and second, the powerful influence of a spirituality which not infrequently reminds one of Asia rather than Europe.

The concept of the Church as a powerful institution, hierarchically organised and constituting something sufficiently resembling an empire to make it appear a rival to the secular state, is a legacy from Rome. If Byzantium was the second Rome, its loss to Christendom meant that the centre of gravity of Eastern Orthodoxy shifted to Moscow, which thus became in some Russian Orthodox eyes 'the third Rome'. While the Orthodox churches do not acknowledge a supreme head, or Pope, and the five patriarchs of Jerusalem, Antioch, Alexandria, Constantinople and Moscow are in theory on terms of equality, nevertheless within Russia itself the position of the patriarch was closely similar to that of the Pope in southern Europe; he was the head of a hierarchical institution. 'The Orthodox Church', writes Timothy Ware, 'is a hierarchical Church. An essential element in its structure is the Apostolic Succession of bishops.' Ware goes on to explain that 'a bishop is appointed by God to guide and to rule the flock committed to his charge; he is a "monarch" in his own diocese' (Ware, 1963; 252f.). So far as the scope of such hierarchical power was concerned, the Church in Russia was reckoned to be not inferior to the secular state, but on an equality with it. As in Byzantium, Church and State constituted 'a dyarchy or symphony of two co-ordinated powers, *sacerdotium* and *imperium*, each supreme in its own sphere' (Ware, 1963; 124). This was symbolised in the two equal thrones which used to be placed in the Assumption Cathedral of the Kremlin, 'one for the Patriarch and one for the Tsar'.

It was this institutional-power aspect of Russian Christianity which, when pushed too far by the seventeenth-century Patriarch Nicon (1605–81), resulted in the subjugation of the Church by the emperor Peter the Great, who reigned from 1682 to 1725. So greatly had Nicon sought to extend the patriarch's power that Peter abolished the office altogether, and thus settled the issue of Church-state power-rivalry. In 1721 Peter issued a declaration, known as the *Spiritual Regulation*, to the effect that the office of patriarch was to be replaced by a commission of twelve men nominated by him, to be known as the Holy Synod. Any member of the commission could, of course, be dismissed at any time by the Tsar. Meetings of the Synod were to be attended by the Tsar's representative, the chief procurator, who would not take part but would 'observe' on behalf of the Tsar. This official came to be known as 'the Tsar's eye' and did in fact wield considerable power in the Church. During the nineteenth century the complete subservience of the Church dignitaries to the emperor was abundantly clear in the relationships which existed between one procurator in particular, who was a colonel of the guards, and the members of the Synod, whom he treated 'as if they were cavalry subalterns' (Florinsky, 1959; ii, 798).

Thus from 1721 the Orthodox Church in Russia was a department of the state. Unlike some other 'establishment' churches, however, the Russian Church's relationship was one not of privilege but of subjugation. During the eighteenth century one of the main results of this was that the admiration of the upper class for all things French and, to a lesser degree, for things European, meant an 'ill-advised Westernisation' of Church art, music and theology (Ware, 1963; 128). By the reign of Alexander I (1801–25) there had appeared in Russia 'a body of genuinely Westernised people' (Zernov, 1961; 175). During the nineteenth century a reaction to this arose within the Russian Church. One of the leading figures was Alexey Khomiakov (1804–60) a wealthy landlord, poet, amateur physician, and orientalist (he compiled the first Russian–Sanskrit dictionary). 'For Khomiakov the Church was not an institution, but a living organism. He dismissed as wrong the search for an external source of infallibility in which the Christian West had been engaged since its separation from the Orthodox Church' (Zernov, 1961; 187). Those who joined together in the movement of which he was the leader were known as the Slavophils. It was a minority movement, but a similar rediscovery of those elements in the life of the Russian Church which are more characteristic of the East, than of Western Christendom, was a marked feature of the nineteenth century, quite apart from the Slavophil movement. There was a growth in monastic life: in 1810 there were 452 monasteries; in 1914 there were 1,025 (Ware, 1963; 130). With this went also a development of the principle of spiritual direction, exercised in Russia by the staretz, a religious figure in many ways like the guru of Asia. One of the greatest of these startsi was St Seraphim (1759–1833) whose life and activities are seen by Ware, rather significantly, as resembling those of Antony of Egypt – where monastic life had developed partly from an Asian, possibly Buddhist stimulus. Another feature of this kind was the emphasis by nineteenth-century Russian Orthodoxy on the practice of the 'Jesus Prayer' – that is the continual repetition of the words 'Jesus Christ, Son of God, have mercy on me', a form of religious exercise which has parallels in the use of the mantra in Asian religion, and especially in Amidism (*6.48*).

Thus the nineteenth century was a period in the history of Russian Orthodoxy when, in spite of subjugation to the state, and perhaps even to some extent because of it, there was a turning away from the religious ideas and institutions of the West and a rediscovery of, and a re-emphasis upon, elements of spirituality which were more characteristic of the East than of Europe.

Another aspect of the recovery of religious vitality in Russia during the nineteenth century was the rise of sectarian movements characterised by a rejection of state supremacy in religion, and of the need for priests and sacraments, and an emphasis upon the interior spiritual life. The beginnings of what is sometimes called Spiritual Christianity in Russia are to be found as early as the seventeenth century, such as the rise of the Dukhobors, or 'Wrestlers by the Spirit'. Count Leo Tolstoi's interpretation of Christianity as a way of peaceful non-resistance to violence, and his rejection of the need for sacraments, had an affinity with the Dukhobors. The official Russian Church disliked Tolstoi and lost no opportunity to discredit him. Significantly, perhaps, it was a Hindu, Mahatma Gandhi (*7.27*), who was strongly influenced by Tolstoi's version of Christianity, and incorporated it into his own reformed version of Hinduism. The attitudes of the authorities to the Dukhobors led many of them to emigrate to Canada in 1899.

7.15 *Nineteenth-century Christian missions*

Not until it was eighteen centuries old did Christianity begin to make any large-scale contact with the Orient. Buddhism, emerging just five centuries before Christianity, had by the second century of the Christian era begun to enter China, and before long was strongly established among the Chinese and the Koreans. Islam arose six centuries later than Christianity, and in the same area, but before two centuries had passed Islam had begun to establish itself and to grow steadily, in north-west India and in South India and Ceylon. But apart from the small fairly static community of Syrian Christians in South India, and some Nestorians in China, the entry of Christianity into the Orient did not begin seriously until the end of the fifteenth century and beginning of the sixteenth.

By that time the Great religious traditions of Hinduism, Buddhism and Islam had already made advances in Asia, and between them commanded the allegiance of large numbers of the population of India, South-East Asia and China, where they had replaced the earlier Little Traditions of primitive tribal religion. Christianity thus arrived rather late on the scene; it was not until after 1800 that its Asian missionary effort seriously began, and it was in those areas where tribal cultures were still untouched by the other Great Traditions that it made most of its converts during the modern period. There were a few attempts to spread the Christian faith among the peoples of the already well-established Great Traditions, attempts which were not highly successful but which had important consequences for our contemporary religious situation.

The reasons for the great expansion of Christian missionary activity from the beginning of the nineteenth century onward are various. For two centuries until then Europe had been 'discovering' Asia, and the European presence was now fairly well established. The rise of Protestantism in Europe is closely connected with the presence of Europe in Asia (and Africa), for the principal reason for that presence was desire for commercial profit. The growth of Evangelicalism, especially in England, is a second important factor. Both to the Calvinist Puritan, and the Evangelical of more Methodist persuasion, profit-making was a righteous activity, almost a religious duty. In 1797 Charles Grant, a director of the East India Company, had written:

> In considering the affairs of the world as under the control of the Supreme Disposer, and those distant territories . . . providentially put into our hands . . . is it not necessary to conclude that they were given to us, not merely that we might draw an annual profit from them, but that we might diffuse among their inhabitants, long sunk in darkness, vice and misery, the light and benign influence of the truth, the blessings of well-regulated society, the improvements and comforts of active industry? . . . In every progressive step of this work, we shall also serve the original design with which we visited India, that design still so important to this country – the extension of our commerce. (Edwards, 1961; 109)

Out of considerations such as these emerged the decision to confer upon the inhabitants of India the benefits of English education – that they might read the Bible and be weaned away from idolatry and superstition; also that there might be a ready supply of educated natives to fill minor administrative posts and, as Macaulay said in a speech in 1833, that they might eventually proceed to self-government, for as he shrewdly pointed out, it would be far better for them to be ruled by their own kings, leaving the English free to get on with the business of trading with them. 'It would be . . . better for us that the people of India were well governed and independent of us . . . that they were ruled by their own kings, but wearing our broadcloth. . . . To trade with civilised men is infinitely more profitable than to govern savages.'

Belief in the enlightening power of education was for many of the evangelical officials and administrators closely connected with belief in the Christian Gospel. A great stimulus was thus given to the setting up of schools and colleges, both government and missionary. Some of the Hindus, who predominated in the areas of strongest British influence (Calcutta, Bombay and Madras), took advantage of the new education offered (7.20). Muslims were more reserved in their attitude, even where English schools and colleges were accessible to them; they feared that the intention was to win them away from Islam to an alien culture. The tone of Christian evangelical missionary preaching had already aroused the suspicions of the Muslims and, in time, of Hindus also. Lord Minto, governor-general 1807–13, had been led to complain about this in a letter to the chairman of the East India Company. Sending a missionary tract as an example of the approach used, he drew attention to the 'miserable stuff addressed to the Hindus, in which without one word to convince or satisfy the mind of the heathen reader, without proof or argument of any kind, the pages are filled with hell fire, and hell fire, and still hotter fire, denounced against a whole race of men for believing in the religion which they were taught by their fathers and mothers' (Edwards, 1961; 106).

By 1830 the vernacular newspapers were bitterly opposed to Christianity on account of its more bigoted representatives, and this resentment by Hindu and Muslim alike of the insulting attitude of the missionaries was a contributory factor to the Mutiny of 1857. After that event the confidence of the various religious communities of India was restored to some extent by Queen Victoria's proclamation that none should 'be in any wise favoured, none molested or disquieted by reason of their religious faith or observance, but that all alike shall enjoy the equal and impartial protection of the law.'

The result of the kind of encounter which took place between nineteenth-century Christianity and the great religious traditions of Asia was that missionary activities, meeting with little or no response among more cultured and influential Asians, turned to the lower classes of society and to the less sophisticated tribal peoples of the remoter hill and jungle areas, where a greater gain in terms of converts was found. This was to some extent also an embarrassment. As Bishop Stephen Neil points out: 'Almost every mission started with an attempt to reach the higher castes; when movements started among the poor, they were viewed with anxiety and a measure of embarrassment by the missionaries, who saw that their whole cause might be prejudiced by the influx of masses of ignorant and despised people' (Neil, 1964; 364). This happened quite frequently whenever the leaders of the tribes were converted, as the figures for the German Rhenish mission in the Batak area of Sumatra, for example, indicate. After the first twenty years of missionary activity, up to 1881, 7,500 converts had been gained; in the next twenty years this became a mass movement, with an influx of 103,000. Since Protestant Christianity had in view the conversion of individuals, and their being brought into the Church one by one *as individuals*, such mass movements presented problems with which Protestantism was ill-equipped to deal. In some areas, such as Sumatra, initial Christianisation was followed by the adherence of these peoples to Islam (7.38).

The years after 1858 were the period of the greatest Christian missionary activity throughout Asia and Africa. In China the treaties of 1858 opened the doors for trade and missionary activity; in Africa the missionary travels and journeys of exploration of David Livingstone kindled enthusiasm for European and American Christian activity in the interior of what was regarded as 'the Dark Continent'.

The most vigorous missionary organisations stemmed from those areas of society where religious vitality was strongest; and in Britain and the United States during the nineteenth century this was predominantly among Methodists and the growing Nonconformist churches of the industrial areas. Their adherents – and therefore their potential missionaries – were drawn largely from the lower-middle and working classes, and were not necessarily men of educated mind, nor did they have great opportunities to become so; men of the calibre of

William Carey, the cobbler who became a great orientalist in the course of his missionary activity, are rare. Moreover, after the early years it was mostly among the lower classes of natives that they worked. This, combined with the evangelical's conviction of being in full, absolute, and exclusive possession of the truth, meant the development towards the religious traditions of Buddhism, Hinduism and Islam of what can only be described as 'the missionary attitude'. Since funds for the maintenance of missionary work had to be coaxed from not always very enthusiastic supporters in the homeland, this has meant that 'the missionary attitude' to the religious faiths of Asia has tended to lay great emphasis on the dire need of the adherents of these faiths for the blessings of Western religion. In this way, any clear idea of the true nature of these faiths and the civilisations which they have produced has been rendered impossible for many people in the West; only in recent times has a more accurate view begun to supersede the idea of the benighted heathen in his blindness bowing down to wood and stone (a description which, by the hymn-writer's criteria, would have to include, of course, Rabindranath Tagore, Aurobindo Ghose, S. Radhakrishnan, Mohammad Iqbal, Dr Malalasekera, and U Thant, to name only a few).

Roman Catholicism entered Asia principally, as we have seen, through Portuguese colonial expansion from about 1500 onwards. During the nineteenth century, however, Roman Catholic missions following in the wake of Protestantism were developed; instead of missionary activity being the concern primarily of the religious orders, as hitherto, it was now given a wider basis, and was supported very much more by the whole body of the faithful and paid for by the pennies of the poor. France took the lead in this respect, and one of the pioneer organisations was the Society for the Propagation of the Faith, founded in 1822 in Lyons. Indo-China, from Burma to Vietnam, was an important area in which French Roman Catholic missionaries worked; there were also missions in India itself and in China.

The Eastern Orthodox Church also developed missionary activities from about the middle of the nineteenth century. The Altay mountains in Central Siberia were the scene of some of the earliest missionary work, undertaken at first by a saintly monk and linguist, Makary Glukharev (1792–1847), and then by his disciples, Landisher and Vladimir, so that eventually more than half the inhabitants of the Altay mountains became Christians. Another pioneer missionary of this kind was John Veniaminor (1797–1879), as a result of whose work in Alaska (part of Russia until 1864), many Aleutians were converted to Christianity. The most outstanding success of Russian Orthodox missions was in Japan, from 1868 onwards, when at the end of the Tokugawa period Japan was once more open to the outside world. By 1912 there was an Eastern Orthodox community in Japan of about thirty thousand; following the difficult years after the Revolution and those of the Second World War, this has now grown a little to about thirty-six thousand. Christianity, in all its varieties, Protestant, Catholic and Orthodox, has always remained an even smaller minority in Japan than in other Asian countries.

7.16 Judaism in the nineteenth and early twentieth centuries

The French Revolution was by no means for Jews the disaster that it was for the Catholics of France (*7.13*). In 1791 the new French state granted Jews equality of rights with Christians, and thus began the series of such emancipations of Jews from their medieval ghettos which followed in other European countries in the early nineteenth century. In England complete civic equality for Jews was resisted for some time by the bishops of the Church of England, acting in their capacity as members of the Parliamentary House of Lords, but was eventually granted in 1866. Significant of the new spirit which emerged during this century was the Assembly of Notables and Rabbis called together by Napoleon in Paris in 1807, which made an official statement declaring the end of 'the Jewish nation' and declaring individual Jews to be 'citizens of the Jewish religion'; in France their religion was to be regarded as coming within the framework of the state. In this way many of the Jews of France, and in similar ways Jews in other European countries, acquired a new role and a new outlook, that of patriotic citizens of this or that European country. In Germany, however, civic rights were not quickly gained or easily preserved, and many Jews made their way from that country to the United States, especially after the failure of the revolutionary movement of 1848 and the reaction against Jews which followed. In Tsarist Russia the position of the Jews became even more miserable than before. The Christian masses of Russia had few enough political rights; the Jews even less. They were there an unwanted people (Parkes, 1964; 148) and provided a convenient

N   L.H.R.

scapegoat for assassinations which were the work of revolutionaries, such as that of Tsar Alexander II in 1881. With the accession of Alexander III in the same year a number of harsh laws were enacted against the Jews of Russia, imposing on them very severe restrictions of movement, occupation, and of property rights. There were two important results of this discrimination against the Jews. First, the number of Russian Jews emigrating westwards increased, especially to the United States, where by their religious learning and piety they considerably stimulated the Jewish community, and to parts of Britain. Second, an impetus was given to the idea that in the modern world the Jews must have a land of their own; in 1884 at Kattowitz, an Odessan Jew named Leo Pinsker founded the Zion Movement, which from Russia spread to other countries of Europe and to America. The story of the Zionist Movement will be dealt with later (*7.19*); meanwhile it is necessary to note the effect upon Jewish religion of the new conditions which Judaism encountered in the nineteenth century.

7.17 *Jewish reform and counter-reform movements of the nineteenth century*

The emancipation of the Jews in Europe, which began with the French National Assembly's granting of full civic rights to them in 1791, had the effect of liberating them suddenly into the wider world of non-Jewish nineteenth-century civilisation, a process which has been called the explosion of the ghetto. The new situation meant that the individual Jew was involved in what was often a painful tension, between on the one hand the deeply-rooted religious tradition of Judaism, and on the other the contemporary secular world of Europe after the Enlightenment and the Revolution. This tension is reflected within Judaism in the movements of reform and counter-reform which developed during the nineteenth century.

The reform movement began in Germany. Moses Mendelssohn (1729–86) had prepared the way with his translation of the Jewish Bible into good German, and thus encouraged the Jews of Germany to use a language which opened a door into a new world of literature. In this way they became familiar with contemporary scientific ways of thought. The leaders of the reform movement were men who had become convinced that Jewish ways of thought and practice had become archaic and needed to be reformulated, so that the newly emancipated Jews should not drift away from Judaism, and so that Jews should not stand out from the rest of their fellow-Germans as men of an obviously alien culture. The pioneer in this direction was David Friedländer (1756–1834) a disciple of Moses Mendelssohn; his plans for the Germanising of the Jewish religion were extreme and few Jews dared to support him. The first practical reform was introduced by Israel Jacobson (1768–1828), who built a 'Reform Temple' in Brunswick in 1810. The use of the name 'temple', which had until then been applied only to the Temple in Jerusalem, showed that Reform Judaism no longer entertained the idea of its possible restoration and of the Jews' return there; they had now accepted for Judaism the status of a religious sect within the European state. The worship of the new temple was assimilated to that of the German churches, with sermon, prayers and chorales in German, with an organ accompaniment to the singing. Similar developments of Reform Judaism took place in England in the 1840s and 50s, in London, Manchester, Liverpool and Bradford. Another important name in Germany is that of Samuel Goldheim (1806–60), who sought to sweep away a great deal that was Talmudic, especially powers of rabbinic jurisdiction; Goldheim disregarded even the rite of circumcision, as being an alien cultural characteristic. In some ways even more radical was Abraham Geiger (1810–74), for whom 'the spirit of the age' was the primary determinant of the forms of religion, and even more important than the prescriptions of the Bible or the Talmud.

Inevitably this was regarded by more conservative Jews as the betrayal of Judaism, and there arose a counter-reform which aimed at preserving and defending traditional practices and beliefs. Such Jews reacted to the new world which had been thrown open to them by rejecting what they saw as its shoddy goods and inferior values. A French Jewish writer has described their attitude as follows:

> The great masters of Talmudism and Hasidism were too aware of the vanities of the century and of the world to accept any alteration in a dialogue that, although perhaps too sublime for the ears of man, Israel would continue with its God. In many a ghetto of Eastern Europe time stood still from the time of the ardent mysticism of the sixteenth and eighteenth centuries until annihilation by the Nazis. (Chouraqui, 1962; 132)

An intermediate position between the two extremes of over-eager modernisation and absolute rejection of the new was taken by Samson

Hirsch (1808–88) whose middle path is known as Neo-Orthodoxy. He was concerned to remind the emancipated Jews of the great spiritual heritage of Judaism; he was opposed to the new communities of Reform Judaism with their extreme tendencies. Another central but somewhat more reformist movement is known (somewhat confusingly) as the Conservative movement, associated with the name of Solomon Schechter (1830–1915); this has become a prominent feature of American Jewry especially.

It was in the United States that Reform Judaism also developed most vigorously, for here orthodox resistance was much less strong. Reform congregations were founded as early as 1824 in Charleston, and 1842 in New York. Moreover, the greater cultural openness of the American situation removed the need for such rigorous rejection of Jewishness that Reform had felt in Germany; hence the more extreme forms of the European Reform movement were avoided. In America Reform Judaism developed as a liberal religious system modern in outlook but drawing its inspiration and its values from the heritage of Israel.

7.18 Contrasting trends in institutional Christianity in the twentieth century

On 23 August 1948, at Amsterdam, the World Council of Churches came into existence. Many Christians consider this to be the most important religious event of the twentieth century in the Western world. The World Council is the organisational expression of a movement which had been going on since the Missionary Conference at Edinburgh of 1910, a movement to bring together the many churches and denominations of which Protestantism consisted. This plurality of Christian bodies was, it was argued, a scandal and an embarrassment, especially in missionary areas. The movement was strongly supported by evangelicals; the Student Christian Movement had an important part to play in preparing the way, and especially in bringing Anglicans into what was until then largely a movement for co-operation among evangelical Protestant bodies; at the time of its inception the World Council of Churches did not include the Orthodox Church of Russia or the Roman Catholic Church; the latter is still outside the Council. The movement has two main aspects; the first has itself been an important factor in its growth, namely the formation of national Councils of Churches, especially in the United States and Britain, for joint action over a wide area of Protestant church life within the national context; the second has been stimulated by the existence of the World Council, namely the movement towards organic church union. Schemes of union have been worked out for particular groups of churches, and some have been put into effect, notably in the Church of South India. This emphasis on *church* union is a sign of an increase in concern with ecclesiastical structures which now characterises many Protestant bodies which in their earlier and more vigorous periods of growth were much more consciously anti-ecclesiastical.

The first of these two main features, the 'conciliar' movement, is particularly characteristic of American Protestantism and seems to be connected with the emergence of what has been called 'common-core Protestantism', that is, the appearance of a widespread type of faith and practice whose ascendancy 'signifies the erosion of Protestant particularity' (Lee, 1960; 83). Just as it is possible to see the old denominational differences among Protestants as being to some extent the product of social class divisions (Niebuhr, 1929), so also in the later period it is possible to see the emergence of common-core Protestantism as, to some extent at least, the product of a growing cultural unity in American life (Lee, 1960).

It has been pointed out that the period in which Protestant bodies have been coming together in conciliar and unitive movements has also been the period of declining vigour in faith and practice among the older denominations who have been principally concerned. In Britain the main Nonconformist bodies have tended to approximate more and more to the 'church-type'; there has been, writes Erik Routley, (a British Congregationalist) 'a movement towards higher forms of church music, more frequent Communion, and more dogmatically-based Baptism' (Routley, 1962; 38). Bryan Wilson, a sociologist of religion, comments that this approximation to the Established Church may be explained 'in terms of the changing circumstances of Nonconformity and its increasing loss of social base in a society facing steady secularisation, in which religion is becoming compartmentalised, and in which, in becoming marginal to the dominant social concerns, its internal divisions lose meaning and relevance' (Wilson, 1966; 156). In America the declining vigour of faith and practice has been masked to some extent by the social conformity to religious practice in terms of church attendance, and what is almost the social obligation to belong to a religious organisation. To be a complete American, it has been said, includes religious commitment of some kind, usually in one of the three acceptable forms, Protestant, Catholic or Jew (Herberg, 1955). Nevertheless, a recent survey showed that although in the United States 57 per cent of the population are members of a Christian church, and 43 per cent regularly attend church every week, only 35 per cent could so much as name the four Gospels (Argyle, 1958; 35). Something has evidently happened to the Bible-centred Protestantism of earlier days. The basis on which the various bodies forming the World Council of Churches came together would appear to be an absolutely minimal doctrinal requirement, namely *acceptance of Jesus Christ as Saviour and God*, a far cry from the ancient Christian creeds, and from the Calvinistic doctrine of, for example, the Church of England's Thirty-Nine Articles. Much more than this would have been necessary as a doctrinal basis for some of the member churches to accept even fifty years ago.

Over against what seems to many Christian critics of the World Council of Churches its reductionist Christianity there has to be set the enhanced sense of belonging to a world community which membership involves for the member churches. Even in Britain, where the Established Church is still well entrenched in national institutions, there may often be strong disagreements between groups of thoughtful Christians and the policies of a virtually secular government. Through the World Council of Churches its members are aware of being able to express Christian opinions and sometimes even take action on matters of contemporary social or international concern – as Christians, rather than as subjects of a secular state.

The movement which began as predominantly Protestant has now drawn Eastern Orthodoxy more fully into its membership, and because of its obviously important nature has gained the sympathetic interest also of the Roman Catholic Church. This is no doubt partly due to a new theological climate, a greater openness and sympathy among Christians of different traditions; it may also be due to some extent to the increasing pressure of secularisation in modern life and the awareness by all these bodies that Christian ecclesiastical institutions have much in common and much to contend with in an age of secularism.

In contrast to the ecumenical trends in the major, old-established Christian bodies, there has also occurred a rapid growth of new Christian sectarian movements. These are usually offshoots from conventional Protestantism, although not always: the 'Spiritists' of Brazil are in origin Roman Catholics who have combined elements of orthodox

Catholic belief and practice with elements of tribal religion and some of the emotionalism of Pentecostal sects. It is this latter feature which, if anything, provides the common feature among these sects. In addition, they are almost always extremely conservative in their theology and literalist in their use of the Bible. With their high valuation of spiritual ardour and emotion goes their poor opinion of the conventional Protestant bodies in general, for their worldliness and lack of fervour, and of the World Council of Churches in particular for its reduced theology. Other characteristic features of these new sects are their predominantly lay character, in contrast to the organisation of the conventional denominations around a full-time professional ministry; the promise to new adherents of immediate 'spiritual' experience; an intimate group-fellowship into which newcomers are welcomed and quickly incorporated; and an intense seven-days-a-week devotion to the service of God.

Such new sects are widespread; it is said that they are now to be found on almost every continent. They are not so prominent in some areas, for example, in Britain; in countries south of the equator, however, they are said to outnumber conventional Protestants by four to one. In New York the students of Union Theological Seminary found in 1960 that in one of the most thickly populated districts of the city (East Harlem) there were fifty such sectarian groups, meeting in 'store-fronts' taken over for the purpose, while there was not a single Protestant church of the traditional type. This underlines two features of the newer sects: their appeal is largely to the working class, and often to that section of the population found in 'down-town' urban areas, namely poor-class immigrants (possibly from small towns or rural areas); second, they do not need to rely on permanent church buildings or provide formal services of worship; it is largely the quality of the group-life which constitutes their appeal.

Towards the other end of the social scale there is to be found another type of sect, although not nearly so extensive in its world-distribution as the working-class sect. This is the type of which the Theosophical Society provides a ready example: usually there are dozens of such upper-middle-class cults or sects in the big cities of the West, often the primary interest is in some aspect of oriental religion. Their members, too, will usually be persons who fail to find satisfaction in the traditional ecclesiastical bodies. In general there has been a steady growth of these during the twentieth century.

7.19 Religion and the new state of Israel

In Tel Aviv, on 14 May 1948, David Ben Gurion proclaimed the new Jewish state of Israel to have come into being. It was thereupon officially recognised by the United States and the U.S.S.R., and the next day was officially invaded by the neighbouring Arab countries. Of the many questions which arise out of the existence of the new state we are here concerned with what was the religious significance, if any, of this event. First, what place has religion had in the bringing into existence of the new Israel, and second, what place has religion in its continuing life. A brief review of the events leading up to the proclamation of 14 May 1948 will help to answer the first question.

For our purpose the story may be regarded as beginning in 1884 with the founding of the Zion Movement in Russia (*7.16*), (although an earlier beginning might be taken – for instance, the fall of Jerusalem in A.D. 70). Anti-Semitism, which Pinsker called 'Judeophobia' and regarded as an endemic European social disease (Epstein, 1959; 309), did not disappear with the emancipation of the Jews in the various European countries in which they were found. The reason for this may well be that from time to time men need a scapegoat for the economic and political ills of society, and the Jews, because they often constitute an easily identifiable and compact minority, provide the most convenient scapegoat, especially as there is always the lurking idea in men's minds that Jews are somehow 'foreign'. (It is conveniently forgotten that many of the rest of the population, Anglo-Saxons, Scots, Irish, etc., are equally 'foreign' to the countries where they now live.) Jewish agricultural settlements were founded in Palestine in the 1880s, and from time to time the influx of immigrant Jewish settlers received a boost from some new wave of anti-Semitism, such as that in France which followed the Dreyfus Affair of 1891. It was this, occurring in so otherwise 'enlightened' a country as France, that persuaded a visiting Viennese Jewish journalist Theodor Herzl (1860–1904) that the only solution to Gentile attitudes to the Jews was the setting up once again of a Jewish state, a view argued in his book *The Jewish State* (1896). In 1897 a Zionist Congress was held in Basle, which resulted in the formal declaration of policy: 'Zionism aims to establish a publicly and loyally assured home for the Jewish people in Palestine'. Not all Jews were in agreement with this policy. It was opposed on religious grounds, namely that the return of the Jews to the Holy Land would follow the appearance of the Messiah, and therefore could not and should not be anticipated. Zionists replied that the Jewish state was the form in which Messianic hopes should now be understood. Others, such as the philosopher Herman Cohen (1842–1918), maintained that the Messianic destiny of the Jewish people was to be fulfilled by their presence within various national states as an element working for the unity of all mankind. However, a great stimulus to the Zionist movement came through the initiative of Chaim Weizmann (1874–1952), who created a Jewish National Fund for the purchase of land in Palestine, and whose advocacy of a Jewish national home in Palestine persuaded the British government through its foreign secretary, Arthur Balfour, in 1917, to declare in favour of such a policy. Its implementation was not easy, however, and was strongly resisted by various interests, especially by the Arabs. Then came the tragedy of the Jewish people in Nazi Germany, where they were dispossessed, dishonoured, and put to death (six million in number, of whom many were children under fourteen) for no other crime than that of being Jewish.

After the Second World War the work of rescuing Jews from all over Europe, many of whom were separated from their families, and of making possible their escape from Europe and immigration into Palestine was carried on by the Mossad, a Jewish organisation, until as we have seen, in 1948 the Jewish state was proclaimed. There are now 12 million Jews in the world, of whom 5½ million are in the United States, about 2 million in the U.S.S.R. and a further 2 million in Israel, which thus comprises one of the three largest groups of Jews in the world.

It will be seen, therefore, that the factors which brought the new Jewish state into being and which produced a flow of immigrants into it were not primarily religious. Israel is not, as Pakistan is, a state whose constitution is based on religious principles. There is no 'state religion'; religious freedom is guaranteed to all Israel's citizens (for these include Arabs), and the form of government is democratic. Widespread indifference to religious observances among its Jewish citizens has led some observers to describe Israel not only as secular, in the sense that there is no state religion, but also as 'secularised' in the sense that religious beliefs and observances play very little part in the life of its people. Others are inclined to the view that in Israel the Jewish religious tradition is being rediscovered and reformulated. Isidore Epstein points to the extent of such religious observance as the use of Saturday as a national day of rest, when government offices, public transport, shops, and cinemas all cease to function, and the adherence to Jewish dietary laws in all public institutions (Army, police, hospitals, etc.) as evidence that the Jewish way of life is influencing the character of the state (Epstein, 1959; 319). Religious schools and places of higher learning have been set up, and rabbis and Jewish scholars from various parts of the world are 'all contributing to the enrichment of spiritual life and to the fostering of religious knowledge throughout the length and breadth of the country'. Some observers see a significance in the richness of the many traditions of Judaism which the nation's life now embraces: the Yemenite Jews, with their tradition reminiscent of the Mishna; North African Jews with the liberalism inherited from the religious tolerance of the great days of Islamic Spain; Kabbalists, Talmudists, Hasidim – all are there (Chouraqui, 1962; 135f.). Others consider that the Judaism of the new state is still strongly influenced by the traditions of the ghetto, and that its religion has yet to find expression in ways that are completely relevant to the conditions of the modern world (Parkes, 1964; 234). What is generally agreed among various observers is that the Jews of Israel are rediscovering their own scriptural traditions; there is a fascination with the Bible *as history*, which may well become the basis for a new unity among men of the different religious traditions represented in Israel and the Middle East: Christian and Muslim as well as Jewish.

7.2 HINDUISM IN THE MODERN PERIOD, 1800 TO THE PRESENT

7.20 Hinduism at the end of the eighteenth century

The modern period, from the beginning of British rule in India, has been a time of important developments in the history of Hinduism. In 1805, when the British had become the dominant power in India, the reforms and adaptations which Hindu religion and society were to undergo in response to Western influences had still scarcely begun. At the end of the eighteenth century, Hindu society was in the position of having successfully learnt to adjust to the presence of a large alien religious community, that of the Muslims. Mughal power had waxed and waned; Islam had made an indelible impression on Indian culture; but Hinduism remained the dominant religious tradition. The Hindu sponge may have failed in the case of Islam to absorb the alien element; on the other hand Islam had failed to win all India, and Hinduism remained firmly entrenched as the religion of the masses throughout the greater part of the subcontinent; it had made some concessions during the Mughal period to monotheistic ideas; but even these were made from within Hinduism's own treasury of beliefs, which included theism, along with polytheism and atheism. The religious practices and social institutions of Hinduism went on as before, largely unaffected by the Islamic presence.

A new and more serious challenge to the Hindu view of life was, however, about to be felt. It came not from European religion, which had made no very great impression on Hindu India, but from English education and the entry which this provided into European thought. But even earlier than the growth of English education, from the second quarter of the nineteenth century onwards, was the effect upon Indians, especially in the areas around Calcutta and Bombay, of contact with English government, methods, and ideas. This process, which went on throughout the nineteenth century, produced three kinds of response from Hindu India.

The earliest response, apparent in the 1820s and 1830s, was almost complete surrender to the values of European liberalism and rationalism by a small minority of Hindus in those parts of India where British influence was strongest, and notably in Bengal. The most characteristic of the Hindus who reacted in this way was Rāja Rām Mohan Roy.

7.21 Rām Mohan Roy: Hindu unitarianism

Rām Mohan Roy (1772–1833) is sometimes described as the inaugurator of the modern age, or the father of modern India, but these are misleading descriptions. A native of Bengal, the gifted son of Hindu parents, he studied Persian and Arabic at Patna, and then Sanskrit. In the service of the East India Company he reached the highest rank possible for an Indian; in 1814, at the age of forty-two, he was able to retire from government service and, living on his private income, to devote himself to various religious and social enterprises. He had a large part in the founding in 1822 of the Hindu College in Calcutta, a secular college where Bengalis could receive English education. So successful was this institution in imbuing its pupils with European liberal ideas that some young Hindus of Bengal began behaving in a blatantly un-Hindu manner in order to shock their conservative elders. Renouncing the whole system of Hinduism they declared themselves free seekers after truth. Rām Mohan Roy's religious position was very close to the unitarianism of some of his English friends. So persuasive an advocate was he that in a discussion with a Presbyterian missionary on the Christian doctrine of the Trinity he won the latter over to unitarian views. In 1827 he founded the British India Unitarian Association, later the Brāhma Samāj, or 'Spiritual Association'. In his campaigning for social reform he was a prominent advocate of the abolition of satī (the voluntary immolation of Hindu widows). He believed very strongly in the virtues of British rule, and it is for this reason that he is unlike most of the Westernised Hindus of the latter part of the nineteenth century who took part in the struggle for swaraj or independence. But it has to be remembered that he died in 1833 (in Bristol, on a visit to England), twenty-four years before the outbreak of the Mutiny of 1857; it was only after the Mutiny that British rule really became imperialistic. His religious attitude, and that of the Brāhma Samāj movement which he founded, consisted of a spiritual monism of the kind found in the Upaniṣads, influenced also to some extent in Rām Mohan Roy's case by the Islamic doctrine of the unity of God and by the unitarian views of some of his Christian friends. He was a firm opponent of the polytheism of popular Hindu practice, and especially opposed to the Hindu use of idols. It was an intellectualised religion, austere and cultless, which had much in common with eighteenth-century European deism.

7.22 Europeanised Hinduism: later developments

This early response of some Hindus to European thought and practice – iconoclastic, critical of authority and of Hindu social tradition – was continued in the Brāhma Samāj movement after Rām Mohan Roy's death.

The Brāhma Samāj was never, however, in any sense a mass movement. It was an association of those who had come under the influence of the liberal and individualistic outlook of early nineteenth-century Europe. V. P. Varma evaluates it thus: 'It was a deeply individualistic protest and signified the rise of individual reason, heart and conscience against what it considered degrading and barbarising customs' (Varma, 1964; 39). The history of the movement is best told therefore in the history of the ideas and attitudes of some of its outstanding individual members, and of these the two most representative are generally taken to be Debendranath Thakur (Tagore) and Keshab Chandra Sen.

Debendranath Thakur (1817–1905) represented those who were more inclined to emphasise the value of the Upanisads as a source of mystical religious teaching. Debendranath rejected the polytheism and ceremonial ritual of the Vedas; he was critical also of the idea of the empirical world as sheer māya, or illusion; his thought had a great affinity with the theology of Rāmānuja (*6.14*). He was opposed to the rigours of the caste system, but on the other hand he sought to give the Brāhma Samāj movement a more definitely Indian basis, and to eliminate Christian influences.

Keshab Chandra Sen (1838–84) represented a different tendency, one which sought to reconcile indigenous Indian ideas with Christian teaching, and to do this more deliberately and consciously than Rām Mohan Roy had done. He was the son of a very Westernised Bengali family, and studied at the Hindu College of Calcutta. In 1866, when he was twenty-eight, he withdrew from the Calcutta Brāhma Samāj and inaugurated a movement which later (in 1880) became known as the Nava Vidhana or New Dispensation. The new movement was characterised by a religious eclecticism, expressed in the anthology of scriptures of various traditions – Christian, Zoroastrian and Islamic, as well as Hindu, which Keshab put together under the name of *Śloka-saṃgraha* (compendium of verses), published in 1866. He even embodied in the ceremonies of the new movement a form of baptism and a communion service based on Christian models. On the other hand he was not opposed to rituals involving the use of idols. Half his heart, he said, was in sympathy with Europe, and the other half with Asia. The movement which he led was limited to an educated and Western-educated minority, and its importance lay chiefly in liberalising the attitudes of Hindu intellectuals to caste, the social position of women, child-marriages, temperance and similar matters. In 1875, nine years before his death, he came under the influence of Rāmakrishna, and moved away from Christianity in the direction of a more positively

Vedāntist position. In protest against the use of idolatrous rituals, and against the autocratic nature of Keshab's leadership another group broke away from his movement in 1878 and formed the Sādhāran (General) Brāhma Samāj upon a more equalitarian and democratic basis. The name Nava Vidhana which Keshab gave to his movement in 1880 indicated his intention to replace the Christian church with this Indianised facsimile, with its own revelation, apostolic order, missionaries and doctrines of sin and salvation.

7.23 Reformed Hinduism: the Ārya Samāj

A few years before the events just mentioned were taking place in Bengal, another new movement had emerged on the other side of India, in the area around Bombay. This was the Ārya Samāj, formed in 1875 by Dayānanda Saraswati (1824–83). Its name indicates the intention of the movement: to work for the restoration of Aryan Vedic religion (*1.33–1.35*), and to reject all the later developments of post-Vedic Hinduism. The earlier response of educated and thoughtful Hindus to European influence, which had been one of admiration and wholehearted acceptance, was giving way to something rather different. It was not necessary to Europeanise Hindu religion and culture, it was now being recognised; Hinduism might stand in need of reform, but the inspiration for such reform could be found in an appeal to the Vedic tradition. This was the attitude adopted by Dayānanda, the son of a brāhman family of Gujerat. Idol-worship, untouchability, child-marriage and other corrupt features of Hinduism were not to be found in the Vedas, he argued. He claimed also that the study of the Vedas should be made open to all, and not to brāhmans only. For reasons such as these he was later known by his followers as 'the Luther of India'. The Ārya Samāj which he founded continued after his death to provide a channel for those Indians who were concerned for the reform of Hinduism without resort to foreign ideas or models. Its strength was in the west of India and the Punjab, but even so its members were but a small minority even of educated Hindus. The influence of the Ārya Samāj, however, was important beyond its numerical size; its reassertion of India's own Vedic heritage coincided with growing Hindu dislike and distrust of British imperial rule in the last quarter of the nineteenth century, and led to the militant Hinduism associated with the name of B. G. Tilak (*7.25*).

7.24　Hindu universalism: Rāmakrishna and Vivekānanda

Gradually Hinduism was recovering from its initial exposure to European thought, an exposure which had been the more severe in that the alien influence had come in a subtle, secular form, rather than in the recognisable and resistible form of a closed system of belief and practice such as Islam or Christianity. In the latter half of the nineteenth century the pressure of Western ways of thought was still as strong as, if not stronger than, before but now Hindus were recovering their composure and were learning how to meet subtle challenge with even subtler weapons from their own armoury. The part played by Christian missions in this process is capable of more than one interpretation. In general, the policy of the missions was to point out the shortcomings of Hinduism and the superiority of Christianity. With the enlargement of British governmental control there went at first a fear among both Hindus and Muslims of religious discrimination against their faiths. This was set at rest by Queen Victoria's proclamation on the subject (*7.15*), but the long-term effect of Christian propaganda, proceeding from an ever enlarging missionary force, was to develop a Hindu resistance to Christian ideas once the first wounding effects of Christian criticism had been absorbed. Regained Hindu confidence found expression in the Rāmakrishna Mission, founded in 1897. Rāmakrishna (1834–86) was in every sense the representative Hindu holy man: a brāhman of Bengal, schooled only in Bengali; with an ardent devotional and mystical attachment to the mother-goddess Kālī, at whose temple near Calcutta he served as a priest; deeply influenced by the monism of Shankara; given to asceticism and meditation. What really places him in the India of the nineteenth century is his awareness of other, non-Hindu, non-Indian faiths, notably Christianity, and also Islam. It was his attitude towards these that became, after his death in 1886, one of the principal features of the movement founded in 1897 by one of his most able and accomplished followers, Vivekānanda. Rāmakrishna's attitude was, in brief, the Hindu affirmation that all the many forms of faith in God are different paths to the same goal. This may be called universalism, but it is *Hindu* universalism, for it proceeds from characteristically Hindu assumptions about the underlying unity of the manifold, and the relative nature of all formulated creeds. It is an attitude which replies to Christian and Islamic exclusiveness by affirming the adequacy of Hinduism – on the grounds of its catholicity. It was this message which Vivekānanda carried to the Parliament of Religions which met in Chicago in 1893, and which he there proclaimed with impressive eloquence.

The Rāmakrishna Mission, with what has been called its 'religion of Mysticism and Charity' (Rādhakrishnan, 1941) became the visible embodiment of a new, awakened Hinduism – awakened by Christianity and by government agencies to social concern for the sick and the needy especially, but awakened also to the need for a religion of reconciliation, a religion of tolerance and charity. Its dispensaries and welfare centres throughout India and the neighbouring lands express the first; its well-stocked public libraries and lecture halls exist to encourage the second; the name of its journal published in Calcutta, *Prabuddha Bhārata* (Awakened India), indicates the Mission's continuing overall purpose.

7.25 Militant Hinduism: B. G. Tilak

The more aggressive aspect of Hindu India's awakening is to be seen in the activities of Bal Gangadhar Tilak (1856–1920). To adapt a phrase of the apostle Paul, Tilak may be described as 'a Hindu of the Hindus'; the aim of all his activities was that Hindus in every part of India should be united 'into a mighty Hindu nation'. Although he proclaimed the eternal, unchanging nature of Hindu religion (the term 'sanatana dharma', he said, 'shows that our religion is very old – as old as the history of the human race itself'), he also instituted and organised two new religious festivals; one in honour of the Hindu god Ganesh, and the other in honour of the Hindu Maratha hero and opponent of Mughal rule, Shivaji. The Ganesh festival was inaugurated by Tilak so that it was a direct imitation of the Muslim festival of Muharram. To the Muslim historian (as to Muslims generally) 'the object was to make it pointedly offensive to the Muslims and to leave no doubt in the mind of the Hindus that the aim ... was to prepare them for a struggle against the Muslims' (Qureshi, 1962; 250). The extolling of a Hindu who had fought fiercely against Muslim rule also indicates clearly enough what kind of Hinduism was here finding expression; a variety rather different from the benevolent universalism of Rāmakrishna, but one which had a wide appeal and following, especially in Tilak's native

Mahārāshtra and in Bengal. Militancy was a Hindu virtue in Tilak's view; accused of fanning hatred against non-Hindus, and of being implicated in assassination plots, he was imprisoned twice by the British. The second of these periods was spent in the jail at Mandalay in Burma, where he wrote a long commentary on the Hindu scripture which appealed to him most – the Bhagavad-Gītā. His interpretation of it emphasised the necessity for political action in the name of religion, and that in such a cause the most violent action was fully justifiable. That he may justly be called a Hindu of the Hindus is evident from the title by which he was, and still is, popularly known by his co-religionists: Lokamanya (Honoured by the People).

7.26 *Modern Hindu hero-worship*

There is more than one India, and there were many places where far from the excitement and turbulence stirred up by Tilak and his followers Hindu village life continued almost unchanged throughout the period of British rule. In such places the villagers' appreciation of the benefits of such rule sometimes took a very characteristically Hindu form: the deification of the officials of the Rāj. Thus, Tilman Henckel, an Englishman who was district officer of Jessore in Bengal, and whose administration of the district was notably just and fair, was subsequently honoured as a god by a class of poor salt-manufacturers who had previously been much oppressed; an image of Henckel was made, which these people then worshipped (O'Malley, 1935; 171). A British officer in the Punjab, John Nicholson, was venerated by his Indian troops even during his lifetime; in spite of the flogging with which Nicholson punished such action his sepoys would sometimes fall down and prostrate themselves before him in worship or prayer. After his death some of them formed a sect known as the 'Nikalsenis'. Another officer, Colonel William Wallace, who died in 1809 and was buried in the cantonment at Sirur, in the Poona district, is revered as a holy man; 'all Hindus of Sirur and its neighbourhood, except Brahmans and Marwaris, worship at the tomb' wrote L. S. O'Malley in 1935, 'while at harvest time the villagers bring first-fruits of the grain as food for his spirit' (see further, O'Malley, 1935; 176). Attempted interference with these practices by an American missionary was promptly followed by his death from cholera, 'which, of course, greatly enhanced Wallace's posthumous reputation'. Missionaries themselves, however, have also on numerous occasions been deified and worshipped. Queen Victoria, whom most of her Indian subjects had never seen, was regarded by many of them with the greatest veneration. 'Even during her lifetime she received a kind of apotheosis. Hindu women are known to have prayed to her for sons' (O'Malley, 1941; 86).

Here then was another aspect of the British impact on India, not only the impression made by British power from the decisive year of 1857 onwards, but also the effect upon unsophisticated Indians of outstanding or unusual personalities, an effect which showed itself in hero-worship. This tells us as much or more about Hindu villagers and sepoys as it does about the British; it is an interesting piece of modern evidence of the tendency which unsophisticated people have to deify the great. It also helps us to understand the basis of Mahātma Gandhi's wide popularity with the masses, and therefore the tremendous influence he was able to exert.

7.27 Neo-Hinduism: M. K. Gandhi

To the story of modern Hinduism, and the gradual emergence of that curious blend of reform, adaptation, reappraisal and aggressive re-assertion which has come to be called neo-Hinduism, belong a number of other names. Included among them are those of M. G. Ranade (1842–1901) and G. K. Gokhale (1866–1915), partners in religious and social reform; B. C. Chatterjee (1838–98), who into the cult of the mother-goddess introduced the concept of the divine Motherland, India; Aurobindo Ghose (1872–1950), mystic and Hindu nationalist; and Rabindranath Thakur (Tagore) (1861–1941), the youngest but one of Debendranath Thakur's fifteen children, poet, playwright, Nobel Prizewinner for literature, whose steady conviction it was that from Asia, the cradle of the world's great religions, must come mankind's spiritual renewal. But all of these represented, or appealed to, special sectors of Hindu society; none of them is quite so fully the representative of neo-Hinduism as M. K. Gandhi.

Known by Indians as Mahātma (Mahā, great; ātman, soul), Mohendas Karamchand Gandhi (1869–1948) had earlier in life been a student in London for three years, a barrister in South Africa for more than twenty, and a newspaper editor. He returned to India in 1915 at a time when Tilak's policy of violent nationalism was still one of the strongest influences in all-India Hinduism. Gandhi was a man of different spirit. He too regarded the Bhagavad-Gītā as one of the great sources of religious ideals and values, but his interpretation of it, unlike Tilak's, was strongly influenced by the New Testament, by Tolstoi, and by Ruskin. Gandhi, on his return to India, adopted peasant dress and a very simple mode of life. In this way he illustrated his own message: that India had been corrupted by her contact with Western materialistic civilisation, and must return to simplicity of life and to spiritual values. He believed that the encouragement of India's village industries, especially the hand-spinning of cotton cloth, was a way by which India could escape the evils of industrialisation, and did all in his power to realise his plan. He devoted himself also to the cause of the untouchables, those who were relegated by Hindu caste society to the very lowest place, where their status was barely that of human beings. Among his plans for combating peasant poverty was the prohibition of liquor. Above all, the method which Hindus should use in their struggle for freedom from foreign rule must be, he insisted, non-violence. From the time of Tilak's death in 1920, Gandhi became the undisputed moral leader of Hindu India; not only of the intellectuals, or of the nationalists, or of the new middle class, or of the peasants, but of all of these. In popular estimation he was a saint, at least: to the untouchables and the peasants, an incarnation of God, come to put right the evils of the world; he was, to them, another illustration of the principle announced in the Bhagavad-Gītā by the Lord Krishna: 'As often as virtue declines or vice increases I create myself anew, and I appear again from age to age for the preservation of the just, the destruction of the wicked, and the establishment of virtue.'

When independence came to India in 1947, however, it was to a land partitioned into the Republics of India and of Pakistan (7.39). The communal violence between Hindus and Muslims which accompanied partition is a complex chapter in the modern political history of Asia: to Gandhi it was simply a bitter grief and a denial of a great deal that he had sought to establish. He fasted, as he had done many times before during the struggle for independence; this time in an effort to bring the two sides to their senses and end the violence. He had tried to teach India a different method from that advocated by Tilak; but Hindu and Muslim communalism were forces too strong to be tamed even by a Gandhi. From Mahārāshtra, the same area of India as both Tilak and

Gandhi, came the fanatical Hindu nationalist who, opposed to Gandhi's policy of conciliation towards Muslims, shot the Mahātma dead at the close of his open-air prayer meeting on 30 January 1948.

7.28 Hinduism in the new India

In many respects it is a new India which has come into being since 1947: geographically depleted by the loss of those areas in the north-west and the north-east which have become Pakistan; constitutionally democratic and secular; in theory, economically and politically free to develop as an independent modern state – with all the complicated relationships with other world powers in which that involves her. In this new India Hinduism too is undergoing changes which are to some extent a continuation of trends that were already present in the period of British rule, and to some extent the result of the new situation.

Modern India is officially a secular state. This means that no one religion has a place of privilege, but that all the religious traditions now found in India are accorded respect: every religious denomination has freedom to practise and to propagate, and there is no discrimination among citizens on religious grounds. Since Hindus form an over-whelming majority of the population, there are some among them who hold that Hinduism should at least be given preferential treatment; the more extreme wing, represented by the political parties Rashtriya Swayamsevak Sangh (RSS), and the Hindu Mahāsabha, are opposed to the present separation of the Indian state from Hindu religion. Other Hindu intellectuals are opposed to the principle of a secular state on grounds of private and public morality. Representative of this point of view, which has behind it the strength of Hindu tradition, is Professor P. Sankara Narayan of the University of Madras, who in 1957 expressed the classical Hindu view as follows:

> In the last analysis, religion alone can answer the question, Why should I be moral? The justification of morality is to be sought in the sphere of religion and this holds good both in the private sector of the individual and in the public sector of the State. It is this idea that is emphasised by the Hindu view of the character of a state, that not the least of its duties is *dharma samstthapana*, the establishment of the reign of religion in the hearts of its subjects. Loud and frequent announcements of the 'secular' nature of the State are likely to sap the springs of morality in religion. It

is neither proper nor expedient for a State to forswear its association with religion and parade its purely 'secular' character.

He sees the Hindu spirit of tolerance as the answer to the problem of assuring equal rights for different religious traditions within a single state:

> Necessary as it doubtless is to be impartial to all religions, it ought not to be beyond human capacity to devise a scheme by which the fundamentals of religion have a determining place in the secular administration. Else, spiritual values will be starved to their ultimate annulment in the hearts and minds of men. In this context the Hindu idea of identity in difference, of manifold paths to the same goal is a useful guide in approaching this not unsolvable, though knotty problem. (Devanandan and Thomas, 1957; 72–4)

Another major criticism of the secular constitution of modern India comes from the extreme Hindu orthodoxy associated with the political right wing, mentioned above. Briefly, this consists of opposition to the secular state's policy with regard to caste. The view of the extreme Hindu orthodoxy is that the caste system is an essential part of Hindu religion, and that in seeking to impose a social pattern in which caste is disregarded, the secular state strikes at the root of Hindu religion. Against this view, and in support of the present policy is the whole tradition of Hindu reformers from Rām Mohan Roy (7.21) to Mahātma Gandhi (7.27), whose view was that the rigid structure of caste and sub-caste was not a necessary feature of Hindu religion. This view has recently found vigorous expression in the writings of K. M. Panikkar. Constantly reiterated, his argument is that 'religion has but little to do with the social institutions of the Hindus, and a man can remain a Hindu even if he repudiates its social institutions. Many sects of Hinduism actually so repudiate them and are still considered Hindu, which is clear enough evidence that these institutions are unrelated to religion' (Panikkar, 1961; 49).

Meanwhile secular forces of the kind that are common to all developing societies in a technological age are at work to undermine the barriers of caste and sub-caste. Life in the cities and in the growing industrialised areas makes the observance of caste distinction difficult, if not virtually impossible. Even in rural areas these same forces are at work. A survey of village life in a traditionally strong Hindu area – Tanjore, in South India – leads an American anthropologist Kathleen

Gough to conclude that the social and economic structure of caste is
breaking down even there:

> It is clear that, in general, the social structure of the Tanjore village is
> changing from a relatively closed, stationary system, with a feudal
> economy and co-operation between ranked castes in ways ordained by
> religious law, to a relatively 'open' changing system, governed by
> secular law, with an expanding capitalist economy and competition
> between castes which is sometimes reinforced and sometimes obscured
> by the new struggle between economic classes. (Marriott, 1955; 52)

If the caste system has been a blot on the name of Hindu religion, as
the reformers have insisted, then what is happening today in the
operation of these 'secular' forces may be seen as a purifying and a
liberation of religion, enabling it to express more clearly its essential
moral and spiritual insights.

Meanwhile, as Hindu religion seeks to adapt itself to the increasingly
urban conditions which are developing in many parts of India, new
movements and patterns of religious association are emerging which
may have great potential for the future of Hinduism. Among the most
notable of these are the congregational, devotional meetings in private
houses, known as bhajans (a word cognate with Bhagavad, and bhakti)
(*3.34*). Milton Singer has described the recent growth in popularity of
these devotional meetings in the area of Madras City (Singer, 1963).
The devotional meetings are true to the bhakti tradition in their
indifference to caste and sect distinctions, and in providing a means of
cultivating and strengthening a devotional religious attitude. 'Each local
bhajan group', writes Singer, 'usually begins with a family household',
but 'it quickly expands to include neighbours and friends from office
and shop who are not kin and who may even come from a different
caste, sect or linguistic region.' There are various levels of association.
'The weekly bhajan remains essentially a neighbourhood group; the
monthly bhajan overflows neighbourhood lines, and the annual bhajan
festival draws crowds from all parts of the city' (Singer, 1963; 213). He
considers the question whether or not these are likely to become the
basis of a new casteless and sectless ecumenical form of Hinduism, and
concludes that this is unlikely, since sectarian forms are already
beginning to appear among them; but he adds that to many Hindus the
bhajans constitute 'the timely instrument of an integrative and unifying
religious movement'.

7.29 Hinduism outside India

Up to the present time Hinduism can hardly be called a missionary religion, that is, in the Western sense of a proselytising faith. Hindus are found outside Indian territory: notably in parts of South-East Asia and East Africa, but this is because they or their forebears have settled in those regions as immigrants and have continued to regard themselves as Hindus, and to practise their ancestral rituals. But broadly speaking Hinduism does not seek to make converts to the Hindu community outside the motherland. To a large extent this has been because in the past to be a Hindu has meant necessarily to be integrated into Hindu society. As a religious system Hinduism may be seen as a Great Tradition which has developed over a long period of time on the basis of the many local Little Traditions of village India, and therefore depends for its life on the nourishment which it derives, as it were, from the soil of India. There has to be some connection with the soil of India, even though, as in the case of immigrant communities in other lands, it is an hereditary link. The outward forms of Hinduism, 'the worship in temples, the great festivals, the outward symbols of sects and groups, the mutts, monasteries and ashrams', these, says Panikkar, 'are the things which differentiate Hinduism from all other religions' (Panikkar, 1961; 125). Without these it would no longer be Hinduism.

Nevertheless, there are forms in which Indians are seeking to convey to the Western world what some of them hold to be the unique and vitally important contribution which Hindu religion can and should make to world society. There is, of course, the Western vogue for yogic exercises, but these are usually carried out by Westerners simply as a form of physical or mental culture, and are not necessarily related to the school of religious philosophy which gives yoga its religious aspect in India. If there is one form of Hinduism which is to be regarded as being for export to the West, it is Vedānta (4.21). This has in fact its missionaries, notably the swāmis of the Rāmakrishna Mission who are to be found in some of the larger cities of the Western world, and here and there a few pundits of the Ārya Samāj. Beyond these identifiable forms of Hindu influence on the West – which are still only barely marginal – there is, however, the indirect influence which is exerted through Hindu literature, both through English and other European translations of Hindu religious classics, and also through the writings of outstanding modern authors: Indian, such as Sir S. Radhakrishnan, Aurobindo Ghose, and Western interpreters of Vedānta, such as Gerald Heard, Christopher Isherwood and Aldous Huxley. In general this influence may be said to be one which supports a view of life which sees behind the manifold and transient forms of empirical existence a reality that is unchanging, blissful and eternal.

7.3 ISLAM IN THE MODERN PERIOD, 1707 TO THE PRESENT

7.30 Islamic reform: the setting

A.D. 1707 was the year of the death of Aurangzeb the Mughal emperor at the age of ninety. Aurangzeb, the last really great name among the Muslim rulers of India, who by his puritan legislation had tried to check the moral decline of Islamic society in India, was followed by a succession of corrupt and ineffective rulers until, in 1858, the emperor Bahadur Shah was deposed by the British and exiled to Rangoon, where he died in poverty. The corruption of Islam in India, which was evident in Aurangzeb's time, and which continued into the eighteenth century, was eventually during that century challenged by movements of revival from within Indian Islam. They were contemporaneous with similar movements of revival elsewhere in the Muslim world – in Central Arabia and in the Yemen. In the nineteenth century came the modernist reform movement in Egypt associated with the name of Muhammad Abduh and his Syrian pupil Rashid Rida, a movement which had a strong influence upon Islam in South Asia, especially in Indonesia.

These various movements for the reform of Islam which occurred during the eighteenth and nineteenth centuries have two outstanding common features: one is the rejection of the accretions which Islam had suffered during its medieval period, and the other is the reformulation of Islamic belief and practice in terms of modern thought and civilisation. A further feature which occurs in many although not all of these movements is the political aim, that of the restoration of Muslim government. The background to all this is European colonial expansion in Asia and the Middle East during these two centuries. This provided the occasion, the stimulant, or possibly the irritant; but the Islamic reform movements of this period are not *simply* due to the impact of the West; they are equally the result of resources provided from within Islam itself.

The revival of Islam in India, which began in the dark days of the mid-eighteenth century when the Muslim empire was rapidly disintegrating and when faithful Muslims were, in the words of Fazlur Rahman, 'almost literally left in a dismal wilderness, not knowing whither to turn', continued into the nineteenth and twentieth centuries and may perhaps be seen as having as one of its results the emergence of the modern state of Pakistan in 1947.

7.31 Early reform movements in India and Arabia

Five years before the emperor Aurangzeb died, there was born one who became known as the leader of Muslim reform in India, Wali Allah of Delhi (A.D. 1702–62). Shah Wali Allah was a Sufi thinker, writer and teacher. He was responsible for a reformulation of Islam on a broader basis than that of the traditional theology. In his system 'a broad, humanistic sociological base is overlain by a doctrine of social and economic justice in Islamic terms and crowned by a Sufi world-view' (Rahman, 1967; 203). He was concerned also to purify Indian Islam of the many alien beliefs and practices which it had acquired from its Indian environment. The influence of his work was widely felt through his writings and through his pupils. His hope for Indian Islam was the restoration of Muslim government, and to this end he urged his views on leading Muslim rulers and soldiers. In a period of depression for Muslims in India it was Wali Allah who gave them a vision of a renewed and reinvigorated Islam. A modern Pakistani historian, Professor S. M. Ikram, considers that 'more than anyone else he is responsible for the religious regeneration of Indian Islam' (Ikram, 1964; 262). The movement which he began was continued after his death by his sons and his disciples.

The other notable reform movement of the eighteenth century was that which owed its inspiration to al-Wahhab of Arabia (1703–92). In early manhood al-Wahhab travelled in Iraq and Persia, and after returning to Arabia at about the age of forty he began, by preaching and writing, to advocate a purified Islam. In a treatise entitled *The*

Book of Unity he attacked many features of popular Islamic religion in the Middle East, such as worship by Muslims at the tombs of saints, belief in the powers of saints, Muslims' calling upon the Prophet and the saints to make intercession for them, and various other forms of what he held to be superstitious practice. With this went an attack upon moral laxity, and upon the accretions to Islamic belief for which the Sufis and the philosophical and theological schools had, in his view, been responsible. The movement which he began was characterised by its rejection of all Muslim medieval authorities and tradition, and appealed exclusively to the authority of the Qur'an and the Sunna; all else was held to be superfluous. As a result of the opposition of some of his own kinsmen al-Wahhab moved to eastern Arabia, and there his views found acceptance by the local chief, ibn Sa'ud. It was this which gave reality to his programme of reform, and enabled the Wahhabi movement to bring the holy cities of Mecca and Medina within its field of influence. The present Saudi Arabian dynasty is descended from this early convert of al-Wahhab's. This movement, too, was carried on by his disciples after the death of its leader, and it continued to be of some influence in Arabia. It was by no means generally accepted by Arab Muslims, and in fact was strongly opposed by those whose moral laxity it challenged, and by those who did not accept its puritanical attitude to the popular cults. Thus, the Wahhabis were driven out of Mecca about the year 1813. Nevertheless the challenge of the Wahhabi movement to moral corruption within Islam, and its emphasis upon the importance of the moral element in Muslim life and thought, had a lasting effect, in that this became an almost universal feature of subsequent reform movements, both in Arabia and elsewhere in the Muslim world.

7.32 Some religious issues leading to the events of 1857

Old prejudices die hard, and in some British ears the words 'Indian Mutiny' may still suggest the idea that Muslims are a stubborn, sullen, rebellious people dominated by irrational superstitions. Just how arbitrary in the case of Islam is the line which Westerners like to draw between religion and politics may be seen very well in the case of the Indian Muslims' situation in the mid-nineteenth century. It is only by recognition of this dual aspect of Islam, the political and the religious, which we have had occasion to note several times already, that one can make sense of Indian Muslim history, and of the kind of reform movements which emerged in the nineteenth century.

From the beginning of the century Mughal power continued to decline. The capture of Delhi by the British in 1803 emphasised how low Muslim power had sunk. In the same year Wali Allah's son Abd'al Aziz (1746–1824) issued a declaration announcing that India was no longer dar-al-Islam, that is Islamic territory; it had become dar-al-harb, alien territory, and must therefore be regained so that an Islamic society could once again be set up. One of the notable achievements of Wali Allah's sons was their translation of the Qur'an into idiomatic Urdu, so that it might be read and understood by the Muslim rank and file. The interlinear method of translation which they adopted, with one line in Arabic followed by its translation into Urdu, had the effect of enabling the ordinary Indian Muslim to gain some familiarity with the Arabic original of his holy book.

Another religious reform movement parallel to that which owed its inspiration to Wali Allah in north-western India was one which emerged in East Bengal from about 1820 onwards. This was inaugurated by Sharīat Allah, a Bengali Muslim who returned in that year from pilgrimage to Mecca, where he had studied for some years under famous and learned Muslim theologians. In East Bengal he built up a following from among the lowest classes of Muslims, and the community thus formed adopted certain well-defined objectives. First, they pledged themselves to perform regularly and faithfully the religious duties required of them as Muslims. These duties are known as the farā-id, so the group became known as the farāidīs. There was also the negative aim, of renouncing various practices which had come to be adopted by East Bengali Muslims under the strong influence of the Hindu environment, practices which were alien to Islam, especially certain celebrations and festivities. The movement aimed at purifying Islam not only from Hindu but also from Sufi practices and influence. It included also certain socio-economic reforms among its objectives; these came from the conviction that inequality of wealth was contrary to the spirit of Islam. Finally, it had the aim of restoring Muslim political power in Bengal; as in north-west India, so here also it was declared that the land in which these Muslims lived had, under the British, reverted to the status of dar-al-harb, and had to be reconquered for Islam.

Not only in Bengal, of course, but everywhere in what had been the

Mughal empire the memory of past grandeur lingered in the memories of Indian Muslims; it was not merely the lost grandeur they lamented, however, but the loss of a genuinely Islamic society, ruled by Muslims, however individually unworthy some of these might have been.

A new threat had now appeared. From about the beginning of the nineteenth century Christian missionaries from Europe began their activities in India, and in Bengal in particular. This led Muslims to fear that the growth of British political power would mean also an attempt to convert the people of India to Christianity. There was some justification for their view. Mr Mangles, the chairman of the Board of Directors of the East India Company, said in Parliament in 1857: 'Providence has entrusted the extensive empire of Hindustan to England that the banner of Christ should wave triumphant from one end of India to the other' (Qureshi, 1962; 226).

In 1835, as a result of Macaulay's famous recommendation, English was declared the official language of India and the medium in which education in India was to be carried out. It was not long before Indians began to avail themselves of the entrée into Western literature and learning which this provided, but it was the Hindus rather than the Muslims who took advantage of the opportunity. For one thing, the areas of strongest British influence, Bombay, Madras and above all Calcutta and West Bengal, were areas of predominantly Hindu population. Another reason was that Hindus were less suspicious than Muslims of the alien culture to which such education exposed them – in the early days, at least. Militant Hindu resistance, represented by the Ārya Samāj, belongs, as we have seen, to the latter part of the nineteenth century (7.23). From the early days Muslims were less willing to share in the 'blessings' of Western culture offered in Christian missionary or government schools. The Muslim suspected, as Qureshi points out, that if he sent his children to these schools they would be taught to despise their own faith, and be 'weaned away from the religious values of Islam' (Qureshi, 1962; 224). Certainly among the Hindus there was in the mid-nineteenth century a considerable crop of conversions to Christianity. One of the aims of the British educational policy was to provide recruits for the colonial government service, and these were in fact found from among the Hindu rather than the Muslim community. Thus Muslims, in addition to their sense of humiliation at the loss of their empire, now had also the feeling that they were being discriminated against in favour of the Hindus.

7.33 Beginnings of a new era for Muslims

It is all the more remarkable, in view of what has just been recounted, that there were Muslims who believed in the possibility of better relations with the British. The most notable and influential of these was Sayyid Ahmad Khan, born in Delhi in 1817, a greatly venerated name among Indian Muslims (Qureshi, 1962; 236–52). In a book published in Calcutta in 1860, *The Causes of the Indian Revolt*, he sought to show British readers that the fundamental cause of the revolt had been British failure to understand the religious views and moral sentiments of the Muslim population and the extent to which these had been affronted by the course which government measures had taken. He believed too that Muslim aversion to the British administration was due to ignorance of the nature of Christian civilisation, and therefore set out to write an interpretation of the Bible to show Muslims that the two religious systems, Islamic and Christian, had much in common. A few years later he visited England and studied for a while at Cambridge. Here he came upon the account of Islam given by Sir William Muir in his book *The Life of Muhammad*. Muir, like that other Western critic of Islam, Ernest Renan, looking at the later stages of medieval Islamic society saw only what seemed a backward and inferior system of thought and practice, based on a primitive religion of Bedouin tribesmen. Sayyid Ahmad Khan therefore undertook to correct this view in a work which was published in London in 1870 under the title of *Essays on the Life of Mohammed*. It was a book characterised by 'fair literary argument and the beginning of scholarly exegesis' according to Sir Alfred Lyall, and constituted a sincere attempt to give Western readers a rational account of Islamic religion and its values.

Sayyid Ahmad Khan was convinced of the ultimate compatibility of modern scientific knowledge and the religion of Islam. It was such knowledge, he was convinced, that explained the greater progress of the West, rather than any superiority of Christianity over other religions. On his return to India, therefore, he embarked upon the building at Aligarh of a centre of learning where modern knowledge and Islamic culture might be fruitfully related to each other. This became known as the Mohammedan Anglo-Oriental College, an institution which 'played an important role in the development of the Muslim community after it had reached so near the brink of the abyss. . . .

It brought up a generation of Muslims who were aware of the new developments in the world and its thought without undermining their fundamental loyalty to Islam' (Qureshi, 1962; 242). By many of the more conservative Muslim religious leaders of India, however, the ideas and teaching of Sayyid Ahmad Khan were regarded with great suspicion and dislike. He was an outstanding early 'modernist' among Indian Muslims. He was criticised for dabbling in theology, for which it was said he had no qualifications. Nevertheless he was a learned man, with sincere religious convictions, and with a firm belief in the value of Islamic society, and it is to him that a great deal of the credit must be given for the awakening of the Muslims of India to a new understanding of the possible place of Islamic religion in the modern world.

A Muslim of similar views concerning the need for relating intellectual and scientific thought to the values of Islamic religion was his contemporary, Jamal al-Din al-Afghani (1839–97). Faith in the God revealed in Islam was for Afghani blended with a conviction concerning the importance of the right moral and social ordering of the life of man, and of rational and scientific methods. Afghani's role was not so much to demonstrate the compatibility of science and Islamic religion (in the sense that this was one of the main actual preoccupations of the Aligarh movement founded by Sayyid Ahmad Khan), as the strengthening of Islam socially and politically. His name is associated particularly with the 'pan-Islam' movement, that is, the reassertion of the unity of the Muslim world as a safeguard against the invasion of Islam by alien forces, political, cultural and religious. He was also an exponent of the idea of the 'people's government' within Islam, as the most effective guarantee of political cohesion and strength; in this connection his influence was felt in Egypt, in Persia, in Turkey and in India.

7.34 Islamic reform in Egypt

The stimulus towards Islamic reformulation which contact with Western civilisation had given to Indian Muslims was felt also in Egypt – another country which at this time was being subjected to European colonial expansion. Here the reform and reinterpretation of Islam was largely led and inspired by Muhammad Abduh (1849–1905), a disciple of al-Afghani (7.33), who during the 1880s co-operated with him in the production of an Islamic journal. Muhammad Abduh was a trained theologian and a teacher at the famous Muslim centre at Cairo, al-Azhar. More securely perhaps than Sayyid Ahmad Khan he had a foot in both worlds, that of traditional Islamic orthodoxy (thus a man to whom some at least of the Egyptian ulama were prepared to listen), and that of modern knowledge. Faith and reason, he maintained, do not conflict but co-operate for the advancement of both true religion and a well-ordered society. He argued that Islam is a religion which calls upon man to use his reason to investigate the world of nature, since this is God's creation. The reformulation of Islamic thought which he believed was possible and necessary was not, however, easily to be achieved, and his ideas met with considerable opposition from the more conservative of the ulama. H. A. R. Gibb sees two consequences of Abduh's influence: one, the growth of secular modernism in the Islamic countries of the Middle East, with a tendency towards the separation of religion and the state; the other the growth of a fundamentalist theological party known as the Salafiya which rejected all medieval authorities and took its stand upon the Qur'an and the Sunna alone. One of the leaders of this movement was a disciple of Abduh named Rashid Rida (1865–1935), and under his leadership the Salafiya movement approached more and more closely to the puritan fundamentalism of the Wahhabis. The movement exerted a wide influence by means of its journal, *al-Manar*, which circulated throughout the Muslim world of the Middle East and South Asia, where it appealed not to the most highly educated but to religiously enthusiastic middle-class Muslims.

7.35 Muslim India: the late nineteenth century

To return to India: we noted in an earlier section (*7.23*) the growing strength of Hindu communal self-awareness seen for example in the Ārya Samāj, founded in 1875; it is now possible to see that while this was to some extent due to the self-assertion of cultural forces having deep and ancient roots in the history of India, it was also the response to a revived Muslim communalism, which had by this time recovered from the shock of the loss of political power. Sayyid Ahmad Khan (*7.33*), liberal in outlook and generous in spirit as he was, nevertheless has to be recognised as 'the first modern Muslim to suggest that Hindus and Muslims constituted two separate nations in India' (Ahmad, 1964; 265). The Indian National Congress, the political organisation which was largely responsible for winning India's independence from British colonial rule, was established in 1885 on a broad basis which included both Hindus and Muslims. But when, two years later, a Muslim was elected to its presidency, it seemed to Sayyid Ahmad Khan that there was a danger that Muslim participation in the Congress would lead to a blurring of essential issues and would prove detrimental to the Indian Muslims' hopes of the recovery of an *Islamic* society. In speeches delivered at Lucknow in 1887 and Meerut in 1888 he declared his policy of political separation as the only way for the preservation of essential Islamic interests, a policy which immediately found widespread support throughout Muslim India. The growing aggressiveness of the more extreme Hindus led by Tilak (*7.25*) after the riots of 1893 served to strengthen the demand which Muslims were now making, in pursuance of this policy of separatism, for regional political representation. In response to this Muslim demand the British government eventually conceded a separate electoral area for Muslims in East Bengal, only to withdraw the concession shortly afterwards in 1911, in response to bitter Hindu opposition. Sayyid Ahmad Khan had died in 1898, but his place as the intellectual champion of Islam in India had been taken by Amir Ali (1849–1928), who in 1877 founded the 'National Muhammedan Association' with its headquarters in Calcutta, a movement having an appeal to younger middle-class Muslims. Amir Ali exerted considerable influence through his writings, notably *The Spirit of Islam* published in 1891. Developing a line of thought already suggested by Muhammad Abduh in Egypt, Amir Ali argued that Islam was essentially a pro-gressive, civilising force. Had it not been prevented from spreading into Europe by 'the barrier which was raised against it by a degraded Christianity', he wrote, it would have proved its progressive character there also. 'Islam, wherever it has found its way among culturable and progressive nations, has shown itself in complete accord with progressive tendencies, it has assisted civilisation, it has idealised religion' (Amir Ali, 1922; 180). Unitarianism (*4.16*) he saw as a kind of European Islam, without Islam's religious discipline. While he wrote with Western readers to some extent in mind, it was primarily to Indian Muslims that his work was addressed, with the purpose of showing them that in Muhammad they had a Prophet of whom they could be proud, and in Islam a religion that enlightens and elevates mankind (W. C. Smith, 1947; 49 f.).

7.36 Muhammad Iqbal and the Muslim League

The Muslim League, founded in 1906, had as its main purpose the promotion of the political aspect of Indian Muslim aspirations. It served also, however, as a channel for the general effort and thought of all those Muslims in India who were convinced that their destiny lay in a separate political and cultural community united by common allegiance to Islam. Its most outstanding leader was Muhammad Iqbal (1873–1938), although his pre-eminence rests more upon his achievements as poet and philosopher. His poetry is ranked next to the Qur'an in its influence upon the Indian Muslim intelligentsia of the twentieth century, and Iqbal is generally acknowledged as the spiritual founder of the state of Pakistan. Like Sayyid Ahmad Khan he had spent a time studying in Europe, at Cambridge and in Germany. He is said to have been influenced by the work of Bergson and of Nietzsche, but the more important formative influence, apart from the Qur'an and his pious Muslim upbringing in the Punjab, was the work of the medieval Muslim mystic Jalal ud-Din Rumi (6.36). He was, however, strongly critical of the influence of the Sufis, and considered that their quietism and inaction more than anything else had been responsible for the weakening of Islam. His interpretation of what it meant to be a Muslim was in decidedly this-worldly terms: strife with evil is the purpose of human existence, and it is this that Islam makes possible. He had no time for beliefs that did not express themselves in action. In his earlier years he was a great advocate of Hindu–Muslim unity, but later on he came to the view that the force of extreme and reactionary Hinduism was a threat to the existence of the Muslim community in India, and hence, from 1930, when as president of the Muslim League he made a notable speech on the subject, he became a great advocate of the idea of a separate Muslim state embracing north-west India and the adjacent regions. He was, nevertheless, a man of great breadth of vision to whom nationalism was the most destructive of all the false gods worshipped by man (Qureshi, 1962; 263). Since he was a Muslim his attitude to life was framed in Muslim terms, but this was in fact only the starting point for what for him was a religious view of much wider dimensions. In his own words:

> My real purpose is to look for a better social order and to present a
> universally acceptable ideal [of life and action] before the world, but it is

o   L.H.R.

impossible for me, in this effort to outline this ideal, to ignore the social system and values of Islam whose most important objective is to demolish all the artificial and pernicious distinctions of caste, creed, colour and economic status. . . . No doubt I am intensely devoted to Islam but I have selected the Islamic community as my starting point not because of any national or religious prejudice but because it is the most practicable line of approach to the problem. (Wheeler, 1962; 198)

The influence of Iqbal provided some of the higher idealism motivating the Muslim League's struggle for a separate independent Islamic state to be formed when British rule in India was withdrawn. There were no doubt other motives, such as fear of being dominated by Hindus, a fear which was fed by the growing strength of the Hindu extremists. The history of that struggle, especially in its culminating stage in the closing years of the Second World War, lies outside the scope of this book; we are here concerned only to point out that this is a major example of how religious issues have affected human history: there is, of course, the other side of the picture namely the way that political, social and economic factors have affected religious issues. With that side of the story, so far as Pakistan is concerned, we shall deal later (*7.39*).

7.37 Modern syncretistic sects: Babism-Baha'ism, and the Ahmadiya

The modern period has seen the growth of several sects which might be considered as further examples of reform movements in Islam in the modern period; an additional reason for their mention is that two of them, Baha'ism and the Ahmadiya movement, are both active in the West and constitute two more of the multitude of sects to be found in the Western world.

The founder of Babism was a Muslim named Sayyid Ali Muhammad who was born in Shiraz, in southern Persia, in 1819. At the age of twenty-four he assumed the title 'Bab', which means 'the Gate' through whom knowledge of the Twelfth Imam was to be gained. Later, after a pilgrimage to Mecca, he declared to the religious authorities in Persia that he had superseded Muhammad as the Prophet of God and had inaugurated a new era. His preaching was addressed mainly to the middle classes (he himself was the son of a grocer) and gave a high place in his ideas to the activity of trade; his ideas were heterodox from an

Islamic point of view in that he regarded interest on loans as lawful. He proclaimed also that commercial correspondence should not be tampered with. Recent research suggests that in the 1840s Persia was undergoing a severe economic crisis and that the Babi movement was partly a response to this. The Bab and his followers at first hoped to convert the religious leaders and rulers of Persia to their ideas. The result was, however, that the Bab was pronounced insane and put in prison. After this the movement took on an increasingly radical character, as the Bab's followers advocated the abolition of private property. The Bab was removed to another prison, and finally, in 1850, was shot. There were various risings and conspiracies as a result, which were violently dealt with by the Shah and his government. The followers of the Bab then divided into two factions; the majority-group was led by one of the most prominent of the Bab's disciples, Baha-Allah (1817–92), and developed into a sect whose doctrines were rather milder and vaguer, of a somewhat universalistic humanitarian nature, but no longer Islamic in any orthodox sense. The Bab had produced a new holy book, the *Beyan*, which superseded the Qur'an, and consisted largely of the laws governing the life of the new theocracy. This in turn was superseded by a new and fuller revelation produced by Baha-Allah, known as the *Kitab Akdas*, the 'Most Holy Book', which also took the form of regulations for a theocratic community. Most of the adherents of the Bahai faith are found in Persia, although there are some in other Muslim countries and, as has already been noted, some are even to be found in Europe and America.

The Ahmadiya movement, or Quadiyani sect, was founded by Mirza Ghulam Ahmad (1839–1908), has the support of only a very small minority of Muslims, and is regarded by the majority as heretical. At about the age of forty Mirza Ghulam Ahmad began to engage in controversy with the Hindu Ārya Samāj supporters, and also with Christians. In 1889, when he was fifty, he declared himself to be the Messiah whose advent is foretold in the Qur'an. He proclaimed a revived and reformed Islam in keeping with the conditions of a modern technological society. He gained a certain following which after his death became divided; one half, the Quadiyani, continued to uphold the claim of the founder to be the Messiah; the other half, centred on Lahore, formed a new 'Society for the Propagation of Islam', and eventually moved towards reconciliation with traditional Sunni Islam. Both halves of the movement have engaged in missionary activity not only in India but also in the West. Perhaps one of the most significant features of the history of the movement is the very slight measure of success it has had – almost negligible – in spite of its claim to present a form of Islam for the modern age.

7.38 Islam in Indonesia

Indonesia, with its seventy-seven million Muslims forming something like ninety per cent of the total population, is obviously a numerically important sector of the Muslim world. The growth of Islam in Malaya and the South-East Asian archipelago was a gradual process from the fourteenth century C.E. onwards, the chief agents of which were traders from South India and Arabia. The process has continued steadily throughout the nineteenth and twentieth centuries, and during this period the Islamisation of Indonesia has increased not only in its extent but also in depth, that is, in deeper penetration into the life of the people. Islam's initial strength in Indonesia was in the ports to which the traders came and in which they settled, and from these urban centres it spread out into the countryside. As in the earlier period, so in the nineteenth and twentieth centuries this expansion has been effected by Muslim traders, minor government officials and teachers.

One of the most important factors was the increase in the number of Muslim pilgrims from Indonesia to Mecca from the middle of the nineteenth century onwards. In 1852 the Dutch government rescinded the order requiring the payment of 110 florins for a passport by any Indonesian wishing to make the pilgrimage to Mecca (Arnold, 1913; 410), with the result that from that date many more Indonesian Muslims began to make the pilgrimage. A further factor was the greater opportunities of steamship travel which were open to pilgrims from about this time onwards. By the 1880s the Indonesians were the largest and most active group of pilgrims from any part of the Muslim world to be found residing in Mecca. By the year 1926–7 they constituted more than forty per cent of Mecca's foreign population. Throughout the past century, therefore, Indonesia has been exposed to a steadily growing stream of returning pilgrims (hajjis) who have brought back to Indonesia the influence, first, of the Wahhabi reform movement still active in Arabia, and then that of the Egyptian modernist reforms emanating from Al-Azhar in Cairo associated especially with

Muhammad Abduh (*7.34*). Some Indonesians during their travels in the Middle East managed to include a period of study at the great university of Cairo itself. The same improved facilities for sea travel also brought increasing numbers of Arab traders from the Hadhramaut area of southern Arabia to Indonesia, to settle there and to infuse their very orthodox Islam into the Indonesian situation.

The growth in numbers of Muslims in the various parts of Indonesia has been one result of such influences. In some places, in Sumatra for example, this has been at the expense of the Christian community, where an initial Christianisation of heathen tribes has paved the way for their later conversion to Islam by Muslim missionaries far more skilled in relating the Islamic faith to the tribal life of these people (Arnold, 1913; 374). But in most of Indonesia it has been the school which has served as the channel for the new enthusiasm flowing into Indonesia from the Middle East.

During the earlier period the typical Islamic school of Indonesia was the pesantrén (from the word 'santri' by which Muslims are known in Indonesia). The pesantrén was an institution very similar to the Buddhist monastery in its combination of religious and educational activities, and in fact was derived directly from the tradition of Buddhist monastic centres of medieval Java; that is, places where holy writings were studied, where travellers were refreshed and given lodging, and where local boys received instruction and education. As a result of the increasing numbers of returned pilgrims, more knowledgeable about their religion, more aware of its essentials, and bringing with them Muslim literature from the Middle East, these pesantréns gradually became centres of a more orthodox Islamic teaching, which thus displaced the somewhat mystical tradition from South India which had characterised them until that time.

Alongside the pesantréns, however, there gradually grew up a somewhat different type of Islamic school, modelled in the case of Indonesia on government and Christian schools, and intended by reformist Muslims to provide an education both more liberal and more modern than that of the pesantréns with their strongly medieval flavour, and also more purely Islamic in the kind of religious teaching imparted: pure, in the sense of more Qur'anic and less mystical and Sufistic. Secular subjects (arithmetic, history, geography, Latin script), were taught, and Islamic religious instruction was given in the form of exposition of the Qur'an and its precepts, rather than a verse-by-verse chanting of the Arabic text which was the method followed in the pesantrén.

Such schools, given by the reformers who established them the name of madrasa to indicate their genuinely Islamic character, were instrumental in the spread of modernist religious ideas. In this the urban Muslims have led the way. Largely men of the middle classes, they are principally interested in Islamic religion as a moral code, a social doctrine, and a source of values for a modern culture. In the twentieth century rural Islam has more and more followed this urban lead and there are now said to be schools of the madrasa type in almost every Muslim village in the rural areas of Java, for example (Geertz, 1962; 104).

Another important factor in the vitality of Islam in Indonesia in the twentieth century has been the formation of religious organisations. The most notable of these is the association known as Muhammadiya. This was founded in 1912 by a returned pilgrim, and in the same year a parallel organisation with a predominantly political character was founded, known as Sarekat Islam, or 'Islamic Union'. From 1923 onwards the Muhammadiya grew very rapidly and by the 1930s had some nine hundred local branches, supported largely by middle-class members (tradesmen, school-teachers, clerks, etc.) who welcomed the modernising emphasis of the movement, and the important place given to reason in its intellectual programme. The activities which the Muhammadiya organisation sponsored grew continually: schools, religious publications, orphanages, asylums and hospitals, special organisations for women and girls, a boy-scout movement, and mass open-air meetings. Through these various media the strength of Islam was built up in many villages and towns of Java, and its adherents were made increasingly aware of their role as Muslims and that they belonged to a unique, exclusive and universal religion. The Muhammadiya, while it was religiously radical, was politically conservative and did not encourage emphasis on the political aspect of Islam. The idea of an Islamic state in Indonesia has had its champions in the period of independence, but it has not had the widespread support which the idea had, for example, in India. When the Indonesian Republic failed to come up to the expectations of some Muslims that it would be an Islamic state, a party of violent revolt called Dar Ul Islam emerged in western Java, northern Sumatra and southern Celebes, with the aim of forcing the government to adopt a 'purer' Islamic constitution. Many

Indonesian Muslims, however, are unconcerned about the political aspect of Islam. Among Muslim intellectuals in Indonesia some have to a large extent lost interest in Islam, and either have become indifferent or have consciously adopted an atheist and in some cases communist outlook. Others, still interested in Islam, have expressed vigorous criticism of it and are looking for a reinterpretation more appropriate to modern thought than the old-fashioned liberalism of the Egyptian reform movements; a few have been attracted to the thought of Muhammad Iqbal (7.36) as it is expressed in his book, *The Reconstruction of Religious Thought in Islam.*

7.39 Islam in the Indo-Pakistan subcontinent since 1947

As the result of a long and exceedingly complex series of events, political, economic, religious, the hopes of many Muslims in the subcontinent of India were realised when in 1947 a separate, sovereign Islamic state known as Pakistan was carved out of what had been British India and the princely states. The idea of the Islamic state, believed by many to be integral to the religion of the Prophet, had once more returned as a reality. At least, Pakistan was a state which *set out* to be Islamic, which existed for the purpose of becoming fully Islamic; for it would not be such immediately. But by the mid-1950s there were many who were beginning to feel that the attempt was not succeeding. The problem was how to create a genuinely Islamic state, based on the values and the law of Islam, amid the pressures of the modern world – secularist, international, economic, technological, to name a few.

In the struggle for independence the traditional religious leaders, the ulama, had played some part, it is true, especially those connected with the Dar al-ulum (an institution of higher learning) at Deoband; these formed the spearhead of the popular movement for Muslim independence and thus contributed to the eventual setting up of Pakistan. But the moulding of the new state was largely in the hands not of traditionalist conservative ulama such as these, but of Western-educated, liberal-minded Muslims who had been trained for secular occupations, the leaders of the Muslim League political party. These men, comments Wilfred Cantwell Smith, were fitted for making the new state viable; they were not fitted for making it Islamic.

The principle of government on which the new state emerged was that of democracy. Its policies, it was believed, were to express the will of the people – that is of the *Muslim* people who were its citizens. In acquiring the competence which qualified them to run a state its leaders had cut themselves off to a very considerable degree from the Muslim basis of their support. On the other hand the traditional religious leaders, the ulama, remained absorbed in 'the forms, the idiom, the milieu, the personnel of an earlier age' (W. C. Smith, 1957; 226). The divergence was manifest in the educational realm; secular education on the one hand and classical Islamic education on the other each had their distinct methods, subjects studied, teachers, and pupils. The stresses in the situation lay not in the impact of modernity upon traditional Islam, but in the rigid separation of the two. The result, comments Wilfred Cantwell Smith, has been a 'failure to generate an interpretation of Islam that could serve as an effective, realistic, meaningful ideology, or framework for ideology' (W. C. Smith, 1957; 227f.). The failure has been on both sides; not only have the secular, bourgeois leaders of Pakistan pursued the interests of their own class or. family; the ulama also have contributed nothing positive. In 1953 rioting broke out in the Punjab which was ostensibly directed against the unorthodox Ahmadiya sect (7.37); the riots served as an outlet for the disappointment and discontent felt by the rank and file Muslims at the failure of the political leaders to fulfil the hopes of the people for a genuinely Islamic state; the unorthodoxy of the Ahmadiya sect served as a symbol against which orthodox Muslims could direct all their resentment. After the riots a court of enquiry was set up. Its report, known as the Munir Report from the name of the court's president, mentioned among other things the failure of the ulama in the difficult contemporary situation, in that they were unable 'to give realistic guidance on elementary matters of Islam', and that no two of them could even agree on the definition of a Muslim!

Another manifestation of orthodox Islamic discontent is that of the Jama'at-i-Islami (Community of Islam) movement, founded by Maulānā Maudūdī (1903–) (Mujeeb, 1967; W. C. Smith, 1957). This began in 1941 as an alternative organisation to the Muslim League. At that time Maudūdī was opposed to the League on the grounds that its policy involved the setting up of a nationalistic Indian Muslim state, and that nationalism was incompatible with Islam. Since the establishment of Pakistan in 1947 Maudūdī, who has continued to be the inspirer and guiding force of Jama'at-i-Islami, has had to change his ground somewhat and now advocates what may be called the thorough Islamisation of the government of Pakistan and its purging from all Western moral, social and political values and practices. His ideas have been expressed in numerous pamphlets and books and in a monthly journal issued from Lahore. By profession a journalist, he has gained a reputation for Islamic scholarship in spite of having had little formal schooling. His view of Islam is that it is essentially a revealed faith, having a social system as its corollary, what he calls a 'theo-democratic' state; this has a fixed, once-for-all character, and is the God-given means for the reformation of human society. The Islamic state which he describes is an ideal which has in fact never existed; an Indian Muslim writer has commented that 'any reference to history or actual fact is incompatible with the method Maulānā Maudūdī has adopted' (Mujeeb, 1967; 402). This Islamic state which Maudūdī advocates is to be ruled by a Muslim who is elected by his Muslim fellow-citizens on the grounds of the purity of his faith and the righteousness of his conduct – an interesting modern reappearance of the political doctrine of the Kharijites (*5.17*). The Islamic state, Maudūdī maintains, has no frontiers, and any Muslim anywhere in the world is entitled to its citizenship. In the present situation, therefore, the aim of Maudūdī and his followers has to be the conversion of the existing state of Pakistan into the truly Muslim universalist state. In the furtherance of this aim he appeals immediately to that section of Muslims in the subcontinent which he considers most likely and able to respond: in his view ninety per cent of the Muslims of Pakistan are poor, and ignorant of the true nature of Islam; of the remaining ten per cent approximately half are relatively uncontaminated by Western values and ideas, and it is to this section that he appeals primarily. Support for the Jama'at-i-Islami is found mainly in the cities, among the lower middle class; a certain amount of support comes also from urban malcontents of various kinds, and from some young Muslims, attracted by the idealism of his programme and the personal honesty and integrity of life which is a much-emphasised feature of the Jama'at-i-Islami membership. According to Wilfred Cantwell Smith this movement is 'one of the most significant developments in contemporary Islam and one of the most significant forces in contemporary Pakistan' (W. C. Smith, 1957; 235n).

7.4 BUDDHISM IN THE MODERN PERIOD, 1800 TO THE PRESENT

7.40 Ceylon in the British colonial period

The beginning of the nineteenth century coincided with the establishment of British colonial rule in Ceylon. In 1796 the British East India
Company succeeded in gaining control of the coastal areas which until
then had been under Dutch rule, and in 1802 this territory came under
the control of the British crown. In 1815 the British extended their rule
beyond the coastal area which the Portuguese and the Dutch had
controlled, and by defeating the Kandyan kingdom in the central area
brought the whole of Ceylon for the first time under a European
government.

British attitudes to Buddhist religion in Ceylon were of two kinds:
liberal and tolerant, represented by the commercial and governing
British community in the island; and evangelical and intolerant,
represented by British Protestant missionaries, and by the government
at Westminster in the early part of the nineteenth century. Three
features of Buddhist life in Ceylon made it particularly vulnerable to the
European presence: its dependence on the support of the Sinhalese
kings; the economic basis of the Sangha, which required for its healthy
functioning an undisturbed and fairly prosperous peasantry; and its
involvement in the indigenous local cults and beliefs of Ceylon
(*6.45*; *6.46*). Under the Dutch and Portuguese governments Buddhist
life had already suffered dislocation from the reduction of the Sinhalese
political structure and loss of royal patronage in much of Ceylon,
although patronage continued in central Ceylon so long as the diminished kingdom of Kandy survived. The British, in displacing the
Kandyan kings, at first accepted responsibility for the control of
Buddhist institutions as a proper part of the function of the ruler of
Ceylon. In Article 5 of the Kandyan Convention (an agreement made
by the British in 1815) it was stated that 'the religion of the Buddhoo
professed by the chiefs and inhabitants of these provinces is declared
inviolable and its rites and ministers and places of worship are to be
maintained and protected'. This tolerant attitude of the British, who
at this stage were interested mainly in commercial profit and with

strengthening their position in Asia against their French competitors, had the effect of encouraging numbers of Sinhalese families who had in the Portuguese period been forced to become nominal Christians and adopt Portuguese names to return to their original Buddhist faith and culture; this was in fact the accelerating of a process which had begun in the latter part of the period of Dutch rule, when similar tolerance had been shown towards Buddhism. From this time onwards can be discerned the beginning, although slight, of Buddhist recovery in Ceylon (Mendis, 1963; 112).

The Sangha, however, was at a very low ebb, especially in the coastal provinces where the economic basis of its support had been badly upset during the Portuguese and Dutch periods. But in 1802 it was given a new infusion of life by the introduction from Burma of monks able to give Buddhist ordination into the Amarapura nikaya (or sect), procured by a Ceylonese Buddhist novice of the Salagama caste, who went to Burma with five others and returned to Ceylon to provide such ordination to all castes. This was contrary to the practice of the until then predominant Kandyan nikaya, which ordained only members of the Goigama caste (to such an extent had Buddhist Ceylon become infected by the Hindu caste system from southern India).

Christian missionary activity was established in Ceylon in the second decade of the nineteenth century. The missionaries soon began to take strong exception to the British government's having assumed responsibility for the protection of the religion of the majority of the Sinhalese people. The duties which the government had undertaken in this connection included the appointing and dismissing of monks in official positions, the enforcing of the decisions of certain Buddhist monastic chapters, the protection of the religious ceremonies at Kandy, supervision of Buddhist temporalities on behalf of the monasteries, and patronage of the pirivenas or Buddhist institutions of higher learning. To missionaries of such enthusiastically Christian disposition as Spence Hardy this was a very shocking situation. Moreover, the openness of Sinhalese Buddhism to the indigenous culture of Ceylon gave it, in the eyes of these missionaries, a clearly idolatrous appearance; Buddhist tolerance in this matter, wrote Spence Hardy, 'must have been greatly offensive in the sight of Him before whom idolatry is the abominable thing, utterly hated' (Hardy, 1860; 321). Buddhist life and practice was, in the view of the missionaries 'opposed to the truth', that is, to the '*only* way of salvation by faith'; it must be utterly destroyed in Ceylon and throughout the world, for it was part of 'the empire of hell'. Such British Christian imperialism eventually succeeded in gaining the support of like-minded evangelicals in Whitehall and Westminster. Meanwhile Christian missions in Ceylon were growing considerably in the extent of their activities and in the support received from the West to carry on their work. This, and other factors such as the use of English as the language of administration and education, made Buddhist recovery doubly difficult, since the Buddhist leaders used only the Sinhalese and Pali languages, and were thus cut off from some of the new developments in public life and education.

About the middle of the nineteenth century the evangelical dislike of British protection for Buddhist institutions, coinciding with equal misgivings among liberals and secularists in Britain about government involvement in religious affairs, resulted in the repudiation of the Kandyan agreement. The British government dissociated itself from Buddhism, but without providing the proper machinery by which the Buddhists of Ceylon could organise the affairs which the British were now abandoning.

In spite of these handicaps, however, Buddhism in Ceylon did continue to show signs of revival. In 1839 a new Buddhist institution of higher learning, the Parama Dhamma Cetiya Pirivena, was set up at Ratmalana. In 1865 a reformed sect of Buddhist monks was founded, the Ramanya nikaya; since the traditional method of reforming the life of the Sangha through government supervision was no longer possible, and because this disability was already resulting in a deterioration of the purity of the monastic life, the matter had to be taken in hand by those Buddhists who had a mind to, 'without tarrying for any'. The Ramanya sect represents also a return to a basic 'pure' form of Buddhist life, in contrast to the amalgam of Buddhist and indigenous forms which is characteristic of Sinhalese Buddhism. In the years 1872 and 1876 two more pirivenas were established, the Vidyadaya and the Vidyalankara; these are today Buddhist institutions of university status. In the early 1870s the opposition of learned Buddhists to the ideas and values and social practices of the West, which they regarded as selfish and immoral, took the form of public disputations with Christian missionaries and clergymen, and in these public controversies some of the latter were worsted (Ludowyk, 1962; 277: Mendis, 1963; 164). Then in 1880 Colonel Olcott, of the American Theosophical Society, arrived in Ceylon to take part in the defence of Buddhism, and was instrumental in gathering together a number of lay Buddhists of Ceylon to form the Buddhist Theosophical Society, an organisation which has played an important part in Buddhist revival in Ceylon since that time.

Moreover, there were British officials and administrators in the Civil Service of Ceylon who, in the tradition of learning, research and writing which has often characterised their kind, developed an appreciation of the Buddhist culture of Ceylon. Among their number were T. W. Rhys-Davids, the great Pali scholar, W. T. Stace, the philosopher, and Leonard Woolf. These and others like them were, says Ludowyk 'an intelligent, responsible and enlightened body of men', who, he adds, 'came closest of all their fellows to knowing and understanding the country where they served' (Ludowyk, 1962; 232).

7.41 India and Burma in the British colonial period

Considerable space has been devoted to the one relatively small country of Ceylon, partly because the clash of Buddhist and modern Western influences can be most clearly seen there, and is most fully documented, and partly because of the important influence which Ceylon has in modern times exerted in other parts of the Buddhist world.

One of these has been India. The most notable movement of Buddhist growth in India took place in the period of independence, after the end of British colonial rule (7.46). But mention must be made at this point of the founding and growth in India of the Mahā Bodhi Society. India is a predominantly Hindu country, but with its fourteen states and its 400 million population it includes a variety of religious traditions; apart from the Muslims, who in the whole subcontinent number approximately 120 million, there are of course the Jains, the Sikhs, the Jews, the Christians – and the Buddhists. Some of these Buddhists, in Bengal and Assam, where Buddhism has never entirely disappeared, constitute a direct link with the early period of Indian Buddhism. Others, in Kashmir and the Darjeeling district in north Bengal, are overspills from Tibet. In the heartland of Buddhism, however, namely the lower Ganges valley and Bihar, there were so few Buddhists during the British colonial period as to be negligible. This meant that the ancient sites connected with the life of the Buddha, notably Gaya, the place of the Buddha's enlightenment, had by the nineteenth century fallen into neglect. In 1885 this fact was pointed out by Sir Edwin Arnold (the author of the long poem about the Buddha, *The Light of Asia*), in a series of articles in the London *Telegraph*. The British authorities had restored the temple at Bodh-Gaya, but the place was in the hands of Hindu Shaivites, who were exploiting it as best they could as a centre of pilgrimage. A young Buddhist of Ceylon, Anagarika Dharmapala, then about twenty-one, hearing of this, visited Bodh-Gaya and was so dismayed at what he saw that he pledged himself to the task of restoring it to Buddhist hands as a worthy place of pilgrimage. He returned to Ceylon in May 1891 and there gathered together a group which became the Mahā Bodhi Society. An international conference of Buddhists was called together at Bodh-Gaya by the new society, and representatives came from China, Japan, Ceylon and East Bengal. The Society set itself the task not only of restoring Bodh-Gaya as a Buddhist place of pilgrimage but also of making the Buddha-Dharma known once again throughout India, and even possibly wherever English was spoken. A journal was launched in the following year in furtherance of this aim. The Society set up headquarters in Calcutta, and in the famine of 1897 undertook relief work, appealing for help to all the Buddhist countries of Asia. Further branches of the Society were opened in 1900, two in India, at Madras and Kusinagara, and one in Ceylon, at Anuradhapura. Substantial financial help came from wealthy Americans. A series of legal actions were undertaken for securing the temple at Bodh-Gaya for the possession of Buddhists, but these were resisted by the Hindu landlord, and in spite of the powerful advocacy given by Sir Edwin Arnold and Colonel Olcott (7.40) the Society had no success in this direction during the period of British rule. However, the publicity given to the case aroused the interest of educated Bengalis in Buddhism; a Buddhist vihara was built in Calcutta, and was opened in 1920; and at Sarnath near Benares, the place of the Buddha's first public preaching of the Dharma, which by the early twentieth century had become a grazing ground for pigs, and surrounded by jungle, a Buddhist vihara was built in 1931, to which were added in subsequent years a library, a free dispensary, a primary school and a training college.

During the period of British colonial rule in India Burma also became a part of the Indian empire: first, the coastal areas of Arakan and of the south, then the Rangoon area and lower Burma, and finally, in 1885, the central area around the capital at Mandalay where the Burmese kings had their court. They, together with about eighty-five per cent of the Burmese, were Buddhists. Until 1885, therefore, the Buddhist Sangha in Burma enjoyed royal patronage and protection. What is more, the medieval Buddhist cosmology (4.29) was still an important feature of Burmese popular belief and culture, and according to this the royal palace and throne represented Mount Meru, the centre of the cosmos. The defeat and dethronement by the British of the last Burmese king, Thibaw, constituted an ideological crisis for the mass of the Burmese Buddhist people, the effects of which have continued in various forms into recent times. E. Sarkisyanz summarises what it meant to the Burmese:

> When the Palace stopped being a cosmocentric symbol, the traditional semi-Ptolemiac world conception centering on Mount Meru collapsed. With it fell the prototype of the historical Burmese state. The word 'revolution' (in an astronomical sense) is first used by Copernicus and Galilei. As in the Occident, so in Burma the history of political revolutions corresponds to the process of man's turning away from cosmic archetypes associated with 'Ptolemaic' views of the universe. Ever since the Mandalay Palace is no longer the centre of the universe, ever since the constellations are no longer grouped around the Cosmic Mountain Meru, Burma's society and culture was being shaken by revolutionary transformations when that Buddhism which had been a 'cosmological morality rooted in spatial-temporal regularity' came to be questioned. (Sarkisyanz, 1965; 107)

In this way a political and military event – the British defeat of Thibaw and the capture of Mandalay – had had an ideological and religious entail reaching far beyond its apparently 'secular' character. Religion in Burma had come to be identified with a certain kind of cosmology; the dislocation of the cosmology has to some extent meant the weakening of traditional religion among the Burmese. Another consequence has been a predisposition towards the support of Messianic movements which have arisen in various parts of Burma from time to time, for associated with this cosmological tragedy is the notion of a coming Buddha-king (Buddha-Rāja). But, as Sarkisyanz comments, it was also possible for many Burmese Buddhists to view the end of the Mandalay kingdom rationally, as another example of the Buddhist notion of the impermanence of all things. In fact, having to accustom themselves to a Buddhism without a royal 'cosmocentric' patronage, many Burmese Buddhists have returned to the more rational basic principles of the Theravāda, and this has in turn helped towards the modern renaissance of Buddhism in Burma. Another contributory factor in Buddhist revival was the struggle for independence from British colonial rule, in which Buddhism was seen to be a large part of the cultural heritage the Burmese were struggling to maintain and defend against what to them was decadent and immoral Western materialism. As in Ceylon, so in Burma also there were among British civil servants men of scholarly bent who developed great sympathy for the religion and culture of the people they lived among; a notable example was Fielding Hall, whose book *The Soul of a People*, with its very perceptive and sensitive presentation of Burmese Buddhism, was influential in the reawakening of the Burmese to the value of their religious heritage. One final point to be noted in connection with the struggle for independence into which the Burmese were forced by British colonial rule is that as this developed during the early part of the twentieth century it tended to bring Burmese Buddhism into an alliance with Asian Marxism, which, because the latter was anti-imperialist, anti-capitalist and anti-Christian, had a strong appeal for many of the younger Burmese Buddhist intellectuals, and the effects of this alliance have continued into the life of independent Burma.

7.42 *China and Vietnam*

Revival and reform have been characteristics of Buddhism in China and Vietnam during the modern period, especially since the revolution of 1911 which brought the Republic of China into being. Buddhist thought and practice, so long dominated by Ch'an (*5.23*) which placed a low value on intellectual pursuits, was challenged by a new intellectual climate in which whatever was conservative and traditional was being rejected, and more especially in the 1920s by the infusion of Marxist ideas into the Chinese 'cultural renaissance'. In response to the challenge a remarkable Chinese Buddhist monk emerged, named T'ai-hsu (1889–1947), who succeeded in rallying his fellow Buddhists and inspiring them to carry out a programme of reform. His aims are expressed in his own words as follows: 'Aroused by the destruction of temples ... I launched the movement to defend the religion, propagate the faith, reform the order and promote education' (Chan, 1953; 56).

In 1929 he organised the Chinese Buddhist Society, which by 1947 had a membership of over four-and-a-half million. He emphasised the international character of Buddhism and opened up new contacts between Chinese Buddhists and those of other Asian countries particularly Ceylon, Thailand and Japan. It was his conviction that 'Buddhist doctrine is fully capable of uniting all the existing forms of civilisation, and should spread throughout the world so that it may become a compass, as it were, for the human mind' (Hamilton, 1946; 297). Institutes for the training of Buddhist leaders were set up in various parts of China, with the aim of reforming the Buddhist Sangha, and in these Institutes large numbers of new leaders were trained (Ch'en, 1964; 456f.), and Buddhist texts were studied in a way that had not happened for a very long time. A notable feature of the revival which was thus stimulated was the appearance of increasing numbers of Buddhist periodicals devoted largely to the exposition of Buddhist thought and to the refuting of critics. Between 1920 and 1935 fifty-eight such periodicals were in publication.

The revival was apparent in two areas of Chinese Buddhism in particular: a rediscovery of the monistic philosophy of Mahāyāna Buddhism and the awakening of interest in Buddhist philosophical ideas among young intellectuals; and secondly, a revival of religious life in the Pure Land tradition (5.22), with a growth of new societies which existed for the purpose of revitalising what had become merely formal outward practices and the achievement of deeper religious experience and holiness of life. In the 1930s between sixty and seventy per cent of China's lay Buddhists are estimated to have belonged to these Pure Land groups (Ch'en, 1964; 460).

Stimulated to some extent by this Buddhist revival in China, similar movements appeared from 1920 onwards in Vietnam. These movements took formal shape in 'Associations for Buddhist Studies' founded in Saigon in 1931, in Hue in 1932, and in Hanoi in 1934. In these laymen and monks met together to work for the purifying of monastic life and the return to proper Buddhist disciplines, and for the training of a new generation of pious and well-instructed monks (Mai-Tho-Truyên, 1959; 807). Numerous periodicals and translations of Buddhist canonical texts, both Theravādin and Mahāyānist, began to be published, using Vietnamese rather than, as in past days, Chinese language. Here as in China there was a great revival of interest in the devotional Buddhism of the Pure Land school, and a decline in the influence of the Ch'an. The movement came to a halt at the outbreak of the Second World War, but was resumed in 1948. From about 1950 Buddhist monks from Vietnam began to go abroad to study, much more than formerly, mainly to India, Ceylon and the West. At about this time also various organisations and periodicals aimed at the modernisation of Vietnamese Buddhism began to appear. In 1951, after a national conference of representatives from the Buddhist organisations of northern, central and southern Vietnam, the All-Vietnam Buddhist Association was formed. Since 1963 the Buddhists of Vietnam have had unwelcome world publicity thrust upon them. In that year, President Ngo Dinh Diem, a Roman Catholic in control of a nation a substantial proportion of whom are Buddhists, unwisely attempted to forbid the public celebration of the Buddhist festival of Wesak. (This represented a far more serious religious affront than if the President of the United States, for instance, were to forbid the celebration of Christmas.) The Buddhists protested; the government took military action against a number of Saigon pagodas. From then onwards Buddhist monks have been increasingly drawn into public affairs in Vietnam. In November 1963 the Diem regime was overthrown, and the popularity which Buddhist leaders enjoyed after this might have made possible the rebuilding of a Buddhist Vietnamese society after these long years of French colonial and Roman Catholic domination. American intervention in the affairs of Vietnam has, however, at the time of writing, physically and morally devastated the country. Buddhist monks and nuns have now achieved notoriety by their protests against this foreign destruction of their culture and people in order to defend American democracy. Their protest has frequently taken the form of suicide by self-immolation. The Vietnamese monks and nuns who make this ultimate form of protest for the sake of their religion are reviving an ancient Chinese Mahāyāna cult. It is a practice which possibly originated in India and made its way with the Mahāyāna to China. An Indian ascetic is said to have burned himself to death in Athens around the year 20 B.C. (A knowledge of this or some similar event is perhaps reflected in St Paul's words: 'Though I give my body to be burned, but have not love, it profits me nothing.') A Ceylonese Buddhist, Walpola Rahula, commenting on this practice, acknowledges that those monks who took this course did so 'in order to protect and perpetuate their religion' and that it demanded of them 'immense courage, faith, determination, inner purification, and development through lone purification', but that nevertheless 'it is not in keeping with the pure and original teaching of the Buddha.' However, he adds, 'it is better to burn oneself than to burn others.'

7.43 Japan, 1868–1947

The circumscribed condition of the Buddhist Sangha during the long period of the Tokugawa regime (1603–1867) (*6.59*) prevented any growth, but with an assured, fixed income the Sangha did just keep alive. In 1868, with the beginning of the Meiji (literally 'Enlightened Government') period, the Sangha was disendowed and for a while even appeared to be in danger of being destroyed:

> A reign of persecution was started. Buddhists were driven out of the syncretic Shinto sanctuaries which they had been serving for ten centuries or more. Buddhist statues, scriptures, and decorations in those temples were taken out and set on fire or thrown into the water. The 'purification' of the Shinto temples was achieved and the severance of Buddhism and Shinto ruthlessly carried out, thus bringing to an end Ryobu Shinto, which had ruled the faith of the nation for ten centuries. (Anesaki, 1930; 334 f.)

Buddhism survived, however. The danger stirred leading monks to come together in common action to preserve their religious life and traditions, and after a while the frenzy of Shinto restoration abated. Buddhist ideas and practices were deeply rooted among the people, and the effect upon Buddhist leaders of their initial period of persecution was to stir them not only to resist, but also to a new and more vigorous advocacy of their faith. The opening up of Japanese life to the outside world once again which was a feature of the regime brought a decade of full exposure to European thought, culture and religion, but it was followed by a reaction against Europeanisation and Christianity. This was a conscious reaction, expressed through patriotic organisations created for the purpose, and a feature of the movement was the re-affirming of the religious traditions of Japan, especially of Buddhism. This special valuation of Buddhism was due to the fact that its philosophy was considered to have a special and striking affinity with certain trends in advanced European secular thought, namely the evolution theory of Darwin, the agnosticism of Spencer and the logic of Hegel. Thus Buddhism gradually regained its status as one of the major religious traditions of Japan, a status which in 1868 it had seemed in danger of losing altogether, although from the closing years of the nineteenth century onwards a strong opposition to all religion began to arise. This was from the ultra-nationalists, a group of heterogeneous elements whose common theme was described as 'Japanism' (Nippon Shugi) and whose creed was 'the glorification of the state and the rejection of all spiritual ideals aiming at anything beyond it'. It was this spirit which led Japan into the Second World War, and it is important to remember that this happened *in spite of* the place which Buddhism had held in the life of the nation for some centuries. By the second quarter of the twentieth century Buddhism was still a recognised feature of the life of Japan, but it could no longer be said to be exercising any pronounced or positive influence on the national life. Its condition in 1928 was described by Anesaki as follows:

> It is hopelessly divided and each branch of Japanese Buddhism remains faithful too much to the subtleties of its ancient teaching, not simply the spiritual legacy of its founder but much more its traditions and conventions accumulated during the centuries of its existence. Ecclesiastical Buddhism, represented by its sects and sub-sects amounting to nearly sixty, still retains much of the indolence it acquired under the high patronage of the government which it enjoyed during the past three centuries. The reinvigorated Buddhism of several revivals and various social works is almost entirely the work of those outside the organised bodies, or of those who have revolted against them. [Finally he adds] Its weakness in face of the industrial regime is too evident to need comment. (Anesaki, 1930; 406 f.)

7.44 Thailand in the modern period

Like Japan, Thailand ('the land of the free') reached the twentieth century without having been subjected to Western colonial treatment. Unlike Japan, Thailand had a tradition of Buddhist rulers, and of royal patronage and protection of the Buddhist Sangha; in other words, of Buddhism as the state religion. The modern tradition of royal patronage may be regarded as having begun in 1782 with King Rāma I who in the first decade of his reign promulgated ten edicts declaring to the Thai nation his intention to purge the Sangha of unworthy members, to purify monastic practice, and to encourage study and meditation.

Broadly speaking this has continued to be the policy of the Thai royal house to the present day. Prince Dhanivat writing in 1965 expressed it thus: 'The constructive protection of the Church given by the monarchy lies principally in the civil aspect wherein the state supports the Church in the performance of its duties and in education.' It is customary for kings of Thailand, like the great majority of the male population, to spend a period in their youth as members of the Sangha, living in a monastery; in this way they come to have a close personal interest in the affairs of the monks. There is also a more formal link between the royal government and the Sangha in the Religious Affairs Department of the Ministry of Education. This culture, in the form of art, architecture, and literature, is almost entirely Buddhist, and the religious element is much in evidence in public life in the form of processions with banners and music, and temple festivals at set times in the year. For the majority of the people of modern Thailand Buddhism has provided them with the framework of life, a heritage which 'meets emotional needs and provides answers to the mysteries of life. . . . supplies a doctrine of man, a metaphysics, a moral law, and an ultimate goal' (Wells, 1960; 6).

Only recently, however, has Thailand begun to experience the effects of modern technology and Western secularism. This has occurred mainly in the urban areas, and notably in the capital, Bangkok, since the end of the Second World War. But industrialisation and the secularising of life that usually goes with it have so far touched the Thai people as a whole only very lightly. A visitor to Bangkok in 1958 was told by a university lecturer that 'extremely few Buddhists had any real intellectual knowledge of the Buddhist scriptures, and that the religion did not make great demands on them. Superstition had almost become a religion in its own right, and as a directive force was confused with Buddhism. Astrology governed the life of thousands' (Thomson, 1961; 125). It is therefore difficult to forecast how Thai Buddhism would respond to a thoroughgoing encounter with Western secularism, and no other country in Buddhist Asia can serve as a guide.

7.45 Ceylon since independence

Buddhism had been disabled institutionally and handicapped educationally during the period of colonial rule in Ceylon, more perhaps than in any other country in Asia, for Europeanisation had been greatest in Ceylon. These were disabilities which could not easily be removed. The upper classes of Ceylon, to whom the British handed over the reins of government, were English-educated, highly Westernised and in some senses more European than Sinhalese. The view of one of them was that Ceylon was 'a little bit of England'. But the majority of the middle class had remained predominantly Sinhalese and Buddhist, and it was these who now looked for the restoration of Buddhism's place in the life of Ceylon. The revival which had begun in small ways in the mid-nineteenth century began to bear fruit. But it was by no means an automatic process, nor was it initiated by the ruling class of the newly independent Ceylon in any way comparable to the royal patronage of religion in the pre-European period, or in contemporary Thailand. To some extent it was the disappointment of the middle-class, largely Sinhalese-educated Buddhists of Ceylon, that more was not being done to restore Buddhist values and institutions to their proper place in the life of the nation that stirred them to action and was responsible for an accelerated revival of Buddhism.

It was in Ceylon in 1950 that the World Fellowship of Buddhists was formed, with the aim of bringing together Buddhists of various countries in a common endeavour to promote Buddhist ideas and values throughout the world. But there was much to be done in this direction in Ceylon itself. An All-Ceylon Buddhist Congress had been organised and in April 1954 this body set up a Committee of Enquiry, 'to enquire into the present state of Buddhism in Ceylon and to report on the conditions necessary to improve and strengthen the position of Buddhism, and the means whereby those conditions may be fulfilled'. The Committee was made up of six leading monks and six laymen. It held sittings throughout Ceylon between June 1954 and May 1956, and travelled approximately 6,300 miles. Its Report published in February 1956, under the significant title *The Betrayal of Buddhism*, while recognising that the most creative and fruitful period of Buddhist history in Ceylon had been prior to 1505 and the coming of the Portuguese, did not envisage a return to the pattern of state Buddhism or the restoration of institutions that had perished under colonial rule. The Ceylon historian G. C. Mendis comments on the Report that 'the Buddhist Commissioners in many respects make a definite break with the past'. The spirit of the recommendations is summed up in the Report's final paragraph:

... we wish to state with all the authority at our command that this struggle which the Buddhists must make is *not* a struggle to obtain a favoured position at the expense of other religious groups, however much we may have suffered at their hands in former times. We ask for ... the right to be allowed to profess and practise our religion without let or hindrance, material or spiritual, secular or religious, in a free and democratic Ceylon.

In the years since 1956 there has been a continuing sense among the sincere Buddhists of Ceylon that there was much to be done – in the purifying and reforming of the Sangha, to begin with. This was brought home dramatically by the murder of the Prime Minister of Ceylon, S. W. R. D. Bandaranaike, by a bhikkhu who had been disappointed in his ambition of preferment. This event produced a shock of horror and a public demand for the purging of the Sangha. On the other hand lay Buddhists have been active in the rediscovery of Buddhist teaching and practice, especially in relating the Abhidhamma (*3.22; 6.43*) to modern thought and in emphasising the importance of meditation. A notable example of this is a work by a retired member of the Government Medical Service, W. F. Jayasuriya, in which he relates Buddhist psycho-physical analysis and moral philosophy to modern medical and scientific knowledge (Jayasuriya, 1963).

Ceylon has also played a larger part than any other Buddhist country in making known to some of the non-Buddhist areas of the world the principles and practice of Buddhism. Ceylonese monks have left their own land to reside in London and Washington and other Western cities, as well as India; and monthly journals such as *World Buddhism* published in Colombo are read by increasing numbers in Europe, America and other parts of the English-speaking world.

7.46 India since independence

In the post-war period Buddhism has certainly risen in status in India. This has been at two different levels of Indian society. First, among the intellectuals, and here a characteristic case would be that of India's post-war Prime Minister, Pandit Nehru. Of a Kāshmiri Brāhman family, he, like many of Ceylon's post-war leaders, was as much English as Asian in his education, tastes and outlook. At his death in 1964 he was cremated with Hindu rites, but during his lifetime he does not seem to have been a Hindu by belief or practice. He himself said that the one religion which attracted him was Buddhism. Another indication of the respect which Buddhism is given among the educated class in India was the publication in 1956 by the government of India of a special volume, *2,500 Years of Buddhism*, in honour of the Buddha-Jayanti, or 2,500th anniversary of the Buddha's enlightenment (or victory, 'jayanti', over Māra the Evil One) according to the Theravāda reckoning. A large number of Indian scholars contributed to the volume and the President of India, Dr Radhakrishnan (who himself has translated and commented on Buddhist texts) wrote a foreword acknowledging India's continuing debt to the Buddha.

The other level at which there has been a Buddhist recovery in India is among the former 'untouchable' castes (4.20). This may really be said to have begun with the conversion of Dr B. R. Ambedkar, a cabinet minister in the government of the post-war, secular state of India, and the leader of the untouchables. On 14 October 1956, at Nagpur, he formally declared his adherence to Buddhism, together with a large number of the movement which he led. This event was followed by a fast-growing number of similar conversions among untouchables, and Buddhist monks began to arrive to undertake the task of instructing these new adherents and exhorting them to fulfil their duties as Buddhist laymen. By 1965 there were about four million ex-untouchable caste Buddhists in India, mainly in Mahārāsh-tra, but similar movements are going on in other states of the Indian Republic. Sangharakshita, a Buddhist monk from north-east India who has had much to do with this new movement, has commented that formerly these untouchable castes, as the result of centuries of con-ditioning by caste Hinduism, regarded themselves as low and despicable. 'But with conversion to Buddhism all that is changed at a stroke, overnight. . . . For the first time he feels free. As a result of this feeling of freedom, of liberation from age-old shackles, a tremendous energy is released which finds expression in all fields of life, social, political, cultural and educational, as well as religious.'

A final brief word must be said concerning Tibetan Buddhism which now finds itself transplanted to Indian soil. Although China claims Tibet politically, it is with India and South-East Asia that Tibet's real affinities lie. When, in the 1950s, the modern Chinese war-lords overran the territory of Tibet, it was to India that her people, both monks and laymen, fled. There they found refuge from the persecution they experienced in their own land under the Chinese communists, and there they found a welcome from a country which, while itself no longer Buddhist, yet takes pride in one of its greatest sons of old, the Buddhist emperor Aśoka *(3.26)*. In the hill country of north India Tibetan Buddhists are fashioning a Buddhist community, the existence of which within the borders of India may well be a factor of potential importance in the future of Indian Buddhism.

7.47 Burma since independence

In post-war Burma, with its long tradition of Buddhist history and its large Buddhist majority in the population, the story has been rather different both from that of Ceylon and of India. In 1947, when Burma achieved independence, the days of the Burmese kings were not so very long past. It was only sixty-two years since Thibaw had been defeated and dethroned by the British and the palace at Mandalay abandoned, and although there would not have been many in 1947 who still remembered the days of the Burmese kings there would have been some; and there were certainly many, who in 1947 were in the prime of life, who had heard their fathers speak of those days. While there had, under British rule, been an acceptance by Buddhists of the new situation and a coming to terms with it, there were also strong enough memories of the Burmese Buddhist kingdom to provide powerful hopes that the old days of Buddhism were to return with independence.

It is this which explains the great popularity of the pious Buddhist, U Nu, who was Prime Minister of Burma for most of the period up to 1962. It explains too the importance attached by so many of the Burmese Buddhists (eighty-five per cent of the total population of the Union of Burma) to the idea of making Buddhism the state religion. This was in fact achieved during the last years of U Nu's premiership, against the opposition of minority religious groups – and paradoxically with a great display of armed force. On the day the necessary Bill came before the Parliament of the Union in Rangoon the streets of the city were deserted for fear of the violence that was expected, and it was the tanks and armoured cars and infantrymen of the Burmese Army who were most in evidence. Soon after U Nu was deposed by the Army coup of March 1962, the measure was withdrawn. A great deal of the agitation for making Buddhism the state religion had come from the more vociferous sections of the Sangha; under the Army regime from 1962 these have been resentful but less demonstrative.

Meanwhile in quieter ways, the recovery of Buddhism after the dislocation it suffered under British rule and its adaptation to the modern world has gone on. There has been a continued interest in and study of the Abhidhamma among the more learned monks, and government examinations in the Abhidhamma are held, for which all are encouraged to sit. There has been an even greater emphasis upon the practice of meditation in certain sections of the lay community. Meditation centres for laymen have sprung up in many places, notably near the great centres of Rangoon and Mandalay, and increasingly these are resorted to by Buddhist civil servants, teachers, and others of the professional or semi-professional class. A notable piece of missionary work on behalf of Buddhism was undertaken by a retired service officer, Colonel Ba Than (now Dhammika – ? 'evangelist' – U Ba Than). Unlike many Buddhists in Burma who have talked of the importance of missionary work in the West, Ba Than has turned his attention to the non-Buddhist tribes of the frontier and hill areas of Burma. A Buddhist writer in the Rangoon *Guardian* commends the realism of U Ba Than's enterprise, for, he comments 'the future of the Buddhasāsana [Buddhist religion] in Burma is dark and gloomy. There is much to be done for the *renascence* of the Buddhist church. Young men are becoming sceptical about the teaching of the monks and their ignorance of Buddhism is appalling.' This was perhaps an unnecessarily pessimistic picture but it expressed the mood of some of the more thoughtful Buddhists of Burma.

The Sixth Buddhist Council held in Rangoon in 1956–7 to commemorate the Buddha-Jayanti year was partly an attempt to provide Burmese Buddhism with a stimulus, partly an attempt to assure the Burmese people that their government under U Nu as Prime Minister was taking seriously its role as protector and promoter of the faith. In addition the government had established the Buddha Sāsana Council to co-ordinate the various aspects of encouraging and propagating the religion, some of which have already been mentioned, such as Buddhist studies, missionary work, maintaining of pagodas, and so on. All this is based on the assumption expressed by a Burmese cabinet minister, U Win: 'The prosperity of a religion . . . depends on the presence of a ruler who is genuinely inclined to promote it.' This assumption is an inheritance from Burma's past. It may or may not be true of the modern world; its unqualified acceptance would throw serious doubt on the prospects for the survival of Buddhism in those countries whose governments are, at best, religiously uncommitted.

7.48 New religions of Japan since 1947

On New Year's Day 1946, soon after the defeat of Japan in the Second World War, the emperor of Japan broadcast a message to his people in which he renounced his divine status as emperor. The tie between Shinto religion and the Japanese state was thus officially brought to an end. In the course of the change-over to democratic institutions, the United States General MacArthur gave permission for the Japanese to form religious groups quite freely, however they might wish. All religious denominations in Japan are required to register with the Ministry of Education, and in 1945 the number registered was forty-three, made up of thirteen Shinto, twenty-eight Buddhist and two Christian. By 1951 this had increased to a total of 720 made up of 258 Shinto-type, 260 Buddhist, 46 Christian and 156 'others'. This looks like an explosion of some magnitude, but can be explained to some extent as the result of greater variety in classification, and also of the registering of groups which had previously existed only 'underground' and had not registered. Ten years later, in 1961, the total number of denominations had settled down to about 170, as against 43 in 1945. When all the necessary allowances have been made the fact remains that a very considerable number of new religious movements or sects have come into existence in Japan in the post-war period.

Undoubtedly one of the basic factors has been the 'crisis of meaning' which the Japanese people experienced in the years following 1945. The shock of Japan's defeat, and the loss over-night of the national figure-head, the divine emperor, have produced a sense of loss of all stability. Père Heinrich Dumoulin suggests that 'Japan's defeat in the last war and the subsequent collapse of a traditional order has shaken many to the core so that the chaos of post-war time is also experienced as a personal crisis of existence' (Dumoulin, 1963; 21).

Similarly Miss Carmen Blacker, on the basis of her personal observation in Japan, notes that all the new religions appear to have as their starting point the feeling of anxiety, insecurity, and the fear of the unknown which afflicts so many people in post-war Japan (Blacker, 1962). There are few social services (except for those provided by certain large organisations for their own employees) and little security. To the shock of defeat and the unsettled post-war conditions has thus to be added the fact that living is insecure. Such general conditions as these frequently produce a situation of acute individual crisis for the Japanese, a feeling of being at the end of one's tether, of not knowing where to turn; in the Japanese expression, the experience of 'all eight ways blocked'. It is this personal crisis which usually provides the occasion for entry into one of the new religious sects, which are 'religious' in the very general sense that they offer their adherents a way of coping with the difficulties of life. Usually the moment of personal crisis is observed by some friend or neighbour who is already a member of one of the new groups, and the opportunity is seized of commending its attractions to the potential convert.

Common elements in the appeal of the new sects are: first, a very simple, positive message which forms the central teaching, often consisting of emphasis upon some single virtue, such as faith or humility, as the universal solvent of problems; and second, the prospect of actual mundane benefits here and now. The latter is often made possible by the large funds which many of the new sects have built up. There is no clear line of demarcation between what the West regards as 'religious' and 'secular' concerns. For many people in Japan the appeal of the new sects lies in their ability to provide alternative solutions 'to the economic as well as the spiritual ills of unorganised workers'. Sheldon comments: 'Labour leaders complain that when union members are converted they lose their fighting spirit.' The majority of the converts to the cults are of low social status. Here one would seem to have confirmation of the Marxist view of religion as an expression of the protest of the oppressed soul (that is, socially and economically oppressed), and of Troeltsch's view that new religious sects most commonly find their adherents among the dispossessed.

A futher reason for the appeal of the sects lies precisely in their *newness*. The old religious traditions of Japan are regarded by many industrial workers as spiritually bankrupt. On the other hand Western religion – in its traditional Christian forms – is not seen by the Japanese worker or peasant as having much relevance to his situation (Howe, 1964). Norbeck points out that 'Total membership in the numerous Christian sects totals only about seven hundred thousand persons, less than the membership of any one of a number of the new Japanese sects that have risen to prominence since the end of World War II' (Norbeck, 1965; 18).

The new sects can be classified according to three main types, although there are no clear distinctions; first there are those which are in some way derived from a Buddhist milieu, historically, and this is usually the Nichiren (6.48) type of Buddhism (the least 'Buddhist' and most Japanese); second, there are those which stem from the Shinto tradition in some way; and third, those with no clear historical roots in any one tradition. Hammer describes post-war Japanese religion as both 'a living museum and a living laboratory'; that is, new blends of faith are constantly being thrown up out of old materials to form what he describes as 'transitional compounds' (Hammer, 1961). Even those sects which have some historical connection with Nichiren Buddhism or with Shinto display their eclectic quality.

The largest numerically and the best known of these newly arisen sects is the Soka Gakkai (Value-creating academic-society). The movement was founded in 1931 but its leader was put in jail and only in 1945 when he was released did it really begin to grow. By 1965 it claimed a membership of thirteen million persons. It offers the panacea of faith to all who find themselves in the situation of 'all eight ways blocked'. The object of faith is a sacred formula Namu Myoho Rengekyo inscribed by the Buddhist leader Nichiren on a strip of paper. It is strongly nationalistic in character, it has also a strong millenarian quality and proclaims a coming millennium towards which men must direct all their efforts. Its appeal is felt largely by small traders, business men and certain special groups of industrial workers, notably miners. It has a strong appeal also to young people for whom there is a special youth corps. The technique by which its converts are won is known as Shaku baku, and consists of bombarding the potential convert with high-pressure propaganda until his resistance is overcome and he is 'converted'. A large headquarters at Mount Fuji provides spiritual refreshment for those who can make the trip from time to time. Its three most important features are: faith, activity, organisation. The last of these now includes political organisation, and its vast membership has enabled it to return its own candidates to parliament. The movement seems to have no clear political programme, but seeks mainly to fill the house with men of integrity and 'sound judgment'. It is feared and disliked by other sections of Japanese society on account of this political activity, especially now that the Soka Gakkai constitutes the third largest group in parliament, after the Liberals and the Socialists.

While most of the spectacular achievements in the post-war period are to be found among these new sects of the Soka Gakkai type, the older traditional faiths have also experienced a mild revival. There has been a growth of more specifically Shinto sects (with the end of state Shinto) and among the Buddhists there has been a limited degree of revival: lay people have learnt to take a more active part in Buddhist organisations, groups have been organised for study, or fellowship or retreats; Buddhist scholars have devoted themselves to the reinterpretation of Buddhist ideas, and this has helped to bring about a deepened religious concern; there has also developed a new interest in Buddhism outside Japan, and an awareness of Buddhism in its international dimension. It is significant that all this post-war vitality of religious movements has occurred in the Asian country which has been undergoing the most rapid industrialisation – so rapid that it is now a serious and often successful rival to the industrial nations of the West.

7.49 Buddhism and modern thought

An important and interesting feature of Buddhism in post-war Ceylon has been the growing literature of exposition of Buddhist thought, of a fairly popular kind, for English readers both in Ceylon and elsewhere. It is particularly significant that nowadays this is produced by both English-speaking monks and laymen; perhaps at least as much comes from the latter. Outstanding among such laymen is Dr G. P. Malalasekere, formerly Professor of Pali at the University of Ceylon, and more recently the diplomatic representative of his country abroad, first in Moscow and then in London, and a governor of the School of Oriental and African Studies of London University. He was one of the lay members of the Buddhist commission of 1954 (7.45), and the first President of the World Fellowship of Buddhists, which was founded in Ceylon. Dr Malalasekere's writings are characterised by both scientific scholarship of the highest order and a deep conviction concerning the Buddhist view of life and its importance for the modern world. What is noteworthy about the presentation of Buddhist ideas that is found in his work is the high place he gives to integrating them with modern scientific thought. In order to do this effectively, he says, Buddhist doctrines must be given continual reformulation and re-interpretation. Moreover, as a Buddhist he welcomes the increasing attention given by Western scientists to the human mind; it is here that he finds the convergence of scientific and Buddhist thought most likely. It is noteworthy too that much of the writing of this thoroughly Buddhist scholar and man of affairs reveals a keen concern with the processes and patterns of contemporary history.

Another important exponent of Buddhism in terms of modern science is Dr W. F. Jayasuriya, whose book *The Psychology and Philosophy of Buddhism* is an exposition of the Abhidhamma (*3.22*) for an educated English readership and intended to appeal especially to those who have received some training in science. The book originated in a series of talks broadcast by Radio Ceylon. The Buddhist Abhidhamma is expounded as a system of science. The traditional method of analysis is taken as a starting point: there are four categories in the Buddhist analysis, namely cognition, mental factors, matter and nibbāna. These four groups are the 'reals'; the first three groups are mundane and exist in a context of strict causal relationships; the fourth is supra-mundane, 'existing without cause, and hence external'. Another way of describing the first three groups, in Buddhist terminology, is to say they are conditioned phenomena; this is in agreement with (what Jaya-suriya regards as) 'the deterministic position of most contemporary scientists that no event is without a cause', for 'if we did not believe in Causality there would be no Science' (Jayasuriya, 1963; 5). It is the unique achievement of the Buddha, he claims, to have perceived this truth more than two thousand years ago. Where Buddhist analysis goes beyond that of natural science, says Jayasuriya, is in respect of the fourth category: 'the Buddha claimed in addition that there was one Unconditioned or Uncaused element, namely Nibbāna, which comes into its own only when we have understood the conditioned elements.'

Other examples of contemporary lay Buddhist writing could be quoted, but even from this brief extract it will be seen what is the general tenor and direction of such modern exposition. Whether the agreement between Buddhist Abhidhamma and modern scientific thought is ultimately as close as such writers would claim or whether there is only an initial or superficial resemblance makes no difference to the fact that for many of those to whom such modern Buddhist writing is addressed it seems that here is a system of religious thought and practice which is both scientifically respectable and spiritually satisfying. It is noteworthy, too, that such laymen of the Theravādin tradition find the Abhidhamma fully sufficient as a religious and philosophical system, and see no need to venture further into the field of metaphysical speculation as the Mahāyānists did (*4.33–4.35*).

Summary and comment on Chapter Seven

Traditional forms of religious belief and practice maintain their existence in the modern world with varying degrees of vitality: this much our survey can thus far be said to have shown. We must now consider whether it is possible to draw any useful conclusions from so general a survey. In particular, the question arises as to whether it is possible to suggest any reasons for these variations in vitality, either within one tradition of religion – between, for example, Thailand and Ceylon, or Pakistan and Indonesia, or Israel and the United States; or across the frontiers of religious tradition, as between Japan (where new religions are booming) and Great Britain (where religious institutions are mainly old and depressed).

One of the possible lines of inquiry that suggests itself is that of the varying relations between religion and the state, and what bearing this relation may have on the vitality of religion in the modern world. If we look first at the 'Indianised' area of South Asia, that is, those countries which have in the past come under the cultural influence of India (India, Pakistan, Ceylon, Burma, Thailand and Indonesia), we shall be studying an area that is both geographically compact, and also religiously varied, in the types of tradition represented (Hindu, Buddhist, Muslim), and also in the varying degrees of vitality within those traditions. If any useful general conclusions can be drawn concerning the variations in a relatively homogeneous cultural area, they can then be tested elsewhere.

Geographically, the area is large, but no greater in extent than, say, the United States. Its economy is mainly rural and agricultural rather than industrial, although it contains one or two important industrial areas, mostly in India. Its population is predominantly peasant, but with a recently emerged, or emerging, middle class, mainly in India, Ceylon and Indonesia.

Within this area Islam is the dominant religious tradition in Pakistan and Indonesia, with an important minority of about 40 million Muslims in India. Pakistan has 82 million Muslims, and Indonesia about 88 million, where they form ninety per cent of the population. For Muslims the question whether the state shall be religious or secular would seem to be important, in view of the close connection between political and religious leadership in Islamic tradition, and of the fact that in origin Islam was, so to speak, the sect that became a state. Islamic theory would appear to require a form of government which could be described as 'theocratic' (so long as the term is dissociated from its secondary meaning, that of the rule of a priestly class). In practice, however, theocracy, if by this we mean government strictly in accordance with divine precepts, through the medium of the Prophet or his successors (caliphs), has not been characteristic of Islam since the Umayyads seized power in A.D. 661 (*5.18*). Nevertheless, minorities of Muslims have from time to time affirmed that this is the only form of government proper to Islam. In modern times such a minority is to be found in the 'theocratic' sects: the Bab movement in Persia in the early nineteenth century (*7.37*), the Ahmadiya and some Shia groups, although, as we have seen, some of these are now only very loosely 'Islamic' (*7.38*).

However, the idea that Islamic religion requires for its proper fulfilment an Islamic state, even though this be democratic in constitution, found expression in 1947 in the creation of the state of Pakistan. The twenty years of its existence have not, as we have seen (*7.39*), provided much evidence that Islamic religion flourishes in a modern Islamic state, although it has to be remembered that in the eyes of some Muslims, Pakistan is still far from being Islamic in fact. Nevertheless, Pakistan is constitutionally Islamic in a way that Indonesia is not; yet it would be difficult to maintain that Islam is healthier or more vigorous in Pakistan.

Indonesian Muslims, the majority of whom do not seem to be very much concerned about making their country constitutionally Islamic, have tended to devote their efforts to voluntary Muslim organisations such as the Muhammadiya and in doing so have in effect given their assent to an alternative type of relationship between Islamic religion and the state – namely that of the Muslim individual in a free, democratic society. This, too, is the relationship which is emerging in Islam in the Republic of India, which in the view of some observers may

P

prove to be a more significant and important development than that of Pakistan (*7.39*).

Turning to the Buddhist countries of South Asia we find a somewhat similar pattern. At one extreme is the classical, medieval pattern which is still maintained in Thailand, with Buddhism as the state religion and the necessity for the monarch to be a Buddhist written into the constitution. At the other extreme is Ceylon, where the medieval pattern was broken with the coming of European imperial rule, and where after independence it has not been restored, but instead, Buddhism is regarded as the way of life practised by the majority of the citizens in this free democratic republic. In between the two extremes is Burma, where too the medieval pattern was broken by the British, and where after independence an attempt was made to restore it; an attempt which has now been abandoned. Nevertheless there remains a hankering after the medieval idea of the Buddhist-Brāhmanical ruler who was also a cosmic figure, and this, as we have seen, has given rise to sporadic messianic movements. If in the case of Buddhism one asks where is the religion strongest and most vigorous, it is difficult not to answer that it is so in Ceylon, where the constitutional Buddhist state now no longer exists (*7.45*). In putting the answer thus one has to allow for the possibility that other factors, besides that of the free relation between religion and the state in Ceylon, have contributed to the vitality of Buddhism there. Some that might be considered are: the longer period in Ceylon in which Western education has been stimulating Buddhist minds to a new kind of response, compared with Burma and Thailand; the geographical features which with the building of roads throughout Ceylon have made easy communication possible, and produced a community in which ideas can be cross-fertilised more readily; and perhaps most important, the presence in Ceylon of a sizeable middle class, the class that tends to be the upholder of traditional religion and also tends to produce progressive restatements of its ideas and attitudes.

It is worth noticing that of these factors in Ceylon which may be held to have contributed to the vitality of Buddhism there, two are found also in Indonesia: one is, as has already been mentioned, that there is no official state patronage of Islam; the other is the emergence of a middle class which has promoted new religious activities and re-formulations of orthodox belief.

In this matter of the relationship between religion and the state a tentative conclusion may therefore be suggested: that the vitality of a religious tradition is not enhanced by too close an identification with the state. On the other hand attention has to be given to the fact that it is equally unlikely to be enhanced where the religion is subject to persecution by the state. The prospect for Buddhist religious life in Tibet is such that Tibetans, both monks and laymen, continue to escape when they can to the more congenial atmosphere of India, where Tibetan Buddhism is managing to maintain its existence. In the U.S.S.R., while the Orthodox Church continues to exist, although in a much reduced and circumscribed form, religious persecution especially of the Protestant sects continues sporadically. At the time of writing communications reaching the Western Churches from the Baptists of the Soviet Union reveal a continuing campaign by the authorities against them over the past five years, a campaign which has taken the more extreme forms of persecution, imprisonment and torture.

The optimum conditions for the future free development of religious life might therefore be thought to exist in those countries of the non-communist world where religious institutions are free from state patronage or state control. The most obvious example of such a situation is in the United States. Certainly religious institutions appear to be more lively and more widely supported there than in those countries of the West where Christianity or Judaism receives state patronage and protection — in Britain, for example, or Israel. It can be argued, however, that in this connection appearances in the United States are misleading. Bryan Wilson, for instance, suggests that there are special reasons for the success of institutional religion in that country, and that these are closely connected with the fact that religious institutions provide the most convenient form of social 'belonging', of identifying oneself as a complete American, in a society which is very mobile, both socially and geographically. He takes a critical view of the religiously superficial nature of most of the booming religious institutions, and adds the (mainly impressionistic) comment that the United States is 'a country in which instrumental values, rational procedures and technical methods have gone furthest, and the country in which the sense of the sacred, the sense of the sanctity of life, and deep religiosity are most conspicuously absent' (Wilson, 1966).

This brings us to the issue which provides the most important single problem in the study of religion in its modern context throughout the

world, especially in industrial society, namely that of the phenomenon
which has come to be known as *secularisation*, and how it is to be regarded.

The problem arises from the fact that the term as used in this
connection has conflicting connotations. For Wilson it means 'the
process whereby religious thinking practice and institutions lose social
significance' (1966; xiv). He acknowledges, however, that the same
range of phenomena which he interprets in this way may be seen by
other observers in a different light. Those who regard religion, as some
sociologists do, as a necessary function of any human society (so that
without some form of religion, quasi-religion, or other functional
substitute for religion the society concerned would disintegrate), would
see the present decline in support for the institutional forms and practices
of religion in the West as a phase of transition between one pattern of
institutionalised religion and another, and not a final evaporation of all
religious concern. Certainly, as will have become apparent from this
introductory study, this is not an unfamiliar situation in the history of
religion; as one religious structure disintegrates it is often, though not
always, succeeded by another. This functionalist argument, from the
nature of religious history in the past and throughout the world, is
countered by Wilson with the assertion that though human societies
until now may have needed some sort of religious system to provide
social and psychological cohesion, this cannot be accepted as an argument concerning what is happening now, for, he says, human needs
can change; or at least they do not necessarily continue to be felt in the
same way. But he acknowledges, and it is in the light of the religious
history of mankind a very important acknowledgement, that there is a
problem which is left unsolved when men in a modern industrial
society have no religious framework to life, and have to live 'in a
world in which ultimate explanations and ultimate satisfactions are
denied them'. In saying this he is implicitly acknowledging the strength
of the objection that might be made against his view that religion may
cease to be one of man's needs: namely, that he has made the entirely
gratuitous assumption that it is *proven* that religion is not a permanent
need of man. This is by no means proven; the run of the historical
evidence, including that from modern times, is against it, and the onus of
proof lies with those who would challenge the functionalist view. Even
in the case of modern Europe the evidence is ambiguous and capable of
more than one interpretation.

Harvey Cox, in his book *The Secular City*, has in fact suggested that what is happening in the modern West is the liberation of religion from mythological and quasi-magical ways of thinking and acting, and the liberation of religious life and practice from the ecclesiastical forms in which it had become imprisoned. In his view 'secularisation' must be clearly distinguished from 'secularism'; the latter is an ideology or a quasi-religion, dogmatic, exclusive and intolerant as ideologies usually are. Secularisation on the other hand, which is a term to describe what is happening to conventional religion in the modern world, according to Cox, is a continuation of the process begun in Biblical religion, whereby man's life is set free from the social tyrannies and false world-views of paganism.

It is significant that something of the same kind of process which Cox sees with Christian eyes is happening in Ceylon, where the introduction of modern scientific knowledge and medicine is having a corroding effect on the old indigenous pagan beliefs and practices, which Buddhism also has been slowly and quietly undermining through the centuries. Modern thought is not having this effect on Buddhism however, but rather is enabling it to be expressed less ambiguously, and without the admixture of paganism which has characterised it in the past. New social and educational patterns may well lead, however, to a restructuring of Buddhism in Ceylon, and elsewhere; especially in connection with the emergence of a sophisticated middle-class lay intelligentsia. It would certainly be as shortsighted and unwise as it would be un-Buddhistic for Buddhists to assume that the structure of their institutions is sacrosanct.

The same is true for Western religion. It would be a mistake to identify the reality of religion with any one institutional form which it may have assumed in the past: the national Churches, or the confessional denominations of Christianity, for example. Ecclesiastical leaders sometimes convey the impression that the disappearance of the Church in its present form would be the ultimate tragedy in the religious life of man; or that religion will die out if it is not kept going and organised on an authoritarian ecclesiastical and dogmatic basis. This kind of view, besides showing a singular lack of faith in the God who is proclaimed as 'living', could also be the reverse of the truth. It may be that religion will die out wherever this *is* the case.

Epilogue: Religious Belief and the Future

THE comparative study of religion is an academic discipline and is not properly undertaken in order to promote or boost any one particular kind of religious belief. What such study can do, however, is to provide us with a less restricted and parochial view of religion than that in which we were brought up (this includes those brought up as humanists or atheists), a wider range of evidence than we might have had otherwise, and some understanding of the historical development and consequences, good and ill, of the various forms of religious belief which exist in the modern world. In this way the comparative study of religion can materially assist the religious thinking of the modern generation.

There are some who would have universities teach only Christian theology. For example, Laurence Bright, O.P., recently dismissed the idea that comparative religion could take the place of Christian theology as the proper approach to the study of religion in an academic context by saying that religious systems other than Christianity do not lie 'at the roots of our culture', and that it 'is artificial to treat Buddhism or Hinduism as other than of slight importance for the majority of people in the West'. (*Slant*, London, Dec. 1966/Jan. 1967, p. 14). This is a curiously weak argument but not uncommon among theologians. It also assumes a static view of the situation. The inhabitants of Britain at the beginning of the Christian era might have objected that this new faith from the Mediterranean did not lie at the roots of their culture. Because Buddhism is a view of the human situation which had its origins in an area which is geographically remote from Britain (though less so now than it used to be), it can therefore be of little interest to little Englanders. One has to note also that Christian theology, which is assumed, rightly or wrongly, to lie 'at the roots of our culture', has a rapidly declining appeal in its orthodox church-theological form as a convincing and coherent view of life. A religious knowledge teacher in a girls' grammar school in Cheshire recently conducted an enquiry among the sixth-formers to find out where their interests lay in the field of religion, and was surprised to find that, as he put it,' there seemed to be about forty potential Buddhists among them'. However inaccurately they may have heard about Buddhism, they were evidently not discouraged from an interest in this alternative to the theology they had been brought up in by the fact that it did not lie at the roots of English culture.

From the brief survey of religious beliefs and traditions which has been undertaken here it is possible to distinguish three main types of developed belief, each of which has a body of adherents in the modern world. First, there is the simple, majestic transcendentalism of Islam: a ruthlessly logical belief in the one, undivided god who is utterly omnipotent, who created and rules over all things, so that everything which happens is his will, who is in no way affected by anything men may or may not do, and who, when the moment comes that it pleases him to do so, will dispose of this world and its inhabitants according to his own predetermining of their fates. Second, and in contrast with this, is the Buddhist doctrine that man's destiny is to become 'awakened' (Buddha) to the nature of his cosmic situation; that he is to achieve this by the suppression of evil tendencies and the encouragement of good tendencies, both through moral conduct and meditational practices; in this way man will eventually come to partake of a life that is no longer individualistic but of a universal kind. In both of these types of religious belief the time-process is not of primary importance; there is little sense of historical development, although there is slightly more in Buddhism than in Islam. Finally, there is the messiah doctrine which focuses in Jesus of Nazareth; here the pattern of existence seen in the life and death of Jesus is affirmed as the pattern of a new humanity which has yet to emerge, and towards the emergence of which there is a power at work who 'fathers' the new man. Jesus is he-who-is-to-come (the Christ), and men are called upon to place their lives within the realm of this developing new humanity in confident expectation of the day that is to come.

These three types of religious belief may be characterised as (1) the theology of the omnipotent; (2) the anthropology of the 'awakened'; and (3) the christology of Jesus, or the new man. Empirical Christianity has, however, tried to combine elements of both (1) and (3), for various discernible, historical, social and political reasons; incompatible elements of belief have to be found room for within ecclesiastical

Christianity, in unstable and uneasy co-existence; so uneasy in fact that an intelligent child of ten finds the tenets of orthodox Christian theology highly unsatisfactory and contradictory.

An important point made by Bryan Wilson in his study of religion and secularisation is that a religious system cannot be emotionally reassuring (as it should be) if it is intellectually unsatisfying. There is plenty of evidence that in Western Europe people desire to find a coherent and meaningful system of values; in overwhelming numbers, however, they vote with their feet against ecclesiastical orthodoxy. Antony Flew, in his book *God and Philosophy*, has set out very clearly the logical weakness of Augustinian Christian theology; the replies made by orthodox theologians and philosophers appear to the present writer to have been largely casuistical, issue-evading and unconvincing. Those who adhere to orthodox Christianity usually do so nowadays for reasons other than that of the coherence of theology; because they need *some* sort of a refuge from nihilism and secularism, because they have been visited and asked to come to church by a friendly represent-ative, because they have personal or family ties, and so on. Identified with the church for these kinds of reasons they then seek to understand and make sense of its ideology, not always, however, with great success, as anyone who has talked to generation after generation of students knows. So long as the proper concerns of religious discourse in the West are held to be the upholding of the particular, Western, and historically-conditioned theology of one ecclesiastical institution and its sacred books and formularies, this situation is likely to continue, and religious belief will languish more and more.

We have seen that for many centuries now Judaism, Christianity and Islam have accepted the belief which has passed into their scriptures (and thus been hallowed) from ancient Near Eastern religion, that of the absolute potentate who is affirmed to be the creator-deity. Islam alone is fully consistent in its logical development of this belief, that is in maintaining that nothing man has ever done or can do will ever affect this Almighty Being in any way whatsoever. So far as Christian faith is concerned this belief in an all-powerful cosmic lord accords ill with the special insight of the early Christians regarding the cosmic meaning and the ultimate supremacy of the crucified Jesus, as the Christ who is to come, and the new view of deity which this entails. Modern scientific ways of thought have now invaded Christian thinking at least, and Christian theology is at last beginning to divest itself of this ancient pagan encumbrance which it has borne for so long. The result has been a certain sense of release, expressed in the idea of the 'death of God', the death, that is to say, of this absolute potentate whose nature and being Christians had been trying for so long to reconcile somehow with the original conviction that in the righteous, suffering, crucified Jesus men were given a glimpse of the 'open secret' of the universe.

The controversy concerning the 'death of God', associated with the names of van Buren, Altizer, and Hamilton especially, has been interpreted by some observers as an aspect of secularisation – in this case, the secularisation of theology. This agrees with Harvey Cox's use of the term, to mean release from magical and non-Christian ecclesiastical structures and the beliefs which underlie them. There is a fundamental liaison between, on the one hand, the potentate concept of God, and on the other all the paraphernalia of cosmogony, magic, the debasement of man and the denial to him of any virtue whatsoever, and an authoritarian ecclesiastical type of religion. Much of this emerges in disguised form in Augustinian types of religion, Catholic or Calvinistic. The view of God and of man's situation which was held by those who had known Jesus of Nazareth was, however, radically new. This can be apprehended most clearly in the mood of expectancy which had been engendered among them. There is a strongly forward-looking emphasis in the New Testament writings. St Paul writes to the Christians of Philippi of his confidence that the 'good work' which has been begun in them will be continued 'until the day of Christ'. To those at Rome he writes of the whole creation waiting 'with eager longing for the revealing of the sons of God', and goes on to speak of the whole creation suffering, as it were, its birth-pangs as a new creation comes into being; included in this cosmic travail are those who already have an 'earnest' or a 'pledge' in their experience of the Holy Spirit; even they too 'wait for adoption as sons'. To the Christians in Galatia he writes concerning the ongoing spiritual life as something which is to continue 'until Christ be formed in you'. He reminds the Christians of Colossæ that 'when Christ who is our life appears, then you will also appear with him in glory'. Similarly, John, the writer of the First Epistle which bears his name, says: 'We are God's children now; it does not yet appear what we shall be, but we know that when he appears we shall be like him.'

The Christian revelation can thus be seen to have two important distinguishing characteristics; it is radical in its view of God; and it is open-ended towards what is yet to come. First, it is radical, in that it entails a new conception of God, not as the power who reigns like a potentate, but the power who produces the Christ-humanity. This is seen first in Jesus, who is to be 'the first-born among many brethren' as the Epistle to the Hebrews puts it, so that God's Christ is also the corporate new humanity which is yet to appear. The appearance of this *new humanity* is the cosmic goal towards which all the life of mankind moves, so that the life of the present is always to be understood in the light of this 'until'. The early Christians had caught a glimpse of the Christ who is to come, 'the Messiah', and through him had glimpsed what to them was a radically new conception of the nature of God. (It is for this reason that the modern theologian Karl Barth emphasises endlessly that all Christian theology – or talk about God – must start from the Word-made-flesh, that is, from the datum provided in Christ, and from nowhere else.) The Christ who is to come is the new humanity; to put it another way, this is a corporate conception, Jesus of Nazareth together with his 'many brethren', the glorified 'new people'. The time-scale of the Christian expectation has been expanded since the days of the first disciples, but the essential principle, the expectation of the appearing of the sons of God as the cosmic climax, remains. The authentic Christian revelation is therefore also open-ended. There is much more yet to be known and experienced; a little has been glimpsed, but there are yet 'those things which eye has not seen, nor ear heard and which it has not entered into the heart of man to conceive, but which God has prepared for them who love him'; the little light has yet to grow into 'the perfect day', the eschatological day of Christ. Among the Christian fathers it is Irenaeus, the first great theologian, who most clearly represents this optimism concerning the nature and destiny of man.

There had been a similar insight in early Buddhism. The ideal, the new type of humanity, the nibbuta-man, had been seen exemplified in one life, it was claimed, and the highest destiny of men was to be found as men listened to the Buddha-word, followed the Buddha-sāsana and, denying the old, private life of selfish individualism, entered into the fuller and wider life of nibbuta-humanity, in which the fundamental roots of evil, namely greed, hatred, and illusion, were conquered and exterminated by the power of the positive forces of good, namely generosity, magnanimity and clear insight.

There is thus a double aspect to the 'death of God' theology. It may serve to emphasise that the concept of God which is finally proving to be untenable in the light of man's scientific understanding of the nature of the universe is a concept which is also alien to authentic Christian revelation; it may serve also to point to the original emphasis among Christians, that beyond the news of this 'death' is the expectation of new birth, the coming into being of a humanity whose nature has been briefly glimpsed in Christ.

It may be that the encounter of religions, East and West, may assist the necessary reinterpretation. Religious truths do not always immediately come into their own, sometimes they wait, preserved and cherished in one particular tradition, until the time of opportunity and need comes, when they become part of the heritage of a much wider society. It may be that the words and the way of the Buddha have much to contribute at this moment of history to the religious life of the West. Karl Barth, in one of his later writings, has pointed out that there are other witnesses to the truth of Christ outside the Bible and outside the Church. He speaks of the community of Christ recognising 'with joy something of its own most proper message' or 'being forced to recognise this with shame because by [these other voices] it is shown and made to realise the omissions and truncations of its own message' (*Church Dogmatics*, iv, 3(1), 124). Perhaps one of the most important and urgent functions of the comparative study of religion is to assist this widening of horizons, this sharing by East and West of their deepest religious insights, and thus help to save men from that bleak and nihilistic secularism, whose tenets have already deeply affected the thinking and the ways of living of Western man. The results are seen in the world wars which have erupted from the West, the increasing chronic alcoholism, and, more recently, the growing drug addiction; these are but the more sensational ways of escape from what is felt to be the meaninglessness of existence. In other quarters there is a suspicion that religion in the West has betrayed man at the most important point in life, and consequently a tendency to find meaning in Eastern religion. Yet there is still readiness to accord honour to the figure of Jesus Christ, and to believe that in this man human life finds meaning and purpose. So long as this is so there is hope that in spite of ecclesiastical orthodoxy the truth will out, the false god of Christian theology will be rejected, and a new chapter in the history of human spiritual progress will open.

The West has its own traditions of spirituality, just as has the East. But Latin Christianity has accepted a tradition of another kind, which the East has not, a tradition of institutional and intellectual authoritarianism. We have seen that in the fourteenth century these two traditions within the Latin Church began to emerge as alternatives, but in the convulsions which shook the Church in the sixteenth century the emphases of the Catholic mystical tradition were lost sight of; Catholics and Protestants alike became preoccupied with institutional forms, dogmatic orthodoxy, and political advantage. Perhaps the greatest need today is for the West to recollect the wisdom it once had and has almost lost in the pursuit of power (and latterly in its concessions to secular ideologies, concessions which are themselves due to spiritual impoverishment). Western religion could, if it were not too proud to do so, find itself fortified in the recovery of its own spirituality by considering the testimony of the traditions of the East.

General Bibliography

The following list includes both works referred to in the text (by means of the author's name and date of publication), and also works recommended for further reading.

Ahmad, Aziz, *Studies in Islamic Culture in the Indian Environment*, Oxford, 1964

Amir Ali, *The Spirit of Islam*, London, 1922 (repr. 1967)

Anesaki, M., *History of Japanese Religion*, London, 1930 (repr. 1963)

Arberry, A. J., *Sufism: An Account of the Mystics of Islam*, London, 1950
  Revelation and Reason in Islam, London, 1957

Ardrey, Robert, *African Genesis*, London, 1961

Argyle, Michael, *Religious Behaviour*, London, 1958

Arnold, T. W., *The Preaching of Islam*, 2nd edn., London, 1913

Aston, W. G., *Shinto, The Way of the Gods*, London, 1905

Aung, S. Z., *Compendium of Philosophy*, London, 1910 (repr. 1956)

Baeck, Leo, *The Essence of Judaism*, New York, 1948

Bary, W. T. de (ed.), *Sources of Indian Tradition*, New York/London, 1958

Basham, A. L., *The Wonder that was India*, London, 1954

Baynes, N. H., 'Constantine', in *Cambridge Ancient History*, vol. xii, ch. xx, Cambridge, 1939

Bendix, R., *Max Weber: An intellectual portrait*, 1959

Benveniste, Émile, 'Traditions indo-iraniennes sur les classes sociales', in *J. Asiatique*, 1938

Bethune-Baker, J. F., *An Introduction to the Early History of Christian Doctrine*, London, 1903

Bettenson, H., *Documents of the Christian Church*, Oxford, 2nd edn., 1963

Bevan, Edwyn, *Jerusalem Under the High Priests*, London, 1904
  Christianity, London, 1932

Bhāndārkar, R. G., *Vaishnavism, Shaivism, and Minor Religious Sects*, Strassburg, 1913

Blacker, Carmen, 'New Religious Cults of Japan', in *Hibbert Journal*, lx, July 1962

Brandon, S. G. F., *The Fall of Jerusalem and the Christian Church*, 2nd edn., London, 1957
  Creation Legends of the Ancient Near East, London, 1963

432   *General Bibliography*

Breasted, J. H., *Development of Religion and Thought in Ancient Egypt*, London, 1912

The Dawn of Conscience, New York, 1935

Bright, John, *A History of Israel*, London, 1960

Brown, Peter, *Augustine of Hippo*, London, 1967

Bullough, Sebastian, *Roman Catholicism*, London, 1963

Burrows, Millar, *The Dead Sea Scrolls*, London, 1956

More Light on the Dead Sea Scrolls, London, 1958

Carpenter, J. Estlin, *Theism in Medieval India*, London, 1921

Chan, W. T., *Religious Trends in Modern China*, New York, 1953

Chattopadhyaya, D., *Lokayata: A Study in Ancient Indian Materialism*, New Delhi, 1959

Ch'en, K. K. S., *Buddhism in China*, Princeton, 1964

Childe, V. Gordon, *New Light on the Most Ancient East* (new edn.), London, 1952

Chouraqui, André, *A History of Judaism*, New York, 1962

Coedès, Georges, *Les États Hindouisés d'Indochine et d'Indonésie*, Paris, 1964

The Making of South-East Asia, London, 1966

Conze, E., *Buddhist Meditation*, London, 1956

Buddhism, 3rd edn., London, 1957

Buddhist Scriptures, London, 1959

A Short History of Buddhism, Bombay, 1960

Buddhist Thought in India, London, 1962

Copleston, F. C., *Aquinas*, London, 1955

Cronbach, A., *Reform Movements in Judaism*, New York, 1963

Cronin, V., *The Wise Man from the West*, New York, 1955

A Pearl to India, New York, 1959

Dasgupta, S. N., *History of Indian Philosophy*, vol. i, Cambridge, 1922

Indian Idealism, Cambridge, 1933 (repr. 1962)

Davids, T. W. Rhys, *Buddhist Suttas* (Sacred Books of the East, vol. xi), Oxford, 1881

Buddhist India, 8th edn., Calcutta, 1959

Devanandan, P. D., and Thomas, M. M., *Human Person, Society and State*, Bangalore, 1957

Dibelius, Martin, *Studies in the Acts of the Apostles*, London, 1956

Dix, Gregory, *The Shape of the Liturgy*, London, 1945

Dodd, C. H., *The Apostolic Preaching and its Development*, London, 1936

Dumoulin, Heinrich, 'Technique and Personal Devotion in the Zen Exercise', in *Studies in Japanese Culture*, ed. J. Ringgendorf, Tokyo, 1963

Drekmeier, C., *Kingship and Community in Early India*, Stanford Univ. Press, Cal., 1972

Duchesne-Guillemin, J., *The Western Response to Zoroaster*, Oxford, 1958

Dutt, Sukumar, *The Buddha and Five After-centuries*, London, 1957
  Buddhist Monks and Monasteries of India, London, 1962
Edwards, M., *Asia in the European Age, 1498–1955*, London, 1961
Eichrodt, W., *Theology of the Old Testament*, vol. I (trans. J. A. Baker), London, 1961
Eliade, Mircea, *Yoga, Immortality and Freedom*, New York, 1958
Eliot, C., *Hinduism and Buddhism*, 3 vols. London, 1921 (repr. 1957)
  Japanese Buddhism, London, 1935 (repr. 1959)
Epstein, I., *Judaism*, London, 1959
Farquar, J. N., *Modern Religious Movements in India*, London, 1929
Fisher, H. A. L., *A History of Europe*, London, 1936
Fitzgerald, C. P., *The Chinese View of their Place in the World*, London, 1964
Florinsky, M. T., *Russia: A History and an Interpretation*, New York, 1959
Frankfort, Henri, *Kingship and the Gods*, Chicago, 1948
  Before Philosophy: The Intellectual Adventure of Ancient Man, Chicago, 1946 (repr. London, 1963)
Gavin, F. 'The Eucharist in East and West' in *Liturgy and Worship*, ed. W. K. Lowther Clarke and Charles Harris, London, 1932
Geertz, Clifford, *The Religion of Java*, Glencoe, 1960
Gibb, H. A. R., *Modern Trends in Islam*, London, 1947
Gilson, E., *History of Christian Philosophy in the Middle Ages*, London, 1955
Goonesekere, Lakshmi R., 'Abhidhamma', in *Encyclopaedia of Buddhism*, ed. G. P. Malalasekere, Ceylon, 1961
Grunebaum, von, G. E., *Unity and Variety in Muslim Civilisation*, Chicago, 1955
Hall, D. G. E., *A History of South-East Asia*, London, 1955 (3rd edn. 1968)
Hamilton, C. H., 'Buddhism', in *China*, ed. H. F. MacNair, Univ. of California, 1946
Hammer, R., *Japan's Religious Ferment*, London, 1961
Hanson, A. (ed.), *Vindications*, London, 1966
Hardy, R. Spence, *Eastern Monarchism*, Edinburgh, 1860
Hare, E. M., *Woven Cadences of Early Buddhism*, Oxford, 1945
Herberg, Will, *Protestant, Catholic, Jew*, New York, 1955
Hick, John, *Evil and the God of Love*, London, 1966
Holtom, D. C., *The National Faith of Japan*, London, 1938
  Modern Japan and Shinto Nationalism, Revised edn., New York, 1947 (repr. 1963)
Hooke, S. H. (ed.), *Myth and Ritual*, London, 1933
Hori, I., 'On the Concept of Hijiri (holy-man)', in *Numen*, vol. v, Leiden, 1958
Hottinger, A., *The Arabs*, London, 1963
Howe, S., 'New Writings on Japan's Religions', in *Pacific Affairs*, Summer 1964
Ikram, S. M., *Muslim Civilisation in India*, New York/London, 1964

James, Fleming, *Personalities of the Old Testament*, London, 1947

Jayasuriya, W. F., *The Psychology and Philosophy of Buddhism*, Colombo, 1963

Jayatilleke, K. N., *Early Buddhist Theory of Knowledge*, London, 1963

Jeffery, A., *The Qur'an as Scripture*, New York, 1952
  Islam: Muhamad and his religion, New York, 1958

Jones, Rufus M., *Studies in Mystical Religion*, London, 1923

Josephus, *The Works of Flavius Josephus* (trans. W. Whiston), Edinburgh, n.d.

Karunaratne, W. S., 'Abhidhamma' in *Encyclopaedia of Buddhism*, ed. G. P. Malalasekere, Fascicule A–Aca, Colombo, 1961

Katsh, A. I., *Judaism and the Koran*, New York, 1954

Kelly, J. N. D., *Early Christian Creeds*, London, 1950

Kent, John, 'Christianity: Protestantism', in Zaehner, 1959

Kirk, K. E., *The Vision of God*, London, 1931

Kosambi, D. D., *The Culture and Civilisation of Ancient India*, London, 1965

Kramer, Samuel Noah, *History Begins at Sumer*, London, 1958

Lee, Robert, *The Social Sources of Church Unity*, New York, 1960

Leff, G., *Medieval Thought: St Augustine to Ockham*, London, 1958

Leur, J. C. van, *Indonesian Trade and Society*, The Hague/Bandung, 1955

Levy, R., *The Social Structure of Islam*, Cambridge, 1957

Lightfoot, R. H., *History and Interpretation in the Gospels*, London, 1934

Lindblom, J., *Prophecy in Ancient Israel*, Oxford, 1963

Ling, Trevor, *The Significance of Satan*, London, 1961
  Buddhism and the Mythology of Evil, London, 1962
  Buddha, Marx and God, London, 1966

Liu Wu-Chi, *A Short History of Confucian Philosophy*, London, 1955

Ludowyk, E. F. C., *The Story of Ceylon*, London, 1962

McNeill, J. T., Spinka, M. and Willoughby, H. R., *Environmental Factors in Christian History*, Chicago, 1939

Mai-Tho-Truyên, 'Le Bouddhisme au Viêt-Nam' in *Présence du Bouddhisme*, ed. René de Berval, Saigon, 1959

Malinowski, B., 'Magic, Science and Religion', in *Science, Religion and Reality*, ed. J. Needham, London, 1926

Manson, T. W., *The Teaching of Jesus*, Cambridge, 1931
  'The Life of Jesus: A Study of the Available Materials', in *The Bulletin of the John Ryland Library, Manchester*, vol. 27, no. 2, June 1943

Marriott, McKim, *Village India* (American Anthropol. Association Memoir No. 83), Menasha, Wisconsin, 1955

Mendis, G. C., *Ceylon Today and Yesterday*, 2nd edn., Colombo, 1963

Migot, André, 'Le Bouddhisme en Chine', in *Présence du Bouddhisme*, ed. René de Berval, Saigon, 1959
  Tibetan Marches (trans. P. Fleming), London, 1955

Moore, G. F., *Judaism in the First Centuries of the Christian Era* (2 vols.), Cambridge, Mass., 1927

    The Literature of the Old Testament, London, 1914 (2nd edn., revised, 1948)

Mowinckel, S., *He That Cometh*, Oxford, 1956

Mujeeb, M., *The Indian Muslims*, London, 1967

Murti, T. R. V., *The Central Philosophy of Buddhism*, London, 1955

Neil, S., *A History of Christian Missions*, London, 1964

Niebuhr, H. Richard, *The Social Sources of Denominationalism*, New York, 1929

Nock, A. D., *St Paul*, London, 1946

Norbeck, Edward, *Changing Japan*, New York/London, 1965

North, C. R., 'Pentateuchal Criticism', in *The Old Testament and Modern Study*, ed. H. H. Rowley, London, 1951

Noth, Martin, *The History of Israel*, 2nd edn. (trans. P. R. Ackroyd), London, 1960

Nyāṇamoli, *The Path of Purification* (trans. from the Pali *Visuddhimagga* of Buddhaghosa) Colombo, 1964

Nyanaponika, *Abhidhamma Studies*, Colombo, 1949

O'Malley, L. S., *Popular Hinduism: The Religion of the Masses*, Cambridge, 1935

    (ed.), *Modern India and the West*, Oxford, 1941

Otto, Rudolph, *The Idea of the Holy*, London, 1923

Panikkar, K. M., *Hindu Society at Cross Roads*, 3rd (revised) edn., Bombay, 1961

Parkes, James, *A History of the Jewish People*, London, 1964

Payne, E. A., *The Śāktas*, Calcutta, 1933

Petrie, W. M. Flinders, *Personal Religion in Egypt before Christianity*, London, 1909

Piggott, Stuart, *Prehistoric India*, London, 1950

Piyadassi, *The Buddha's Ancient Path*, London, 1964

Pratt, James Bissett, *The Pilgrimage of Buddhism*, New York, 1928

Prestige, G. L., *Fathers and Heretics*, London, 1940

Qureshi, I. H., *The Muslim Community of the Indo-Pakistan Sub-Continent* (610–1947), The Hague, 1962

Rad, von, Gerhard, *Old Testament Theology*, vol. i, Edinburgh and London, 1962

Rādhakrishnan, S., 'Hinduism and the West', in *Modern India and the West*, ed. L. S. O'Malley, Oxford, 1941

Rahman, F., *Islam*, London, 1967

Rahula, Walpola, *History of Buddhism in Ceylon*, Colombo, 1956

Redfield, Robert, *Peasant Society and Culture*, Chicago, 1956

Reichelt, Karl Ludwig, *Religion in a Chinese Garment*, London, 1951

Renou, L., *Religions of Ancient India*, London, 1953

Richardson, H. E., *Tibet and its History*, London, 1962

Ringgren, H., *Israelite Religion* (trans. David Green), London, 1966
Robinson, J. A. T., *Twelve New Testament Studies*, London, 1962
Robinson, T. H., *Prophecy and the Prophets*, London, 1923
Routley, Erik, *Hymns and Human Life*, London, 1962
Rowley, H. H. (ed.), *The Old Testament and Modern Study*, London, 1951
    Prophecy and Religion in Ancient China and Israel, London, 1956
Runciman, S., *A History of the Crusades*, Cambridge, 1951–1954
Russell, D. S., *Between the Testaments*, London, 1960
Sarkisyanz, E., *Buddhist Backgrounds of the Burmese Revolution*, The Hague, 1965
Sastri, K. A. Nilakanta, *Development of Religion in South India*, Orient Longmans, 1963
Scholem, G., *Major Trends in Jewish Mysticism*, rev. edn., New York, 1941
Scott, J. G. (Shway Yoe), *The Burman: his life and notions*, 3rd edn., London, 1909
Sen, K. M., *Hinduism*, London, 1961
Shryock, J. K., *The Origin and Development of the State Cult of Confucius*, New York, 1932 (repr. 1966)
Singer, Milton, 'The Radha-Krishna *Bhajans* of Madras City', in *History of Religions*, vol. 2, no. 2, Chicago, 1963
Slater, Gilbert, *The Dravidian Element in Indian Culture*, London, 1924
Slater, R. H. L., *Paradox and Nirvana*, Chicago, 1951
Smart, Ninian, *Historical Selections in the Philosophy of Religion*, London, 1962
    Philosophers and Religious Truth, London, 1964 (1)
    Doctrine and Argument in Indian Philosophy, London, 1964 (2)
Smith, Vincent A., *The Oxford History of India*, 3rd edn., Oxford, 1958
Smith, Wilfred Cantwell, *Modern Islam in India: A Social Analysis* (rev. edn.), London, 1947
    Islam in Modern History, Princeton, 1957
Smith, William Robertson, *Lectures on the Religion of the Semites*, 3rd edn., London, 1927
Snellgrove, David, *Buddhist Himalaya*, Oxford, 1957
Srawley, J. H., *The Early History of the Liturgy*, Cambridge, 1947
Stein, Burton, 'The Economic Function of a Medieval South Indian Temple', in *Journal of Asian Studies*, xix, no. 2, Feb. 1960
Stevenson, S., *The Heart of Jainism*, Oxford, 1915
Stone, Darwell, *A History of the Doctrine of the Holy Eucharist*, 2 vols., London, 1909
Straelen, Henry van, *The Religion of Divine Wisdom*, Kyoto, 1957
Swanson, Guy, *The Birth of the Gods*, Michigan University Press, 1960
Sweetman, J. W., *Islam and Christian Theology*, Part One, vol. ii, London, 1947
Thapar, Romila, *A History of India*, vol. i, London, 1966
Thomas, Bertram, *The Arabs*, London, 1937

Thomas, D. Winton, *Documents from Old Testament Times*, London, 1958
Thomas, E. J., *The Life of Buddha*, 3rd edn., London, 1949
   The History of Buddhist Thought, 2nd edn., London, 1951
Thomson, Ian, *Changing Patterns in South Asia*, London, 1961
Trevelyan, G. M., *English Social History*, 3rd edn., London, 1946
Varma, V. D., *Modern Indian Political Thought*, 2nd edn., Agra, 1964
Walker, G. S. M., *The Growing Storm*, London, 1961
Wand, J. W. C., *A History of the Modern Church*, 6th edn., London, 1952
Ware, Timothy, *The Orthodox Church*, London, 1963
Warfield, Benjamin B., 'Augustine', in *Encyclopaedia of Religion and Ethics*,
   Edinburgh and New York, 1909, vol. ii.
Warren, Max, *Social History and Christian Mission*, London, 1967
Watt, W. Montgomery, *Free Will and Predestination in Early Islam*, London, 1948
  Muhammad at Mecca, London, 1953
  Muhammad at Medina, London, 1956
   'The conception of the charismatic community in Islam', *Numen* (Leiden)
   VII, fasc. I, Jan. 1960
  Muhammad, Prophet and Statesman, London, 1961 (1)
  Islam and the Integration of Society, London, 1961 (2)
  Islamic Philosophy and Theology, Edinburgh, 1962
Weber, Max, *The Protestant Ethic and the Spirit of Capitalism*, London, 1930
  The Religion of China, Glencoe, 1951
  Ancient Judaism, Glencoe, 1952
  The Religion of India, Glencoe, 1958
  The Sociology of Religion, Boston, 1963
Wells, K. E., *Thai Buddhism*, Bangkok, 1960
Wensinck, A. J., *The Muslim Creed*, Cambridge, 1932
Wheeler, H. Mortimer, *Early India and Pakistan*, London, 1959
  Civilizations of the Indus Valley and Beyond, London, 1966
Wheeler, Richard S., 'The Individual and Action in the Thought of Iqbal', in
   The Muslim World, London, 1962
Wilhelm, Richard, *A Short History of Chinese Civilisation*, London, 1929
Williams, G. H., *The Radical Reformation*, London, 1962
Wilson, Bryan, *Religion in Secular Society*, London, 1966
Wittfogel, Karl, *Oriental Despotism*, London, 1957
Wright, Arthur F., *Buddhism in Chinese History*, n.p., 1959
Yang, C. K., *Religion in Chinese Society*, Berkeley and Los Angeles, 1961
Zaehner, R. C., *Zurvan: A Zoroastrian Dilemma*, Oxford, 1955
  (ed.) *The Concise Encyclopaedia of Living Faiths*, London, 1959
  Hinduism, London, 1962
  Hindu Scriptures, London and New York, 1966
Zernov, N., *Eastern Christendom*, London, 1961

Sectional Bibliography: Suggested Further Reading

Details of the books here referred to by author and date will be found in the General Bibliography.

Chapter One

1.1 Brandon, 1963. Frankfort, 1946. Kramer, 1958. Piggott, 1950. Wheeler, 1959, 1966.

1.2 Bright, 1960. Eichrodt, 1961. Noth, 1960. Ringgren, 1966. Rowley, 1951.

1.3 Basham, 1954. Dasgupta, 1922; 1933. Kosambi, 1965. Sen, 1961. Zaehner, 1962.

1.4 as for 1.2.

1.5 as for 1.3.

Chapter Two

2.1 Lindblom, 1963. Robinson, 1923. Weber, 1952. And as for 1.2.

2.2 Zaehner, 1955; 1959.

2.3 Chattopadhyaya, 1959. Conze, 1957. Davids, 1959. Dutt, 1957. Eliot, 1921. Kosambi, 1965. Thomas, 1949.

2.4 Anesaki, 1963. Aston, 1905. Liu Wu-Chi, 1955. Reichelt, 1951. Stevenson, 1915. Wilhelm, 1929.

Chapter Three

3.1 Bevan, 1904. Burrows, 1956. Russell, 1960. And as for 1.2.

3.2 Conze, 1962. Dutt, 1957; 1962. Jayatilleke, 1963. Nyanaponika, 1949. Thomas, 1951.

3.3 Basham, 1954. Kosambi, 1965. Thapar, 1966. Zaehner, 1962.

3.4 Bevan, 1932. Dodd, 1936. Hanson, 1966. Lightfoot, 1934. Manson, 1931; 1943. Scott, 1909.

Chapter Four

4.1 Bethune-Baker, 1903. Bevan, 1932. Dix, 1945. Hick, 1966. Kelly, 1950. Prestige, 1940.

4.2 As for 3.3.
4.3 Conze, 1960; 1962. Dutt, 1957; 1962. Murti, 1955. Smart, 1964.
     Thomas, 1951.

Chapter Five

5.1 Arnold, 1913. Jeffery, 1958. Levy, 1957. Rahman, 1967. Thomas, 1937.
     Watt, 1953; 1956; 1961 (1) Wensinck, 1932.
5.2 Anesaki, 1963. Coedès, 1966. Dutt, 1962. Eliot, 1921; 1935.
     Snellgrove, 1957. Thomas, 1951. Wright, 1959.

Chapter Six

6.1 Basham, 1954. Eliot, 1921. Sastri, 1963. Thapar, 1966.
6.2 Copleston, 1955. Epstein, 1959. Gilson, 1955. Jones, 1923. Leff, 1958.
     Runciman, 1951–54. Smart, 1962; 1964 (1). Walker, 1961. Ware, 1963.
     Zernov, 1961.
6.3 Arberry, 1950. Arnold, 1913. de Bary, 1958. von Grunebaum, 1955.
     Hottinger, 1963. Ikram, 1964. Watt, 1961.
6.4 Anesaki, 1963. Chan, 1953. Ch'en, 1964. Conze, 1960.
     Eliot, 1921; 1935. Sarkisyanz, 1965. Thapar, 1966.
6.5 Anesaki, 1963. Arnold, 1913. de Bary, 1958. Niebuhr, 1929.
     Sastri, 1963. Ware, 1963. Williams, 1962.

Chapter Seven

7.1 Bettenson, 1963. Chouraqui, 1962. Epstein, 1959. Florinsky, 1959.
     Lee, 1960. Parkes, 1964. Wand, 1952. Ware, 1963. Wilson, 1966.
     Zernov, 1961.
7.2 Farquar, 1929. Marriott, 1955. O'Malley, 1935. Qureshi, 1962.
     Singer, 1963. Varma, 1964.
7.3 Ahmad, 1964. Ali, 1922. Arnold, 1913. Geertz, 1960. Gibb, 1947.
     Ikram, 1964. Mujeeb, 1967. Qureshi, 1962. Rahman, 1967.
     Smith, 1946; 1957.
7.4 Anesaki, 1963. Chan, 1953. Ch'en, 1964. Hammer, 1961. Mendis, 1963.
     Pratt, 1928. Sarkisyanz, 1965. Wells, 1960.

Index and Glossary

Note: Foreign names and terms, where used in their original linguistic form (that is, transliterated but not anglicised) appear in italics; thus, *Kṛṣṇa*

Names of authors mentioned in the Bibliography are shown in capitals, thus, AUNG, S. Z.